ALSO BY JEFFRY D. WERT

Cavalryman of the Lost Cause: A Biography of J. E. B. Stuart

The Sword of Lincoln: The Army of the Potomac

Gettysburg: Day Three

A Brotherhood of Valor: The Common Soldiers of the Stonewall Brigade,
C.S.A., and the Iron Brigade, U.S.A.

Custer: The Controversial Life of George Armstrong Custer

General James Longstreet: The Confederacy's Most
Controversial Soldier—A Biography

From Winchester to Cedar Creek: The Shenandoah Campaign of 1864

A Glorious Army

ROBERT E. LEE'S TRIUMPH, 1862–1863

Jeffry D. Wert

Simon & Schuster

NEW YORK LONDON TORONTO SYDNEY

Simon & Schuster
1230 Avenue of the Americas
New York, NY 10020

First Simon & Schuster hardcover edition April 2011

SIMON & SCHUSTER and colophon are registered trademarks
of Simon & Schuster, Inc.

For information about special discounts for bulk purchases,
please contact Simon & Schuster Special Sales at 1-866-506-1949
or business@simonandschuster.com.

The Simon & Schuster Speakers Bureau can bring authors
to your live event. For more information or to book an event,
contact the Simon & Schuster Speakers Bureau at 1-866-248-3049
or visit our website at www.simonspeakers.com.

Designed by Paul Dippolito

Manufactured in the United States of America

3   5   7   9   10   8   6   4   2

Library of Congress Cataloging-in-Publication Data
Wert, Jeffry D., 1946–
A glorious army: Robert E. Lee's Triumph, 1862–1863 / Jeffry D. Wert.—
First Simon & Schuster hardcover edition.
p.   cm.
Includes bibliographical references and index.
1. Confederate States of America. Army of Northern Virginia.
2. United States—History—Civil War, 1861–1865—Regimental histories.
3. United States—History—Civil War, 1861–1865—Campaigns.
4. Lee, Robert E. (Robert Edward), 1807–1870—Military leadership.
I. Title.
E470.2.W45 2011
973.7'42—dc22
2010046544

ISBN 978-1-4165-9334-8
ISBN 978-1-4165-9847-3 (ebook)

To my mother, Kathleen M. Wert,
and my mother-in-law, Ethel L. Long

Contents

Preface and Acknowledgments

In May 1863 Robert E. Lee confided to a subordinate, John Bell Hood, "There never were such men in an army before." Lee wrote those words within weeks of the army's recent victory at Chancellorsville. At that time, at the midpoint of the Civil War, the Army of Northern Virginia had come to embody Confederate nationalism and to fire southern aspirations of an independent nation. In less than a year Lee, his lieutenants, and the common soldiers who followed them had redirected the war's course in the East.

Lee assumed command of the army on June 1, 1862. In the estimation of his foremost biographer, Douglas Southall Freeman, his appointment marked "the turning point of the war in the East." During the next thirteen months the Confederate commander and his army crafted a record of achievement unmatched by any army in the annals of American military history. They won four major victories—the Seven Days, Second Manassas, Fredericksburg, and Chancellorsville—held the bloody ground at Antietam, and were on the march to a reckoning at Gettysburg.

My book examines that span of time, from the weeks immediately before the Seven Days Campaign through the three-day engagement at Gettysburg. A final chapter covers the twenty-one months of warfare after Gettysburg, which ended for Lee's army at Appomattox Court House. My intent is not to offer detailed tactical studies of each battle, for there are excellent works on all of the engagements, but to offer a narrative and analysis of the fighting, with a focus on leadership and on the experiences of men on the firing lines. I have drawn heavily from the letters, diaries, and memoirs of the army's veterans and from the fine recent scholarship of fellow historians.

In a sense this is an exploration, a search for answers to questions and controversies. I address Lee's strategic and tactical boldness, its cost in staggering casualties, the performances of his senior lieutenants—Stonewall Jackson, James Longstreet, Jeb Stuart, A. P. Hill, and Richard Ewell—the morale and discipline of the men in the ranks, the roles of brigade and regimental commanders, and the misfortunes and failings of the Union Army of the Potomac. My judgments and conclusions will surely not end the debates nor resolve the controversies. The craft of history is never stagnant; it is ongoing, offering new insights and fomenting more disagreements. I hope my book contributes to the discussions.

Decades ago, as a college freshman, I first read Freeman's three-volume *Lee's Lieutenants: A Study in Command.* Although I was already a Civil War buff, my fascination with the Army of Northern Virginia began when I sat hour after hour with Freeman's elegant prose. Since then the writing of history has taken me with Lee's men as they defended an unfinished railroad bed at Second Manassas, stood in the sunken road at Antietam, manned a stone wall at Fredericksburg, crossed farmers' fields toward Cemetery Ridge at Gettysburg, and marched the final steps on a road at Appomattox. This book is a return for me. I am surely not alone in being drawn back to their story.

As always, my book has benefited from the assistance of others. All errors of omission and commission are, however, entirely mine.

I wish to thank the archivists and librarians at the institutions cited in the bibliography for their assistance and understanding. The following individuals deserve my particular gratitude and recognition:

Joseph Pierro, a historian, author, and a friend, for reading the entire manuscript, offering perceptive insights, and improving my writing.

Horace Mewborn, a historian on operations of Lee's cavalry and a friend, for commenting on sections of the manuscript and posing insightful questions on it.

Robert K. Krick, the modern authority on the Army of Northern Virginia and a friend, for sharing copies of material with me.

Ted Alexander, the chief historian at Antietam National Battlefield and an old friend, for reading my chapter on the Maryland Campaign and sharing with me his unequaled knowledge of the operations.

Daniel Laney, Civil War preservationist and historian and valued family friend, for poring over most of the manuscript, correcting my errors, and challenging my conclusions.

Robert Gottlieb, chairman of Trident Media Group, and my agent, for his advice and constant efforts on my behalf.

Bob Bender, my editor, for all that he has done for me in our association of more than twenty years and for always making my work so much better.

Johanna Li, associate editor, for her kindness, assistance, and tireless patience.

Our son, Jason Wert, our daughter-in-law, Kathy Wert, our grandchildren, Rachel and Gabriel Wert, our daughter, Natalie Wert Corman, and our son-in-law, Grant Corman, for their love, support, and all that they mean to Gloria and me.

My wife, Gloria, my best friend and cherished love, who has shared all this work throughout these many years. Without her, none of this is possible or of meaning.

Our mothers, Kathleen M. Wert and Ethel L. Long. For all that mothers do and for all that they mean to Gloria and me, this book is dedicated to them.

A Glorious Army

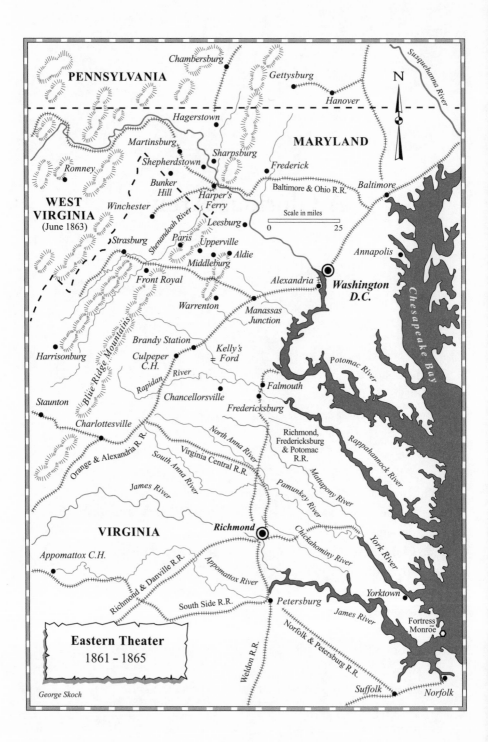

Prologue

The musketry and artillery fire had died away with nightfall on May 31, 1862. For several hours during the day the fighting had raged in the woodlots and clearings around Seven Pines and Fair Oaks Station, several miles outside of Richmond, Virginia. The combat's fury and the bloodletting surpassed anything in the experience of those trapped within its confines. A Virginia soldier confessed to his wife that it was a "miracle" that he passed through unscathed as "every body else was falling around us." A regimental commander who survived the conflict's four years admitted afterward that the engagement was "one of the bloodiest of my war experience."[1]

The day had not gone as planned by the attacking Confederates. Muddy roads and flooded bottomlands from the previous night's thunderstorms, a misunderstanding of orders, and piecemeal assaults had hampered the Southern operations and shaped the struggle. Consequently the error-plagued offensive did not go forward until early afternoon, hours behind schedule. The attackers gained successes, overrunning a Union redoubt and wrecking the enemy's front line. But Federal resistance stiffened, and reinforcements blunted a final Rebel thrust. The opposing ranks lay close to each other at day's end, with more carnage awaiting sunrise.[2]

The Confederate commander, General Joseph E. Johnston, rode away from his headquarters late in the day to examine the terrain and the army's lines. Johnston had spent the entire morning and most of the afternoon waiting anxiously for word of the attack at Seven Pines. Instead of learning for himself why his orders had miscarried, he remained at headquarters. It was not until nearly 3:00 P.M. when the commander received a dispatch that reported the action. Now, as he rode on his personal examination of the situation, a piece of an artillery shell struck him in the chest, breaking some ribs. Staff officers secured a litter, and the painfully wounded general was carried to the rear.[3]

Confederate President Jefferson Davis and his military advisor, General Robert E. Lee, met the litter party. The relations between Davis and Johnston had been strained for months, exacerbated by disagreements over military policy and both men's proud and thin-skinned personalities. At this moment, however, Davis spoke kindly to the wounded general, expressing his hope that Johnston would soon be able to return to duty.[4]

With the expectation that fighting would continue the next day, Davis assigned Johnston's senior subordinate, Major General Gustavus W. Smith, to command of the army. In the past, when confronted with responsibilities in the field, Smith had become indisposed with unspecified illnesses. Davis had little confidence in his generalship, but Smith would have to do for the present. The president also knew that no other ranking officer in the army could replace Johnston until the wounded general recovered.[5]

Davis started back toward the Confederate capital, accompanied by Lee. Since March Lee had served as the president's military advisor, and during those months the two men had developed a mutual trust. At some point, as they rode through the darkness, Davis asked Lee to replace Smith and to assume command of the army. It was to be a temporary assignment.[6]

So it was—a beleaguered chief executive turned to a general whose standing with the public had been diminished because of a failed campaign in western Virginia in the fall of 1861. At the time newspapers derisively called him "Granny Lee" for his perceived indecisiveness and even timidity. Unlike Johnston or Smith, however, Lee possessed the confidence of Davis, having worked well with the difficult president. And, with a crisis at hand, Davis had no one else.[7]

The magnitude of the crisis extended far beyond the lines at Seven Pines and Fair Oaks. For months a darkening, foreboding shadow had settled in across the Confederacy. Defeat had followed defeat—forts Henry and Donelson, Nashville, Shiloh, New Orleans, and Roanoke

Island. Finally, with the Union Army of the Potomac at the outskirts of Richmond, the independence of the Confederacy seemed to be a short-lived dream. In words unspoken, Lee had been asked to stay the darkness. He and those who awaited him in the army's ranks would do more. At about midday on June 1, 1862, Robert E. Lee dismounted at army headquarters. It marked the beginning.[8]

Chapter One

The Man and the Army

A MEMBER OF THE 4TH South Carolina, writing home on June 2, 1862, noted the appointment of Robert E. Lee to command of the army and stated: "I know little about him. They say he is a good general, but I doubt his being better than Johnston or [James] Long-street." The South Carolinian undoubtedly spoke for thousands of his comrades. Few officers or men had served with Lee in the antebellum army, and fewer had sat with him in councils or ever spoken to him. An officer who knew Lee and his family, Brigadier General James Ewell Brown "Jeb" Stuart, had confided earlier, "With profound personal regard for General Lee, he had disappointed me as a General."[1]

Lee was fifty-five years old, a son of the Revolutionary War hero "Light Horse" Harry Lee. An 1829 graduate of West Point, ranking second in his class, Lee served primarily on engineering and staff assignments in the antebellum army. During the Mexican War he rendered distinguished service as an officer on General Winfield Scott's staff. Scott regarded his fellow Virginian as the finest officer in the Regular Army. In April 1861 Union authorities offered Lee command of an army, but when Virginia seceded, Lee resigned his commission, traveled to Richmond, and was appointed commander of the state's volunteer forces. He directed the mobilization with skill until Virginia formally joined the Confederacy.[2]

In late July President Jefferson Davis assigned him to conduct operations in western Virginia, where the Federals had achieved minor successes. The duty was difficult and frustrating for Lee. The mountainous terrain, foul weather, feuding subordinates, sickness, and undisciplined troops resulted in disappointment and failure. By year's end, Lee was in South Carolina, overseeing the construction of coastal defenses. At last, in March 1862, Davis recalled Lee to Richmond as his advisor on military affairs.[3]

A day after he assumed command of the army, Lee confessed to his daughter-in-law, "I wish his [Johnston's] mantle had fallen on an abler man." Despite this modest assertion, Lee was an enormously talented man. Edward Porter Alexander, the army's chief of ordnance, stated, "No one could meet Lee and fail to be impressed with his dignity of character, his intellectual power, and his calm self-reliance."[4]

A handsome man, Lee possessed an imposing physical presence and a reserve that shielded an essentially private man. But in his dealings with government officials, fellow officers, and common soldiers, he was habitually courteous and kind. A staff officer said that he was "approachable by all." A private who had served under him in western Virginia remembered that Lee "soon won the affection of all by his politeness and notice of the soldiers." Another officer believed "no man was so tender to the faults of others as he was or so ready to assume his own."[5]

Lee's dignified calm, noted by many, resulted from a "remarkable self-control," in the words of Walter Taylor, a member of Lee's personal staff. "General Lee was naturally of a positive temperament, and of strong passions," continued Taylor, "and it is a mistake to suppose him otherwise; but he held these in complete subjection to his will and conscience." When angered, Lee revealed it with a "little nervous twist or jerk of the neck and head," a reddened face, a brusque manner, and clipped words. His ill humor or "occasional outcropping of temper" fell mainly upon his staff members, who called him "The Tycoon" out of his hearing.[6]

Few things irritated Lee more than the mounds of paperwork that he had to deal with daily as an army commander. As he soon demonstrated, he understood the workings of an army, the constant requirements of supply, ordnance, and organizational changes. His work habits acquired over decades as a soldier stood him well; he was attentive, industrious, and meticulous. Henry Heth, a general and friend, asserted "Lee was the embodiment of order and punctuality." As the strains on Southern resources deepened, the demands on his time and skills mounted. A hallmark of his generalship was his ability to maintain the army's prowess despite the crippling scarcities of rations, clothing, ordnance, and animal fodder.[7]

Walter Taylor served on Lee's personal staff through most of the war, until the end at Appomattox. For him, a defining characteristic of the general was his "sublime devotion to duty." In the soldier's trade, duty governed a man's life and prescribed its limits. For Lee, it was an uncompromising principle; it meant to him, in the words of the historian Joseph Harsh, a "pragmatic acceptance of the hand dealt him by fate." The performance of his duty would, like a lodestar, lead the way.[8]

Harsh has argued that Lee's "greatest assets grew from the strength of his own character." His most renowned biographer, Douglas Southall Freeman, attributed his consummate skill as a general, however, to his intellect. "The accurate reasoning of a trained and precise mind is the prime explanation of all these achievements," wrote Freeman. "Lee was preeminently a strategist, and a strategist because he was a sound military logician."[9] In time Lee's personal attributes and habits inspired confidence and instilled loyalty.

Lee possessed an intellect of exceptional depth and discernment. He excelled at deductive reasoning. He sifted through reconnaissance reports, information from spies, captured documents, Northern newspaper articles, and prisoner interrogations to formulate strategy across a broad landscape. Where opponents might see the dim outline of possibilities, Lee perceived opportunities. With his character strengths, intellectual acumen, and the training and experience of a career soldier, he would be a formidable enemy, a general with an aptitude for the art of warfare.[10]

By the time Lee assumed command of the army, he had formulated ideas on overall Confederate strategy. During the previous several months he had witnessed the string of Union victories and the loss of Southern cities and territories as the Davis administration followed a defensive strategy. By June 1862, in the view of the historian Gary W. Gallagher,

Rebel "armies had been losing ground in every quarter . . . as a cancer eating at southern morale and will." Perhaps worst of all, the North's largest force, the Army of the Potomac, lay at Richmond's doorstep.[11]

Joseph Johnston supported a defensive strategy. He told fellow generals "that the true policy of the Confederacy was to *save men* & only fight at an advantage—that we had plenty of territory, but no troops to spare." In March he withdrew the army from the Centreville, Virginia, area, abandoning and destroying more than a million pounds of critically needed foodstuffs and forage. When the Federals disembarked on the Peninsula east of Richmond in early April, Davis ordered Johnston's army to the capital and down the Peninsula to confront the 100,000 Federals. Within weeks, however, Johnston retreated toward Richmond, trailed by the enemy. Finally, confronted by a possible advance of a second force south from Fredericksburg, Johnston struck at Seven Pines and Fair Oaks.[12]

Johnston's passive defensive strategy had resulted in the conflict in the East being perched on the edge of the Confederate capital. If the Union commander, Major General George B. McClellan, closed the vise tighter and rolled up heavy cannon to within range of the city, Richmond could be doomed. This had been the inherent danger in Johnston's withdrawal into the defenses. As Gallagher has argued in a study of the Confederate war effort: "Even leaving aside surrendered troops strategically defensive campaigns often drained manpower at a rate almost equal to that lost by the side on the offensive. The problem lay in the fact that defenders usually reached a point where they had to attack in order to avoid a siege."[13]

Lee had watched with mounting concern Johnston's withdrawal up the Peninsula into the fieldworks outside of the city. With Major General Thomas J. "Stonewall" Jackson Lee had fashioned an offensive operation in the Shenandoah Valley that had stalled, for the present, an overland advance by the Federals from Fredericksburg. When Davis and his advisors discussed the possible abandonment of the city, at a May 14 Cabinet meeting, Lee stated his position on the security of the capital, exclaiming with uncharacteristic fervor, "Richmond must not be given up; it shall not be given up!" The passion of his words stunned his listeners.[14]

Charles Marshall, Lee's military secretary, wrote later, "It was a saying of General Lee that Richmond was never so safe as when its defenders were absent." An integral component of Lee's strategic views was an unbending commitment to the defense of the capital. He understood clearly the strategic, industrial, and symbolic importance of Richmond. If Confederate independence were to be attained, Richmond must not fall. The security of the capital lay well beyond its environs.[15]

Lee saw the civil conflict for what it had become, a struggle between two democratic societies. Each side had to sustain the support of its respective populaces, their willingness to accept the sacrifices and casualties to achieve ultimate victory. He directed his strategy against the will of the Northern people. In the enemy's newspapers he watched the political climate closely. He believed an overall military victory lay beyond the resources of the Confederacy. The goal of independence could be achieved only by a political settlement with the Lincoln administration. In turn Lee realized that Southern civilian morale could be upheld only by battlefield victories.[16]

In the struggle between North and South time was the silent enemy of the Confederacy. A protracted war meant almost certain defeat for the eleven seceded states, whose human and economic resources paled before those of the Union. The harvests of Northern farms, the furnaces of steel mills, the web of railroads, and the reservoir of manpower composed the sinews of an unsheathed, terrible sword of military power. If the will of the Northern citizenry held firm, the outcome appeared inevitable.[17]

Against these long odds Lee would act. When the time came, he led the army down a fork in a road no other Confederate general dared to follow. Within the broad offensive-defensive strategy of the Confederacy, Lee rejected the passive defensive stance of the previous winter and spring. As he wrote to Davis later in the war, "If we can defeat or drive the armies of the enemy from the field, we shall have peace. All our efforts & energies should be devoted to that object." It was his belief then; it was his belief in June 1862.[18]

Within days of Lee's assuming command of the army, Porter Alexander spoke with Captain Joseph C. Ives of Davis's staff. Alexander inquired if Lee was audacious enough as a general, believing that such an attribute was an *"absolute requisite"* if the South, with its inferior resources and manpower, were to have *"any chance* at all" in gaining independence. "Alexander," replied Ives, "if there is one man in either army, Federal or Confederate, who is head & shoulders, far above every other one in either army in audacity that man is Gen. Lee, and you will very soon have lived to see it. Lee is audacity personified. His name is audacity, and you need not be afraid of not seeing all of it that you will want to see."[19]

A private from Texas subsequently compared Lee's temperament to that of "a game cock," adding that the "mere presence of an enemy aroused his pugnacity and was a challenge he found hard to decline." James Longstreet described it as "headlong combativeness," and Alexander called it Lee's "combative instinct." Perhaps the Confederate commander possessed an innate aggressiveness; perhaps his soul burned when confronting an opponent on a battlefield. In his words, he strived to "destroy," "ruin," "crush," and "wipe out" enemy forces.[20]

Lee's aggressiveness or boldness arose from his reasoned assessment of how the numerically inferior Confederacy could achieve independence. To await the onslaught of Union might was to await a slow death. A realist acting on the disadvantages faced by all Confederate field commanders, Lee chose boldness, a calculated gamble that, with a series of battlefield victories and heavy enemy casualties, could discourage the Northern populace. "Lee's willingness to take the risk of action lay at the core of his generalship," the historian Charles Roland has written.[21]

Audacity meant risky, even desperate measures, but these offered opportunities. The offensive allowed Lee to dictate operations and to seize and to retain the strategic or operational initiative in the theater. He could frustrate Union plans, form the contours of a campaign, and maneuver the Federals onto fields advantageous to his own army. Celerity of movement and the concentration of forces became hallmarks of his strategic operations. Together they presented the possibility of inflicting a decisive, if not fatal, blow upon the enemy. According to the historian Harsh, Lee would "force the issue," and so "control the tempo of the war."[22]

Jefferson Davis and pro-Confederate Southern civilians supported an offensive strategy; they too wanted to force the issue. Recent Union victories and advances into Southern territory had drawn criticism of the Davis administration and sapped civilian morale. Southerners believed in the region's military heritage and the prowess and bravery of their soldiers. Newspapers urged aggressive action. In his June 2 letter to his daughter-in-law Lee expressed not only his belief but mirrored the thoughts of his fellow countrymen, that they must "drive our enemies back to their homes."[23]

With such a purpose, with personal attributes unmatched by any other Confederate commander, and with authority from the president over a theater of operations not given to Joseph Johnston, Lee and a handful of staff officers dismounted at army headquarters east of Richmond at about midday on that Sabbath, June 1, 1862. Uncertainty about him hung over the city and the army. The Richmond *Examiner* railed against his appointment, but a clerk in the War Department jotted in his diary, "This may be hailed as the harbinger of a bright future."[24]

Gustavus Smith relinquished command of the army to Lee and would leave the army permanently the next day. Davis had preceded Lee to the headquarters, and the two men surely conferred before the president returned to the city. Lee went to work.[25]

The order that appointed Lee read, in part, that he "will assume the immediate command of the armies of Eastern Virginia and North Carolina." His authority embraced Johnston's five infantry divisions, Major General Benjamin Huger's division from Norfolk, Stonewall Jackson's Valley District command, and the 33,000 troops in the departments of North Carolina and Henrico. By the last week of June, a new infantry division, the "Light Division" of Major General Ambrose Powell Hill, had been organized, and an additional twenty-seven regiments joined Lee's force outside of Richmond. By the opening of the Seven Days Campaign, Lee had amassed 112,000 present for duty, as compared to George McClellan's Union army of slightly more than 100,000. Lee's was the largest army ever assembled by the Confederacy.[26]

In October 1861, Johnston's command had been designated the Department of Northern Virginia. Over time the units were referred to as the Army of the Potomac, the same designation as that of the Union army in the East, and as the Army of Northern Virginia. On the day Lee assumed command he issued Special Orders No. 22, appealing to the officers and men "to maintain the ancient fame of the Army of Northern Virginia," and so it would be known. Continuing, Lee directed, "Commanders of divisions and brigades will take every precaution and use every means in their power to have their commands in readiness at all times for immediate action."[27]

In fact, the army was ill-prepared for "immediate action." The fighting at Seven Pines and Fair Oaks lasted into the afternoon of June 1. When it ended, Confederate casualties exceeded 6,000; Union losses, some 5,000. A Southern staff officer described the two-day engagement as a "waste of life and a great disappointment." In a letter to his mother Lieutenant Colonel William W. Bentley of the 24th Virginia complained, "Everything is managed so badly when going into battle." The army's senior leadership had mishandled the attacks, resulting in the Federals achieving a tactical victory.[28]

The problems within the army extended into its very fabric. Johnston had been a popular commander but a poor administrator, neglecting paperwork and procedures. Discipline was lax; desertions depleted units, and illnesses stalked the camps. Major General Daniel Harvey Hill grumbled to his wife on June 10, "There are hundreds and thousands of skulkers, who are dodging off home or lying around the brothels gambling saloons & drinking houses of Richmond." Writing at the same time, a South Carolinian described "a great deal of sickness in our army, and soldiers are dying at the hospital almost daily."[29]

Colonel Robert H. Chilton, Lee's chief of staff, described the army as a collection of "*undisciplined individuality*" when Lee assumed command. "It was extremely wasteful," Chilton said, "little observant of the relations which should exist between commanders and the commanded, and absenteeism without proper authority, prevailed largely amongst both officers and soldiers, which greatly reduced effective strength." Like Chilton, James Longstreet attributed the difficulty with discipline to the spirit of individuality of the troops.[30]

Many veterans, the volunteers of 1861, stood in the ranks, but thousands of recruits had joined the army within the past two months. In February 1862, the Confederate Congress had enacted a national conscription law, the first of its kind in American history. The legislation granted the men the opportunity to transfer to another unit and to elect their company and regimental officers. The reorganizations occurred during April and May, resulting in the replacement of 155 field officers by newly elected men. "The whole effect," wrote Porter Alexander, "was very prejudicial to the discipline of the army."[31]

Whether green recruits or veterans, soldiers grated against authority. A Virginian argued that he and his comrades were ready to fight, "but never ready to submit to the routine duty and discipline of the camp or the march." Private John Casler of the 33rd Virginia said that each Southern-born man "felt himself a king." A Georgian wrote: "A feeling of very democratic equality prevailed. . . . Officers were no better than the men." He added, "The process of disciplining them took away none of their personal spirit or their personal interest in the war."[32]

They came into the army from a society whose touchstones of belief were duty, honor, and liberty. The political controversies of the 1850s deepened their sense of the South's cultural superiority. With the outbreak of the war they enlisted in defense of their homes, of their individual and states' rights, and of the institution of slavery, the economic, political, and social foundation of their way of life. "In these revolutionary times," wrote a Virginia volunteer, "individual life is much less regarded than ordinarily. The issues are so momentous that the blood of the present generations must be the purchase money."[33]

"We were rather a devout army," contended a staff officer. Their faith reassured them of the righteousness of their cause. "Religion supplied the overarching framework for southern nationalism," the historian Gallagher has observed, "as Confederates cast themselves as God's chosen people." In turn, they viewed the enemy as "ungodly," a "depraved Yankee race," "wretches," and "devils." Their belief in ultimate victory, willed by God against such a foe, was to sustain them in their worst times, amid the worst of the carnage.[34]

Defense of home and family was woven into the certitude of their cause and contrasted with the barbarity of Northerners. Explaining to his sons why he had enlisted in the 2nd Virginia, Lieutenant Samuel Moore answered for many fathers: "They [the Yankees] might go into the State of Virginia, and burn our houses and kill all the men and the women and children, and do a great deal more harm, and I am sure I would rather see a thousand of them killed around me, than to know that they had done any harm to my wife and dear little boys." A Virginia infantryman expressed similar reasons to his wife. "I feel that it is for you that I fight, that while I render my country service I am as a shield between my love, my darling & danger."[35]

Although the Yankee "devils" too believed in the justness of their cause and of God's blessing upon it, the defense of their homeland instilled in these Confederates a heightened fighting spirit or élan in battle of inestimable value. They had shown it at Seven Pines and Fair Oaks, fiercely charging the Federal works and a redoubt. One story, most likely apocryphal but ringing with truth, circulated in Richmond after the battle of a Yankee prisoner exclaiming, "The Southern soldiers would charge into hell if there was a battery before them—and they would take it from a legion of devils!"[36]

To an astute observer, those Rebels had the makings of a formidable opponent. They had embraced the cause, said one of them, with "fervent feeling." But the illusions of a quick victory and a short war had passed with the reality before them. They remained undisciplined in camp, straggled on marches, and bristled under the authority of officers, whom they often viewed as their equals. "I never had any doubt that our people would make good fighters," stated James Longstreet after the war, "but I knew that the issue must at least be put upon organization." Like a steel blade tempered in a forge, organization meant the molding, if not recasting, of an army composed of fiercely independent souls. That task fell to Lee and his subordinate officers.[37]

The army's officer ranks, from regimental to divisional command, consisted of a core of professionally trained or experienced men. Scores of them had attended or were graduates of West Point, Virginia Military Institute (VMI), South Carolina Military Academy (today's Citadel), North Carolina Military Institute, and other antebellum private military schools. Veterans of the Mexican War, prewar army and navy, and state militia units held commissions. More of these educated or experienced officers served with the army in Virginia than with any other Confederate command.[38]

In the reorganization of the army in April and May roughly one-third of the majors, lieutenant colonels, and colonels with prewar education or service were removed through elections. The number of experienced captains and lieutenants voted out at company level is difficult to quantify. As noted previously, the turnover of officers caused a further erosion of discipline in the ranks. But a majority of experienced officers secured reelection, often at a higher rank; for instance, nearly every Virginia infantry and cavalry regiment had VMI alumni on their rolls. The presence of such men provided the army with, in the words of the historian Richard McMurry, "a much sounder command and administrative structure than . . . any other Civil War army."[39]

The army was composed of units from all eleven of the Confederate states and Maryland. By the beginning of the Seven Days Campaign, Virginia accounted for a small plurality of infantry regiments and battalions, trailed by units from Georgia and North Carolina. In fact, the majority of infantry units hailed from the lower South, from South Carolina to Texas. Conversely Virginia had organized a large majority of the artillery batteries and nine of the fourteen cavalry regiments. The assignment of so many foot soldiers from beyond the borders of the Old Dominion indicated the importance of the theater to Confederate authorities.[40]

With the influx of reinforcements and the reorganization of units during June, the army had thirty-five brigades of infantry. Nineteen of the brigade commanders were graduates of the United States Military Academy, Virginia Military Institute, and the South Carolina Military Academy. Among the West Pointers, John Bell Hood, Jubal A. Early, Richard H. Anderson, George Pickett, William Dorsey Pender, Charles Field, Isaac Trimble, and Cadmus Wilcox were destined for division or corps command. Graduates of VMI included brigadiers of outstanding promise, Robert E. Rodes, Samuel Garland Jr., and William Mahone.[41]

Among the remaining sixteen brigade commanders, half of them had served in the Regular Army and/or were veterans of antebellum conflicts. The other eight generals included three graduates of either Princeton or Yale, a militia officer, and four politicians, most notably the Georgians Howell Cobb and Robert Toombs. Like many of the professionally trained brigadiers, men such as Maxcy Gregg, Lawrence O'Bryan Branch, Joseph Kershaw, James Kemper, James Archer, Ambrose R. Wright, and George T. Anderson became reliable, if not

excellent, combat leaders. With a few exceptions, Lee's brigade commanders—men generally in their early to midthirties—were talented
men, unmatched by Union officers of similar rank.[42]

The army's senior leadership and infantry division commanders
were composed entirely of West Point graduates. Until resigning their
commissions in 1861, most of them had been career officers in the Regular Army. Except for William H. C. Whiting, all of them had been
with the army in Mexico, many earning a brevet or temporary rank for
distinguished service. Several would help to forge the army's character
and be an indelible part of its history, while others would be gone from
it after one campaign.[43]

If Lee were to correct the army's administrative and discipline problems and weld it into a weapon, he had to rely on his senior officers.
He knew none of them well, nor they him. Lee had sat in meetings
with James Longstreet, offered advice on operations to John Bank-
head Magruder and Benjamin Huger, and by correspondence crafted
with Stonewall Jackson and Richard S. Ewell the Shenandoah Valley
campaign. The others—Daniel Harvey Hill, William H. C. Whiting,
David R. Jones, Ambrose Powell Hill, and Lafayette McLaws—Lee
knew either through reports or by reputation. In time, in councils, and
by observations on a battlefield, Lee would evaluate their strengths and
weaknesses. For the present the defense of Richmond would take the
measure of all of them.[44]

The army's artillery and cavalry commanders, by contrast, had
known Lee since their cadet years at West Point. The chief of artillery, Brigadier General William N. Pendleton, had been in the class
behind Lee, graduating in 1830. Pendleton left the army within a few
years to become a teacher and then an Episcopalian minister. When his
native Virginia seceded, he organized a battery and commanded it at
First Manassas. Johnston appointed him to the post for his administrative ability, not for his tactical control of cannon on a battlefield. A day
after Lee assumed command of the army, he kept Pendleton as chief of
artillery.[45]

No subordinate commander enjoyed Lee's personal affection more
than the twenty-nine-year-old cavalryman Brigadier General Jeb Stuart. A Virginian, Stuart was a cadet at West Point when Lee served as

its superintendent. Stuart's best friend was fellow classmate Custis Lee, Lee's oldest son, whom Stuart joined often for Saturday dinners at the family's quarters. Later Captain Stuart served under Lee in the capture of abolitionist John Brown at Harper's Ferry, Virginia, in October 1859. He joined fellow Virginians in Confederate service, was appointed lieutenant colonel of cavalry, and led his regiment with distinction at First Manassas. In the fall of 1861 Johnston organized the army's mounted regiments into a brigade and assigned Stuart to command. The army commander called the horse soldier "a rare man."[46]

This was the army that Robert E. Lee joined on Sunday, June 1, 1862. If Richmond were to be saved, if the Confederacy were to survive, a trial awaited both him and them. Despite the administrative and discipline problems, the shortages of supplies, ordnance, and quality firearms, the fiber of these officers and men defined the army. Duty, honor, the cause, and the safety of loved ones kept them in their camps, behind fieldworks, and along skirmish lines. Months earlier Lee had written to a son, "All must be sacrificed to the country." An army was to be reborn, fittingly on a Sabbath day.[47]

Chapter Two

Seven Days

PRIVATE A. W. STILLWELL of the 5th Wisconsin described the month of June 1862 as "digging, entrenching, mortifying, and dying in the Chickamoniny swamps." Since Stillwell and his comrades in the Union Army of the Potomac had reached the Chickahominy River on May 17, they had edged slowly, methodically closer to Richmond. Such an approach suited Sergeant Charles E. Perkins of the 2nd Rhode Island who thought that the army commander, Major General George B. McClellan, "wants to save all the men he can. . . . I like to go slow and sure for I know what it is to go in a hurry and come back in a hurrey for I remember I went to buls run once and came back agane and I don't want to see eney more such cind of work."[1]

"Slow and sure" had been McClellan's preferred method of operations since the army's arrival on the Peninsula two months earlier. Once the army crossed the Chickahominy River, which coursed southeasterly across the Peninsula to the James River, McClellan ordered engineer details to repair damaged bridges and to construct new spans across the stream. He established the army's main supply base at White House on the Pamunkey River, using the single-track Richmond and York River Railroad to haul the supplies from the base to the army's camps. Expecting the overland advance of Union troops from Fredericksburg,

McClellan posted three infantry corps north of the Chickahominy and two corps south. It was this division of the enemy army that prodded Joseph Johnston to attack the Federal Third and Fourth corps around Seven Pines and Fair Oaks.[2]

Stonewall Jackson's offensive in the Shenandoah Valley, however, disrupted Union plans. President Abraham Lincoln postponed the movement of Major General Irvin McDowell's 30,000-man force from Fredericksburg, instead sending units from that city against Jackson. McClellan correctly viewed Jackson's operations as a diversion. The War Department did, however, transfer one infantry division from McDowell's department to McClellan, giving the army about 115,000 officers and men present for duty. After the engagement at Seven Pines and Fair Oaks, McClellan shifted the bulk of his infantry and artillery south of the Chickahominy, leaving Major General Fitz John Porter's Fifth Corps and the newly assigned division isolated north of the river at Mechanicsville. The Federals meanwhile shoved closer to the Confederate works and hauled up artillery to pound the Rebels.[3]

While confronting McClellan on the lower Peninsula at Yorktown, Joseph Johnston wrote to Robert E. Lee: "We are engaged in a species of warfare at which we can never win. It is plain that Genl M'C will adhere to the system begun near Alexandria, & depend for success upon Artillery & Engineering. We can compete with him in neither. It is necessary therefore that we adopt a different system. We must assume the offensive." Johnston had tried and failed before falling wounded. His burden before McClellan's "species of warfare" was now Lee's.[4]

From his assumption of command of the army, Lee planned to retake the strategic, or operational, initiative in Virginia and to strike the Federals. He, not his cautious opponent, would dictate the war's course in the region. It fit his strategic views; it fit the expectations of the Southern people. To him, Confederate soil must be held for logistical and political reasons. The deeper advance of Union forces into the Confederacy caused the loss of valuable foodstuffs and livestock and disheartened Southerners and encouraged Northerners. As soon as possible he intended, he explained to Jefferson Davis, "to bring McClellan out."[5]

The accomplishment of that strategic goal required the establishment of order in the army. The task was prodigious, unceasing. He issued instructions, directing officers at all levels of command to tend to the welfare and comfort of the men, the reorganization of the quarter-master and commissary departments, and the return of stragglers from Richmond, a place of "awful wickedness as well as noble Christian virtue." He improved the efficiency of the artillery with the formation of reserve artillery battalions and ordered the preparation of maps. During his initial days in command his correspondence addressed such details as tents, picket duties, shovels, and axes. It took time, but Lee's administrative imprint upon the army reflected his constant attention to and ability in dealing with the workings of such a force.[6]

The paperwork and duties at army headquarters fell to Lee's small personal staff. General staff officers handled the commissary, quarter-master, and ordnance departments. Six officers constituted Lee's head-quarters staff, or inner circle: colonels Robert H. Chilton and Armistead L. Long and majors T. M. R. Talcott, Walter Taylor, Charles Marshall, and Charles Venable. Lee preferred a Spartan lifestyle, and his small coterie of aides seemed to reflect this. "There was an utter absence of the rigid formality and the irksome ceremonial," recalled Taylor of the headquarters.[7]

The historian Robert E. L. Krick has argued, "There is reasonable doubt that Lee really understood how undermanned his staff was, or even recognized that he had too few personal staff officers to help him administer the army." Lee selected each aide, and fortunately for him, he chose well. They were men of "exceptional intelligence" and tire-less work habits. In time Lee organized staff duties: Long and Marshall served as secretaries; Taylor handled paperwork and screened visitors to headquarters; Venable and Talcott joined Lee on his daily rides through the camps or on the march; and Chilton acted as chief of staff. They were few, but they were talented officers.[8]

Lee began planning on how "to bring McClellan out" when he directed the army's chief engineer, Major Walter Stevens, to examine the lines, to place cannon at commanding points, and to oversee the construction of additional fieldworks. "My object," he informed Stevens, "is to make use of every means in our power to strengthen ourselves and enable us to fight to the best advantage." The major had the authority to requisition working parties from division commanders.[9]

Under Stevens's direction work on the entrenchments began within days. Soldiers assigned to the duty grumbled about the labor and derisively called the army commander the "King of Spades." "Our people are opposed to work," Lee wrote to Davis on June 5. "Our troops, officers, community & press. All ridicule & resist it. . . . There is nothing so military as labour, & nothing so important to our army as to save the lives of its soldiers." The complaints and criticism of Lee's orders missed its purpose: it was not part of a defensive strategy, but an offensive one. "He was building the fortifications there in order to hold Richmond with a small force," Jeb Stuart explained later to a staff officer, "and then attack McClellan's right flank."[10]

On the same day Lee issued his instructions to Stevens, the army commander met with several generals at The Chimneys, a house on Nine Mile Road outside of the city. Present were James Longstreet, John Magruder, D. H. "Harvey" Hill, William H. C. "Chase" Whiting, and Robert Toombs, one of Magruder's brigade commanders. President Davis rode out from Richmond to attend the meeting. Lee had probably already decided to assume the offensive, but he wanted to know the army's condition after Seven Pines and the officers' views on whether to await a Federal attack or to strike the enemy.[11]

The conference, recalled Charles Marshall, was "quite protracted." Lee, who now had a closely cropped, full beard, spoke sparingly. "Gen Lee was extremely reticient & seldom communicated his private views & opinions on pending operations to any one," remembered Longstreet. Instead he and Davis listened. It appears from conflicting accounts that Magruder and Whiting offered pessimistic assessments of the situation, arguing that the Confederate lines should be withdrawn closer to the city. When one general raised the matter of the rumored disparity in numbers between the armies, Lee reportedly rebutted: "Stop, stop. If you go to ciphering we are whipped beforehand." Harvey Hill proposed an assault on the Union left flank around White Oak Swamp.[12]

After the meeting adjourned, according to Harvey Hill in a private postwar letter, Lee said to the subordinate officer, "The troops [are] too raw & portion of them too demoralized by the Seven Pines fight to risk the fall of the Confederacy on a pitched battle." Perhaps he was responding to Hill's idea of an attack against the Federal lines.[13]

When Davis started back to the capital, Lee rode with him for some distance. Days earlier, before Seven Pines, they had discussed an offensive strategy. The president supported the idea of assuming the initiative against the Federals, and as the historian Harsh has noted, "Lee's strategy did not contravene Davis's concepts; it transcended them." Now, as they rode together, Lee proposed a movement against McClellan's right flank, north of the Chickahominy River, which was the opposite of Hill's suggestion. Davis suggested that Lee might need Jackson's troops, currently in the Shenandoah Valley, for the operation.[14]

This shared ride and conversation with Davis exemplified Lee's early, and continuous, efforts to keep the president apprised of his thinking and of army matters. Unlike Johnston, Lee advised and sought the counsel of the acutely sensitive chief executive. Davis had asked to be informed of "what is passing before and around you." Lee replied, "Our position requires you should know everything & you must excuse my troubling you." He was frank and respectful with Davis, a manner the president appreciated. Before long Davis confided to his wife, "Lee is working systematically and operating cordially and the army is said to feel the beneficial effect of it."[15]

On the day after the conference at The Chimneys James Longstreet came to army headquarters, located at High Meadows, the farmhouse of Mrs. Mary C. Dabbs, a widow, about two miles from Richmond on Nine Mile Road. Longstreet had said little during the previous meeting, preferring to speak privately with Lee. In his memoirs he wrote that Lee had set a "wise example" during the conference by not revealing his views. "Public discussion and secrecy were incompatible," thought Longstreet.[16]

A Georgian, the forty-one-year-old Longstreet had been Johnston's most trusted subordinate. "What I *did* notice in you in all the years we served together," Johnston told him after the war, "was promptness of thought and action equal to your resolution." Johnston had entrusted to the major general the main assault force at Seven Pines, upwards of 30,000 troops. But Longstreet misunderstood his orders, directed units onto the wrong road, creating delays, and then gave little personal supervision to the fighting. The size of his command—until that time no subordinate had led so many officers and men in an engagement—

and the wooded terrain contributed to his mediocre performance. He did few things right and none well. To his discredit, he blamed Benjamin Huger afterward for his own failings.[17]

Longstreet's family had called him Pete or Peter, and his friends and fellow officers from the Regular Army knew him as "Pete." An aide said of the general, "He has a good deal of the roughness of the old soldier about him." Physically strong, with seemingly limitless stamina, he stood six feet, two inches tall and weighed about 200 pounds. He was self-confident, thorough in his work—"Whatever he has to do, he does well and quickly," noted the staff officer—industrious, and given to few words. When he spoke, there was a bluntness and assertiveness to him. He and his wife had lost three of their young children to scarlet fever in eight days during the past winter. After this family tragedy his religious faith deepened.[18]

Longstreet conferred with Lee in the commanding general's office, which occupied the back room on the first floor of the Dabbs house. In their conversation Longstreet argued for a movement against the Union right flank, behind Beaver Dam Creek near Mechanicsville. Lee, recalled Longstreet, "received me pleasantly and gave a patient hearing to the suggestions, without indicating approval or disapproval." A few days later Lee wrote to Davis: "Longstreet is a Capital soldier. His recommendations hitherto have been good, & I have confidence in him."[19]

On this same day, June 4, Jeb Stuart submitted his views to Lee, on the military situation basing them, as he put it, on "convictions derived from a close observation of the enemy movements for months past, his system of war, and his conduct in battle as well as our own." The Federals would not advance asserted the cavalryman, until they had perfected their works and brought forward heavy artillery to bear on the Confederate lines. In Stuart's view, the Rebels should "move down with a crushing force upon our front and right flank, thwart his designs, and deliver our capital." "We have an army far better adapted to attack, than defend," he added. He would support, however, whatever course of action Lee chose.[20]

Although Lee wisely solicited the opinions of his senior commanders, he had decided on a movement against the Union right flank before the conference with subordinates, the private meeting with Longstreet, and the receipt of Stuart's letter. He said as much to Davis in their ride together. His words to Hill on that same day about the inexperience and morale of the troops in "a pitched battle" revealed, in part, his thinking. He explained later in his campaign report that McClellan's left wing, south of the Chickahominy, "rendered a direct assault injudicious, if not impracticable." Lee saw the weaknesses of his opponent's position—units of the army separated by a river, with a vulnerable supply line—and seized the opportunity.[21]

Lee fashioned his offensive on two established military principles: a concentration of forces and a turning movement. Civil War officers who had fought in Mexico, like Lee, had witnessed those principles utilized by Zachary Taylor and Winfield Scott. Whether strategically in a theater or tactically across a battlefield, the massing of troops against an opponent's vulnerable point gave a general superiority in numbers, and a turning or flanking maneuver forced an enemy either to retire or to offer battle at a disadvantage.[22]

Lee became a master in the application of both principles. In a broad sense they defined his generalship for two years, before he was forced by another master, Ulysses S. Grant, to wage a defensive struggle. Lee's plans and execution were marked by boldness and relentlessness. He preferred maneuver over frontal assaults, but once he had an opponent reeling he sought, in his words, to "destroy," "crush," or "wipeout" the Federal army. Strategically or operationally, he conducted campaigns to inflict a crippling, if not fatal, blow. Once he gained tactical momentum on a battlefield, he pressed it. His audacity magnified the possibilities.[23]

Here, then, on the edge of Richmond, with a cautious McClellan moving deliberately and with units of the Federal army separated by a river, Lee struck. Afterward he explained his plan in his official report: "It was therefore determined to construct defensive lines, so as to enable a part of the army to defend the city and leave the other part free to cross the Chickahominy and operate on the north bank. By sweeping down the river on that side and threatening his communications with York River it was thought that the enemy would be compelled to retreat or give battle out of his intrenchments."[24]

Lee had begun preparations for the offensive by midmonth. On June 11 he ordered Stuart and the cavalry on "a secret movement to the rear of the enemy." He wanted to know the practicability of an advance beyond the Federal right flank. When Stuart discussed the plan with his commander, he broached the idea of a ride around the Union army. Lee thought it unwise, but only cautioned him in the instructions "not to hazard unnecessarily your command or to attempt what your judgment may not approve."[25]

With 1,200 horsemen and a pair of cannon, Stuart started forth the next day. The riders angled northeast past the enemy ranks and then veered eastward, meeting little opposition. They arrived at Old Church on the afternoon of June 13. Stuart had secured the intelligence that Lee desired. When scouts reported that few enemy troops barred the route south toward the Chickahominy, Stuart led the column toward the river. They captured some wagons and prisoners before eluding their pursuers. The cavalrymen entered Richmond on June 15, greeted by throngs of cheering residents.[26]

Lee wrote that the mounted operation "was executed with great address and daring by that accomplished officer." Stuart had embarrassed McClellan and his army and enthused the Southern public with the daring exploit. The Richmond *Examiner* described it as "one of the most brilliant affairs of the war, bold in its inception and most brilliant in its execution." A Georgia soldier exclaimed, "The whole seems fabulous." The youthful Stuart had become what he aspired to be: a hero of the Confederacy.[27]

The cavalry expedition confirmed previous reports that McClellan had not fortified the Pamunkey-Chickahominy watershed. On the same day he ordered Stuart to conduct his operation, Lee notified Stonewall Jackson that three infantry brigades, fourteen regiments, were being sent to him. With these reinforcements Jackson was to march his main body east, to "sweep down" between the two rivers, and to sever McClellan's supply and communications line. Jackson, who had concluded his Valley campaign with tactical victories at Cross Keys and Port Republic on June 8 and 9, respectively, needed several days to ready his command. On June 19 his 16,500 officers and men marched toward Mechum's River Station on the Virginia Central Railroad.[28]

Jackson preceded his troops, traveling by rail and on horseback. He arrived at army headquarters after midday on June 23, "dusty, travel-worn, and apparently very tired," having been in a saddle for twelve hours and covered fifty-two miles. He was escorted into Lee's office, where the commanding general and Harvey Hill, Jackson's brother-in-law, awaited him. Minutes later James Longstreet and A. P. Hill walked into the back room at the Dabbs house. Lee had summoned them so he could discuss his offensive movement against the Army of the Potomac.[29]

The plan, as presented by Lee, was a bold undertaking. While approximately 25,000 troops manned the Confederate defenses south of the Chickahominy, opposite nearly 70,000 Yankees, the remainder of the army—56,000 officers and men under these four generals—would move against the 30,000 Federals posted behind Beaver Dam Creek. Jackson's Valley command, reinforced by the three brigades, would outflank the smaller Union force near Mechanicsville, opening the passage to the north bank of the Chickahominy for Longstreet's and the two Hills' divisions. As Lee stated in his report, McClellan would have to retreat, abandoning his supply line from the Pamunkey River, or offer battle away from his fieldworks.[30]

Undoubtedly Lee anticipated an engagement or engagements, but in its initial stages this was a campaign of maneuver, a turning movement, to unhinge the Union lines. The audacity of the operation was evident in Lee's commitment of the bulk of his army to the offensive while leaving a numerically inferior force in Richmond's defensive works. If McClellan recognized the disparity in numbers, he could overwhelm the city's defenders and capture the Confederate capital. Finally, Lee's plan was complicated, requiring timeliness of movements and cooperation between units.[31]

When Lee finished outlining the operation, he left the room remarking, in Longstreet's recollection, that "he had other matters to look after for a few minutes." A discussion ensued among his subordinates, centering on the opening date of the campaign. Jackson offered June 25, but Longstreet suggested that that might not be enough time if Jackson encountered obstacles and enemy resistance. "Jackson seemed surprisingly unconcerned about the starting times," observed James I. Robertson Jr., a biographer of the general. The evidence conflicts as to whether Lee returned before the matter was settled, but he made the decision to begin the offensive at 3:00 A.M., June 26. The meeting adjourned at nightfall, with a weary Jackson remounting his horse and riding back to rejoin his command.[32]

The thirty-eight-year-old Jackson was the most acclaimed general in the Confederacy for his victories in the recent Shenandoah Valley campaign. After months of defeat and despair, his operations had lifted Southern morale at home and in the army. His so-called foot cavalry had out-marched and out-fought three Union forces. Porter Alexander maintained later, "I believe it to be unsurpassed in all military history in brilliancy & daring." It had been a remarkable achievement that disrupted Federal plans and forestalled an overland advance of reinforcements to McClellan's army.[33]

A Georgia private said it as well as anyone about "Old Jack," as his men called him: "Jackson was always a surprise. Nobody ever understood him, and nobody has ever been quite able to account for him." Cadets at VMI, where Jackson had taught for a decade, swore that he could see backwards. In April 1861, after Virginia had seceded, he told them, "All I have to say is, that when you once draw the sword in a civil war, throw away the scabbard." A staff officer described him as "serious-minded as he was earnest and strong-willed, reticent and exacting of himself."[34]

Ambition burned in Jackson as fervently as did his belief in an omnipotent God from Whom he sought guidance daily. Devoted to the cause, maniacal in the performance of duty, unbending in discipline—"as hard as rails," thought an aide—and unforgiving of failure in subordinates, he demanded unquestioned obedience of orders. His obsession with secrecy infuriated his senior officers. Brigadier General Richard Taylor, who served under Jackson in the Valley, called him "this damned old crazy fool," and another brigadier considered him to be "tyrannical & unjust." He imposed his will on unwilling soldiers and pushed them to the limits of physical endurance. They cursed him for the hardships, but as a colonel noted in a letter in mid-June: "The privates of the whole army have the most unbounded confidence in him. They say he can take them into harder places and get them out better than any other living man and that he cannot be caught asleep or taken when awake."[35]

Jackson stood nearly six feet tall and had a strong, angular frame. He suffered from rheumatism, dyspepsia, and weak eyesight. He ate sparingly, a bland diet, and drank neither coffee, tea, nor liquor. A private, reticent man, he "stays by himself most of the time," confided an aide. "If silence be golden," Richard Taylor said of Jackson, "he was a 'bonanza.'" When he spoke, he did so in "a low, gentle voice." One of Lee's staff officers described his voice as "a nasal twang peculiar to himself."[36]

An artillery private, seeing the famous Stonewall for the first time during the campaign, confessed in his diary, "He is not a man whom I would take for a great general, if I had to judge from his looks." He wore a nondescript uniform, described by others as "the very plainest garb . . . very seedy," that "isn't worth a dollar." G. Moxley Sorrel, Longstreet's chief of staff, wrote that Jackson was "quite shabbily dressed, but neat and clean—little military ornament about him." Sorrel noticed, however, that "it was the eye full of fire and the firm, set face that drew attention." Old Jack was a contradiction, inexplicable to many, but his blue eyes, ablaze on a battlefield, were those of a warrior. More than a year earlier he had drawn the sword and thrown away the scabbard.[37]

Lee issued the written orders for the operation on June 24, committing the army to an offensive on a scale unprecedented in its experience. In numbers it was the largest force that Lee ever led, nearly equal to his opponent—roughly 80,000 effectives to 90,000 Union effectives. Questions remained, however, about the army's ability to execute a complicated movement. It was still early in the war, and many regiments and brigades had not been tested in combat. The same could be said of the Yankees, but an attacking force required more cooperation between commands than those on the defensive. Confederate artillery batteries could not match their enemy counterparts in ordnance and ammunition. In organization and leadership only Jeb Stuart's cavalrymen had an advantage over their mounted foes, but the wooded terrain of the Peninsula limited their roles.[38]

The Confederate rank and file had been expecting a clash for weeks. Within days of Lee's assignment to command, a Georgian wrote his mother, "We are all expecting a battle most every day, are continuously under marching orders." Morale seemed to be high. Brigadier General William D. Dorsey Pender asserted to his wife on June 25: "Our Generals who have access to General Lee are beginning to gain a great deal of confidence in him. Everything, darling, around Richmond looks bright." A War Department clerk noted that President Davis was "very cheerful" about the impending offensive.[39]

Lee's bold offense miscarried at the outset. In his written orders for June 26 Jackson was to initiate the movement at 3:00 A.M., advancing southeast to Pole Green Church, turning the enemy position behind Beaver Dam Creek, and communicating with a detached brigade of A. P. Hill's division, posted near Jackson's route at Half Sink. When Hill was informed of Jackson's passage, he was to cross the Chickahominy with his remaining five brigades and move on Mechanicsville, clearing the Mechanicsville Bridge for a crossing of Longstreet's and Harvey Hill's division. Jackson, meanwhile would continue "well to his left" and outflank the enemy. Once the commands united, they were to "press forward towards the York River Railroad, closing upon the enemy's rear and forcing him down the Chickahominy." South of the river Confederate defenders had orders to hold the lines "at the point of the bayonet."[40]

At the June 23 meeting Longstreet had said to Jackson that the timely advance of the latter's command "is the key of the campaign." But on this day timeliness was beyond the capabilities of the veterans of the Valley campaign. Their march from the Blue Ridge Mountains toward Richmond had been a nightmare of slow-moving trains, muddy, rutted roads, and supply wagons bogged down miles to the rear. Stragglers by the hundreds, if not thousands, abandoned the ranks, stumbled along far behind the columns, or roamed the countryside in search of food and water. By nightfall of June 25, Jackson's command had halted west of Ashland, sixteen miles from Pole Green Church. Jackson issued orders for the march to resume at 2:30 A.M.[41]

Despite the efforts of Jackson and his officers, the main body of hungry, bone-weary soldiers did not step out until eight o'clock in the morning. Jackson, who had slept only eight hours in three days, tried to push the ranks, but without much success. Jeb Stuart and some mounted units joined the march, swinging wide to cover the left flank. Jackson divided the column, marching the two wings on parallel roads. McClellan had learned of Jackson's approach the day before, and Union cavalry dueled with the vanguard and felled trees across the roads. The marchers passed by Pole Green Church late in the day, halting at Hundley's Corner before sundown. Here Jackson expected to make contact with other divisions and to proceed toward Cold Harbor. To the south the sounds of artillery fire and musketry could be heard.[42]

Although hours behind schedule, Jackson was where Lee had specified. The army commander had based his orders, however, on an inaccurate map, which located Pole Green Church beyond the headwaters of Beaver Dam Creek and the Union position along the stream. In fact, the church was three miles from the headwaters, with woods covering much of the gap. If Jackson were to unhinge the Federal line, he would have to attack. Lee had not ordered an assault, and without any messages from the commanding general during the day, Jackson bivouacked his exhausted troops. The hero of the Valley "appeared to me anxious and perplexed," wrote his chief of staff.[43]

On the south bank of the Chickahominy, opposite Mechanicsville, Lee and his division commanders waited through the morning and into the afternoon on word that Jackson had closed on the Union flank. President Davis and his aides joined Lee, Longstreet, and Harvey Hill near Mechanicsville Bridge. Farther upstream A. P. Hill's five brigades lay back from Meadow Bridge. With each passing hour and no advance by A. P. Hill, Lee's concerns mounted, particularly for the Confederate defenders of the capital. McClellan had undertaken a reconnaissance-in-force the day before, testing the Southern works and igniting a sharp engagement near Oak Grove. The Rebels had repulsed the Union advance, but if McClellan renewed the effort in greater force, the Yankees might break through the lines and march into Richmond.[44]

In his memoir Major Joseph Brent recounted that he delivered a message from John Magruder to Lee, arriving about midafternoon. Before Brent departed, Lee said to him, "I cannot wait longer, and have just sent orders to General [A. P.] Hill to cross at Meadow Bridge." Similarly, the army commander said in a postwar conversation that he attacked at Mechanicsville "in order to occupy the enemy and prevent any counter movement." Lee added that he did so against the advice of his engineer officer, "but he was obliged to do *something*." Conversely Hill stated in his official report, "I determined to cross at once rather than hazard the failure of the whole plan by longer deferring it."[45]

Powell Hill, as he was called, possessed an aggressiveness, an "impetuous ardor," in the words of one officer. He had been promoted to major general within the past month for distinguished service on the Peninsula and assigned to command of what he designated the "Light Division." A Virginian, Hill was thirty-six years old, a West Pointer, a thin man, with deep-set, hazel eyes and chestnut hair and beard. He rarely wore a uniform or insignia of rank. He could be aloof and temperamental, with a prickly sense of honor and right. His men called him "Little Powell."[46]

Whether this officer so new to his rank initiated the movement of his own volition or received orders from the commanding general is difficult to determine. But once Hill's advanced guard seized Meadow Bridge, scattering enemy pickets, his five brigades filed across and pushed toward Mechanicsville. On the plateau above Beaver Dam Creek, east of the village, Union batteries opened fire. The blue-coated artillerists and infantrymen belonged to Major General Fitz John Porter's Fifth Corps, supported by the Pennsylvania Reserve Division. They numbered about 30,000 officers and men and were defending their works on McClellan's order. Their position in Porter Alexander's judgment, was "absolutely impregnable to a front attack."[47]

Harvey Hill's and Longstreet's divisions followed across the Chickahominy, their passage slowed by the broken bridge. Lee and his staff rode ahead into the village, where the Confederate commander met Powell Hill. Perhaps that was when Lee believed, as he said after the war, that "he was obliged to do *something*." Lee either ordered or approved a decision by Hill to advance against Porter's position. Hill committed four brigades to the attack—those of Charles Field, James Archer, Joseph R. Anderson, and Dorsey Pender. Most of the regiments in the brigades had not been in combat before. Later Roswell Ripley's brigade of Harvey Hill's division entered the struggle beside Pender's regiments.[48]

The result was a bloody defeat in the fields west of Beaver Dam Creek. Union gunners scorched the Confederate ranks with shellfire and canister. Federal musketry killed and wounded more Southerners. A Pennsylvania artillerist described the Rebels "laying sweltering in their own blood." Some of the attacking units reached the swampy edge of the creek but could go no farther. The fighting ended at about nine

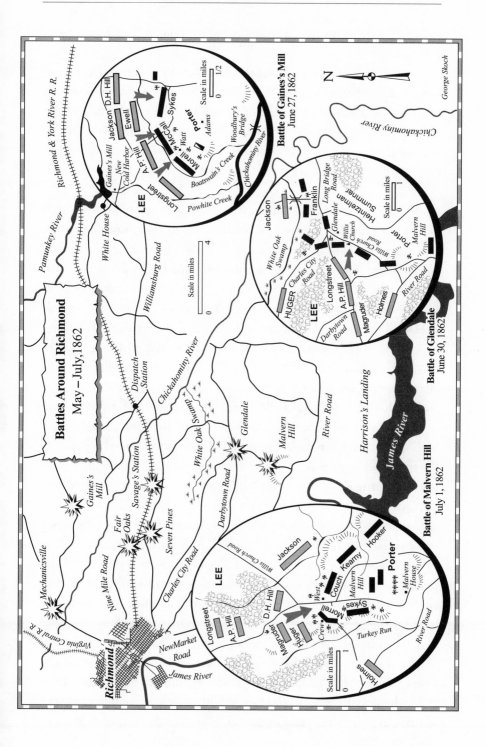

Battles Around Richmond
May – July, 1862

Battle of Gaines's Mill
June 27, 1862

Battle of Glendale
June 30, 1862

Battle of Malvern Hill
July 1, 1862

George Skoch

o'clock. Confederate casualties amounted to about 1,400; Union, fewer than 400.[49]

Harvey Hill offered his assessment of the engagement at Mechanicsville in a postwar article. "The blood shed by the Southern troops there was wasted in vain, and worse than in vain; for the fight had a most dispiriting effect on our troops. They could have been halted at Mechanicsville until Jackson had turned the works on the creek, and all that waste of blood could have been avoided."[50]

It had been a difficult, frustrating day for Lee that ended in futile, costly attacks. Where was Jackson, he could not answer. For his part Jackson reached his assigned destination, heard the sounds of distant combat, and could not fathom their meaning. An inaccurate map and an hours-late start by Jackson had undermined Lee's plans. For unexplained reasons Lee made no effort to learn the whereabouts of Jackson's command. Lawrence Branch, commander of the detached brigade at Half Sink, had made contact with Jackson's right column but never relayed the information to Powell Hill. Ultimately Hill's aggressiveness and Lee's concern for the safety of Richmond triggered the assaults along Beaver Dam Creek.[51]

Despite the command breakdowns and the tactical defeat, operations on the Peninsula had shifted strategically. Unknown to Lee, McClellan had ordered officers at White House to forward supplies to the front and to prepare to abandon the supply base. The Union commander instructed Porter, who had learned of Jackson's presence on his flank at Hundley's Corner, to withdraw to better defensive ground at Gaines's Mill. In his order McClellan stressed to Porter "the absolute necessity of holding the ground." Porter started his command at daylight on June 27, marching four miles southeast to a plateau behind Boatswain's Swamp and deploying his infantry and artillery in a semicircle to cover a retreat route across the Chickahominy. He was to buy time for the passage of the army's wagon trains. With these decisions McClellan ceded the strategic initiative to his opponent.[52]

For a second day, however, maneuver and the security of Richmond shaped Lee's plans. When Porter withdrew, the Confederates at Mechanicsville advanced, Harvey Hill's brigades angling northeast to make contact with Jackson, Powell Hill's and Longstreet's divisions moving on parallel roads in pursuit of the Federals. At about 9:30 A.M., Lee met Jackson at Walnut Grove Church, three miles east of Mechanicsville. When Lee and his staff arrived, Powell Hill's men were marching past, their vanguard skirmishing with the Federals farther ahead. Lee and Jackson conferred for more than a hour.[53]

Lee reasoned that Porter would make a stand to the east behind Powhite Creek. Once again, however, the Confederate commander based his decision on a faulty map that did not show the more defensible ground at Boatswain's Swamp. He ordered Jackson to swing around the assumed Union position with his command and Harvey Hill's division, while Powell Hill and Longstreet pushed Porter's troops toward Jackson's lines. Once again, as at Beaver Dam Creek, a bloody struggle loomed ahead.[54]

The Light Division encountered the Federals at 2:00 P.M. Above open fields and a brush-lined, boggy ravine, the Yankees waited, their infantry ranks stacked in three lines, backed by cannon. Lee ordered an attack, and Powell Hill readied his six brigades. What was about to unfold, said a Pennsylvanian afterward, was "as terrible as human beings can make it."[55]

Brigadier General Maxcy Gregg's South Carolinians went in first. The forty-one-year-old Gregg had been a wealthy lawyer and outspoken advocate of states' rights and secession. Across the fields, into the morass, and up the slope Gregg's men charged. Powell Hill later recalled that their attack was "the handsomest charge in line I have seen during the war." A brigade member exclaimed, "What we had seen before was child's play." The Union musketry and artillery fire tore into their ranks. Blasted back, some of the South Carolinians broke in disorder. Gregg rode among them and rallied them. One of his men called it "the sublimest spectacle I ever saw." They halted at the edge of the ravine, keeping up the fight. One of Hill's aides declared, "Hill is brave to a fault; but as for Gregg, he really loves danger."[56]

Behind the South Carolinians, in succession, came the brigades of Lawrence Branch, Dorsey Pender, Joseph Anderson, James Archer, and Charles Field—regiments from every Confederate state except Texas and Florida. The Southerners came, said a Yankee, with "their piratical flag waiving defiently in the breeze." For two hours the fighting belonged to them and Porter's men. Along sections of the Union lines the Rebels broke through, clubbing and firing in hand-to-hand combat, only to be driven down the slope by enemy counterattacks. Like the South Carolinians, they rallied and hung on below the plateau. Hill lost more than 2,000 killed or wounded.[57]

In his report Lee stated that Hill's men charged "with the impetuous courage for which that officer and his troops are distinguished." Writing after the war, Porter Alexander offered his assessment of what he had witnessed: "We had men good enough & enough of them to have beaten him [Porter] on the very first charge, had one grand simultaneous effort been made. But somehow, God only knows how, everybody else seemed to stand still & let A. P. Hill's division, from 2 o'clock until near or quite four, wreck itself in splendid, but vain & bloody, isolated assaults."[58]

Alexander's criticism did not reflect, however, the actual situation on the battlefield when Hill attacked. "One grand simultaneous effort" could not have been undertaken, as only Longstreet's division was at hand. Lee held these six brigades in reserve while "awaiting anxiously," according to a staff officer, the arrival of Harvey Hill's division and Jackson's command. For a second day misunderstandings and poor communications plagued Confederate operations. It was not until after three o'clock before Harvey Hill's troops approached the battlefield, followed by Richard S. Ewell's veterans of the Valley. Another two hours passed until Jackson's remaining two divisions, strung out and coming up brigade after brigade, shifted into line.[59]

At five o'clock Lee ordered Longstreet to make a diversion against the Union left, but almost from the outset the effort stalled before Yankee firepower. At about the same time Ewell advanced three brigades in piecemeal attacks, which were bloodied and repulsed by the Federals. On Longstreet's left Chase Whiting's two brigades, under Brigadier General John Bell Hood and Colonel Evander Law, moved into position. Powell Hill's battered ranks withdrew to the rear. It was now about seven o'clock, an hour of daylight left, with the ranks of Confederate infantry aligned in a long arc, standing before a hellish slope darkened by lines of enemy infantry and the muzzles of cannon. By Lee's order, they stepped out.[60]

Perhaps now, a dying sun at its back, the Army of Northern Virginia glimpsed the road ahead. In a test of courage on a scale never experienced before, they charged, their yells heralding a warning. They were the Virginians of George Pickett, the North Carolinians of George B. Anderson and Samuel Garland, the Stonewall Brigade, the Alabamians of Cadmus Wilcox, the South Carolinians of Richard Anderson, the Mississippians of Winfield Scott Featherston, and the Texas Brigade. On this day, with their bloodied comrades in the Light Division, they exhibited the valor that was theirs. "No battle-field can boast of more gallantry and devotion," declared Longstreet in his report.[61]

On the crest and along the slope Union cannon and muskets exploded in flame and smoke. A Confederate staff officer described the enemy fire as a "perfect hail." On the Southerners came: "The dead and wounded marked the way of their intrepid advance," reported Lee. At the forefront, in the center of the Rebel lines, were the 4th Texas and the 18th Georgia of the Texas Brigade. At their head and on foot with them, their brigadier, John Bell Hood, urged them forward. He had instructed them not to fire until ordered and to keep moving.[62]

A Kentuckian by birth and a West Pointer, Hood had been colonel of the 4th Texas before promotion to brigadier in March 1862. He was, noted an officer, "a tall, rawboned country-looking man." He had a long face, haunting blue eyes, and a full beard. A Texan described him in battle as "the coolest man I ever knew." Charles Venable of Lee's staff believed that combat "transfigured" him, "The fierce light of his eyes, I can never forget." Members of the Texas Brigade were devoted to him, and he knew each man by name. "Each trusted the other," wrote one of them. "Hood, that the brigade would accomplish all he asked of it—the Texas Brigade, that he would make no demand on it beyond its power."[63]

Through the ravine and up the rise, Hood led the Texans and Georgians. They crossed the first line of fieldworks and surged toward the crest. Close behind them, along the length of the Union defenses, their comrades drove back the Yankees. Porter's ranks unraveled before the onslaught. On the plateau the fighting spiraled into hand-to-hand struggles. Federal reinforcements, sent by McClellan, stiffened the resistance, but they were not enough before the Rebel whirlwind. An ill-

advised mounted charge by blue-jacketed cavalrymen ended in a heap
of dead and wounded men and horses. Porter's valiant troops fled south
across the Chickahominy. Darkness ended the Southern pursuit. Lee's
men captured more than 2,500 Yankees and fourteen cannon.[64]

"No more creditable performance can be found in the history of
the Army of Northern Virginia than the capture of the Federal position near Gaines's Mill by the brigades of Longstreet's and Whiting's
divisions, and better soldiers never fought," asserted Walter Taylor. The
staff officer's praise could have extended to the troops of Powell Hill,
Harvey Hill, and Richard Ewell. "Nothing could surpass the valor and
impetuosity of the men," reported Cadmus Wilcox. Longstreet wrote
similarly, "There was more individual gallantry displayed upon this field
than any I have ever seen."[65]

Such courage and élan exacted a fearful price. Confederate casualties amounted to 8,700 in killed, wounded, and missing; Union losses
approached 6,900. Two acting brigade commanders in Lee's army, colonels Isaac G. Seymour and Samuel V. Fulkerson, were killed. Five regimental colonels fell dead or mortally wounded. Casualties in the 4th
Texas and 1st South Carolina Rifles exceeded 50 percent. That night
an aide of Harvey Hill found Hood, who was sitting on a box and crying,
surrounded by fallen members of the Texas Brigade, which had forged
its reputation a few hours before. Hood said, "Just look here, Major, at
these dead and suffering men, and every one of them as good as I am,
and yet I am untouched."[66]

Porter's fleeing troops had burned the bridge across the Chickahominy before regrouping south of the river. During the night McClellan
met with his corps commanders. Lee's offensive had left the Union generals with two options: they could assault Confederate defenses south
of the stream or they could retreat down the Peninsula. A counterof-
fensive could salvage the three-month campaign and perhaps carry
the Federals into Richmond while the main body of Lee's army was
north of the Chickahominy. But such a strike entailed risk and possibly heavy casualties. Convinced that he was outnumbered—he placed
Rebel strength at a gravely exaggerated 200,000—McClellan would not
or could not take that gamble. He ordered the supply base at White
House to be destroyed and the army to begin marching south to the

James River, where a new depot would be established. The campaign for the Confederate capital was to be abandoned. "If we were defeated," he told the assembled officers, "the Army and the country would be lost."[67]

The Army of the Potomac consisted of willing men led by an unwilling commander. Porter's stands at Beaver Dam Creek and Gaines's Mill showed the mettle of the army's rank and file. Characteristically, McClellan blamed the Lincoln administration for his troubles by delaying the march of reinforcements from Fredericksburg. McClellan's methodical operations before Richmond, however, had presented Lee with the opportunity to reshape the campaign. With his decision to retreat, McClellan defined himself and, to a great degree, his generalship. Ahead was a hazardous enterprise, conducted over poor roads, across White Oak Swamp, slowed by miles of supply and ordnance wagons and ambulances filled with sick and wounded soldiers. It would test the temper of his army.[68]

Lee spent Saturday, June 28, deciphering his opponent's intentions. Skirmishers confirmed that enemy batteries remained on the south bank below Gaines's Mill. Lee could not believe that McClellan would abandon the supply base at White House, so he ordered Richard Ewell's infantrymen and Jeb Stuart's cavalrymen east toward the Richmond–York River Railroad, the Union supply line. Ewell and Stuart sent reports that indicated a Federal retreat, and dust clouds south of the river, which Lee saw, gave more evidence of a withdrawal. Lee hesitated to act, however, until the route of the enemy movement—either east down the Peninsula or south to the James River—could be ascertained.[69]

During the night two Confederate engineers forded the Chickahominy on a reconnaissance. Returning soon after sunrise, they reported that the Federals had evacuated a defensive position south of the river. Lee reasoned that McClellan must be in retreat to the James River and issued orders for a pursuit. He wrote to Jefferson Davis that "though not certain" of the enemy's route, "the whole army has been put in motion upon this supposition."[70]

North and south of the river, Confederate units stirred upon Lee's instructions. Longstreet's and Powell Hill's divisions marched west, crossed the Chickahominy at New Bridge, passed the outskirts of Richmond, and bivouacked for the night roughly four miles west of the road used by the enemy. The divisions of John Magruder and Benjamin Huger, coming out of the city's defenses, marched east on parallel roads toward the Union columns. Jackson was directed to rebuild Grapevine Bridge, cross the river, and move against the Federal rear while Magruder and Huger closed on it from the west. Lee hoped to slow McClellan's withdrawal across White Oak Swamp and to interdict the Yankees' march on the next day.[71]

Magruder's three understrength divisions formed the key component of the Confederate movement. Lee crossed the river, met with Magruder, and evidently urged the major general to act aggressively in an advance east on Williamsburg Road. Magruder believed that Benjamin Huger's division would follow on the road and support him in an action. Lee ordered Huger, however, to march on Charles City Road toward the crossroads at Glendale. Huger could protect Magruder's right flank but was too distant to lend immediate assistance.[72]

The clash occurred in the afternoon west of Savage Station, where Magruder encountered the Union rear guard north of White Oak Swamp. The fighting lasted for two hours, a bloody, blinding struggle in the woods on both sides of Williamsburg Road. The brigades of Joseph Kershaw and Paul Semmes fought the numerically superior Federals to a draw. In the action Brigadier General Richard Griffith, commanding Mississippians, was mortally wounded by a piece of artillery shell and died the next day in Richmond. Magruder's losses amounted to fewer than 400; Union losses approached 600.[73]

During the fighting at Savage Station, Major General David Jones requested support from Jackson. Jones's brigades covered Magruder's left flank between Williamsburg Road and the Chickahominy. On the river's north bank Jackson's troops were repairing Grapevine Bridge and a second span, Alexander's Bridge, named for the Union engineer who had overseen its construction. Work details had not completed the second structure when Jones's message reached Jackson. In a terse reply Jackson said that he could not support Jones "as he has other important duty to perform."[74]

Lee's orders to Jackson specified that he should support Magruder by crossing the river and "push the pursuit vigorously." Before Jackson heard from Jones, he received a copy of a dispatch, written by Lee's chief of staff, Robert Chilton, and addressed to Jeb Stuart. The cavalry general had forwarded it to Jackson. The note said that Stuart should watch the lower river crossings, ascertain if the enemy might move in that direction, and advise Jackson, "who will resist their passage until reinforced."[75]

Jackson misinterpreted Chilton's poorly worded dispatch, concluding that his command should guard the crossings, and if the enemy were to move toward them, his troops could assail the Federals. To Jackson, this was the "other important duty to perform." Magruder informed Lee of Jackson's reply, which the commanding general described later as having "originated in some mistake." Jackson bivouacked his men for the night on the north side of the river and did not begin moving south until 2:00 A.M. on June 30. It was not what Lee had expected.[76]

During the night of June 29–30, the final contingent of the Union army crossed White Oak Swamp, burning the bridge behind it. At Savage Station, 2,500 sick and wounded Yankees, abandoned by their comrades, awaited capture. By the morning of June 30, seven divisions and a brigade of infantry, supported by batteries, numbering about 55,000 Northerners, lay at or around Glendale, where Charles City, Long Bridge, and Quaker roads intersected. Earlier, on June 29, when a cavalry officer informed McClellan that no Confederate troops had been seen west of Glendale, the army commander remarked, "The roads will be full enough tomorrow."[77]

After the war William Allan, a staff officer, wrote of June 30, 1862, "This day marked the crisis in the Seven Days' Battles, for it was on this 30th of June that Lee more nearly grasped the full fruits of his strategy and McClellan more narrowly escaped complete overthrow than on any other." Porter Alexander concurred. "Never, before or after, did the fates put such a prize within our reach." The "crisis" and the "prize" lay at Glendale.[78]

As McClellan had predicted, toward the crossroads came the Rebels. Longstreet's and Powell Hill's divisions, under Longstreet's command, advanced on Long Bridge Road. To their left Benjamin Huger's men moved on Charles City Road, while on the Confederate right Major General Theophilus H. Holmes and two brigades, brought north from

Petersburg, angled southeast to occupy New Markets Heights, securing the army's flank. Jackson, north of White Oak Swamp, was "to pursue the enemy on the road he had taken." Magruder had orders to support Longstreet by Darbytown Road. Lee and President Davis trailed Longstreet's and Hill's columns.[79]

It was midafternoon when the battle began, in Moxley Sorrel's words, "with great suddenness and severity." When Longstreet heard Huger's cannon open fire to his left, he ordered a charge by Colonel Micah Jenkins, in temporary command of Richard Anderson's brigade of South Carolinians. Longstreet regarded Jenkins as "the best officer he ever saw." The colonel and his fellow South Carolinians disappeared into the woods and into a scythe of Union musketry and artillery fire. They faced the Pennsylvania Reserve Division and were slaughtered. Jenkins rode along their ranks, urging them forward, but they looked at him as if to say, "We can go no further." Yet they stood, their ranks thinning with each enemy volley.[80]

Longstreet fed more brigades into the fury. Next came James Kemper's Virginians, followed by Cadmus Wilcox's Alabamians. These Southerners overran Union batteries and breached an infantry line, but enemy counterattacks shoved them back into the woods. A Yankee exclaimed, "To believe any man desires to go into battle, is to believe him a fool." Longstreet had hesitated to commit his entire division and Hill's brigades, anticipating the assaults of Huger and Jackson. But the South Carolinians, Virginians, and Alabamians needed support.[81]

The intensity of the combat forced Longstreet to commit his final three brigades and Powell Hill to order in all six of his brigades. Union reinforcements, upward of 10,000 troops drawn from the rear guard opposite Jackson's command, entered the struggle. "The volume of fire that . . . rolled along the line was terrific," reported Hill. Porter Alexander believed that the engagement had the most hand-to-hand combat he knew of in the war. The Confederates seized eighteen cannon, a host of prisoners, and a few stands of colors, but the valiant stand of their opponent kept Willis Church Road, the retreat route, open, saving McClellan's army. Then, with a suddenness that had marked its beginning, the fighting ceased.[82]

Longstreet stated in his report, "The troops sustained their reputation for coolness, courage, determination, and devotion so well earned on many hotly contested fields." Porter Alexander said that the soldiers fought the Yankees "for all that they were worth." The battle at Glendale, or Frayser's Farm, involved 60,000 men, two Northerners for every one Southerner. Confederate losses amounted to at least 3,500; Federal, about 3,000. Longstreet lost another brigade commander, Winfield Featherston, who was severely wounded in the shoulder.[83]

Among those engaged at Glendale the missed opportunity lingered into the postwar years. Cadmus Wilcox recalled, "It could not have been expected that two divisions should have accomplished what was intended to be achieved by the whole army." Referring to Huger and Jackson, William Allan asserted: "The others accomplished nothing. They did not even prevent reinforcements from going to the Federal centre." The most critical analysis came from Porter Alexander, who declared: "When one thinks of the great chances in General Lee's grasp that one summer afternoon, it is enough to make one cry to go over the story how they were all lost. And to think too that our *Stonewall Jackson* lost them." Alexander went further, alleging that it was at Glendale, not at Gettysburg, that Lee's army missed its finest chance for a victory to end the war.[84]

Huger performed miserably, undertaking feeble attacks on the enemy, but Jackson's failure to force a crossing of White Oak Swamp and to assail the Union rear guard has undergone scrutiny ever since. When his command reached the swamp they confronted a destroyed bridge and a force of Union infantry and artillery, numbering about 22,000 men, in a good defensive position. Jackson's batteries engaged the Federal gun crews, and he accompanied some cavalry across the marsh, viewing the enemy force. When he returned to the north side he "quit," in the estimation of the historian Douglas Southall Freeman: "His initiative died almost in the moment of his return from the south side of the swamp."[85]

But instead of quitting, Jackson seemed incapable of decisive action. Although he had crews work at repairing the bridge and ordered reconnaissance parties in search of other crossing sites, he did little more. When Longstreet sent Major John Fairfax with a request for assistance, Jackson gave no reply and walked away from the staff officer. He ignored reports of favorable locations for a passage of the morass and went to sleep. His greatest failure was in not attempting some effort that would have held the Federal rear guard in place, preventing the departure of nearly half the force to the combat at Glendale. Jackson's opponent, Brigadier General William B. Franklin, contended that had Jackson attacked simultaneously at the wrecked bridge and at a ford a mile upstream, the Confederates "would have embarrassed us exceedingly."[86]

Jackson's performance in this campaign has been framed against his conduct in the army's other operations—the seeming inexplicable compared to the outstanding, even brilliant. A foremost authority on Lee's army, Robert K. Krick, has argued, "The Stonewall Jackson of the Seven Days did absolutely nothing." Krick and other historians have attributed the Valley hero's failings to physical exhaustion caused by a lack of sleep and illness. Jackson, Krick has written, was "exhausted beyond the ability to function adequately." A biographer of the general, James I. Robertson Jr., titled his chapter on the Seven Days "Fatigue." Jackson admitted to his wife in a July 7 letter, "During the past week I have not been well, have suffered from fever and debility."[87]

The numbing strain on Jackson's body and mind culminated, according to Krick, at White Oak Swamp: "The worst of Jackson's days during this bad week clearly came on June 30." Although Robertson accepts that Jackson was exhausted, he has also analyzed the difficulties of the terrain, the natural strength of Franklin's position, and Lee's orders. Robertson has argued that Jackson had instructions to pursue the enemy, not attack him. Lee and Jackson had met that morning, and surely Lee outlined the day's operations. Furthermore the sounds of battle at Glendale could be heard distinctly by Jackson's troops. Lee indicated his expectations when he stated in his report, "Could the other commands have co-operated in the action the result would have proved most disastrous to the enemy."[88]

As Robertson has noted, however, Lee must share blame for the day's outcome: "What happened at White Oak Swamp is fundamentally what happened throughout the Seven Days Campaign: an all but complete breakdown in communications between the Confederate generals." Lee spent much of the afternoon within an hour's horseback ride from Jackson but never sent a staff officer to inquire about the difficulties Jackson faced. Instead, late in the day, he joined Holmes and viewed the Federal units on Malvern Hill. Porter Alexander could have been describing this situation on June 30 when he compared an army to a machine, contending, "If a machine balks at any point he [the commander] may be most promptly informed & may most promptly start it to work."[89]

It was at Glendale, perhaps, that a rarity—the destruction of a major portion of an enemy army—eluded Lee's grasp. The historian Freeman has called the battle "one of the greatest lost opportunities in Confederate military history. It was the bitterest disappointment Lee had ever sustained, and one that he could not conceal." In the end a stubborn Union defense had held, and through the night the blue-coated defenders marched away from the crossroads, joining their comrades on Malvern Hill. The next morning the clanging Confederate machine followed toward a terrible consequence of Glendale's missed chances.[90]

If the fates conspired against the Confederates at Glendale, they crafted a tragedy for them at Malvern Hill. With the entire Army of the Potomac arrayed on its broad, open crest, it possessed, said a Union general, "elements of great strength." Malvern Hill rose 150 feet above the surrounding terrain, with cleared hillsides and fields of ripened grain and shocks of harvested wheat. Marshes and ravines protected the defenders' flanks. Rows of cannon and ranks of infantry held the doors to a slaughterhouse.[91]

The van of the Army of Northern Virginia came into view of their opponents at about midmorning on July 1. Unwell and ill-tempered on this day, Lee had ordered a pursuit, believing that the Yankees were demoralized and vulnerable. According to Cadmus Wilcox, word in the army was, "We were on a hot trail." William Allan contended that to Lee "the object aimed at was the overthrow of the Federal army, not the prevention of its retreat to Harrison's Landing. . . . A united and determined attack with his force on the enemy before they were out of reach seemed to promise the overthrow in part, if not in whole, of the Federal army."[92]

Lee had been forewarned of what lay ahead. He and Longstreet met Harvey Hill at Willis Church during the morning. To his men, Hill was "a fighter from way-back." The division commander had learned from a local minister of Malvern Hill's natural strength. After recounting the civilian's description of the terrain, Hill said, "If General McClellan is there in force, we had better let him alone." Longstreet laughed and jokingly replied to his fellow academy classmate and old friend, "Don't get scared now that we have got him whipped." Lee said nothing, but if a combative officer like Hill had misgivings, his caution should have been heeded.[93]

The Confederates stumbled to one of the saddest places in the army's history. Inaccurate maps, heavily wooded terrain, faulty troop dispositions, erroneous reports, incompetence, and no "concert of action," in Lee's words, combined to pull the army into a bloodbath. An exhausted Lee—he slept for a time under a tree—had difficulty formulating a plan. He examined the Union position and even posted individual units. At his request Longstreet conducted a reconnaissance on the army's right front and located an "elevated point" that could serve as a platform for artillery. He reported to Lee that cannon from this site and from a field along Jackson's line on the army's left could rake the plateau of Malvern Hill in a crossfire and prepare the way for an infantry assault. He estimated that forty to sixty guns could be placed on the elevation.[94]

Lee approved Longstreet's idea. Brigadier General Lewis A. Armistead's brigade of Virginians occupied an advanced position in the center of the army's line. From there they had a good view of the enemy's ranks on the crest. Lee had his chief of staff, Robert Chilton, prepare a written order to division commanders. It read: "Batteries have been established to rake the enemy's lines. If it is broken, as is probable, Armistead, who can witness the effect of the fire, has been ordered to charge with a yell. Do the same."[95]

Whether Lee dictated the order or read it after it had been written is uncertain. It was, however, an astonishing message. "As a combat directive," the historian A. Wilson Green has asserted, "Lee's orders at Malvern Hill are almost unbelievable." The responsibility for an infantry assault rested on the observations and judgment of a brigadier. Armistead never indicated that his division commander, Benjamin Huger, forwarded the order to him.[96]

Skirmishing between infantry units and sporadic exchanges between batteries characterized the action until Confederate gun crews began rolling their pieces into position for the bombardment. From Malvern Hill, Union artillerists unleashed their fury. When the Southern crews answered, the Federals targeted their guns. The Rebels brought fewer than thirty cannon to bear on the plateau, inflicting minor damage. The superiority and the greater number of the Union ordnance soon prevailed, silencing their foes. In his report Lee described "the extraordinary force of that arm" in McClellan's army.[97]

The inability of the Confederates to engage the Federals with more guns symbolized a recurring problem during the campaign: a breakdown in communication. Batteries attached to infantry commands remained idle. The army's artillery reserve of more than twenty batteries stood in a park a few miles to the rear, in woods south of Willis Church, because the chief of artillery, Brigadier General William N. Pendleton, admitted later he could not find Lee for instructions. Thus, in the judgment of the historian of Lee's artillery, "the setting was complete for a tremendous disaster, the certainty of which to an attacking force unsupported by a preponderance of artillery fire would have been patent to a novice who had become familiar with" the Union position on Malvern Hill.[98]

Lee and Longstreet meanwhile surveyed the enemy's right front. Longstreet "understood," as he stated in his report, that Lee had decided against an infantry assault because of the strength of the Federal position. Instead the army commander directed Longstreet to take his and Powell Hill's divisions, which had been held in reserve, to turn the enemy's right flank. As both generals rode back to implement the maneuver, two aides delivered messages to Lee, each one indicating a Union retreat. The information was wrong; the Yankees had not begun a withdrawal but had shifted units on the plateau.[99]

One dispatch came from John Magruder, who reported that Armistead had advanced farther. In fact Armistead's men had managed only to shove back Union skirmishers. Magruder had arrived at the front a short time before and knew little about the terrain or troop deployments. A soldier who saw him at this time thought, "He was the reddest, hottest looking man I ever saw." A nearby battery commander testified later that Magruder "seemed to be laboring under the most terrible excitement."[100]

Robert Chilton penned Lee's fateful order to Magruder: "General

Lee expects you to advance rapidly. He says it is reported the enemy is getting off. Press forward your whole line and follow up Armistead's successes." Thus two pieces of false information triggered one of the worst mistakes in Lee's career. "The attack at Malvern Hill contradicted everything the Confederate commander had been trying to achieve in his first campaign," the historian Joseph Harsh has written. Harvey Hill's advice portended a "terrible disaster."[101]

It was four o'clock in the afternoon or some minutes past when Lewis Armistead's and Ambrose "Rans" Wright's officers and men stepped out. For the next four hours fellow Southerners in thirteen full brigades and regiments from other ones ascended the rising ground toward the crest of Malvern Hill. There was, Lee said, no "proper concert of action among the troops." The brigades charged piecemeal, singly, or in pairs. A Yankee private stated that the Rebels "rushed on in great numbers, seemingly regardless of consequences." He was convinced that they had to be "full of whiskey" to keep coming. After they had been repulsed, asserted a Union officer, "they advanced again with grim, hard-set resolution."[102]

All that they cherished and believed—of home, of duty, of cause, of comrades—they needed on this field before the flames of Yankee cannon and the flashes of thousands of muskets. To stay there, to go forward, to fall back, and to step forth again required a courage that lay in the deepest folds of men's souls. They were engulfed in carnage amid a deafening roar and the screams of falling comrades. Many could not withstand it, panicked, and fled. More, however, remained in the ranks, doing what one general said "was all that could be asked and even more than could be expected of men."[103]

They spoke of it in words haunted by the reality. A Georgia lieutenant confided to his parents that on "that field a tempest of iron & lead was sweeping over it cutting down every living thing." He continued: "Oh what a terrible consuming fire is man's passions when it has full sway. . . . Nothing but a kind Providence saved any of us alive." A Virginia soldier described it as a "perfect hail storm of shell, grape, canister." Another Virginian claimed, "The roar of the artillery was such that our firing was hardly audible." Porter Alexander remembered "the rivers of good blood that flowed that evening all in vain." A veteran recalled, "At no other time did I so realize the horrors of a battle field."[104]

Lafayette McLaws, whose brigades joined in the assaults, said, "It was but a slaughter pen." In a postwar letter to Longstreet, he declared: "As for Malvern Hill, who is going to tell the truth about it, the whole truth. If I ever [were] to write what I saw . . . I would be denounced by our own people as a caluminator." Harvey Hill said as much, writing two years later, "My recollections of Malvern Hill are so unpleasant that I do not like to write about it." In a published account afterward, Hill put it bluntly, "It was not war—it was murder."[105]

Hill and Lee attributed the defeat to a "want of concert among the attacking columns." The vagaries in the terrain and the lack of overall direction almost precluded such coordination among units. Although Lee had ordered in McLaws's troops, the fight was conducted by division and brigade commanders, not by the commanding general. The rank and file later described it as "a criminal blunder" and "useless sacrifice" and wrote "We were very badly led," "The battle ought never to have been fought where it was," and "The reckoning there was awful and apparently for no good." Years later an artillerist wrote in a memoir, "No Confederate cares to say anything about it."[106]

The casualty lists revealed the truth of the forlorn attacks. Confederate losses amounted to 5,650 killed, wounded, and missing; Union casualties barely exceeded 2,100. In numbers engaged the percentage of Lee's fallen at Malvern Hill compared to those lost at Gaines's Mill. That night Lee rode through the army's camps and, according to an account, met John Magruder. Lee asked, "General Magruder, why did you attack?" He replied, "In obedience to your orders twice repeated." The question and the answer illustrated Malvern Hill's tragic cost.[107]

Before midnight on July 2 the Federals began their withdrawal from Malvern Hill, leaving behind wounded comrades and marching toward Harrison's Landing and the protection of gunboats on the James River. Lee met in the morning with Longstreet, Jackson, Stuart, and President Davis. Lee asked Longstreet, "What are your impressions?"

"I think you hurt them about as much as they hurt you," replied Longstreet.

"Then I am glad we punished them well, at any rate."[108]

Discussions of the army's condition continued when a report arrived that confirmed the Union retreat. Stuart left with his cavalry in pursuit.

An "incessant rain" began falling at about midday, the muddy roads slowing the Confederate horsemen. But Stuart's men bagged scores of enemy stragglers along the route. Later that night the cavalry commander informed Lee by courier that he would resume the pursuit at daylight, noting, "McClellan is doubtless awaiting his transports."[109]

The mounted pursuit ended at Evelington Heights, a mile-long elevation near Harrison's Landing. Beneath Stuart and his troops, on "a beautiful plain," sprawled the campsite of the Army of the Potomac, with its vast train of artillery and wagons. Stuart hurried a message to Lee, who responded that the cavalry should "retard" the enemy until the infantry, who were on the march, joined them. Lee praised Stuart for "the vigorous pursuit."[110]

Then, in an action Charles Venable of Lee's staff later termed "a grave error," Stuart brought out a howitzer and began shelling the campsite. "Stuart's fondness for the use of artillery was almost excessive," claimed an aide. Union gunboats returned the fire and, in the words of a cavalryman, "We skedaddled." The general's hasty, if not rash, decision alerted the Yankees to the tactical importance of the heights, and bluecoated infantrymen soon occupied the elevation. Although McClellan and his generals might have recognized the army's vulnerability before Confederate infantry arrived, Major Walter Taylor contended, "Those heights in our possession, the enemy's position was altogether untenable, and he was at our mercy; unless they could be recaptured his capitulation was inevitable."[111]

It is not known if Lee ever expressed any criticism of Stuart's action. The next morning, with the infantry at hand, he and Jackson examined the Union ranks on Evelington Heights. While standing and looking through their field glasses, the two generals came under distant fire from enemy sharpshooters. Jackson argued against any further attacks. "It was deemed inexpedient to attack him [McClellan]," Lee stated in his report, "and in view of the condition of our troops, who had been marching and fighting almost incessantly for seven days under the most trying circumstances, it was determined to withdraw, in order to afford them the repose of which they stood so much in need." The Confederates marched away from their foes, leaving behind cavalry to observe the Federals, ending the campaign.[112]

At Harrison's Landing members of the Army of the Potomac passed the Fourth of July with "not much enthusiasm, but we fired a salute by way of keeping up appearances," according to a lieutenant. George McClellan rode through the camps, inspiring the men with "a new vigor." His subordinates and the rank and file, not he, had executed a skillful retreat. At Glendale and at Malvern Hill, with combat looming, he rode away from the army. He believed to the end that he and the army had been betrayed by the administration in Washington, D.C. There was a blindness to "Little Mac."[113]

In April, McClellan had heard a rumor that Lee had replaced Joseph Johnston in command of the Confederate army. He forwarded the information to Abraham Lincoln, and then stated, "I prefer Lee to Johnston—the former is *too* cautious & weak under grave responsibility—personally brave & energetic to a fault, he yet is wanting in moral firmness when pressed by heavy responsibility & is likely to be timid & irresolute in action." In the Seven Days Campaign he and his army had learned otherwise.[114]

Chapter Three

"To Change the Theater of the War"

ROBERT E. LEE'S JULY 7 congratulatory order to the army read in part: "On Thursday, June 26, the powerful and thoroughly-equipped army of the enemy was intrenched in works vast in extent and most formidable in character within sight of our capital. To-day the remains of that confident and threatening host lie upon the banks of the James River, 30 miles from Richmond, seeking to recover, under the protection of his gunboats, from the effects of a series of disastrous defeats."[1]

The statement summarized the basic facts of the Seven Days Campaign. Lee attributed the campaign's outcome to "the only Giver of all victory," who "has blessed our arms," and to "the courage, endurance, and soldierly conduct of the officers and men engaged." The order ended with these words: "Soldiers, your country will thank you for the heroic conduct you have displayed—conduct worthy of men engaged in a course so just and sacred, and deserving a nation's gratitude and praise."[2]

Lee's army had achieved the first significant Confederate victory since First Manassas in July 1861. On July 4 the Richmond *Enquirer* proclaimed, "From out [of] the gloom and doom of the past, the martial spirit has emerged . . . [and] the skill and valor of our men over our brutal foe is incontestably established." A rival newspaper, the Richmond *Dispatch*, was even more effusive in its praise: "History has no record of such succession of triumphs. . . . Throughout all time they will stand without parallel in the annals of warfare."[3]

The campaign had achieved the immediate objective of preventing the capture of Richmond. In a broader sense, as the Richmond *Enquirer* editorialized, the victory affirmed to Southern folks the prowess of their arms and reinvigorated Confederate morale. Conversely the campaign's outcome stunned Northerners. The defeat, reported the New York *Times*, was "entirely unexpected." The retreat of the Union army "shatters the high hope which the country has of late indulged."[4]

Strategically, with the Army of the Potomac at Harrison's Landing on the James River, the threat to the Confederate capital remained. For the present, if he chose to wield it, George McClellan held the initiative in the region. But beyond the present the failure of McClellan's campaign portended a longer, more inexorable conflict, "a war to the knife!," in the words of a New York lieutenant. A staff officer with McClellan contended perceptively that the army's defeat was "destined to be followed by the effusion of seas of blood."[5]

For Lee and his army, the final week of June marked a historic passage. The Seven Days Campaign, wrote Porter Alexander of Lee, "seems to me perhaps his greatest achievement." A private stated, "Gen. Lee has proven himself the master of the art of war." In a dramatic manner the Confederates had altered what seemed inevitable, the advance of that darkening shadow across the Confederacy. "The 'half-success' at Richmond had a seismic effect on the Confederacy's war for nationhood," the historian Gary Gallagher has concluded. "Lee's debut as a field commander marked the most important watershed in the development of the Army of Northern Virginia—and one of the crucial turning points of the entire war."[6]

The operation's strategic success confirmed Lee's commitment to the offensive, executed by a concentration of forces and a turning movement. When he had assumed command of the army, Lee rejected the idea of a passive defensive stand. He accepted the risks of an offensive strike because he had to be daring. Alexander regarded Lee's audac-

ity "as the *greatest of all* of his greatest qualities," explaining, "Our inferiority in force made [offense] an *absolute requisite* to give us *any chance*
at all." For the first time, along the Chickahominy River, Lee demonstrated the boldness that became arguably the dominant characteristic
of his generalship.[7]

The Confederate commander initiated the offensive with a turning movement, but as the campaign unfolded he sought a killing blow
against the retreating enemy. He attempted such crippling, if not fatal,
strikes at Glendale and Malvern Hill. Although the attacks failed at
both places, they did not dissuade him from his belief in the possible
destruction of the Union army. Like Lee's qualities, as a strategist and a
tactician, his search for that decisive opportunity shaped his operations.
The Seven Days Campaign was merely the beginning.[8]

The defeats at Glendale and Malvern Hill almost assuredly explain
Lee's reaction to the campaign's results. "We of Gen. Lee's staff knew
at the time," recalled Alexander, "that he was deeply, bitterly disappointed, but he made no official report of it & glossed all over as much
as possible in his own reports." Lee confided to his wife on July 9, "Our
success has not been as great or complete as I could have desired, but
God knows what is best for us."[9]

Lee stated in his report, "Under ordinary circumstances the Federal
Army should have been destroyed." Staff officer Walter Taylor described
the Seven Days as "a record of lost opportunities." But neither Lee's nor
Taylor's assessment accurately reflected the reality on the field. Under
the best of circumstances the destruction of McClellan's formidable
command, whose rank and file had fought stubbornly and bravely, was
simply beyond the skill of the Confederates. Only at Glendale did the
Southerners have a chance to inflict a serious, perhaps crippling defeat
on part of the Union army. The failure to do so exemplified the problems that plagued Lee and his lieutenants throughout the operations.[10]

"Every movement of an army must be well-considered and properly
ordered," wrote Lee in a postwar letter. Although his offensive movement had been "well considered," vague orders and the lack of communication and coordination between the independent divisions
undermined the execution. Inaccurate maps, the wooded terrain with
swampy bottomlands, and "the want of correct and timely information,"

in Lee's words, compounded the organizational failures, resulting in disjointed attacks and slowing the pursuit. The army's artillery had been
either underutilized or misused, allowing the superior Union ordnance
to dominate the battlefields at Gaines's Mill and Malvern Hill.[11]

The campaign also exposed the inadequacy of staff work within the
army. From the beginning, at Beaver Dam Creek, to the end, at Malvern Hill, the breakdown in or lack of communications between Lee
and his subordinates was critical, hampering, even preventing, cooperation between units. Primary blame rested with Lee, whose personal staff
was too small for the demands placed upon it. Lafayette McLaws argued
after the war, "The great defect in our army was in staff organization
& its practices." The problem persisted, however, long after the campaign's conclusion.[12]

James Longstreet described the Confederate offensive as "a succession of mishaps." His conclusion had elements of truth to it, but a
more accurate assessment came from Porter Alexander, who wrote in
his memoirs: "We had men enough, & good enough, to have gotten
him [McClellan] & all he had, if we had only been organised up to the
standards which we finally reached. But as yet we were green & had to
learn by experience."[13]

Still, by July 2, with the Union army slogging through mud toward
Harrison's Landing, the Confederates had prevailed, despite the organizational flaws, the miscommunications, the "mishaps," and the failings of subordinates. The Yankees had been driven from Richmond's
environs, and according to Lee's report, his army had captured fifty-two
cannon, nearly 31,000 firearms, 10,000 sets of accoutrements, and 6,000
knapsacks, all vitally needed ordnance and equipment. A modern study
of the campaign has placed the number of seized artillery pieces at forty.
Five thousand or more Federal soldiers had been captured.[14]

The Confederates had achieved victory at a fearful price. Casualty
figures vary slightly, but the most recent book on the campaign calcu-
lates them at 3,478 killed or mortally wounded, 16,261 wounded, and
875 missing, for a total of 20,614. Union losses amounted to 1,734 killed
or mortally wounded, 8,062 wounded, and 6,053 missing, or 15,849 in
all. The higher casualties for Lee's army reflected the reality of Civil
War combat: attackers sustained greater losses than defenders.[15]

The divisions of James Longstreet, Harvey Hill, and Powell Hill—the units that bore the brunt of the assaults, except at Malvern Hill—incurred the highest casualty rates, from 25 percent to nearly 50 percent. One brigadier, Richard Griffith, had been mortally wounded, and seven had sustained wounds; among these were Dorsey Pender, George Pickett, George B. Anderson, and Arnold Elzey. A Georgian captain wrote during the campaign: "I know very well why we lose so many generals. They never send the men where they are afraid and do not go themselves."[16]

At the regimental level casualties among field grade officers were daunting. Nearly 110 colonels, lieutenant colonels, and majors were killed, wounded, or captured. More than one-third of the fallen had been fatally shot, including thirteen colonels or regimental commanders. Southern culture honored bravery and aggressiveness, and soldiers in the ranks expected officers to be in the forefront during combat. Losses at this command level reflected this martial spirit and this measurement of leadership.[17]

"We were lavish of blood in those days," Harvey Hill averred in a postwar article, "and it was thought to be a great thing to charge a battery of artillery or an earth-work lined with infantry." Referring in part to Beaver Dam Creek and Malvern Hill, the former general declared that the assaults "were all grand, but of exactly the kind of grandeur which the South could not afford." In another written piece Hill claimed, "Throughout this campaign we attacked just when and where the enemy wished us to attack."[18]

The more than 20,000 Confederate casualties lent validity to Hill's criticisms. By these assertions Hill inferred that Lee and his senior generals had committed the army to a series of doomed assaults, regardless of the cost in blood. Unquestionably the attacks at Beaver Dam Creek and Malvern Hill were unwise and resulted in costly repulses. At both places, however, miscommunications and the actions of subordinates triggered the offensive strikes. Malvern Hill stands as a prime indictment of Lee's alleged predilection for frontal assaults, but the evidence indicates that he had decided against assailing the Union position until two false intelligence reports indicated that the Federals had resumed their retreat. To be sure, at Malvern Hill Lee "misjudged both the weakness of the enemy and the capabilities of his own army," the historian Joseph Harsh has written.[19]

Lee had predicated his bold endeavor on maneuver, on a broad turning movement that would force McClellan to retreat either down the Peninsula or toward the James River. At Gaines's Mill, the bloodiest engagement of the campaign, circumstances forced him to order attacks on Fitz John Porter's command. By keeping McClellan's attention on events north of the Chickahominy River, Lee negated a possible Union advance against the weakened defenses south of the stream. The Confederate commander and his generals deserved criticism for the disjointed, piecemeal attacks at each battlefield, except for the final charge at Gaines's Mill. Inexperience, shortcomings in organization and leadership, and stout enemy resistance accounted more for the magnitude of Southern losses than Lee's preference for "grand" assaults.[20]

In a letter home a Union soldier offered his own explanation for Confederate casualties, writing that the Rebels "fought more like demonds, than men, charging right up to our guns." The nature of Civil War combat, with its close-in fighting, tested men's will, often to extraordinary limits. Nothing quite gauged the depth of that resolve as when duty required men to align ranks and step out, marching toward an array of enemy cannon and muskets. On each of the campaign's five major battlefields Lee's foot soldiers charged, suffering repulses, or in their phrase, "cut all to pieces" in four of them. At the campaign's end Lee owed his victory, in the estimation of Jennings Cropper Wise, a historian of the army's artillery, to "the sheer *élan* of his lion-hearted infantry."[21]

When they charged they moved against a foe they had come to detest. Their letters burn with hatred toward the Yankees. They called the enemy "vandals," "vile Hessians," "heartless scoundrels," and "a miserable, cowardly race." Some referred to fighting the Federals as "*hog killing time.*" If there is one degree of *hell* hotter than an other," swore an officer, "I think it will be retained for the Vandles who invade our homes, rob & destroy our property." A captain admitted after the campaign, "It did me good to see the wretches routed." A Mississippian writing of the Seven Days declared, "One thing it has accomplished, it has imbred every man of ours with a determination to fight like demons."[22]

The captain who had felt good watching the "wretches routed" confided that it came with a price. "I paid well for it, marching & fighting day & night." Writing on July 4 a staff officer contended, "I never in my life saw men in such a nervous, excitable (or rather totally despondent) condition, from mere fatigue." A member of the 4th South Carolina said in a letter a week later: "A sadness pervades the army. . . . Not one amongst us but has lost a dear relative or friend in this great struggle." An artillerist, offering a similar view, wrote, "The demoralization was great and the evidence of it palpable everywhere."[23]

Despite the courage and will displayed by the men throughout the campaign, thousands of soldiers straggled on the march or abandoned the ranks during the fighting. Men broke down from the physical and mental strain or fled to the rear while their comrades stood amid the carnage. "You would be surprised to know how many skulked behind and returned to camp under the pretense of sickness," grumbled Colonel Alfred H. Colquitt, a brigade commander. The Georgian added, "I witnessed acts of cowardice that is disgraceful to Southern character." Weeks after Malvern Hill many men remained absent from the ranks and were seen daily on the streets of Richmond.[24]

Lee attributed the vast number of stragglers and absentees to "the laxity of discipline in the army." He recognized also that the officers and men had reached their limit and required "the repose of which they stood so much in need." With the Union army dormant at Harrison's Landing, the Confederates settled into camps around the capital. On July 9 Lee wrote to Davis, "We have lost many valuable officers whose places must be supplied, and our thinned ranks must be filled as rapidly as possible." He added that he would "proceed at once to reorganize our forces for active operations."[25]

With upward of 30,000 men not present for duty, Lee acted at once. He forbade leaves of absence, created a special provost guard for each division, and ordered commanders to gather up stragglers. Within ten days more than 13,000 men returned to the ranks. From the War Department he secured the transfer of nearly twenty regiments, or about 14,000 troops, to the army. A clerk in the department claimed of Lee: "So large are his powers that the Secretary of War has but little to do. He is, truly, but a mere clerk."[26]

While Lee strengthened the army's ranks with the return of absentees and the arrival of reinforcements, he also addressed command and organizational issues. It was to be a constant task for the army commander. "The roster of the army changed ceaselessly," the historian Douglas Freeman has written. "Every campaign had to be followed by a reorganization." Lee's method of command gave subordinates latitude in the execution of orders on a battlefield. He expected them to act aggressively, but not injudiciously. Some measured up; some did not. After each campaign the army's leadership underwent a sifting as a result of combat casualties and command failings.[27]

With the approval of Jefferson Davis, Lee relieved of command John Magruder, Benjamin Huger, and Theophilus Holmes. Magruder had been done in by his performance at Malvern Hill, where fellow officers described him as acting "more like a madman than a General commanding in a great battle." A rumor alleged that he had been drunk, which was inaccurate. Huger and Holmes had acted indecisively at Glendale and Malvern Hill, respectively. The War Department assigned Huger to the post of Inspector of Artillery and Ordnance and transferred Holmes to the Trans-Mississippi Department. In the fall Magruder reported to the District of Texas, Arizona, and New Mexico; his assignment to the post had been temporarily suspended during the Seven Days Campaign. Like Gustavus Smith earlier, the three generals were gone from the army.[28]

With the ineffective staff work, Lee's management of the infantry divisions had been difficult, leading to miscommunications and misunderstandings. At times during the campaign he had broadened the authority of James Longstreet and Stonewall Jackson over other units. The Confederate Congress had not authorized the creation of corps, so in the reorganization, Lee formed two unofficial wings and assigned Longstreet and Jackson as commanders.[29]

No subordinate had enhanced his standing with Lee during the battles more than Longstreet. At Gaines's Mill and at Glendale he had demonstrated, in the words of his chief of staff, his "consummate ability in managing troops." In the furor of combat he had remained calm, confident, and tenacious. "He was like a rock in steadiness," recalled Moxley Sorrel, "when sometimes in battle the world seemed flying to pieces." Since Lee had assumed command of the army he and Longstreet had developed a close personal and professional relationship. When the campaign ended, Lee was asked about the major general's performance. "Longstreet was 'the staff in my right hand,'" he answered.[30]

Jackson's lethargic performance, however, troubled Lee. As noted, Porter Alexander claimed that Lee "was deeply, bitterly disappointed." In the postwar years Alexander became one of Jackson's harshest critics of his performance during the Seven Days, but further evidence supports his allegation of Lee's disappointment. Months later Jeb Stuart, Jackson's closest friend in the army, told Jedediah Hotchkiss that Lee had "a rather low estimate of Jackson's ability" after the campaign. Another officer asserted that years later a member of Lee's staff argued "that Jackson ought to have been shot for his failure there."[31]

Despite Lee's concerns about the subordinate, he assigned Jackson to wing command. By rank and his previous accomplishments, no general, except Longstreet, rivaled the Valley hero. The commanding general almost assuredly knew that Jackson was, as one of his men put it, "the idol of the soldiers." When "Old Jack" rode through camps or along marching ranks, he was greeted with cheers. Lee did, however, temporarily reduce Jackson's command from fourteen brigades to seven.[32]

At the divisional level Richard Ewell, Daniel Harvey Hill, and Ambrose Powell Hill distinguished themselves in the campaign. Ewell had served under Jackson in the Shenandoah Valley. A Virginian, he had much of the old Regular Army about him; a soldier believed that he was "the most violently and elaborately profane man I ever knew." At Gaines's Mill his horse was killed under him while he was "charging up and down the line all the while encouraging the men." Curiously, in the Valley Ewell had remarked to a cavalry officer that he would rather command an independent cavalry regiment than the "best division of infantry in the army." "You fellows have some fun," he added, "but I am no better than a darned tin soldier." His abilities, eccentricities, and concern for their welfare endeared him to his fellow tin soldiers.[33]

Like Ewell, Harvey Hill was a man of "a marked and peculiar character," said a staff officer. A spinal injury bent his frame, and dyspepsia soured his personality. He could be blunt and caustic in his speech, but he shared with his brother-in-law, Jackson, a profound religious faith.

An officer described him as "a Puritan in religion and morals, [who] thought even an innocent julep an abomination and a cold dinner on Sunday a special recommendation of Divine favor."[34]

At Gaines's Mill and Malvern Hill the West Pointer and former college professor handled his brigades with skill. Wrote a Rebel, "He had a sort of monomania on the subject of personal courage." Moxley Sorrel, Longstreet's chief of staff, believed him to be "positively about the bravest man ever seen." Sorrel added, however, that Hill "would take his men into battle, fight furiously for some time and then something weakened about him." Hill needed to serve under a more forceful officer, thought Sorrel, such as Longstreet or Jackson.[35]

Hill's opinionated nature, often expressed in intemperate language, made him an unpopular man with some fellow officers. But allowing for the accuracy of Sorrel's statement, his prowess as a combat commander could not be denied. Lee could tolerate acidity in a man to a degree if he fought like Hill. In mid-July, however, the War Department appointed the major general to departmental command in his adopted state of North Carolina. His absence from the army was to be brief.[36]

The third division commander who had enhanced his reputation was Powell Hill. Although his impetuosity at Beaver Dam Creek had resulted in a bloody repulse, he showed at Gaines's Mill and Glendale the leadership and aggressiveness favored by Lee. Within days of the campaign's conclusion, however, articles in Richmond newspapers ignited a serious dispute between Hill and Longstreet, which heated to the point of an arrest and a challenge to a duel.[37]

John M. Daniel, the editor of the Richmond *Examiner*, had served as a volunteer aide on Hill's staff until Gaines's Mill, where he suffered a minor arm wound. Returning to the city, Daniel penned a series of articles on the campaign. Although not present at Glendale, he described the battle, exaggerating the role of Hill and the Light Division, implying that Longstreet had not been on the field during the fighting. The article infuriated Longstreet and his staff members. Longstreet prepared a rebuttal under the signature of Moxley Sorrel and had it published in the Richmond *Whig*. That article angered the inordinately proud and sensitive Hill, who believed that Longstreet had disparaged his troops publicly.[38]

On July 12 Hill asked Lee for a transfer from Longstreet's command, a request endorsed by the wing commander. Lee ignored it. When Hill refused twice to provide information ordered by Longstreet, the latter placed him under arrest. The two generals exchanged private letters, but Hill had become so incensed and antagonistic about his arrest that he challenged Longstreet to a duel. Fortunately Lee intervened under the guise of military necessity, released Hill from arrest on July 25, and restored him to command of the Light Division the next day. On July 27 Hill and his troops started west to join Stonewall Jackson, a more difficult superior officer.[39]

While the Longstreet-Hill controversy boiled, Lee completed the reorganization within the army. In the infantry Richard H. Anderson received promotion to major general and command of Benjamin Huger's former division. Writing of Anderson, Moxley Sorrel stated: "His courage was of the highest order, but he was indolent. His capacity and intelligence excellent, but it was hard to get him to use them." If anyone could prod him into action it was Longstreet, to whose wing he was assigned. Longstreet was also given John Magruder's two divisions under David R. Jones and Lafayette McLaws. At some point Chase Whiting went on sick leave, and John Hood assumed temporary command of the Texas Brigade and Evander Law's regiments. After Gaines's Mill few, if any, brigadiers stood more preeminent as a combat officer than Hood.[40]

At the brigade level Jubal Early returned to the army, having recovered from a shoulder wound received in the Battle of Williamsburg on May 5. A man with "a snarling, rasping disposition" and a "biting tongue," the Virginian possessed unquestioned courage and proven ability. Early replaced the wounded Arnold Elzey in Ewell's division. With this assignment his association with Ewell would shape an integral part of the army's history.[41]

Confederate authorities rewarded Jeb Stuart for his daring enterprise in June and for his performance during the Seven Days with promotion to major general, dated July 25. The commanding general congratulated Stuart and noted, "It is deserved though it has been somewhat tardy." Jackson wrote to his friend: "Permit me to congratulate you upon your well earned promotion. . . . I am desirous of seeing you along the front of my lines. . . . Nothing has yet given a fair opportunity for our cooperation, should any exist, you may expect to hear from me."[42]

In his letter Lee informed Stuart, "I am endeavoring to put the Cavl on a good footing." Earlier Jackson had suggested to Lee that Stuart should be assigned "to the command of all the cavalry" in the army. On July 28 Lee approved the formation of the army's mounted regiments into two brigades, with orders that Stuart would "take General direction of all the Cavalry of this army" and assign Wade Hampton and Fitzhugh Lee to command of the brigades.[43]

The creation of a cavalry division increased Confederate advantages over their mounted opponents. In Stuart, Lee had a matchless light cavalryman at reconnaissance and screening an army. "Stuart was, by nature, intended to lead and command men," wrote an aide. With the appointments of Hampton and Fitz Lee, Stuart had capable brigade commanders. A wealthy South Carolinian who had led an infantry brigade during the Seven Days, Hampton became Stuart's finest subordinate, although they never warmed personally to each other. Fitz Lee, the nephew of the army commander, was one of Stuart's favorites, whose election to colonel of the 1st Virginia Cavalry had been engineered by Stuart in the spring. The two men shared a frolicsome nature and hearty laughter, but Lee's abilities as a horse soldier were limited. To Stuart's discredit, favoritism colored his judgment of officers and men.[44]

Weaknesses in the organization and tactical use of artillery were not addressed during these weeks. New batteries joined the army, and some were redistributed to the infantry. Lee retained William Pendleton as chief of artillery, although the former minister's performance in the campaign had revealed his serious shortcomings as an artillery commander. The attachment of a battery to each infantry brigade remained unchanged. It would be months before the artillery underwent needed organizational overhaul.[45]

The army's rank and file enjoyed the respite during July's heat. Wounded men healed, stragglers rejoined units, and new regiments swelled the ranks. A member of the Stonewall Brigade described the time as "the halcyon days." Ample rations, good supplies, and light duty restored the men's health. In their free time some men gambled, bolder ones sneaked away from camp to enjoy Richmond's pleasures, and some wrote letters to loved ones at home.[46]

They had no illusions, however, about what awaited them. An Alabamian wrote to his sister, "We have always been at our post, ready and willing—but not very anxious, as we have seen a few battlefields." An officer told his folks, "We are now reorganising to capture every Yankeey in Virginia & try the game of invasion ourselves." A Texan recalled that he and his comrades "were soon rested up and fattened so we could stand a long hard drive to the next slaughter pen."[47]

For Jackson's veterans the "halcyon days" ended with marching orders from Lee on July 13. On June 26 the Lincoln administration had consolidated the troops in the Mountain, Shenandoah, and Rappahannock departments into a newly formed Army of Virginia and appointed Major General John Pope as the commander. An academy roommate of Longstreet, Pope had won a pair of minor victories along the Mississippi River in the spring of 1862. Lincoln believed Pope possessed aggressiveness, which was lacking in George McClellan.[48]

The "general object" of Pope's army was to cover the Federal capital and to aid McClellan. Pope asserted later in his memoirs, "I was offered command of a forlorn hope under the most unfavorable conditions possible for success." To augment Pope's command the War Department formed the Ninth Corps, drawing divisions from the departments of North Carolina and the South. Lincoln appointed Major General Ambrose Burnside to command of the corps and ordered it north from the Atlantic coast to Fredericksburg, Virginia. In all, Pope's and Burnside's commands numbered nearly 60,000 officers and men.[49]

With McClellan's Army of the Potomac still at Harrison's Landing, Pope intended to advance south into central Virginia, a movement that would protect Washington, D.C., and threaten Confederate railroad communications to the west. His three corps were scattered across upper Virginia, however, and, in the words of the historian John J. Hennessy, were "in a significant state of disrepair." Nevertheless the vanguard of his army crossed the Rappahannock River and occupied Culpeper Court House on July 12; less than thirty miles to the south lay the vital junction of the Orange & Alexandria and Virginia Central railroads. It was the reported presence of Yankees in Culpeper County that forced Lee to dispatch Jackson and roughly 15,000 troops to the region.[50]

By rail and by foot Jackson's troops headed west. A movement had not been unexpected by the men in the ranks. A few days earlier a sergeant wrote, "Having been with 'Jack' some time [we] know well that—some move will soon be made as he is no man to stay in sight without fighting them in some way or the other." Jackson and the leading contingent of his command arrived in Gordonsville on July 19.[51]

On the day Lee ordered Jackson to confront Pope's advance, July 13, he learned that Burnside had withdrawn most of his command from North Carolina. Lee assumed that this Union force was moving north on ships to reinforce McClellan. If Burnside were indeed headed for Harrison's Landing, the combined force posed a grave threat, once again, to Richmond, while Pope could sever Lee's supply line to the Shenandoah Valley. For now, the strategic initiative rested not with Lee, but with his opponents.[52]

For the next two weeks Lee wrestled with uncertainties. "The reports are so conflicting and sometimes opposing," he informed Davis. Information placed Burnside's troops at Fort Monroe, on the eastern tip of the Peninsula; McClellan undertook daily demonstrations "to deceive, test our strength, or preparatory to real movements," wrote Lee; and from Jackson word came that Pope's destination was Gordonsville. By month's end, however, Lee acted, without solid intelligence and with risk, to break the strategic impasse.[53]

On July 27 Lee ordered Powell Hill's Light Division and a brigade of Louisianans to Jackson. Lee advised Jackson that he had been "reluctant to weaken the force around Richmond without seeing a prospect of striking a blow elsewhere." When Jackson claimed that his force was too weak numerically to confront Pope, Lee decided to send the reinforcements to Gordonsville. In a letter of this date Lee asserted, "I want Pope to be suppressed." He cautioned Jackson: "Cache your troops as much as possible till you can strike your blow, and be prepared to return to me when done, if necessary. I will endeavor to keep General McClellan quiet till it is over, if rapidly executed."[54]

The words "I want Pope to be suppressed" resulted from Lee's reading in Northern newspapers of the Union commander's General Orders No. 11. In it, Pope instructed his subordinate officers to arrest all disloyal males "within their reach" and to give the civilians the choice of signing an oath of allegiance or being expelled beyond Union lines. If a citizen violated the oath, he faced execution without a trial and the seizure of his property. The orders infuriated Confederate officials, including Jefferson Davis, who directed that officers captured from Pope's army were to be imprisoned and exempt from parole. How much Lee's own anger with the order governed his strategy is difficult to measure. "The course indicated in his [Pope's] orders . . . cannot be permitted," he told Jackson, "and will lead to retaliation on our part."[55]

While Jackson awaited the arrival of the reinforcements and readied his command for an advance north toward Culpeper County, apparent Union threats against Richmond mounted. On August 5 Stuart reported the march south of two Federal brigades from Fredericksburg toward the Virginia Central Railroad at Hanover Junction. Stuart's cavalrymen skirmished with the Yankees, who retreated. It had been only a raid, but Stuart reported to Lee that enemy prisoners claimed "Burnside [was] at Fredericksburg, with 16,000 men, to follow on the same route." On that same night Lee learned that McClellan had occupied Malvern Hill with a considerable force from the Army of the Potomac.[56]

Lee rushed five divisions, his entire infantry force north of the James River, to Malvern Hill on August 6. He followed and assumed command on the field. The enemy he informed Davis, was "drawn up in line of battle, his artillery in position, and he apparently was prepared to deliver battle." The next morning, however, the Federals were gone, having withdrawn to Harrison's Landing during the night. The Federals' retreat surprised and confused Lee. Two days later he confided to his daughters in a letter, "I thought they were going to fight the battle over again."[57]

McClellan had intended it only as a reconnaissance-in-force. More important, the advance to Malvern Hill marked his final effort on the Peninsula. Lee could not have known it, but after weeks of a contentious exchange of correspondence and meetings with administration officials, McClellan had been ordered to withdraw from the region. He had been offered a choice of operations: reinforcement of 20,000 troops and a movement on the Confederate capital or abandonment of the Peninsula. When he replied that he needed 50,000 more men, Lincoln ordered the withdrawal. The Union commander objected to the order and stalled, but finally, on August 14, he complied, starting the army toward transports on the Chesapeake Bay.[58]

It had been five weeks since the conclusion of the Seven Days Campaign. Since then, while the army healed, refitted, and reorganized, the enemy had controlled the strategic situation, forcing Lee to act cautiously. The security of Richmond governed his responses to the Federal operations. Protection of the Virginia Central Railroad had necessitated Jackson's move to Gordonsville. Although caution marked Lee's actions, boldness awaited an opportunity.[59]

Back in May, Davis, Lee, and Joseph Johnston had agreed that, if circumstances arose, the Confederates should cross the Potomac River, taking the war into northern territory. In his congratulatory proclamation to the army after the Seven Days, Davis had enjoined the officers and men, "Carry your standards beyond the outer boundaries of the Confederacy." As noted, Lee believed that Richmond was most secure when its defenders were away from its gates. The Seven Days had been the initial stride in an extended offensive. Now, after weeks of countermoves, Lee set the army on a course toward central Virginia, and perhaps beyond.[60]

On August 9 reports placed Burnside's Ninth Corps in Fredericksburg. Whether Burnside was to combine with Pope or act as a defensive force for the Union capital, Lee decided to reclaim the initiative in Virginia. He ordered Longstreet's and Jones's divisions, ten brigades in all, to Gordonsville, assigning Longstreet, his senior officer, to overall command of these and Jackson's units. One half of the army would be with Longstreet, the other half manning the defenses of Richmond. With the Army of the Potomac still at Harrison's Landing, such a reduction in the capital's defenses was "a startling decision," according to the historian Harsh. As he would inform Davis subsequently, Lee's intent was "to change the theater of the war from James River to north of the Rappahannock."[61]

On that same day at Cedar Mountain, eight miles south of Culpeper Court House, Jackson attacked Major General Nathaniel Banks's corps, the vanguard of Pope's army. Two days earlier Lee had written to Jackson: "I would rather you should have easy fighting and heavy victories. I must now leave the matter to your reflection and good judgment." Jackson received Lee's message as his men toiled through oppressive heat and dust-choked roads toward the woodlots and farmers' fields in the shadow of Cedar Mountain. Characteristically, as he had done at Kernstown in March and at Port Republic in June, Jackson fed units into the fighting as they arrived on the battlefield.[62]

It was not "easy fighting," as Lee had hoped. Jackson's own division, under the temporary command of Brigadier General Charles Sidney Winder, bore the brunt of the combat, which began about one o'clock in the afternoon. Banks's troops fought stubbornly. Winder was killed by a piece of artillery shell. When the Rebels' left front broke under a Union charge, Jackson rode into the shredded ranks, waving his sword still in its scabbard and rallying the men. Confederate gun crews, a stout stand by Jubal Early's brigade, and the arrival of Powell Hill's division saved Jackson from possible defeat. The Southerners counterattacked, and the Yankees fled north. Darkness ended Jackson's pursuit.[63]

Jackson began his retreat south on the afternoon of August 11, during a truce in which the Federals tended to their wounded and buried their dead. Union losses approached 2,400, with more than one-fourth listed as captured. Southern casualties slightly exceeded 1,300, nearly all either killed or wounded. The death of Winder was a grievous loss. An officer in the Stonewall Brigade, Winder's official command, said, "He was an excellent officer, a gallant man, and a polished gentleman." Dr. Hunter McGuire, Jackson's medical officer, wrote that the brigadier "was a good soldier, and if he had lived, he would one day have been made Lieut. General. Gen. Jackson felt his loss keenly."[64]

Weeks earlier a Georgia soldier had informed readers of his hometown newspaper, "We believe in Jackson, because, like David of old, he goes forth to battle in the name of the Lord of hosts." At Cedar Mountain, in Jackson's estimation, a kindly Providence once again had favored him and his men and blessed them with victory. To be sure, it had been a signal victory. Jackson's aggressiveness had seemingly broken the will of Pope. The Union commander had proclaimed previously to his army that he came from the West, "where we have always seen the backs of the enemies." "Let us look before and not behind," he declared. "Success and glory are in the advance." Banks's defeat, however, changed the tenor of Pope's dispatches. While he concentrated his units around Culpeper Court House after the battle, he wrote to the War Department, "I will do the best I can, and if forced to retire will do so by way of Rappahannock Crossing." Cedar Mountain had given Lee the initiative in central Virginia.[65]

Jackson's troops had returned to Gordonsville by August 14. By then Longstreet's and Jones's men had spilled off the train cars and were encamped outside of the town. The victor of Cedar Mountain soon reported to Longstreet at the home of a Mr. Goodman and offered over-all command to him. Longstreet declined, however, stating that Jack-son knew the terrain and situation better than he and that Lee would be joining them shortly. Before the two generals met, Longstreet wrote to Lee, proposing a turning movement around Pope's right flank. Whether he discussed the plan with Jackson is uncertain.[66]

The historian James I. Robertson Jr. has asserted that the relation-ship between Lee's two senior generals was strained, fueled by Long-street's jealousy and envy of Jackson's achievements in the Valley. Rob-ertson bases his contention on Longstreet's postwar writings, in which the Georgian argued that Jackson had forged his reputation against second-rate Union generals and "did not appear so well" against more capable antagonists. When Longstreet penned his memoirs and articles, Lee and Jackson had become icons of the "Lost Cause," while he had been made a pariah in the South because of alleged failings at Gettys-burg and his postwar political affiliations. Undoubtedly some bitterness tinged his defense of his generalship, and he made misstatements of facts, trying to enhance his role in the war.[67]

But Robertson's claim lacks creditable and extensive contemporary evidence to support it. Why Longstreet would be jealous of Jackson at this time is difficult to fathom. In their contemporary letters and post-war reminiscences, none of Longstreet's staff officers allude to their commander's envious feelings toward Jackson. Conversely, Henry Kyd Douglas of Jackson's staff stated that the relations between the two gen-erals were "always cordial." Among the army's generals only Jeb Stu-art could rightfully claim a close personal friendship with Jackson. As another aide put it, "He [Jackson] seems to be cut off from his fellow men and to commune with his own spirit only, or with spirits of which we know not."[68]

The army's two senior subordinates were, first and foremost, profes-sional soldiers. Duty and devotion to the cause framed their relationship, but they viewed war in starkly different terms. Jackson practiced this most terrible of trades with a fervency that rivaled his religious convictions; Longstreet, with a dispassionate coolness. Jackson could be driving, relentless; Longstreet, more cautious and deliberate. Neither man harbored romantic illusions about the bloodletting. With Lee they were to shape the army's character.[69]

Lee entrained for Gordonsville at four o'clock on the morning of August 15, arriving later that day. Before he left Richmond, a Union deserter and a report from scouts confirmed that the Army of the Potomac had begun leaving Harrison's Landing, en route east down the Peninsula. Lee ordered John Hood's and Richard Anderson's divisions to Gordonsville. He notified Davis of McClellan's departure and then offered, "This is of itself, I feel, as a great relief, but he ought not to have got off so easily."[70]

When the Confederate commander reached Gordonsville, he met with Longstreet and Jackson at the residence of a Mrs. Barbour in the town. The two subordinates described the situation to Lee. To the north, the Army of Virginia was tucked in a large V laid on its side, formed by the Rappahannock and Rapidan rivers. The apex of the V pointed east, toward Fredericksburg, nine miles from the confluence of the two rivers. Longstreet had proposed earlier to assail the western, or open, part of the V. Lee preferred to strike the closed end, cutting off Pope from Burnside's troops, reportedly moving toward Culpeper County.[71]

The three generals settled on Lee's plan and worked out the details. Longstreet would cross the Rapidan at Raccoon Ford. Jackson would move upstream and cross at Somerville Ford. Jeb Stuart, with the brigades of Beverly Robertson and Fitz Lee, would use Morton's Ford, east of Longstreet, march through Stevensburg, and seize the Orange & Alexandria Railroad bridge at Rappahannock Station, cutting off Pope's main supply and retreat line. If the plan worked, Pope's army would be trapped in the V and could be destroyed.[72]

Jackson advocated an advance the next day, followed by an attack on August 17. Longstreet asked, however, for more time. Though his troops had come by rail to Gordonsville, his commissary wagons, carrying rations for the men, were still rolling on the roads. Jackson offered rations from his wagons. Lee listened and decided on a day's delay, until August 18. For Lee, the final consideration was the cavalry. Fitz Lee's brigade had remained at Hanover Junction, watching for any enemy movement south from Fredericksburg, and most likely could not join the army before August 17. The meeting ended, and Longstreet and Jackson rode away to ready their commands for the movement.[73]

Dust-covered columns of Southern soldiers filled the roads of Orange County, marching north toward the Rapidan fords on August 16 and 17. "Our march cannot be too rapid," wrote Lee's aide, Walter Taylor, on August 17, "as the great desideratum is to strike Pope before 'little Mac' reaches this section. The army is in fine spirits, and I pray I may not be disappointed in expecting much from it." But on that same day Lee admitted in a letter to Davis, "The process is slow and tedious." Supply wagons lagged to the rear, and there were the usual delays with troops on the march. Lee and his staff members ascended Clark's Mountain, a 1,100-foot eminence south of the Rapidan, and gazed upon the enemy's campsites. "In plain view before them," Armistead Long recounted, "lay Pope's army stretched out in fancied security, and to all appearance in utter ignorance of the vicinity of a powerful foe." The Rebels bivouacked for the night of August 17–18 just south of the river crossings.[74]

Jeb Stuart arrived at army headquarters outside of Orange Court House at about noon on August 17, preceding Fitz Lee's brigade from Hanover Junction. His orders were to initiate the Confederate offensive by passing beyond Pope's left flank. After viewing the Federal lines from Clark's Mountain, Stuart and several aides rode in the evening to the crossroads village of Verdiersville, where they expected to find Fitz Lee's horsemen. When the troopers were nowhere to be found, Stuart sent Major Norman FitzHugh in search of the missing brigade. The general and the other staff members then bedded down for the night on the front porch of a nearby house.[75]

The Confederate cavalry officers stirred before daylight on August 18, awakened by the sounds of approaching horses and wagons. Thinking it was Fitz Lee's brigade, Stuart sent two men to meet the oncoming riders. A morning's fog cloaked the ground. Within minutes, however, pistol shots rang out, and Stuart's aides raced back to the farmhouse, shouting that Yankee cavalry were behind them. Stuart and the rest of the group mounted their horses and fled across fields toward woods under gunfire from the Federals. The Confederate general described their escape as "miraculous." On the porch the blue-jacketed troopers found Stuart's hat, cloak, and haversack.[76]

The companies of Union cavalry had crossed the Rapidan River at unguarded Raccoon Ford. During the previous night Longstreet had sent an order to Brigadier General Robert Toombs, instructing him to detail two of his Georgia regiments to picket the crossing site. A former U.S. senator, Toombs possessed a "luminous intellect [that] embraced no soldier's talent," wrote Moxley Sorrel. "The Georgian was for once and all a politician, and in the wrong shop with a sword and uniform on." He was absent from his headquarters when Longstreet's order arrived. Upon his return Toombs withdrew the pickets, alleging that the ford could be guarded "with an old woman and a broomstick." Longstreet later placed Toombs under arrest for disobeying his orders. The Georgian, claimed an officer, had "a great contempt for West Pointers and a great dislike for Mr. Davis."[77]

Toombs's dereliction of duty amounted to more than the near-capture of one of the Confederacy's most renowned and valuable generals. While en route to Verdiersville, the Union horsemen captured Norman FitzHugh, who was riding back to Stuart. As Stuart's chief of staff, FitzHugh had in his possession a copy of Robert E. Lee's orders about the offensive against the Federal army. Pope received the document shortly after noon. Realizing the danger that he faced, the Union commander ordered a withdrawal across the Rappahannock River. Late that afternoon the Army of Virginia began a retreat, which continued through the night and into the next day.[78]

"It can hardly be denied however," concluded Charles Venable, "that if the cavalry had been sooner up . . . there would have been a good opportunity for striking Pope a heavy blow in Culpeper." In his report Stuart criticized his brigade commander with "failure to comply with instructions." While on the march Fitz Lee had detoured through Louisa Court House to collect forage and provisions, adding twenty miles to his march. Evidently, Stuart's orders did not specify the urgency of the brigade being up on August 17, and for this he deserved a share of the blame. When the horsemen appeared on the night of August 18, the brigadier reported that the mounts were exhausted and needed a day's rest.[79]

When army headquarters initially learned of the absence of Fitz Lee's cavalrymen and later of their horses' condition, the commanding general delayed and then postponed the army's forward movement until August 20. At about midday on August 19 Lee received the news of Pope's retreat. He and Longstreet rode together to the summit of Clark's Mountain. To the north dust clouds billowed up, hanging above the roads that led to the Rappahannock crossings. According to Longstreet, Lee "put away his glasses, and with a deeply-drawn breath, expressive at once of disappointment and resignation, said, 'General, we little thought that the enemy would turn his back upon us this early in the campaign.'"[80]

For the present the quarry had eluded them. Below the two generals, on the valley floor, sprawled the bivouacs of their army. Together they had traveled far, in miles and in things immeasurable, since June 1. All Lee had to do was ask, and the army would go farther. When he passed by them in their camps or on the march, they cheered him, whom they now called "Marse Robert" or "Uncle Bob." Several days earlier Jackson had remarked to Stuart that he would "be willing to follow [Lee] blind-folded."[81]

Writing on August 19, a Virginian proclaimed to his sister: "Our men seem confident and in fine spirits. Great confidence in the abilities of our Generals pervades the whole army. It is the general impression, too, that the mass of the Yankee Army is much demoralized and will not fight too well." The next day "Marse Robert" and his men forded the Rapidan and marched north. Many in the dusty ranks probably speculated on their destination. Few, if any, could have predicted where the roads would end.[82]

Chapter Four

Lee's Masterpiece

JEFFERSONTON, VIRGINIA, LAY a handful of miles south of the
Rappahannock River in the Little Fork region of northwest Culpeper
County. The village had about 160 inhabitants, most of Scots-Irish and
German ancestry. It boasted the Jefferson Academy for boys, a Baptist
church, and a store owned by "old Mac." Men from the town and neigh-
borhood had embraced the Confederate cause, enlisting in the Little
Fork Rangers, or Company D, 4th Virginia Cavalry.[1]

The war had never been so near, however, as it was in August 1862.
For weeks the Yankees had occupied Culpeper County, but they had
retreated across the Rappahannock, followed by soldiers of the Army of
Northern Virginia. In recent days the boom of cannon could be heard
from along the river. While congregants gathered in the Baptist church
on Sunday, August 24, artillery fire still echoed in the distance. Outside
of Jeffersonton, in a nearby field, history paused around a map on a table.[2]

It had been four days since Robert E. Lee's army had waded across
the Rapidan fords in pursuit of Union Major General John Pope's Army
of Virginia. When the Federals withdrew across the Rappahannock,
they burned bridges and several houses and rimmed the higher northern
bank of the river with artillery and infantry. Lee's trailing units closed
on the Rappahannock, and clashes occurred at Kelly's, Freeman's, and

Beverly's fords. In one exchange of artillery fire a shell plowed into the ground within a few feet of James Longstreet and Cadmus Wilcox but did not explode.[3]

While Longstreet's troops dueled with the enemy, Jackson's veterans sidled upriver to an unguarded crossing site opposite Warrenton Sulphur Springs. On August 22 Jackson shoved eight regiments and two batteries, commanded by Jubal Early, across the river to the north bank. That night a howling thunderstorm, with downpours, blew in and isolated Early's force. All through the next day details of men labored on a bridge to extricate the stranded units, while Longstreet's infantrymen and artillerists demonstrated against Pope's lines farther downstream. In reaction to Early's incursion, Pope concentrated his divisions around Warrenton and Warrenton Sulphur Springs.[4]

Jeb Stuart, meanwhile, proposed a raid behind Pope's lines to cut the Orange & Alexandria Railroad, the Union general's supply line. When Lee approved, Stuart, 1,500 officers and men, and a pair of cannon rode forth on the morning of August 22. Circling west and north, they passed beyond the Federal right flank and halted near Catlett's Station about 7:30 P.M. Rain poured down from the thunderstorm, which had raised the river in Early's rear. "It was so dark that I could not see a man by my side," swore a Virginia cavalrymen.[5]

With the sounds of hoofbeats muffled by the rain and darkness, Stuart's horsemen swept down on the railroad depot, surprising the outmanned Union guards. "Never had I seen anything like it," exclaimed one of Stuart's aides. "The Yankees were perfectly frantic with fear." The Federals triggered a volley and then fled. The 1st and 4th Virginia Cavalry charged a camp to the south of the station but soon abandoned the attempt, meeting resistance by the enemy. "The great object of the expedition—the destruction of the Cedar Run railroad bridge," reported Stuart, defied all Confederate efforts to either burn it or to wreck it with axes. The Rebels found, however, Pope's headquarters wagon, which contained the general's uniform coat and hat and dispatches.[6]

The raiders started on their return march at three o'clock on the morning of August 23. They halted later in the day at Sulphur Springs and encamped near Early's troops. With Early's units the cavalrymen crossed the river the next day. "Raiding with General Stuart is poor fun and a hard business," grumbled one of his men. "Thunder, lightning, rain, storm nor darkness can stop him when he is on a warm fresh trail of Yankee game." Lee told Jefferson Davis that the Catlett's Station raid "accomplished some minor advantages."[7]

The value of Stuart's expedition lay in the capture of Pope's dispatches to the War Department in Washington. From them Lee learned that his opponent's force numbered 45,000 present for duty. The messages revealed further that Major General Fitz John Porter's Fifth Corps of the Army of the Potomac had arrived at Falmouth, across the Rappahannock from Fredericksburg, and was to join Pope. After reading the dispatches, Lee informed Davis that the Union commander's plan was "to hold us in check until McClellan can join him from the lower Rappahannock." Consequently, Lee added, "the whole [Confederate] army, I think, should be united here as soon as possible." He would order up the divisions of Lafayette McLaws and Harvey Hill, who had been recalled from department command.[8]

Pope's dispatches confirmed what Lee had thought since the Army of the Potomac had begun leaving the Peninsula: the Federal administration planned on some combination of the forces of Pope, Burnside, and McClellan. The Confederate commander could not assault Pope in front or wait until McClellan's units arrived from the Peninsula. Writing to Davis on August 23, Lee outlined his strategic goal: "If we are able to change the theater of war from James River to the north of the Rappahannock we shall be able to consume provisions and forage now being used in supporting the enemy. This will be of some advantage and prevent so great a draft upon other parts of the country." Lee wanted to maneuver Pope farther away from Fredericksburg and reinforcements, while at the same time reclaiming lost territory.[9]

For a second time Lee confronted a reality that underpinned Confederate operations in Virginia: Union numerical superiority must be thwarted by aggressive action. Lee had to select, if not dictate, the time and place for engaging the Federals in battle. As he explained, "It is only by the concentration of our troops that we can hope to win any decisive advantage." With Davis's approval and cooperation, his burden was to attain on the battlefield, within the limits of Confederate manpower, as close a numerical equality as possible.[10]

Lee's strategy at this time, however, encompassed more than pre-venting the merger of Union forces. According to Major Charles Mar-shall, Lee's "object was to cause General Pope to retreat by cutting the railroad behind him, and at the same time to delay the arrival of rein-forcements. By placing his army on General Pope's right flank, he would be able to use the Shenandoah Valley to approach the Potomac and so cause apprehension in the Federal Government for the safety of their capital. This General Lee told me himself." An August 25 letter of Lee's to the War Department lends credence to Marshall's postwar account. In it Lee requested that Major General William W. Loring, commander of the Department of Southwestern Virginia, be "directed to clear the valley of the Kanawha [River] and then operate northwardly, so as to join me in the valley of Virginia."[11]

The boldness of Lee's strategy was daunting. From Pope's corre-spondence he could estimate the numbers that might be arrayed against him. How far Lee planned to take the army is uncertain. Future events indicate that even as he faced Pope along the Rappahannock, he fore-saw carrying the war not only to the Potomac River, but beyond, into Maryland or Pennsylvania. "The theater of war will thus be changed, for a season at least, unless we are overpowered," he told Davis. The task for the present was to get at Pope.[12]

The fashioning of a plan transpired on the afternoon on August 24 in the field outside of Jeffersonton. While staff officers lounged on a nearby hill, Lee, Jackson, Longstreet, and Stuart—"great spirits of the land," a Virginian called them—stood around a table, looking at a map and discussing the proposed movement. An eyewitness described the council between the four generals as "brief." Jackson had joined Lee before Longstreet and Stuart arrived; it would appear that Lee pre-sented his plan to Jackson and then informed the other two officers of the details. Longstreet stated after the war that Lee conceived the plan himself, without prior consultation.[13]

Stuart related a different version of the plan's origins, implying that Jackson had proposed it. In the winter of 1863 the cavalry commander told Jedediah Hotchkiss, the topographer, that Jackson was "entitled to all the credit of the movement round the enemy:" "General Lee had very reluctantly consented to it." Furthermore, Lee asked Stuart if he did not think "it was very hazardous" for Jackson to march beyond Pope's flank.[14]

Although Stuart's account is more immediate to the events than Longstreet's postwar memoirs, the audacious plan belonged to Lee. Arriving late Stuart probably concluded that Jackson had formulated it. Lee instructed Jackson to march his three infantry divisions and artillery batteries up the Rappahannock, swing beyond the Union flank, and in a wide sweep sever the Orange & Alexandria Railroad, Pope's communication and supply link to Washington. Longstreet's wing, meanwhile, would engage Pope's troops along the Rappahannock. When Pope retreated, as Lee expected he would, Longstreet would cross the river and move toward Jackson. Stuart's cavalry would join Jackson's column on the march and screen the infantry and artillery.[15]

The details of the movement, where Jackson planned to strike the railroad, Lee left to the general. By this time Lee's concerns about Jackson's performance during the Seven Days had been resolved, and he trusted the judgment of both of his wing commanders. "General Lee always accorded to his lieutenants great liberty in the exercise of their discretion as to the manner of the execution of his orders," stated Walter Taylor. When Lee asked Jackson when he could start, Stonewall replied, "I will be moving within an hour."[16]

The plan was risky: if Pope detected Jackson's march and deduced that Lee had divided his army, the Federals could overwhelm Longstreet's troops before advancing against Jackson's isolated wing. After the war Lee justified the extremely daring operation: "The disparity . . . between the contending forces rendered the risks unavoidable." He hoped to maneuver Pope out of the region without giving battle; nevertheless he figured that an engagement was likely, and if so he wanted the clash to occur before his opponent received large numbers of reinforcements. Writing of Lee's offensive, Longstreet stated, "The strength of the move lay in the time it gave us to make issue before all of the Army of the Potomac could unite with the army under General Pope."[17]

Before dawn on August 25 Jackson's wing—the divisions of Richard Ewell, Powell Hill, and William B. Taliaferro, twenty-one batteries and a cavalry regiment—started its march. Only Jackson and his topographical engineer, Lieutenant Keith Boswell, knew the destination.

Boswell was familiar with the region and had been instructed by Jackson to determine a direct and "covered route" to the Orange & Alexandria Railroad. The division commanders need only obey orders. Weeks earlier, when Powell Hill's division had joined Jackson, Dorsey Pender grumbled to his wife, "None of Jackson's old officers ever try to divine his movements, and some of the old Army like him."[18]

From Jeffersonton, past Amissville, across the Rappahannock at Hinson's Mill Ford, and on to Orleans, the column snaked. An artillerist described the infantrymen's stride on the march as a "swaying, swinging, panther like step." Jackson issued orders against straggling and left baggage wagons and the men's knapsacks behind at Jeffersonton. Officers pressed the pace, urging the men to close up ranks. Jackson prodded, pushed, and demanded, with characteristic relentlessness.[19]

The van of Jackson's wing, which numbered approximately 24,000 officers and men, reached Salem (present-day Marshall) toward sundown. Throughout the day civilians along the route had watched them pass, some even joining the march for a while. Outside of Salem Jackson dismounted, climbed onto a large bolder, and removed his cap. As his "foot cavalry" approached him, the men cheered, but officers passed the word back through the ranks, "No cheering." Jackson could not have been more proud of them and, turning to a staff member, said, "Who could not conquer with such troops as these?" It was well past nightfall before the miles-long column arrived at the village. The men slept well, having covered twenty-six miles.[20]

The march resumed early on August 26, moving east toward a rising sun. The men had a phrase for advancing against the Yankees: "Give a showing." They must have sensed something was up again with Old Jack. They passed through unguarded Thoroughfare Gap in the Bull Run Mountains and descended into the rolling country miles north of the Rappahannock and Pope's army. At midafternoon Jeb Stuart and two brigades of cavalry overtook the head of the column, having passed through Glascock's Gap, a mile and a half south of Thoroughfare Gap. When Stuart met his friend, he allegedly called out: "Hello Jackson! I've got Pope's coat; if you don't believe it, there's his name." Stuart held up the uniform coat for Jackson, who replied, "General Stuart, I would much rather you brought General Pope instead of his coat."[21]

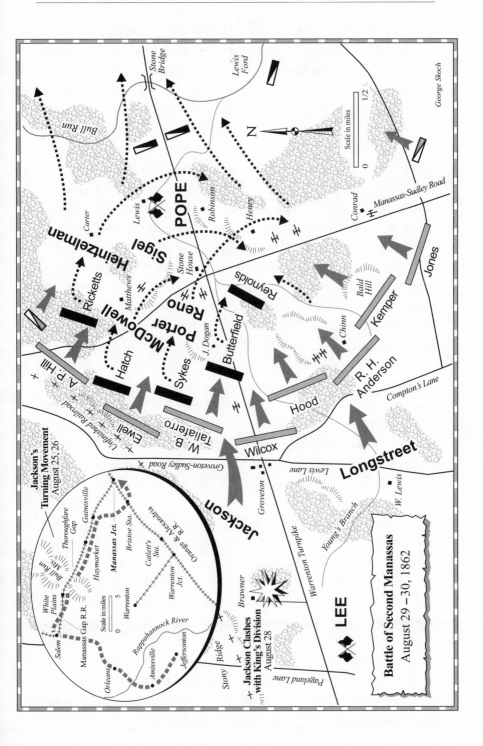

Battle of Second Manassas
August 29–30, 1862

With Stuart's horsemen covering the flanks, the Rebels entered Gainesville and took the right fork toward Bristoe Station on the Orange & Alexandria Railroad. The 2nd Virginia Cavalry, followed by Confederate infantry, swept into the village, scattering a Union detachment after a brief struggle. Within minutes they heard the approach of a train coming from the south and hurriedly piled wooden sills on the tracks. Seeing the danger, the engineer plowed through the barrier under blasts of gunfire and the train disappeared down the line. The Rebels then lifted rails along a section of the track and waited. A second train appeared, was fired upon, and sped past the station, before careening down an embankment when it hit the gap in the rails. Finally, a third train steamed past the station and into the rear of the derailed cars. The Southerners swarmed over the wreckage.[22]

In a grueling ordeal of stamina and fortitude, the Confederates had marched fifty-four miles in thirty-six hours. Despite Jackson's orders and his officers' effort, hundreds, perhaps thousands had abandoned the ranks, unable or unwilling to maintain the pace. "Men dropped exhausted out of the ranks by the wayside, or got hopelessly in arrears in stopping to gather a few ears of corn or an apple, or to dip a cupful of water from a spring; but the column still pressed on," recalled a Virginian. Writing a week later, Dorsey Pender complained to his wife that Jackson "forgets that one ever gets tired, hungry, or sleepy."[23]

Brigadier General Alexander R. Lawton, who commanded a Georgia brigade in Ewell's division, said of Jackson: "He had no sympathy with human infirmity. He was a one-idea man. He looked upon broken-down men and stragglers as the same thing. He classed all who were weak and weary, who fainted by the wayside, as men wanting in patriotism. . . . He was the true type of all great soldiers. He did not value human life where he had an object to accomplish." His troops, believed Lawton, "feared him, and obeyed him to the death; faith they had in him a faith stronger than death." "But be ye sure," he concluded, "it was bitter hard work to keep up with Stonewall Jackson, as all know who ever served under him."[24]

This "one-idea man" and the faithful behind him had accomplished a remarkable feat, seizing the main supply line of the Army of Virginia. An artillerist called the achievement "the great wonder." Moxley Sorrel declared their march was "in swiftness, daring, and originality of execution . . . almost extraordinary." Five miles to the north on the railroad lay Pope's supply base at Manassas Junction, with its railroad cars and warehouses overflowing with quartermaster and commissary stores. With its capture the Union army would have no choice but to abandon the Rappahannock line.[25]

"I deemed it important that no time should be lost in securing Manassas Junction," reported Jackson. Sixty-year-old Brigadier General Isaac Ridgeway Trimble volunteered to seize the supply base with the 21st North Carolina and 21st Georgia. When Jackson asked if he might need more than two infantry regiments, Trimble answered, "I beg your pardon, General, but give me my two Twenty-ones and I'll charge and capture hell itself." Jackson assigned Stuart to overall command of the operation. With cavalrymen preceding Trimble's veterans, the Rebels followed the tracks toward Manassas Junction.[26]

The Confederates attacked the small Union garrison at the supply base at about two o'clock on the morning of August 27. Trimble's Georgians and North Carolinians overwhelmed the enemy infantrymen and artillery crews and scattered a new regiment of Pennsylvania cavalrymen. The 4th Virginia Cavalry, circling behind the junction, overtook scores of fleeing Yankees. The Confederates captured more than 300 prisoners, eight cannon, nearly 200 horses, and the vast stockpiles of supplies. Stuart reported it had been achieved with "little difficulty."[27]

After daylight Jackson marched Powell Hill's and Taliaferro's troops to Manassas Junction. Ewell's division remained at Bristoe Station as a rear guard. In the afternoon Major General Joseph Hooker's division of the Third Corps of the Army of the Potomac appeared, advancing along the railroad tracks from the southwest toward Bristoe Station. Ewell readied his veterans of the Valley and the Seven Days, and they engaged the Federals. Hooker shoved more units into the combat. When Ewell received orders from Jackson to retreat, the redoubtable general and his men executed a skillful fighting withdrawal. It was dusk when the last of Ewell's regiments disappeared into the dying light. The Confederates suffered fewer than 200 casualties; the enemy, more than 300. As a tactician commanding a division Ewell had few equals in Lee's army.[28]

At Manassas Junction, meanwhile, Jackson's other troops feasted on a mountain of various foodstuffs. "What a time was that," recounted a member of the Stonewall Brigade. "Half-starved and worn out, we suddenly found ourselves turned loose among car loads of everything good to eat and drink and smoke." What the men did not consume they stuffed into pockets and haversacks or carried away on their backs. They grabbed clothing, shoes, and candles. Some discovered barrels of whiskey and filled their canteens and "were as happy as lambs with two mammies."[29]

While the Confederates reveled among the warehouses and railroad cars, Brigadier General George Taylor's New Jersey brigade approached the junction from Centreville. Earlier Jackson had deployed infantry and artillery when a Union regiment appeared in his front. These Yankees retreated quickly, before the New Jersey volunteers started forth. Believing that he opposed only Confederate cavalry, Taylor led his men into a bloodbath. They advanced, said a Southerner, in "the prettiest line I ever saw." Then Jackson's gunners blasted them with canister, and the infantrymen triggered volleys that shredded the line. The Federals staggered and broke for the rear. "The enemy seemed to run, every man for himself," bragged a Rebel, "and we ran right after them, shooting as we ran." Taylor suffered a mortal wound, and his brigade incurred more than 400 casualties.[30]

After Ewell's troops arrived at Manassas Junction and scavenged through the depleted stores, Jackson ordered the supply base burned. With the enemy at Bristoe Station and likely en route on Warrenton Turnpike to Gainesville, Jackson readied his command to march. Taliaferro's division left first, followed a few hours later by Powell Hill's brigades. Acting as a rear guard again, Ewell's troops departed at about daylight on August 28. By midday Jackson had concentrated the three divisions on a wooded ridge north of Warrenton Turnpike from Groveton to Sudley Springs. A mile and a half away to the east lay Henry House Hill, the old killing ground of First Manassas.[31]

In his fine study of the Second Manassas Campaign, John Hennessy argued, "The idea of luring Pope into battle dominated Jackson's thoughts and actions on August 28." Although the Confederate general did not address his thinking in his report, the events on this day support Hennessy's conclusion. By the time Jackson finished his deployment on the ridge, he had learned from captured enemy dispatches that Pope's units were marching toward Manassas, with some elements crossing his front on Warrenton Turnpike. Furthermore, Jackson and Lee had maintained contact by courier, and the former knew that Longstreet's command had reached Salem and was approaching Thoroughfare Gap, ten miles southwest of Jackson's position. Instead of eluding the Federals, Jackson readied his veterans behind the bed of an unfinished railroad, which provided them with a natural fieldwork along much of its length.[32]

Jackson's aggressive stand reshaped the campaign. He had accomplished his primary objective, seizing the railroad and forcing Pope to abandon the Rappahannock line. Jackson could retreat north or west, crossing the Bull Run Mountains at Aldie Gap or angling toward Leesburg, reunite with Longstreet's wing, and then advance either into Maryland or the Shenandoah Valley, as Lee had indicated. Instead, Jackson sought a battle with Pope before McClellan's entire Army of the Potomac could combine with the Army of Virginia. By doing so he committed Lee to a general engagement, which the army commander said he wanted to avoid.[33]

Coming toward Jackson's 24,000 officers and men and Stuart's horse soldiers from the south and east were more than 75,000 Federals. Jackson's march had been detected as early as nine o'clock on the morning of August 25. "It seems apparent," Union corps commander Nathaniel Banks wrote to army headquarters, "that the enemy is threatening or moving upon the valley of the Shenandoah via Front Royal with designs upon the Potomac, possibly beyond." Pope accepted Banks's misinterpretation of the movement and forwarded the information to Washington, estimating the enemy force at 20,000. Pope promised to act on the intelligence, but did little. The news of the Rebel capture of Bristoe Station the next day, however, forced him to react. With his supply line severed, he had to abandon his position along the Rappahannock, either moving downriver to Fredericksburg or turning north toward the Federal capital. He reasoned correctly that Lee had divided his army, and an opportunity offered, as he put it, to "crush any force of the enemy that had passed through Thoroughfare Gap."[34]

At daylight on August 27 the roads north from the Rappahannock River filled with Yankees on the march. Rumor put it, noted a private in his diary, "that the enemy had outflanked us and were trying to get in our rear." The Federals moved in three parallel columns, the ranks enveloped in clouds of dust and sweltering heat. "Straggling almost became a mania," recalled one of them. By nightfall, however, they had reached Bristoe Station, clashing with Ewell's troops, Gainesville, and Greenwich. Pope had been informed of a large Confederate force— Longstreet's command—at Salem but issued no instructions to delay or to prevent it from joining with Jackson. The Union commander explained later, "I believed then that we were sufficiently in advance of Longstreet . . . that by using our whole force vigorously we should be able to crush Jackson completely before Longstreet could have reached the scene of action."[35]

Pope's statement belied the fact that he did not know Jackson's whereabouts on the night of August 27. The Union general mistakenly believed that the Confederates remained at Manassas Junction and directed his units toward the abandoned, smoldering supply base on August 28. When Pope arrived at the junction during the day and found no enemy troops, he issued new orders for a concentration at Centreville, where rumors placed the Rebels. Pope's single-minded intention to find Jackson—"We shall bag the whole crowd," he boasted to a corps commander—led him to ignore the danger beyond the Bull Run Mountains and drew his army, as Jackson wanted, toward a reckoning on "the plains of Manassas."[36]

It was an hour before sunset on August 28 when Jackson revealed his presence to the enemy. Before him on Warrenton Turnpike marched the Union division of Brigadier General Rufus King of Major General Irvin McDowell's Third Corps. Jackson, riding back and forth on the ridge, watched a brigade pass by and then ordered forward a battery and William Taliaferro's infantry. "Bring up your men, gentlemen," Jackson instructed. The gunners opened fire, stirring a response from the enemy. Federal artillerists unlimbered cannon and returned the fire. From the roadbed Brigadier General John Gibbon's brigade, comprising the 2nd, 6th, and 7th Wisconsin and 19th Indiana, began ascending through the fields and woodlot of the John Brawner farm. From the crest of the ridge Confederate battle flags appeared in front of gray-coated ranks. So began the Battle of Second Manassas.[37]

It was as though a hellish vortex had settled over the Brawner farm, drawing fellow Americans into a swirling fury of killing and maiming. For two hours, amid the darkening of a day, at times thirty yards apart, three Confederate brigades—Stonewall, Alexander Lawton's, and Isaac Trimble's—and six Union regiments, Gibbon's four and the 56th Pennsylvania and 76th New York, ravaged each other. "My God, what a slaughter!" exclaimed one of Gibbon's Westerners. "I have never known so terrible a fire," asserted Trimble. "Jackson's men fight like Devils," argued a Yankee. Rail fences and a swale in the ground offered some protection, but the opposing lines simply stood at point-blank range and blazed away.[38]

Darkness ended the slaughter. Union losses exceeded 950, of which Gibbon's brigade suffered 725 killed, wounded, or missing. When told the casualty figures that night, Gibbon wept. Except for the 2nd Wisconsin, his men had not been in combat. A demanding officer, Gibbon had outfitted them in the uniform of Regular Army troops, with the long frock coat and tall black Hardee hat. After this day their foes called them "those damned black hats."[39]

Confederate losses amounted to 1,200, or nearly 30 percent. Although Jackson and his subordinates had numerical superiority and the advantage of higher ground, they handled the fighting poorly by attacking piecemeal. In two separate charges the 26th Georgia and 21st North Carolina sustained casualties that exceeded 70 percent. Only two other regiments in Lee's army would incur a higher percentage of loss in a single engagement during the war. Most critically Jackson lost Taliaferro, Trimble, and Ewell to wounds that would disable them for months. Ewell had been kneeling on the ground when a bullet struck his left kneecap and coursed down his leg, splitting the tibia; surgeons amputated the leg above the knee that night. Ewell was irreplaceable at his rank in Jackson's wing of the army.[40]

The engagement at Brawner's farm disclosed Jackson's location to Pope, which by all accounts, Jackson intended. When he ordered his men brought out, the Confederate commander did not know whether or not Longstreet's wing had secured Thoroughfare Gap and passage through the mountain defile. If the enemy held the gap, blocking Longstreet's march, Jackson would confront formidable odds for an indefinite

time. What spared him from the possible consequences of his risky decision were Pope's believing wrongly that Jackson was in retreat and the
disjointed Union operations. By the time Pope's scattered units con-
verged on Jackson's position on August 29, Lee's two wings had been
reunited.[41]

Longstreet's twelve infantry brigades, sixteen artillery batteries, and
the army's entire wagon train had crossed the Rappahannock River at
Hinson's Mill Ford late on the afternoon of August 26, hours before
the Federals began their withdrawal from the river. By the afternoon
of August 27 the van of the column had reached White Plains, having covered twenty-three miles in twenty-four hours. Lee, Longstreet,
and their staffs rode at the head of the marchers, and near Salem were
nearly captured by a Union cavalry patrol. At White Plains they were
encamped seven miles from Thoroughfare Gap. During the evening
Richard Anderson's division and Colonel Stephen D. Lee's artillery
battalion arrived at Salem after a grueling march. Longstreet's command now numbered 30,000 troops.[42]

The pace of the march to White Plains generated postwar controversy. Former officers in the army alleged that Longstreet was slow in
reaching Manassas, forcing Jackson to fight alone for two days. Rooted
in postwar political differences, the criticism had no basis in facts. Lee,
not Longstreet, regulated the speed of the movement. Kept informed
by Jackson of his actions east of Bull Run Mountains, the commanding
general expressed no urgency in reuniting with Jackson. Perhaps most
indicative of Lee's satisfaction with Longstreet's efforts was the advance
on August 28, when the Confederates did not begin marching toward
Thoroughfare Gap until eleven o'clock in the morning.[43]

David Jones's brigades led the march on this day, trailed by the
divisions of John Hood, Cadmus Wilcox, and James Kemper. Known
as "Neighbor" for his affable personality, Jones was a capable officer
who suffered from health maladies. At about 3:00 P.M., Colonel George
T. Anderson's Georgians entered the western end of the gap, pushing
back Union cavalry vedettes. The Rebels climbed the mountain's face
and halted at the stone Chapman's Mill. To the east Federal artillerists opened fire, and three regiments formed into a line of battle and
advanced toward the Georgians. The Yankees belonged to the division

of Brigadier General James B. Ricketts, who had been ordered to hold the gap. Unfortunately for Ricketts's troops, they had arrived too late to man the mountain crests on both sides of the defile.[44]

The Federals resisted stubbornly on the rocky, wooded ground. When additional Confederate regiments ascended the mountains on the Georgians' flanks, the Northerners withdrew to the eastern entrance of the gap. Ricketts held on until after nightfall and then retreated toward Haymarket and Gainesville. The Southerners bedded down in the gap.[45]

Longstreet had his veterans on the march at daylight on August 29. Skirmishers from the 5th Texas covered the front of the column. Behind them rode Lee, Longstreet, and their staffs. At about nine o'clock, between Haymarket and Gainesville, Jeb Stuart and troopers from Beverly Robertson's brigade appeared. Stuart had been sent by Jackson to "establish communications with Longstreet." Lee inquired of Jackson, and Stuart described his position. The three generals examined a map, and Stuart suggested that Longstreet's men turn left at Gaines-ville onto Warrenton Turnpike in order to come in on Jackson's right flank. Lee then ordered Stuart, with Robertson's brigade, to reconnoiter south and east toward Manassas Junction, screening Longstreet's flank in that direction.[46]

Lee and his aides preceded Longstreet's troops, halting at the edge of a woodlot. Dismounting, Lee walked forward alone and surveyed the terrain while skirmishers exchanged fire in front of him. When he returned, according to Major Charles Venable, Lee said to his staff, "A Yankee sharpshooter came near killing me just now." His face bore the mark of a bullet that had grazed his cheek.[47]

Meanwhile Longstreet conducted his own reconnaissance from about a mile from Groveton. Like Lee, he came under enemy fire before returning to a hollow behind the elevation. Lee soon joined him, fol-lowed shortly by Jackson. "A most joyful meeting took place between the three generals," said an eyewitness. They walked up to the crest, where Jackson pointed out his position behind the scar of the unfin-ished railroad and the ground south of Warrenton Turnpike for Long-street's command. Longstreet then rode away on his large bay horse to oversee the deployment of his units.[48]

As Longstreet's infantry arrived—"The whole corps is excited," declared a Virginian—they filed off Warrenton Turnpike. John Hood deployed a brigade on both sides of the road. The divisions of Kemper, Jones, and Wilcox and Nathan Evans's Independent Brigade extended the line south or deployed as a reserve. When their dispositions were completed by noon, the Confederate army's front covered roughly three miles, divided almost equally between Jackson and Longstreet. Unlike the defensive advantages of Jackson's line, Longstreet's position pos-sessed no natural strengths, serving more as a platform from which to launch an attack. Woods, however, concealed Longstreet's ranks. After shuffling into line his footsore, weary men welcomed the halt.[49]

"Our advance to this place (near Bull Run) was one of the bold-est moves of our so-called 'timid' General," bragged Lee's aide, Walter Taylor, in a letter to his sister. Lee's daring operation of dividing his army and sending Jackson to strike Pope's supply line had given him the strategic initiative. Now, with his army reunited, he had brought it into one of the greatest tactical opportunities of the war. Unquestionably, poor, if not inept, Union leadership aided Confederate efforts. But as staff officer William Allan contended with justification in his postwar history of the army in 1862, Lee had "adopted a plan of campaign such as only masters of the art of war may hazard."[50]

"Like most great soldiers, Lee enjoyed warfare," the historian Grady McWhiney has written. "It challenged and excited him to be intrep-idly daring." Longstreet stated it more tersely, saying that Lee "loved a fight, and urged his battle with wonderful determination." It was such at midday on August 29. With Longstreet's deployment completed, the situation on the battlefield stirred Lee's combativeness. As Longstreet remembered in a postwar letter, "We all were particularly anxious to bring on the battle after 12 [P.M.]; General Lee more so than the rest." The Confederate commander "expressed his wish" that an attack be made at once.[51]

Longstreet spoke up, cautioning against an immediate assault. In his memoirs he asserted that the commanding general "always invited the views" of subordinates, particularly those of Jackson and himself. While Lee accepted, if not embraced risks and Jackson often rushed his men into a fight, Longstreet acted more warily, more carefully. He has been criticized for being slow, when thorough more correctly characterized his generalship. Things had to fit for Longstreet before he committed his troops into battle. So when Stuart reported the presence of an unknown enemy force approaching on Gainesville-Manassas road, Longstreet asked to conduct a personal reconnaissance, and Lee consented.[52]

Longstreet rode south to Brewer's Spring, where he reconnoitered on horseback and on foot for an hour. He saw that the Union ranks covered half of his front. "The position was not inviting," he wrote. "I so reported to General Lee." The commanding general "was quite disappointed," recalled Longstreet, and was "not entirely satisfied with the report." Lee thought that the Union flank could be turned. A courier soon arrived with a message from Stuart: the enemy along Gainesville-Manassas road were in considerable numbers and were threatening the army's right flank. Lee decided to see for himself.[53]

Stuart's cavalrymen had been dragging brush along roads, raising clouds of dust, giving the impression of marching infantry. The Federals had halted and deployed skirmishers when Lee and Longstreet arrived on the flank. The two generals saw that the enemy force consisted of at least one corps: Fitz John Porter's Fifth Corps of the Army of the Potomac, the Southerners' foe at Mechanicsville and Gaines's Mill. Lee ordered Wilcox's division shifted far south to strengthen the flank and then rode back to his headquarters. Longstreet watched a fitful skirmish between his men and Porter's before rejoining Lee. The wing commander reported that, in his judgment, the Yankees posed no immediate threat and appeared to be retiring toward Manassas.[54]

As Lee and Longstreet conferred at about 5:00 P.M., the fighting along Jackson's front was intensifying to a climax. The Federals had undertaken a series of assaults on the Confederate ranks, beginning as early as eight o'clock in the morning. The attacks centered on Powell Hill's brigades on Jackson's left and Ewell's division, now under Alexander Lawton, in the center. Weeks earlier a rumor had circulated among Longstreet's men that Jackson had "issued an order to the troops to fight against any odds & be victorious at any cost." Most likely it was unfounded, but if it had been true, obedience to such a summons came on this day.[55]

A string of blue-coated brigades—units from Pope's First Corps, the Ninth Corps, and the Third Corps of the Army of the Potomac—assailed the Confederate ranks along the unfinished railroad bed and the ridge behind it. Much of the critical Civil War combat between opposing infantry occurred within a span of fewer than 120 yards; along Jackson's line the fighting boiled up much closer. At points the fury was hand-to-hand, muzzle-to-muzzle, with men clubbing each other with muskets. A Southerner recounted: "Often the combatants delivered their fire within ten or a dozen paces. . . . The slaughter was too horrible and sickening."[56]

At 3:00 P.M. Brigadier General Cuvier Grover's five Union regiments, veterans from the Army of the Potomac, charged toward the unfinished railroad. They were New Englanders and Pennsylvanians, and they struck a gap between two of Powell Hill's brigades. So suddenly came the Yankees through woods that they surprised and routed Edward Thomas's Georgians. "Those [Georgians] who made a fight were instantly shot or bayoneted," declared a New Hampshire soldier. A North Carolinian in Dorsey Pender's brigade, posted behind the Georgians on the ridge, declared, "It looked for a time as if the entire left wing of the Confederate Army would be overwhelmed."[57]

At the other end of the gap in the line lay Maxcy Gregg's brigade of South Carolinians. An advocate of secession and a Mexican War veteran, the dark-complexioned Gregg was one of Hill's most trusted subordinates. His men had repulsed a late morning attack. When Grover's Yankees scattered Thomas's Georgians, Gregg counterattacked with three regiments. The foes blasted each other, standing at places only a few yards apart. The South Carolinians' volleys, asserted a member of the 1st Massachusetts, were "terrible. Men dropped in scores, writhing and trying to crawl back, or lying immobile and stone-dead where they fell." Thomas rallied his broken ranks, and Dorsey Pender's North Carolinians charged. Caught almost in a circle of hellfire, Grover's men fled rearward, pursued by the Confederates. In thirty minutes Grover sustained nearly 500 casualties, a third of his command.[58]

Grover's isolated attack against three Confederate brigades characterized the piecemeal Union assaults on this day. Grover's troops had reached safety when three regiments of Colonel James Nagle's Ninth

Corps brigade charged Jackson's line, defended there by Lawton's division. Like Grover's men, Nagle's troops overran the unfinished railroad and advanced toward the ridge, only to be met with heavy musketry from the woodline. On their left Virginians and Louisianans wheeled out, raking the Federals' flank. Nagle's men broke toward the rear. At the same time Colonel Nelson Taylor's New York brigade arrived in support before the railroad embankment. The Virginians and Louisianans, however, hit the New Yorkers like a giant hammer, shattering their ranks and sending them in flight.[59]

The final Union effort came at about five o'clock, an assault against Hill's left front by the veteran infantrymen of Major General Philip Kearny's Third Corps division of the Army of the Potomac. The main thrust of Kearny's attack advanced toward the worn-out and thinned ranks of Gregg's South Carolinians. When Gregg saw the Union preparations for a charge, he sent a message to Hill, "Tell General Hill that my ammunition is exhausted, but that I will hold my position with the bayonet." Then, as the enemy started forward, Gregg drew the Revolutionary War sword of an ancestor and walked behind his line, telling his fellow South Carolinians, "Let us die here, my men, let us die here."[60]

Hill notified Jackson that his troops, with cartridge boxes nearly empty, might not be able to repulse another enemy attack. Minutes later the two generals met, each riding toward the other. Differences between them had arisen since the Light Division joined Jackson's command at Gordonsville. To Jackson, Hill's loose discipline was unacceptable; to Hill, Jackson's obsession with secrecy was infuriating. With a crisis at hand they now met. Jackson said: "General, your men have done nobly. I hope you will not be attacked again; but if you are you will beat the enemy back." Suddenly gunfire erupted along the lines. Turning to leave, Hill said, "Here it comes." Jackson replied, "I'll expect their repulse."[61]

Kearny's veterans drove toward the brigades of Gregg, Thomas, and James Archer. The Union attack was powerful and relentless. Once more the opponents lashed each other with musketry at point-blank range. Gregg's South Carolinians and Thomas's Georgians buckled under waves of Yankees. The Rebels found themselves caught, in the words of an officer, in "a semicircle of flame and smoke." They broke. On their right part of Archer's brigade gave way. Then, as Jackson's left front teetered on destruction, Jubal Early's 2,500 Virginians, coming from the right, swept through the shredded ranks and plowed into the Federal line. Early's charge was more than Kearny's exhausted men could withstand, and they fled rearward, finished for the day. When Jackson learned of the repulse, he sent an aide to Hill with the message, "Tell him I knew he would do it." In his report Lee praised Jackson's troops for "their accustomed steadiness."[62]

Lee and Longstreet, meanwhile, had agreed on a reconnaissance-in-force down Warrenton Turnpike. To be sure, Lee did so reluctantly, after urging an attack south of the road for a third time. He must have felt an urgency to relieve the pressure on Jackson's troops, evident by the roar of artillery fire and musketry. For a third time Longstreet objected. "Though more than anxious to meet his wishes, and anticipating his orders," explained the subordinate in his memoirs, "I suggested, as the day was far spent, that a reconnaissance in force be made at nightfall to the immediate front of the enemy, and if an opening was found for an entering wedge, that we have all things in readiness at daylight for a good day's work." Lee acceded to the proposal and issued the orders.[63]

Longstreet chose Hood's two brigades for the operation, supported by Nathan "Shanks" Evans's regiments. Aligned on both sides of the roadbed, the brigades advanced at 6:30 P.M., sunset. Driving toward Groveton, a cluster of houses along the turnpike, the Confederates struck two brigades of Brigadier General John Hatch's division. The collision stunned Hatch's men, who had been ordered in pursuit of an allegedly retreating enemy. The fight unraveled quickly into a confusing struggle in the deepening darkness. It became "so dark that one flag could not be distinguished from another, nor the Yankee troops from Southern soldiers," recounted a Texan. Hood's veterans captured a cannon and several battle flags before the Federals retreated. The Rebels halted for the night a mile in front of Longstreet's line.[64]

After the fighting had ceased, Cadmus Wilcox and his division joined Hood's and Evans's brigades. Wilcox and Hood conferred, agreeing that their troops were too far in advance of the main line. Hood rode back to discuss the situation with Lee, who objected to a withdrawal. Lee had consented to Longstreet's plan as a prelude to a possible attack at daylight and now was unwilling to abandon the ground taken by Hood's men. When Hood informed Wilcox of Lee's answer, Wilcox sought out Longstreet. Accounts conflict as to whether Longstreet, acting as wing commander, ordered a withdrawal or convinced Lee to do so. In the end the brigades pulled back during the night, and the proposed dawn assault was canceled.[65]

The operations south of Warrenton Turnpike on August 29 subsequently fueled acrid controversy in both armies. John Pope accused Fitz John Porter of disobeying a direct order to attack Longstreet's command. In Porter's defense, he faced twice his numerical strength and would have been "easily and thoroughly repulsed," in Wilcox's opinion. Nevertheless, after the Union defeat Pope filed formal charges, and a court-martial found Porter guilty and cashiered him from the army in January 1863. Fifteen years later, however, Porter achieved exoneration from all the charges and had his name restored to the list of army officers.[66]

On the Southern side, former Confederates and many future historians would view the culprit as James Longstreet. His critics accused him of slowness, of thwarting Lee's desire for an attack, and even of dominating the commanding general. They envisioned a connection between his reluctance on the first day at Second Manassas and his recalcitrance on the second day at Gettysburg. In his magisterial, four-volume biography of Lee, Douglas Southall Freeman wrote, "The seeds of much of the disaster at Gettysburg were sown in that instant—when Lee yielded to Longstreet [on August 29] and Longstreet discovered that he would."[67]

Unquestionably Lee urged an offensive strike. The Confederate commander was a warrior and might have seen an opportunity that the cautious Longstreet found too risky. Ultimately, on the afternoon of August 29, the tactical situation on the ground precluded a Confederate advance. Porter wrote to Longstreet after the war that he had welcomed an assault with his infantry and artillery posted and with units of Irvin McDowell's corps in close support: "I am very sure if you had attacked me your loss would have been enormous." The Union presence on the Confederate right flank could not be ignored.[68]

The accusation leveled against Longstreet by his critics "presupposes that Lee was weak, and therefore could be dominated," the historian John Hennessy has averred. "If true—and it was not—then Lee, not Longstreet, deserves criticism for allowing a subordinate to overbear him in the face of good sense and good tactics." Longstreet's argument had validity, and Lee accepted it, albeit with reluctance. Their relationship had evolved since Lee had assumed command of the army, and he welcomed and listened to his subordinate's counsel. In his memoirs Longstreet described their relationship as one of "confidence and esteem, official and personal, which ripened into stronger ties as the mutations of war bore heavier upon us." It had become the same with Lee and Jackson, who, like Longstreet, earned the army commander's trust. Finally, the events of August 30 affirmed Longstreet's judgment.[69]

Saturday, August 30, dawned clear and warm. "A lovely day," said a Virginian. "The morning was so still and quiet that everybody seemed to be on good behavior." Skirmishers and artillery crews interrupted the quiet sporadically, reminding each side of the bloody work to come. Lee expected, even desired, a renewal of enemy attacks on Jackson's position. When the hours passed without evidence of more Union assaults, Lee brought Jackson, Longstreet, and Stuart to army headquarters, situated in the grove of trees south of Warrenton Turnpike.[70]

At the meeting the Confederate senior leadership agreed to await an enemy movement. If Pope did not resume his attacks, Jackson would withdraw after nightfall and march beyond the Union right flank, interposing his troops between Pope's forces and the defenses of Washington. Longstreet would demonstrate against the Federal left front and would follow if the Yankees retreated. Whether Lee considered it is unknown, but Jackson's turning movement might have placed him between Pope's thousands and the missing corps of George McClellan's Army of the Potomac. Lee knew of the Lincoln administration's sensitivity about the security of its capital; it would not have been unreasonable for him to surmise that McClellan's other corps had been ordered there and had arrived. If so, Jackson's men would have been in a precarious position. The proposed movement entailed more risks than Lee and his generals considered.[71]

After the conference Lee wrote to Jefferson Davis, "The movement has, as far as I am able to judge, drawn the enemy from the Rappahan-

nock frontier and caused him to concentrate his troops between Manassas & Centreville—my desire has been to avoid a general engagement,
being the weaker force & by manoeuvring to relieve the portion of the
country referred to—I think if not overpowered we shall be able to
relieve other portions of the country, as it seems to be the purpose of the
enemy to collect his strength here." It was a restatement of the under-
pinnings of his strategy since he had concentrated the army at Gordonsville. He left unstated, however, that a general engagement had
not been avoided. While Lee had made plans for another movement, he
preferred to settle the issue on this field with the army's wings reunited
and on favorable ground.[72]

The inactivity extended past midday. During that time Longstreet
realigned his units, and Jackson withdrew some of his frontline brigades
for a rest, filling their places with troops from his reserve. Colonel Stephen D. Lee's artillery battalion and Richard Anderson's infantry division had arrived on the battlefield. Lee (no relation to the commanding general) rolled his eighteen cannon onto the ridge above Groveton
between Jackson's and Longstreet's ranks. According to Porter Alexander, it was a "beautiful position" from which Lee's crews could sweep
the ground in front of Jackson's right. Anderson's bone-weary soldiers
deployed as a reserve behind Longstreet's left front.[73]

It was three o'clock in the afternoon—Lee had begun preparations for the flanking movement—when the front ranks of a 20,000-
man Union attack force emerged from Groveton Woods, marching
toward the center of Jackson's line along the unfinished railroad. Since
early morning John Pope had struggled with uncertainties. Conflicting
reports either had the enemy in retreat or still in force along the railroad cut. He could have taken up a defensive position and awaited Lee's
next move, but his aggressive temperament evidently ruled out such a
consideration. Instead he jeopardized his army, unable to grasp the reality before him.[74]

Pope knew of Longstreet's presence on the field but mistakenly
believed that his academy roommate's troops had deployed behind
Jackson's line, not as an extension south beyond Warrenton Turnpike.
Porter and the division commander Brigadier General John F. Reynolds tried to persuade Pope otherwise, but, as Porter noted, the army

commander "put no confidence in what I said." Finally, without credit-able evidence, Pope concluded late in the morning that Lee's army was indeed in flight and ordered Porter's Fifth Corps, supported by two divi-sions, in pursuit. The preparations consumed three hours, while skir-mish fire and artillery exchanges mounted in intensity, harbingers of a fury unleashed by John Pope.[75]

At the sight of Porter's ranks, Jackson's infantrymen grabbed their muskets and steeled themselves. To their right Stephen Lee's gunners loaded their cannon. When the Confederate infantry and artillery opened fire, "the first line of the attack column looked as if it had been struck by a blast from a tempest and had been blown away," exclaimed a Rebel. But Porter's veterans kept coming, ascending a long slope toward Louisianans and Virginians. Lee's cannon scorched the flank of the attackers, gouging holes in the ranks. Still the Yankees came. "The yells from both sides were indescribably savage," exclaimed a New Yorker. "We were transformed . . . from a lot of good-natured boys to the most bloodthirsty of demoniacs." He spoke for men on both sides.[76]

The fiercest struggle centered along sections of the railroad bed known as the "Deep Cut" and "The Dump." To the right of the Deep Cut the Stonewall Brigade reeled under the onslaught, broke to the rear, rallied, and counterattacked. Brigade commander Colonel William S. H. Baylor grabbed the flag of the 33rd Virginia and shouted to his men, "Boys, follow me." When the Federals triggered a volley into the Virginians, the blast lifted Baylor off the ground, killing him instantly. Once again Jackson's old brigade recoiled into the woods on the ridge, regrouped, and charged. This time they drove the enemy back, retaking the railroad bed. An excellent and popular officer, Baylor had seemed destined for higher rank.[77]

To the left of the Stonewall Brigade, Colonel Bradley Johnson's Vir-ginians and Colonel Leroy Stafford's Louisianans manned the railroad bed from the Deep Cut to a hundred-yard gap in the fill, known after-ward as The Dump. They clung desperately to their position against a seemingly endless stream of Union regiments. "It is impossible for me to give you an idea of this battle," admitted a Yankee in a letter home. As it had been the day before, the killing and maiming were done at close range. Opposing battle flags stood yards apart. At one point, with ammunition expended, Stafford's Louisianans hurled stones at their foes. "They had a short distance to throw," wrote a Confederate. Colonel John M. Brockenbrough's Virginia brigade rushed forward in support of Johnson's and Stafford's men.[78]

Jackson sent Major Henry Kyd Douglas to Longstreet for reinforcements, requesting that a division be sent. Longstreet had been watching the struggle along Jackson's front and decided that sending an infantry division would take too much time. Instead he ordered three batteries forward beside Stephen Lee's eighteen guns. Under the pounding from Lee's guns, Porter's ranks were already fraying and streaming into the woods. Recognizing the opportunity before him, Longstreet ordered a counterattack by his entire command. His aides hurried along the line, delivering the instructions. At army headquarters the commanding general had concluded the same and issued orders to Longstreet for an advance.[79]

Longstreet said later that Lee "invariably left" the hour and mode of attack to Jackson and himself. On this day the time had come; the execution was Longstreet's. The wing commander designated John Hood's division, posted along Warrenton Turnpike, as the column of direction, with Henry House Hill, a mile or so to the east, as the target. The other brigades and divisions would advance in succession, those units south of the turnpike obliquing left to conform with Hood's movement. Longstreet preferred a tactical formation that hit an opponent with consecutive blows, a hammering by one battle line after another. A Mississippian asserted that when Longstreet "went into a fight he was a whole team."[80]

Each regimental color-bearer stepped in front of the battle lines, moving an eyewitness to exclaim, "The spectacle was magnificent." A member of the 57th Virginia confessed that he and his comrades "thought the day of judgment was at hand." Longstreet called them later "over 30,000 of the best soldiers the world ever knew." They numbered, however, slightly more than 25,000 in the attack force.[81]

"My whole line rushed forward at a charge," reported Longstreet. "The troops sprang to their work, and moved forward with all the steadiness and firmness that characterizes war-worn veterans." Hood's Texas Brigade spearheaded the counterattack, moving down a slope and up a second hillside. On the crest in front of them stood the 5th New York, or "Duryee's Zouaves," and the 10th New York. Skirmishers from the latter regiment fled before the oncoming Rebels. Before these Yankees could clear the fronts of the two regiments, the 5th Texas, Hampton Legion, and 18th Georgia had closed to within forty yards.[82]

At this range the Confederates could hardly miss, and they shredded the ranks of the New York regiments. Singly, in pairs, and then by dozens, the New Yorkers fled down the back side of the hill and through Young's Branch. In ten minutes the Zouaves lost 120 men killed or mortally wounded, the largest loss of life in a regiment in a single engagement in the war. The fallen Zouaves in their blue jackets and red pants reminded a Texan of home, of a "hillside in spring, painted with wild flowers of every hue and color." At the dedication of the regimental monument decades later, a survivor in the 5th New York declared that he and his comrades had stood in "the very vortex of Hell."[83]

Hood's veterans pursued the New Yorkers across Young's Branch and ascended a knoll east of the stream. No infantrymen in Longstreet's wing were better fighters than members of the Texas Brigade. They routed a second Union brigade and overran a battery on the knoll. Shifting to the right, the Rebels scaled the western slope of Chinn Ridge, a broad, uneven height 500 yards west of Henry House Hill. Behind them came Shanks Evans's South Carolina regiments. On the ridge waited a solitary Union brigade, Colonel Nathaniel C. McLean's four Ohio regiments. When the Confederates appeared above the ridge's edge, the Ohioans opened fire. Their volley marked the beginning of a whirlwind that swept across Chinn Ridge for nearly ninety minutes.[84]

Five Union brigades—men from Ohio, Pennsylvania, New York, and Massachusetts—opposed six Confederate brigades: Texans, South Carolinians, Georgians, and Virginians. James Kemper's three brigades, followed by Colonel Henry L. Benning's Georgians of Jones's division, wheeled onto the ridge from the south, coming in on the right of Evans and Hood. Union reinforcements arrived from the north, and the combat flowed back and forth in those directions. A Yankee wrote that the Rebels "were yelling in their peculiar effeminate manner." The musketry swelled into a roar. "Half the time the smoke was so thick," declared a Virginian, "that we could not detect the blue forms of our enemies—and could only tell where they were by their cheers and the occasional glimpse we caught of their flag."[85]

Both sides suffered frightful casualties. Brigadier General Micah Jenkins fell, severely wounded, and Colonel Fletcher Webster, commander of the 12th Massachusetts and the eldest son of Daniel Webster, went down with a mortal wound. Finally, Confederate numbers and fighting spirit prevailed. The Rebels, stated a Union captain, "swept everything before them like a hurricane." It was about 6:00 P.M., and the valiant sacrifice of the Federals on Chinn Ridge allowed Pope and his senior generals to patch together a final line on Henry House Hill, its front ranks lying along Sudley Road and facing west. If these defenders could hold for an hour, nightfall would shield Pope's defeated army.[86]

Lee and Longstreet trailed the counterattack on Warrenton Turnpike and came under Union artillery fire from batteries on Dogan Ridge. Longstreet brought forward gun crews to oppose the Federal cannon. Lee's aide Walter Taylor described the fighting as "sublime." Before the Confederates cleared Chinn Ridge, Longstreet ordered forward the divisions of Richard Anderson and Cadmus Wilcox, directing them toward Chinn Ridge and Henry House Hill. Wilcox misunderstood the instructions, however, sending only one brigade south across the turnpike.[87]

When Longstreet's troops stepped out at four o'clock, Lee sent a message to Jackson: "General Longstreet is advancing; look out for and protect his left flank." At the time, after the repulse of Porter's assaults, three of Jackson's brigades and two brigades from Wilcox's division had advanced to the eastern fringe of Groveton Woods. Before them on Dogan Ridge stood a row of Union cannon. An attack on these guns could have been costly, but it might have relieved some of the pounding taken by Longstreet's units south of the turnpike. Most critically, Jackson's inaction for two hours allowed Union generals to hurry reinforcements across the turnpike and to withdraw to Henry House Hill.[88]

In his report Jackson offered no explanation for the delay. When several brigades advanced at about six o'clock, they scattered four Union regiments and captured eight cannon. The limited success came, however, too late to assist Longstreet. "That it took two hours for the Confederate units north of the turnpike, most of them Jackson's, to move forward stands as one of the battle's great puzzles," Hennessy con-

cluded in his campaign study. "It also stands as one of the most significant Confederate failures on the fields of Manassas."[89]

By the time Jackson pressed forward north of Warrenton Turnpike the
struggle for Henry House Hill was mounting in intensity. David Jones's
two brigades of Georgians struck the Union defensive line along Sudley
Road. Coming off Chinn Ridge, the Georgians wheeled to the right and
charged directly at the "blue-coated hirelings," as a staff officer derisively
termed the Federals. The 15th Georgia of Benning's brigade knifed across
the road, broke through Union ranks, and then clung to the ground. The
advance of the other Georgians stalled, and the foes raked each other
along Sudley Road at distances of fifty yards or less. A Confederate battery
had unlimbered to the right, blasting the left flank of the Union line.[90]

Richard Anderson's division arrived from the west, across Chinn
Ridge. While Ambrose "Rans" Wright's four Georgia regiments moved
in support of Jones's brigades, Virginians under brigadiers William
Mahone and Lewis Armistead crossed Sudley Road beyond the enemy's
left flank and wheeled to the left, facing north. Union regiments rushed
to meet Mahone's and Armistead's threat to unhinge the entire Federal
line on Henry House Hill. A "terrific fire," in Mahone's words, blazed
along the opposing ranks in the gathering darkness. The ramrod-thin
Mahone fell wounded, but his men's musketry forced the Yankees rearward. For unexplained reasons Anderson did not press forward against
the exposed flank. Along Sudley Road the depleted and weary ranks
of the Georgians began receding toward Chinn Ridge. Far to the Confederate right Beverly Robertson's cavalrymen routed four regiments of
enemy horsemen in one final action.[91]

Nightfall spared the Federals, who retreated across Bull Run to Centreville, where they met the Second and Sixth corps from the Army
of the Potomac. Rain fell overnight, bringing, said Longstreet, a "nasty
and soggy" morning of August 31. Lee conducted a personal reconnaissance along Bull Run. While he was standing with Jackson and Longstreet, someone shouted the alarm of Yankee cavalry. Reaching for the
reins of Traveller, Lee tripped, falling forward and bracing himself with
both hands. The pain was instant; he sprained his left hand and broke a
small bone in his right. With his hands in splints, the army commander
would have to ride in an ambulance for more than a fortnight.[92]

Despite the weather and mud and the men's fatigue, Lee moved to intercept the Federal retreat between Centreville and Washington. While Longstreet's troops demonstrated before the Union lines at Centreville, Jackson's command marched north, struck Little River Turnpike, and turned east toward Fairfax Court House. Stuart's two brigades screened Jackson's column, gathering up enemy stragglers, wagons, and ambulances. Throughout the day reports filtered back to Pope's headquarters of Confederate cavalry and infantry on Little River Turnpike. The Union commander reacted the next morning, September 1, by shifting units to cover the retreat route and sending Brigadier General Isaac Stevens's Ninth Corps division toward Ox Hill to check Jackson's march.[93]

The final clash of the Second Manassas Campaign occurred late on the afternoon of September 1, at Ox Hill, in a drenching thunderstorm. Neither side gained a tactical advantage, but Confederates killed Stevens and Philip Kearny, who had led his division forward in support of Stevens's troops. Jackson suffered about 700 casualties; the Federals roughly 500. Dorsey Pender told his wife in a letter, "None of us seemed anxious for a fight or did ourselves much credit." Longstreet's men arrived during the fighting, and Lee's army bivouacked for the night.[94]

Valor had walked the plains at Manassas, demanding a terrible price. A modern calculation lists Union casualties as 1,724 killed or mortally wounded, 8,372 wounded, and 5,958 captured or missing, for a total of 16,054, or 21 percent of Pope's command. Confederate losses amounted to 1,481 killed or mortally wounded, 7,627 wounded, and 89 captured or missing, totaling 9,197, a casualty rate of 19 percent. A surgeon with Jackson's command observed astutely in a letter on August 31, "Their [Federals'] loss is much greater than ours in numbers but not equal in worth."[95]

Records and accounts testify to the critical nature of Confederate losses. From Cedar Mountain on August 9 to Ox Hill on September 1 nearly eighty regimental field officers had fallen in battle; at least a fifth of them were regimental commanders. In Richard Anderson's three brigades that attacked the Federals on Henry House Hill, every field officer except one was either killed or wounded. No field officer had been spared in Isaac Trimble's brigade, and a captain led each of the four regiments. Total casualties surpassed 600 in the brigades of Maxcy Gregg, George T. Anderson, and Nathan Evans. The Texas Brigade incurred losses of more than 570, with the 5th Texas losing more men than any regiment in the army. In fact Longstreet's wing suffered more casualties in its counterattack than Jackson's command did in its two-day defense of the unfinished railroad.[96]

Moreover six generals had been wounded: division commanders Richard Ewell and William Taliaferro; brigade commanders Isaac Trimble, Charles Field, Micah Jenkins, and William Mahone. Colonel William Baylor of the Stonewall Brigade had died in defense of the railroad cut. By the end of the campaign "the subordinate army command was suffering more from attrition than ever it had," concluded Douglas Southall Freeman. In fact since June, either through transfer or as a casualty, the army had lost seven division and twenty-six brigade commanders. By nightfall on September 1 fewer than half of the regimental, brigade, and divisional commanders held the appropriate rank.[97]

In those three months, however, the Army of Northern Virginia had shifted the conflict in the Old Dominion from the environs of Richmond to the outskirts of Washington, a distance of roughly 100 miles. The accomplishment was not lost on those with the army. "We ransack history in vain for a more brilliant campaign than this," boasted a newspaper correspondent to readers in Georgia. Dorsey Pender wrote to his wife on September 2, calling the operation "the most brilliant and daring feats of Generalship and soldiership ever performed. The boldness of the plan and the quickness and completeness of execution was never beaten." In another letter Pender asserted that Lee's campaign surpassed any of Napoleon Bonaparte's. In his history of the army Porter Alexander described Second Manassas as "a beautifully played game on Lee's part."[98]

From the planning in a field outside Jeffersonton to Jackson's march on August 31, the campaign clearly revealed Lee's commitment to strategic, or operational, maneuver. "The defensive turning movement, best exemplified in Lee's Second Manassas campaign," the historian Archer Jones contended, "was a valuable military innovation and fully in harmony with Confederate political gains." The Confederate commander had disrupted Union plans, relieved sections of the state from enemy occupation, and achieved what he called "a signal victory." When Jackson committed the army to a battle at Manassas, Lee accepted the tactical situation before him, despite his expressed desire to avoid an engagement. With the wings of the army reunited on August 29, Lee controlled the battlefield if his opponent chose to stand and to fight. When Pope stood, Lee came the closest he ever would to the destruction of a Union army.[99]

"The history of the achievements of the army," Lee stated in his report, "from the time it advanced from Gordonsville leaves nothing to be said in commendation of the courage, fortitude, and good conduct of both officers and men." The Seven Days had marked the beginning. Second Manassas marked the emergence of an army characterized by outstanding senior leadership and the bravery and fighting prowess of its rank and file. Not all the problems of the previous campaign had been rectified, but somewhere on the dusty roads of central Virginia and amid the horror at Manassas, the elements of an army were forged. In the judgment of Porter Alexander the campaign's significance was that the officers and men "acquired that magnificent morale which made them equal to twice their numbers, & which they never lost even to the surrender at Appomattox."[100]

The army's success owed much to its two senior subordinates, Stonewall Jackson and James Longstreet. Lee's creation of two wings, or unofficial corps, gave both men the organizational structure to utilize their talents. As he had done in the Shenandoah Valley in the spring, Jackson had imposed his will upon an opportunity, pushed his men with an unmatched determination, and chosen the battleground. He had limits as a tactician, but he could steel men in combat like few others. His delay in supporting Longstreet's attack on the afternoon of August 30 counted against his performance. In Jackson's defense, he might have believed that his men were too worn out after the grueling flank march and two days of fierce combat. Had he complied with Lee's instructions sooner, however, it might have counted more for the army.[101]

From the time James Longstreet arrived on the battlefield on the morning of August 29, his instincts and judgment were sound. His advice to Lee on that day, opposing an attack, proved to be measured and correct. When his troops went forward on the afternoon of August

30, they executed one of the war's finest counterattacks. According to Moxley Sorrel, Longstreet displayed his "consummate ability in managing troops" in combat. Longstreet himself described Lee's achievement as "clever and brilliant," regarding it as the Confederate commander's masterpiece of the strategic offensive and the tactical defensive. It was the method of waging war that best suited the careful and cautious Longstreet.[102]

The performances of division and brigade commanders were uneven. Richard Ewell and Powell Hill distinguished themselves once again. Ewell's wound, however, would keep him away from the army for more than eight months. Although he unofficially commanded two brigades, John Hood's conduct on August 30 was, in Freeman's estimation, "magnificent." James Kemper and William Starke, who succeeded a wounded William Taliaferro, did well for the first time at that command level. Conversely, Richard Anderson showed a lack of aggressiveness that would too often mark his leadership. At the brigade level Jubal Early and Maxcy Gregg excelled.[103]

Conducted over a broad swath of territory and culminating in a battle on relatively open terrain, the campaign offered opportunities for the cavalry and artillery not present during the Seven Days. Jeb Stuart and his two brigades of cavalrymen appeared to be everywhere, scouting and screening Jackson's wing in particular. Stuart detected the march of Fitz John Porter's corps on August 29, which forced Lee at that time to delay his attack plans. Union cavalry was no match for Stuart's horsemen. As for the army's batteries, the tactical handling of guns in combat had improved, and the contribution of the gun crews was vital. Stephen Lee called Second Manassas the "finest battle to date for the Confederate artillery."[104]

Unquestionably the Confederate victory at Second Manassas was attained against a Union army cursed by dissension among its senior generals and a commander whose single-mindedness fashioned a near disaster. To Pope's credit, he reacted aggressively to Jackson's seizure of the railroad, but then became fixated on trapping the Confederate raiders. His failure to defend Thoroughfare Gap with a strong force was a critical, if not inexcusable, misjudgment. Once the battle was joined at Manassas he misread, time and again, the tactical situation, ignored the advice and warnings of his officers, whom he distrusted, and seemed incapable of or unwilling to countenance any facts at variance with his own conclusions. Simply put, the Union army lacked any generals comparable to Lee, Jackson, and Longstreet.[105]

The Union defeat at Second Manassas ignited a controversy in Washington. On September 1, in a message to the War Department, Pope declared, "I think it my duty to call your attention to the unsoldierly and dangerous conduct" of "many" officers of the Army of the Potomac. Pope meant particularly Fitz John Porter, but Abraham Lincoln and his Cabinet members questioned George McClellan's conduct during the campaign's critical days. McClellan was at Alexandria with the Second and Sixth corps. Whether he deliberately withheld these two corps from reinforcing Pope in the hope that he would be defeated has been the subject of historical dispute. Lincoln confided to his secretary John Hay at the time, "Unquestionably McClellan has acted badly toward Pope! He wanted him to fail! That is unpardonable." Four Cabinet officers signed a letter accusing McClellan of incompetence and deliberate disobedience of orders.[106]

Lincoln agonized over a decision. Early on the morning of September 2, he and Henry W. Halleck, the Union general-in-chief, went to McClellan's residence, where Lincoln offered him command of the capital's defenses. McClellan accepted. Lincoln informed the Cabinet at a midday meeting, stating that he alone was responsible for the decision. He explained to Hay: "We must use the tools we have. I must have McClellan to reorganize the army and bring it out of chaos. McClellan has the army with him." On that same day, to the west, Robert E. Lee looked north, beyond the Potomac River.[107]

Chapter Five

The Army's Finest Hour

THE ARMY OF NORTHERN Virginia marched away from its bivouac sites around Chantilly, Virginia, toward Leesburg in Loudoun County on September 3, 1862. On that same day Robert E. Lee wrote to Jefferson Davis. The commanding general began the letter with words of momentous import: "The present seems to be the most propitious time since the commencement of the war for the Confederate Army to enter Maryland. The two grand armies of the United States that have been operating in Virginia, though now united, are much weakened and demoralized."[1]

Lee continued, explaining the situation before him. With the enemy behind the defenses of Washington, he said, "I had no intention of attacking him in his fortifications, and am not prepared to invest him." The army could not remain in the Chantilly area because it lacked supplies, and he had ordered it into Loudoun County, where the army could garner forage and provisions and threaten a Union force in the Shenandoah Valley. At Leesburg, "if found practicable," the army could cross into Maryland. "The purpose, if discovered," Lee noted, "will have the effect of carrying the enemy north of the Potomac, and, if prevented, will not result in much evil."[2]

There were difficulties, admitted Lee: "The army is not properly equipped for an invasion of the enemy's territory. It lacks much of the material of war, is feeble in transportation, the animals being much reduced, and the men are poorly provided with clothes, and in thousands of instances are destitute of shoes. Still, we cannot afford to be idle, and though weaker than our opponents in men and military equipments, must endeavor to harass if we cannot destroy them. I am aware that the movement is attended with much risk, yet I do not consider success impossible, and shall endeavor to guard it from loss."[3]

The victory at Second Manassas had opened the possibility of carrying the war to Northern soil, a strategic goal shared by Lee, Davis, and the Southern populace. The Confederate commander indicated, however, that at Leesburg he had options. He could cross the Blue Ridge into the Shenandoah Valley, but that movement offered few immediate strategic gains and would distance him from the main Union army. He could withdraw into central Virginia along the Rappahannock River, but that would negate a major aim of the previous campaign.[4]

In fact, according to Charles Marshall in a postwar letter, "General Lee had nothing left to do after the battle [of Second Manassas], except to enter Maryland." Lee and the army had come too far not to press the strategic advantage they had achieved. By crossing the Potomac River east of the mountains, the Confederates could threaten Washington and Baltimore and draw the Union army out of Washington's earthworks. Once in the border state, Lee planned to march west across the mountains and to move north toward Pennsylvania. Central to his thinking, Lee stated in his letter to Davis, was "to harass if we cannot destroy" the Union army. He said after the war, "I went into Maryland to give battle."[5]

The boldness of the movement into Maryland exceeded the daring of the Seven Days and Second Manassas campaigns. An urgency factored into Lee's thinking. As he stated to Davis, he believed that the Union armies in Washington "are much weakened and demoralized." The Federals would need time to reorganize and to undertake active operations, allowing the Confederates time to maneuver and to choose when and where to offer battle. Lee's reasoning, however, might underestimate the enemy's capacity to reenter the field. In turn, the success of the forthcoming campaign relied on the capability of his army. He

had asked much of them before, and they had given much. Lee's audacious offensive beyond the Potomac hinged on an army that had already
stretched its physical and material limits to a critical edge.[6]

"We were in wretched plight," recalled a South Carolinian. The
men were simply exhausted; diarrhea and dysentery were rampant. Esti-
mates put the number of sick and wounded who would have to be left
behind as high as 5,000. Thousands of stragglers had left the ranks during the previous weeks. Many were barefoot, with pieces of clothing
serving as uniforms. When a Marylander saw them, he described them
as "these bundle of rags, these cough-racked, diseased and starved men."
Another Marylander, a young boy, watching them pass, said the Rebels
"were the dirtiest men I ever saw, a most ragged, lean and hungry set of
wolves."[7]

If they entered Maryland, Captain Greenlee Davidson of the Stonewall Brigade feared, "we will soon starve." The knapsacks belonging to
him and his comrades in Jackson's command remained behind at Jeffersonton, and the army's quartermaster and commissary wagons trailed
and would not overtake the army until September 8. Ammunition for
the artillery was in short supply; Lee had cautioned Longstreet during
the counterattack on August 30 to be sparing of it. Longstreet wrote in
his memoirs that the men were "worn by severe marches and battles,
and in need of rest."[8]

Lee believed he could not give them time for mending and refitting.
With the trials ahead, beyond the Potomac, what mattered most was
the men's confidence in themselves, which had sunk deep into their
marrow and into the soul of the army. They gave voice to it. On the
battlefield at Manassas a South Carolinian in the Hampton Legion told
a prisoner: "We will foute [fight] you until we are all dead, Yank! And I
reckon the women will foute you after that." Encountering the Rebels
after they had crossed into Maryland, a Union surgeon wrote what they
had said: "They all believe in *themselves* as well as their generals, and are
terribly in earnest. They assert that they have never been whipped, but
have driven the Yankees before them whenever they could find them."[9]

"I shall remember with pride," a soldier in the 4th Texas declared in
a letter to his wife on September 2, "that I belonged to the great army
that fought before Richmond so gloriously, that made twice memorable

Manassas plains & entered Maryland for its liberation." A fellow Texan wrote home the next day: "One more fight and I think the war will be over. . . . We move toward the enemy in a short time." A staff officer contended later, "The ragged and dirty soldiers hailed with joy the advance to the Potomac." The army he added, had "unbounded confidence in itself and its leaders." The campaigns of Seven Days and Second Manassas, asserted Colonel Bradley Johnson, left men who "were as hard and tough as troops ever have been, for the process of elimination had dropped out all of the inferior material."[10]

The men's morale, experience, and fighting prowess were the bedrock of the army, formed at Gaines's Mill, Glendale, Malvern Hill, Cedar Mountain, and Second Manassas. But those bloody fields had exacted a daunting rate of attrition among regimental, brigade, and division commanders. When the reinforcements joined the army and Lee reorganized units, only four of the nine infantry divisions were commanded by major generals. Among brigade commanders, twenty-one of forty held the rank of brigadier. In the 179 full-size regiments, sixty-eight commanders were colonels. Jackson's wing had a slightly higher percentage of lower grade officers in command than Longstreet's wing.[11]

The army that gathered in Loudoun County numbered roughly 70,000 officers and men. Having been ordered forward by Lee two weeks earlier, the infantry divisions of Lafayette McLaws and Harvey Hill, the Reserve Artillery, and Wade Hampton's cavalry brigade had arrived. A soldier with McLaws said in a letter, "We have had an extraordinary march for severity," and an Alabamian asserted to his family, "The march up to Maryland liked to have ruined me." Within days Brigadier General John G. Walker's 5,000-man division joined the army in Maryland.[12]

On September 4 Lee readied the army for the movement into Maryland. He reduced the number of wagons to those absolutely needed for each regiment. In the artillery unfit horses were removed, crews reassigned to other batteries, and battalions transferred to Jackson's and Longstreet's commands. In all, seventy-eight regular batteries and three horse artillery batteries accompanied the army. Lee appointed Lewis A. Armistead to command of the army's provost guard, with the duty of rounding up stragglers. In the same order Lee warned stragglers that they would be punished and enjoined "the gallant soldiers" to aid "their officers in checking the desire for straggling among their comrades."[13]

The main body of the army, led by Jackson's veterans, began crossing the Potomac at White's Ford on September 5. "The water being limestone," wrote a soldier, "it was as clear as crystal. The men removed their shoes, socks, and 'britches.'" Staff officer Thomas G. Pollock watched as the men, in ranks of four, waded into the river. "I never expect as long as I live to witness such a spectacle." "No body spoke," he explained, because "it was a time of great feeling." Pollock rode into the current, then turned in his saddle and looked to the rear. The column of marchers stretched as far as he could see. He confided to his father, "I felt, I was watching what must be the turning point of the war."[14]

When the men reached the Maryland riverbank, they cheered. A band played "Maryland, My Maryland." Jedediah Hotchkiss, Jackson's topographer, boasted to his wife in a letter, "The passing of the Rubicon was not more memorable for we were really advancing." Jackson, wrote Hotchkiss, was "more than usually attentive to all that passed." Writing the day before, a Virginian had observed, "Jackson next to Lee is the favorite here and I think Jackson inspires more enthusiasm in the men than Lee." Hotchkiss thought that there was "fewer straggling than I almost ever saw."[15]

In Leesburg, meanwhile, at the residence of Henry T. Harrison, a distant kinsman of Lee, the commanding general had a letter prepared for Davis. "As I have already had the honor to inform you," he stated, "this army is about entering Maryland, with a view of affording the people of that state an opportunity of liberating themselves. Whatever success may attend that effort, I hope, at any rate, to annoy and harass the enemy." A local physician visited the Harrison home and attended to Lee's injured hands, applying new splints and giving him slings for his arms.[16]

The next morning, September 6, Lee, Longstreet, and the wing commander's troops headed toward the Potomac crossings. "You may expect to hear of wonders performed by the consolidated, veteran armies of Longstreet and Jackson," predicted a soldier with the column. In his memoirs Longstreet affirmed that the army "was then all that its leaders could ask, and its claim as master of the field was established." A

Georgian noted, however, "Many of our men did not cross the river for want of shoes."[17]

By September 7 the campsites of the Army of Northern Virginia sprawled south and east of Frederick, Maryland, by the Monocacy River. Farther to the east Jeb Stuart's three cavalry brigades and three batteries of horse artillery, about 4,500 officers and men, strung a cordon of vedettes, or picket posts, from New Market on the army's left flank, through Hyattstown in the center, to the Urbana-Barnesville area on the right. Stuart had orders to confuse the Federals by threatening Baltimore and Washington and closely watching their movements. The horsemen remained on the broad arc until September 11.[18]

Lee had established army headquarters at Best's Grove, a stand of oak trees about two miles south of Frederick. The Confederate commander issued a proclamation to the people of Maryland, announcing that his army had entered their state to assist them "in throwing off the foreign yoke" of Federal authority. In this pro-Union section of the state, however, the reaction was decidedly mixed. Some of the soldiers purchased shoes and clothing with Confederate money, but many Marylanders "turned the cold shoulder *every where*," in the view of one officer. The hoped-for a influx of recruits from the state amounted to fewer than 200.[19]

Stonewall Jackson arrived at army headquarters on the afternoon of September 9; most likely Lee had requested a meeting with the subordinate. An artillerist who saw the famous Stonewall in Maryland remarked, "Jackson looks as if wading the Potomac and other streams has in no wise improved his appearance." Three days earlier Jackson had been "stunned and severely bruised" when he spurred a "gigantic gray mare," given to him by a Marylander, and rider and horse fell to the ground. The general's favorite mount, Little Sorrel, had been stolen recently and was not yet recovered. The injury forced Jackson, like Lee, to use temporarily an ambulance.[20]

Lee informed Jackson that the army would march west, cross South Mountain, and operate in either the Hagerstown or Cumberland valleys. His intent was to draw the Army of the Potomac farther away from the Federal capital before possibly engaging his opponent in a battle. The Confederates' supply line would be relocated from east of the mountains to the Shenandoah Valley, with its base at Winchester. To secure the flow of supplies Lee proposed the capture of the 13,000-man Union garrison at Harper's Ferry, located at the confluence of the Shenandoah and Potomac rivers. He had expected the isolated enemy force to withdraw from the indefensible town, which lay at the bottom of a bowl formed by three heights. In Washington, however, it had been determined, over the opposition of George McClellan, to defend Harper's Ferry.[21]

Lee proposed dividing the army, assigning a force to the Harper's Ferry movement, while the remaining units crossed South Mountain and halted around Boonsborough. Jackson objected to the plan. "At the council held at Frederick," he told Harvey Hill months later, "I opposed the separation of our forces in order to capture Harper's Ferry. I urged that we should all be kept together." Jackson argued further that the army should remain east of the mountains. Evidently Jackson had asserted to Hill days earlier that the Confederates should advance into Pennsylvania and "give them a taste of war."[22]

Whether Lee explained his reasoning to Jackson is unknown, but the commanding general presented his thinking in his report: "The advance of the Federal army was so slow at the time we left Fredericktown as to justify the belief that the reduction of Harper's Ferry would be accomplished and our troops concentrated before they would be called upon to meet it." Lee expected that the capture of the Union garrison could be completed by September 12 or 13.[23]

The two generals discussed the details of the operation. When they completed the work, Lee heard the voice of Longstreet outside the closed headquarters tent and asked his other wing commander to join them. During their march together to Frederick, Lee had broached the plan to Longstreet. "I objected," Longstreet later recounted, "that the move would be very imprudent as we were then in the enemy's country, that he would be advised within ten or twelve hours of our movement, and would surely move out against us in our dispersed condition." Both of them left it at that for the present.[24]

Once inside the tent, Longstreet heard the specifics of the plan. "They had gone so far," he wrote of Lee and Jackson, "that it seemed useless for me to offer any further opposition." Instead he suggested that the entire army be used in the movement to Harper's Ferry. When Lee rejected the recommendation, Longstreet countered that Richard Anderson's division be added to the five divisions assigned to the detached force and that his two divisions and Harvey Hill's command be kept together. Lee agreed to this and said written orders would be issued. The meeting—one of the most momentous in the army's history—concluded.[25]

The commanding general incorporated his operational ideas in Special Orders No. 191, distributed to the army later, on September 9. The orders directed Jackson, with three divisions and artillery, to recross the Potomac upriver from Harper's Ferry and to close the western approaches to the town. The divisions of Lafayette McLaws and Richard Anderson were ordered to march down Pleasant Valley and to seize towering Maryland Heights, across the river from the site of John Brown's failed October 1859 raid. Like Jackson's command, John G. Walker's division was to reenter Virginia and occupy Loudoun Heights, east of the Shenandoah River. Longstreet's two divisions were to cross South Mountain with the reserve, supply, and baggage trains and halt at Boonsborough. Trailing Longstreet, Harvey Hills's five brigades were to act as the army's rear guard. Stuart's cavalry would cover the route of march and gather up stragglers. The army would move the next day, September 10.[26]

In a postwar article Longstreet asserted, "The division of the army to make this attack on Harper's Ferry was a fatal error." The old warrior went even further in another piece, declaring that Lee's decision was "not only the worst ever made by General Lee, but invited the destruction of the Confederate army." Longstreet's criticisms benefited from the clarity of hindsight, but the operation was a potentially dangerous gamble, predicated on a timely capture of Harper's Ferry and a ponderous advance of McClellan's army. Unquestionably the discovery of a copy of Special Orders No. 191 by the Federals altered the campaign's course. Nevertheless, Lee compounded the boldness of the advance into Maryland with the dispersal of his divisions, based on an optimistic, and ultimately unrealistic, timeframe for the "reduction of Harper's Ferry." In his fine campaign study Joseph Harsh concluded: "The decision Lee made on the 9th put at risk his campaign in Maryland and possibly even the safety of his army. It did so at the time he wrote Special Orders, No. 191, and long before events prevented these orders from a timely execution—or before they fell into the hands of his enemies."[27]

Before daylight on September 10, coming from the north, east, and south, the Confederates started passing through the streets of Frederick, heading west. Jackson's troops led the march on National Road, followed by the veterans of Longstreet, McLaws, Anderson, and Harvey Hill. "Much speculation as to our destination," jotted an officer in his diary. When Longstreet's men filed past the civilian onlookers, a regimental band played "The Girl I Left Behind Me." With the entire army, except for Walker's division and the main body of Stuart's cavalry, on the single road, the column stretched for thirteen miles.[28]

Throughout the next two days the various commands marched toward their assigned destinations. By nightfall on September 12 units of the army lay scattered, dozens of miles apart, with Lee's timetable in shambles. His orders anticipated the capture of Harper's Ferry on this day, but none of the three columns had closed on the Union garrison. After swinging farther west in an attempt to bag a Federal detachment at Martinsburg, Virginia, Jackson had halted several miles west of Harper's Ferry. On Maryland Heights McLaws's advance had stalled before enemy defenses and the rugged terrain. After marching and countermarching, Walker's small division had bivouacked eight miles from Loudoun Heights.[29]

In Maryland, meanwhile, Harvey Hill's five brigades guarded Turner's Gap in South Mountain and rested at the mountain's base around Boonsborough. To the east, across the mountain range, Stuart's cavalrymen were receding before mounting Union pressure. "I do not wish you to retire too fast before the enemy," Lee instructed Stuart on this day, "or to distribute your cavalry wide apart." But it was too late, as the Federals had entered Frederick. Finally, a report of an enemy militia advancing from Pennsylvania toward Hagerstown had brought Longstreet's two divisions north from Boonsborough. During the march to Hagerstown Lee and Longstreet rode together. At one point, with evident frustration, Longstreet grumbled to Lee, "General, I wish we could stand still and let the damned Yankees come to us!"[30]

Time pressed against the Confederates, they were behind schedule, and the vanguard of McClellan's army had reached Frederick. Most critically the ranks of the Army of Northern Virginia had been thinning with each successive mile during those three days. While in Frederick Lee had written to Davis: "I need not say to you that the material of which it [the army] is composed is the best in the world, and, if properly disciplined and instructed, would be able successfully to resist any force that could be brought against it. Nothing can surpass the gallantry and intelligence of the main body." He noted, however, "One of the greatest evils, from which many minor ones proceed, is the habit of straggling from the ranks. The higher officers feel as I do, and I believe have done all in their power to stop it. It has become a habit difficult to correct."[31]

The straggling had begun during the Seven Days, worsened on the roads to Second Manassas, and swelled into a flood in Maryland. As Lee indicated, the efforts of officers could not stanch the bleeding. Hunger, exhaustion, and illness pulled men from the ranks in droves, human eddies flowing away from the marching columns back across the Potomac into Virginia. Their letters at the time and memoirs later were frank in discussing "a great curse of the army." Officers and men foraged and even plundered for food. A South Carolinian recalled that he and his comrades chewed tobacco to alleviate hunger pangs. For barefoot men, claimed a Virginian, the state's rocky roads were "more than most of us were used to." A North Carolinian believed that every regiment in the army lost soldiers to the "curse."[32]

The extent of the straggling and desertion was staggering. Before the army had crossed into Maryland, thousands had abandoned the ranks. A newspaper correspondent with the army described the situation beyond the Potomac, "Candor compels me to say that the straggling and desertion from our army far surpasses anything I had ever supposed possible." An Alabamian believed that "the army then was little better than a mob." Writing in early September, a soldier averred, "I would not have believed without actual experience, that flesh, blood and muscle could stand what we have stood." In fact too many could no longer withstand the marching in bare feet, the lack of food, and the cumulative strains of weeks of campaigning. At least 20,000, probably closer to 30,000 Confederates either remained behind in Virginia or returned there during the campaign. Their absence put at risk the entire army.[33]

The consequences for a depleted and divided Confederate army loomed graver on Saturday, September 13. At Harper's Ferry Jackson's troops approached from the west and deployed before Union defenders on Bolivar Heights. To the east, across the Shenandoah River, Walker occupied Loudoun Heights with infantry but needed another day to haul artillery to the crest. After an all-day struggle McLaws's veterans wrested Maryland Heights from the Federals and closed the road from the town at its eastern end. Like Walker, McLaws could not place cannon on the 2,000-foot-high Loudoun Heights until September 14. The operations against the garrison at Harper's Ferry took on the characteristics of a siege.[34]

At Frederick meanwhile George McClellan rode into the community. On September 6 Lincoln had restored him to command of the Army of the Potomac and the Army of Virginia. McClellan then integrated John Pope's corps into the Army of the Potomac and assigned dozens of new regiments to brigades. Within days of his reappointment to command, he started his 95,000-man army in pursuit of the Rebels. When he entered Frederick, throngs of civilians cheered him, even holding up children for him to kiss. Before noon an officer handed the general a copy of Lee's Special Orders No. 191, which had been discovered by a soldier in the 27th Indiana in a field outside of town. The copy was addressed to Confederate Major General D. H. Hill and wrapped around three cigars. Who lost the copy remains unresolved.[35]

When the Union commander received the copy, he was addressing a group of local citizens. He stopped to read it and then exclaimed, "Now I know what to do." One of McClellan's staff officers attested to the document's authenticity; having served with Robert H. Chilton in the antebellum army he was familiar with the handwriting of Lee's chief of staff. McClellan wrote to Abraham Lincoln: "I have the whole Rebel force in front of me but am confident and no time shall be lost. . . . I think Lee has made a gross mistake and he will be severely punished for it. The Army is in motion as rapidly as possible. I hope for great success if the plans of the Rebels remain unchanged. . . . I have all the plans of the Rebels and will catch them in their own trap if my men are equal to the emergency. . . . Will send you trophies."[36]

The orders did not reveal either the strength of Lee's army—

McClellan's cavalry commander had put the number at an unrealistic 120,000—or whether the Confederates had followed the routes specified by Lee. Consequently, McClellan spent the afternoon seeking further corroboration of the order's details. He directed Brigadier General Alfred Pleasonton, the cavalry commander, "to ascertain whether this order of march has thus far been followed by the enemy." The sound of gunfire from Harper's Ferry indicated that the garrison had not surrendered. It was in the early evening when Pleasonton reported that the evidence indicated that the enemy had complied with Lee's orders.[37]

To relieve the troops at Harper's Ferry, McClellan decided to advance on Turner's Gap, Boonsborough, and Crampton's Gap, eight miles south of Turner's Gap. Eighteen hours passed, however, from the time McClellan was handed the copy of Lee's order until his units marched on the morning of September 14. His efforts to obtain additional intelligence on the afternoon of September 13 were reasonable, but the situation clamored for aggressiveness. He should have, with minimal risk, pushed his infantry columns closer to the gaps. At no time, however, could McClellan have struck a contingent of the Confederate army unless Lee chose to stand and give battle. Although fortune had given McClellan the strategic initiative, Lee could still dictate whether there would be an engagement at a time and place of his choosing.[38]

It was past nightfall when a courier delivered a message from Jeb Stuart to Lee at Hagerstown. Hours before, a Southern sympathizer had found Stuart at the eastern base of South Mountain. Stuart's cavalrymen had been skirmishing with their mounted opponents in the valley around Middletown since early morning. Approaching Stuart, the Marylander related that he had been standing outside of McClellan's tent when the Union general read a document and exclaimed that he now knew what to do. It remains uncertain whether Stuart surmised that McClellan possessed a copy of Special Orders No. 191. Although his message to Lee has not been found, Stuart apparently concluded that the Federal commander had learned that Lee had divided his army and that the enemy was moving to the relief of the Harper's Ferry garrison.[39]

Shortly after Lee received Stuart's dispatch a message arrived from Harvey Hill at Boonsborough, reporting that the entire Federal army appeared to be bivouacked on the valley floor east of Turner's Gap.

Lee had spent the day waiting anxiously on news from either Jackson or McLaws on the seizure of Harper's Ferry. Now the threat to his dispersed army was critical. Lee admitted later that McClellan's change in tactics had surprised him.[40]

Lee summoned Longstreet to the headquarters tent, gave him the messages from Stuart and Hill, and then stated that they would defend the South Mountain gaps. He wanted Longstreet to march at daylight with his two infantry divisions and artillery to Boonsborough, thirteen miles to the south. Longstreet disagreed, arguing that his command and Hill's should withdraw to Sharpsburg, where they could threaten the flank and rear of the Federals as they marched down Pleasant Valley toward Harper's Ferry. Lee "would not agree," said Longstreet, and ordered the advance. Returning to his tent Longstreet put his argument in writing and sent the note to army headquarters. Lee did not reply.[41]

Sometime after midnight on September 14 a second message from Stuart arrived at army headquarters. In it (the dispatch is missing) Stuart either implied or stated positively that McClellan had obtained a copy of Special Orders No. 191. The dispatch confirmed for Lee why his opponent was acting with unaccustomed aggressiveness. Whether or not McClellan possessed a copy of the orders, the campaign turned against the Confederates when the Union army reached Frederick. Lee could not abandon the campaign and retreat into Virginia, as he believed he had come too far to do so. He was thus left with one choice: buy time for the completion of the Harper's Ferry operations and the reuniting of his army by slowing the Federal passage through South Mountain.[42]

Lee's instructions to Stuart and Hill were unequivocal: "The gap must be held at all hazards until the operations at Harper's Ferry are finished. You must keep me informed of the strength of the enemy's forces moving up by either." Although "the gap" was unspecified, Lee meant Turner's Gap, where he expected Stuart and Hill to conduct its defense. The cavalry commander was convinced, however, that the main Federal thrust would be at Crampton's Gap and the road into Pleasant Valley in the rear of McLaws's and Anderson's troops. Soon after daylight on September 14, Stuart rode south toward the mountain defile, apparently without notifying Hill. The defense of Turner's Gap and Fox's

Gap, a mile to the south, fell to Harvey Hill, of whom Porter Alexander said, "There is not living a more honest fighter."[43]

Hill rode to the crest of South Mountain before sunrise on September 14. Colonel Alfred H. Colquitt's brigade of Georgians and Alabamians had spent the previous day and night on the mountain at Turner's Gap. Hill ordered them down the eastern face to the mountain's base and into line. Before long Brigadier General Samuel Garland Jr.'s North Carolinians arrived and were deployed at Fox's Gap. Hill's other three brigades were miles to the rear. In all, Hill commanded fewer than 5,000 officers and men.[44]

A North Carolinian wrote of Hill, "The clash of battle was not a confusing din to him, but an exciting scene that awakened his spirit and his genius." One of his veterans observed in a postwar letter to the general, "If you had a fault as a division-commander, it seems to us to have been the fortunate one of excess of determination and pugnacity in the face of appalling difficulties and danger." The former soldier did not specify a particular engagement, but this day on South Mountain fit the description.[45]

Union Ninth Corps troops advanced on Fox's Gap at about nine o'clock, clashing with the 5th Virginia Cavalry and a battery of horse artillery, left behind by Stuart, and Garland's North Carolinians. South Mountain rose 1,300 feet in elevation, and its scarred face, with wooded hollows and knolls, thick underbrush, and entangled patches of mountain laurel, aided the defenders. But the Federals kept pushing back the beleaguered Rebels. While standing with the 13th North Carolina on the front line, Garland was struck and killed. Hill described the brigadier in his report as "the most fearless man I ever knew." The attackers scattered the North Carolinians and reached the crest, where the Old Sharpsburg Road passed through the gap.[46]

Fortune intervened for Hill. The Union attack stalled on the crest before the fire of the horse artillery and a pair of cannon sent in by Hill. A patchwork force of Rebels supported the guns. Amid the smoke and tangled underbrush the Federal officers, believing they had encountered another battleline, asked for reinforcements. To the north, at Turner's Gap, Colquitt's men awaited a slowly developing assault by the Union First Corps.[47]

With Garland's ranks broken and Colquitt's line facing an over-whelming enemy force, Hill ordered forward his three brigades from Boonsborough. Brigadier General George B. Anderson's North Caro-linians arrived first and were shifted to the right. Behind them the Alabama regiments of Brigadier General Robert E. Rodes moved over the crest in support of the left flank of Colquitt's troops, who were now engaged in a fierce struggle along National Road. When Brigadier Gen-eral Roswell Ripley's brigade came up, Hill directed it toward Ander-son's command. In Hill's words, he had "played the game of bluff" until these units reached him.[48]

After a grueling march from Hagerstown in which hundreds of men fell exhausted in the heat and dust, the two leading brigades of Long-street's divisions arrived at Turner's Gap at midafternoon. Hill sent them toward Fox's Gap and assigned Ripley to overall command of the action. The fighting there dissolved into a bungling, confusing affair. The Yankees renewed their attacks, piercing a gap in the Confederate ranks and driving them rearward. Ripley's brigade became disoriented in the wooded terrain and angled away from the combat. Hill declared to Longstreet in a postwar letter that Ripley "was a coward and did nothing." A Georgia colonel stated, "Ripley gave himself but little con-cern about what was going on."[49]

The situation at Fox's Gap stabilized at last with the appearance of John Hood and his redoubtable fighters. Hood had been placed under arrest by Longstreet in a dispute with Shanks Evans over captured ambulances at Second Manassas. When Hood's men reached the west-ern foot of South Mountain, they saw Lee, who had preceded the troops in an ambulance, and shouted to the commanding general, "Give us Hood!" In response Lee temporarily suspended the brigadier's arrest. When the Texans heard the news, they yelled, "Hurrah for General Lee! Hurrah for General Hood! Go to hell, Evans!"[50]

Hood's presence on the crest solidified the Confederate right flank. To the north, at Turner's Gap, Colquitt's and Rodes's veterans clung to the ground against mounting odds. The fighting lengthened into the night, the opposing lines marked by musket flashes. A Yankee attested that the "sides of the mountain seemed in a blaze of flame." The envelop-ing darkness ended the clash. Longstreet had joined Hill on the crest and informed Lee that he could not hold the position another day without reinforcements. Lee had none and ordered a withdrawal. According to Moxley Sorrel, it was "a bad night" on the mountain as the Rebels filed down the western face, leaving behind their dead and wounded. Confederate cavalry formed a rear guard and remained on the mountaintop.[51]

The defense of Turner's Gap and Fox's Gap had cost the Confederates 1,950 in killed, wounded, and captured; the Federals, about 1,800. In his report Hill praised his troops' stand "as one of the most remarkable and creditable of the war." He deserved blame, however, for not sooner ordering forward the brigades of Anderson, Rodes, and Ripley. The Federals' hesitation to press the advance on the crest at Fox's Gap and their slowly developing attack at Turner's Gap spared Hill from a likely defeat. The stubborn fighting by Colquitt's and Rodes's men and the timely arrival of Longstreet's troops salvaged the day for the Confederates.[52]

Longstreet, Hill, and Hood rode off the mountain ahead of the troops and met with Lee. Almost certainly they discussed the condition of the officers and men and the likely enemy movement across South Mountain in the morning. "After a long debate," in Hood's words, Lee decided that the retreat should proceed through Sharpsburg to the Potomac River and into Virginia, the campaign in Maryland would be abandoned. After the meeting Lee sent messages written by Robert Chilton to Jackson and McLaws, dated 8:00 P.M., September 14. In them Lee directed Jackson to withdraw from Harper's Ferry and to proceed to Shepherdstown, where he could cover the retreat of the units with Lee across the Potomac. The dispatch to McLaws read: "The day has gone against us and this army will go by Sharpsburg and cross the river. It is necessary for you to abandon your position to-night."[53]

Two hours later Lee learned of the Federal's seizure of Crampton's Gap and their advance into Pleasant Valley. As noted, Jeb Stuart rode to the defile, where he had sent Wade Hampton's cavalry brigade on September 13. On that day the gap had been manned by Colonel Thomas Munford with 400 troopers, 300 infantrymen, and six cannon. When Stuart arrived, he learned "that the enemy had made no demonstration toward Crampton's Gap up to that time." The inactivity by the Federals persuaded him that they were marching directly along the

Potomac River, bypassing South Mountain, to Harper's Ferry. He dispatched Hampton's 1,200 horsemen to cover the roads along the river and instructed Munford to "hold it [the gap] against the enemy at all hazards." Once again Stuart had misjudged the Yankees' intentions. Leaving the defense of Crampton's Gap to Munford's small force, he rode on to Maryland Heights.[54]

The Federals were marching, however, to Crampton's Gap. They did not reach Burkittsville, east of the gap, until after midday. McClellan had instructed Major General William B. Franklin, Sixth Corps and acting wing commander, "to attack the enemy in detail & beat him." McClellan expected Franklin to act energetically; instead he halted the march in violation of orders until a trailing division joined his corps. When they appeared before the gap, one of Munford's men noted: "As they drew nearer, the whole country seemed to be full of bluecoats. They were so numerous that it looked as if they were creeping up out of the ground." Only a few hours of daylight remained when Franklin's infantrymen attacked.[55]

For two hours the Confederates valiantly resisted the enemy assaults. Munford described the fighting as "the heaviest I ever engaged in, and the cavalry fought here with pistols and rifles." When McLaws heard the sounds of battle, he sent Brigadier General Howell Cobb's brigade to Munford. Cobb's Georgians and North Carolinians arrived in time to be swept to the rear with Munford's broken ranks. McLaws and Stuart rode toward the gap and tried to rally the men. Darkness prevented a Union pursuit, giving McLaws time to patch together a defensive line across Pleasant Valley. McLaws did not like Stuart personally, and he remarked to the cavalry commander, "Well General, we are in a pen, how am I to get out of it?"[56]

The news from Crampton's Gap temporarily altered Lee's plans. Instead of Longstreet's and Hill's divisions, one-third of the army, marching through Sharpsburg to the Potomac, now they would halt at Keedysville, a small village three miles southwest of Boonsborough on the road to Sharpsburg. From there they could move against the enemy flank if the Federals crossed South Mountain and turned south toward McLaws's and Anderson's position on Maryland Heights. The security of those two divisions was foremost in Lee's plans.[57]

The withdrawal from Boonsborough began minutes past midnight on September 15. The bone-weary Confederates stumbled through the morning's darkness. Overcome with exhaustion, uncounted numbers lay down in the fields and slept. Some managed to rejoin their comrades; others were captured hours later by the trailing Yankees. While en route Lee received a dispatch, dated 8:15 P.M., September 14, from Jackson, who wrote that he expected "complete success to-morrow." With the morning's light Lee saw that the terrain around Keedysville provided no good, natural defensive position. He ordered the column on to Sharpsburg.[58]

As the Southerners crossed Antietam Creek, less than a mile east of Sharpsburg, they filed to the north and south, deploying into line on a string of ridges and hills. When Lee in his ambulance passed a group of soldiers, he reportedly said to them, "We will make our stand on those hills." He stated in his report that the halt and deployment on the western side of Antietam Creek "reanimated the courage of the troops." A staff officer said likewise, noting in his diary on this day, "Men in a grand humor for a fight."[59]

Shortly after noon a courier delivered a dispatch from Jackson to Lee. Dated 8:00 A.M., the message read, "Through God's blessing, Harper's Ferry and the garrison are to be surrendered." The fate of the Union troops had been sealed late on September 14, when Powell Hill's division moved beyond the Federals' left flank into the rear of their position on Bolivar Heights. In all the Confederates captured 11,500 prisoners, seventy-three cannon, 13,000 stands of arms, and large quantities of military equipment and supplies. The garrison's cavalry force, led by Colonel Benjamin F. "Grimes" Davis, had escaped during the night, passing beneath Maryland Heights. During their ride they passed through Sharpsburg and farther north seized dozens of Longstreet's ordnance wagons.[60]

In his dispatch Jackson informed Lee that five of the six divisions at Harper's Ferry "can move off this evening as soon as they get their rations." Powell Hill's officers and men would remain to parole prisoners and secure the captured property. "To what point shall they move?" asked Jackson. Although no reply from Lee has been found, the commanding general certainly ordered Jackson's two divisions and those of

McLaws, Anderson, and Walker to Sharpsburg. The retreat to Virginia had been postponed.[61]

Meanwhile to the east, on National Road in Turner's Gap, blue-coated columns had been descending the mountainside. A Massachusetts lieutenant passed by Rebel dead and described them to his wife in a letter: "Such a filthy looking set I ever saw. The people here say that their whole army is the most forlorn looking set they ever saw." At Boonsborough the Yankees encountered Fitz Lee's cavalry brigade, acting as the Confederates' rear guard. Lee's horsemen had reached Boonsborough late on September 14, after an ill-advised attempt, ordered by Stuart, to operate beyond the right flank of McClellan's army as it approached Frederick. Consequently, Lee's regiments were removed from the campaign for two days.[62]

Union cavalry scattered Fitz Lee's Virginians in "a general stampede" through Boonsborough. Lee rallied two regiments and counterattacked. In the swirling action the 9th Virginia Cavalry's Colonel William H. F. "Rooney" Lee, son of the commanding general, had his horse killed under him and fled on foot to escape capture. The Virginians retreated toward Sharpsburg. "This was an awful day for our Brigade," wrote a Rebel, "as the loss was heavy & injury inflicted on the enemy must have been slight."[63]

The Federals halted at Keedysville, where McClellan arrived at about one o'clock in the afternoon amid cheers from his troops. Like Lee, he had learned of the surrender of the Harper's Ferry garrison. He examined the Confederate ranks on the bluffs above him. He had at hand the First, Second, Ninth, and Twelfth corps and two divisions of the Fifth Corps—in all about 60,000 officers and men. Late in the day he ordered two of Franklin's three Sixth Corps divisions, posted in Pleasant Valley, to join the main army. Three days earlier McClellan had written to his wife, "My only apprehension now is that the secesh will manage to get back across the Potomac at Wmsport [Williamsport, Maryland] before I can catch him." From Keedysville, however, it looked as if Lee was offering battle.[64]

Before McClellan, beyond Antietam Creek, stood the thinned ranks of a proud, defiant army. Ten days earlier, ill-supplied, ill-shod, ragged and dirty, they had carried the hopes of the Southern people and

Confederate nationalism across the Potomac River. The hardships of the campaign had reduced their numbers to a stalwart core of hardened veterans. Despite their "destitute condition," they were "in high spir-its," believed an officer, "and always ready to rush into a fight." So there they stood, upon orders from "Marse Robert."[65]

Robert E. Lee's decision to give battle at Sharpsburg, or Antietam, embodied, perhaps more than at any other time and place, the combat-iveness of the man and the audacity of the general. Ezra A. Carman, a Union veteran of the engagement and its first accomplished historian, wrote of Lee, "His daring was never more fully shown than when he made up his mind to fight at Antietam." Writing of the campaign in his memoirs, Longstreet thought that Lee "found it hard, the enemy in sight, to withhold his blows." After the capture of Harper's Ferry the army should have returned to Virginia, in Longstreet's estimation.[66]

Porter Alexander termed the decision "the greatest blunder that Gen. Lee ever made." With the army's reduced strength, Alexander contended, Lee could expect a drawn battle as the best "possible out-come." If the Federals broke the Southern lines, forcing a retreat, the army had one avenue of escape, Boteler's Ford on the Potomac, a deep, rocky crossing three miles west of Sharpsburg. In Alexander's judgment, Lee risked the destruction of his army.[67]

Historians have rendered similar assessments. An early critic of Lee's generalship in the war was the British army veteran and historian Sir Frederick Maurice. In the 1920s Maurice wrote, "Of all Lee's actions in the war this [Antietam decision] seems to me to be the most open to criticism." Like Alexander, Maurice argued that the Confederates' best hope was to "beat off" the Federals. The foremost modern historian of the army, Robert K. Krick, believed that Lee's determination to offer battle was "probably [his] worst of the war," with no reasonable chance to accomplish anything. In his campaign study Joseph Harsh offered this explanation for Lee's gamble, "He expected to win."[68]

In postwar interviews and correspondence Lee addressed the issue. He told an interviewer that Sharpsburg was forced on him by McClel-lan's "finding out [my] plans and moving quickly in consequence." It had been Lee's intent to engage the enemy west of South Mountain in the Hagerstown or Cumberland Valley. In his thinking, however, the finding of the "lost order" altered the campaign's direction. He accepted the reality of a withdrawal into Virginia after September 14, but changed his mind with the capture of Harper's Ferry. He gave an explanation in a letter to Stonewall Jackson's widow, "In view of all the circumstances, it was better to have fought the battle in Maryland than to have left it without a struggle." Lee added that when her husband arrived at Sharpsburg on September 16 and heard Lee's reasoning for making a stand, Jackson "emphatically concurred with me."[69]

Undoubtedly, as Harsh maintained, Lee expected to win; it could not have been otherwise. But that expectation of victory rested with his army, "a tired and weakened force." He had admitted to Davis in a September 13 letter, "Our ranks are very much diminished—I fear from a third to one-half of the original numbers." In his report Lee placed the number at fewer than 40,000 officers and men. The general's biographer, Douglas Freeman, described the Confederates at Sharpsburg as "this ghost of an army."[70]

When all of the infantry divisions, except Powell Hill's, reached Sharpsburg on the morning of September 17, Lee counted about 35,500 infantry, artillery, and cavalry on the battlefield. The reported numbers present for duty within infantry regiments and brigades revealed the attrition through straggling and casualties. Several regiments mustered fewer than sixty officers and men around their battle flags: 3rd South Carolina Battalion counted fifteen; 8th Virginia, twenty-two; and an adjutant commanded the fifty-four members of the 19th Virginia. The average strength of a Confederate infantry regiment at Sharpsburg was roughly 165 officers and men.[71]

"The fact is I believe," remembered Private John Dooley of the 1st Virginia, "that our army was in a more deplorable condition than any one except the individual soldiers were willing to admit." Nearly a third of the infantrymen carried antiquated .69 caliber smoothbore muskets, while other foot soldiers held .54, .57, and .58 caliber rifle muskets of various kinds. Within the artillery nearly half of the cannon were smoothbores with limited range. In fact forty-five guns were the obsolete six-pounders of the antebellum era. Only five of the fifty-nine batteries had guns of uniform caliber and types. By contrast, rifled pieces constituted the majority of Union ordnance.[72]

Lee's chosen battleground lay within a broad loop of the Potomac River, which limited enemy flanking movements. The landscape possessed no dominant natural features, but woodlots, hollows, rock outcroppings, and ripples in the ground provided protection for the defenders. Antietam Creek, spanned by four stone-arch bridges, was shallow and a modest barrier to fording troops. The bluffs above the stream served as natural towers for infantry and artillery. A ridge extended north from Sharpsburg, with its 1,300 inhabitants. Hagerstown Turnpike scarred the ridge, its roadbed framed by post-and-rail fences. For decades farmers had tilled the rich soil, and fields of corn and pastures quilted the ground.[73]

Tuesday, September 16, passed in relative quiet, but artillery exchanges and a late afternoon skirmish foretold the coming madness. Lee welcomed Jackson with the divisions of brigadiers Alexander Lawton and John R. Jones, who had rejoined the army at Frederick, and John Walker's two brigades. The troops of Lafayette McLaws's and Richard Anderson's commands were en route but would not arrive until the next morning. Lee considered a turning movement north toward Hagerstown, but gave up the idea after a reconnaissance by Stuart.[74]

Periodically during the day Lee conferred with Jackson, Longstreet, and Stuart at the Dr. Jacob Grove residence in the village. Between meetings Jackson oversaw the posting of units on the army's left in the fields and woods beside Hagerstown Turnpike, while Longstreet rode along the bluffs above the creek, examining the Federal lines. During one of the artillery duels Longstreet watched the fire, "perfectly indifferent to the bursting shell," claimed a nearby Georgian. When completed, the Confederate line resembled a rough, inverted L, with Jackson's men defending the base north of town and Longstreet's soldiers extending it south from the bend to a lower ford on Antietam Creek. Stuart's horsemen guarded the flanks. The Confederate position's major advantage was that it expedited the movement of units from one wing to the other along interior lines.[75]

East of Antietam George McClellan spent the day surveying the Southern position. He ruled out an assault on this day, finally deciding on an initial assault on the Confederate left for the morning of September 17. He expected Lee, as the Union offensive progressed, to shift units toward the threatened sector, giving the Federals an opportunity

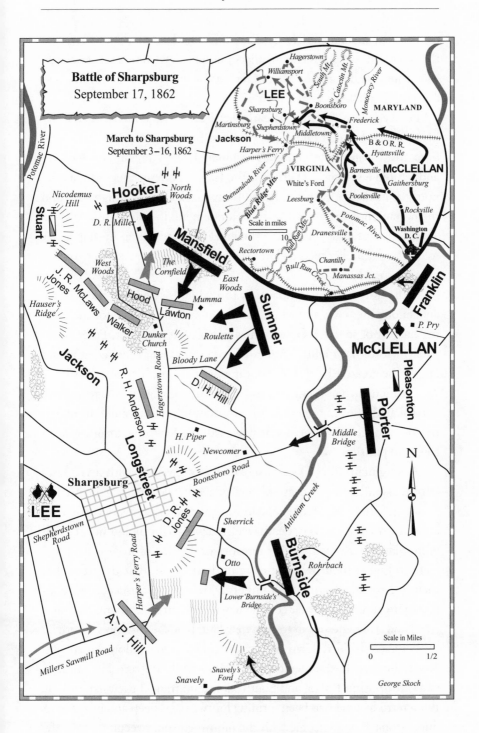

Battle of Sharpsburg
September 17, 1862

March to Sharpsburg
September 3–16, 1862

George Skoch

to strike the weakened right flank and center. McClellan, however, neither met with his corps commanders nor issued written orders to clarify their roles. He designated Major General Joseph Hooker's First Corps as the initial attack force.[76]

Hooker's three divisions, nearly 9,000 officers and men, began moving north and west at midafternoon, crossing Antietam Creek upstream from the Confederate center. Their march drew enemy artillery fire and ignited a skirmish. Halting at the Joseph Poffenberger farm, a mile north of Jackson's lines, the Federals bivouacked for the night. Behind them, marching in the darkness, Major General Joseph Mansfield's two Twelfth Corps divisions forded the creek and moved up in support. A soldier with Hooker recorded in his diary, "We all knew we were on the eve of a great battle."[77]

A drizzling rain fell, followed by fog, which settled into the hollows and among the trees, as if white-clad specters had gathered for the coming harvest of souls. A Georgia newspaper correspondent, Peter Alexander, wrote that night: "From all I see around me, I feel certain that one of the greatest battles of the war will be fought here tomorrow. . . . The Antietam river [sic] is in our front; the Potomac in our rear. If we are defeated, the army must perish; if successful, the stream in front and the Blue Ridge at whose base it flows will prevent any pursuit. It is an awkward position."[78]

A Virginian, John Dooley, spoke of what awaited with a veteran's knowledge: "I believe that soldiers generally do not fear death less because of their repeated escape from its jaws. For, in every battle they see so many new forms of death, see so many frightful and novel kinds of mutilation, see such varying fortunes in the tide of strife, and appreciate so highly their deliverance from destruction, that their dread of incurring the like fearful perils unnerves them for each succeeding conflict, quite as much as their confidence in their oft tried courage sustains them and stimulates them to gain new laurels at the cannon's mouth."[79]

For those bedded down amid the drizzle and fog, fellow Americans, North and South, the memory of Gaines's Mill, Malvern Hill, Brawner's Farm, Chinn Ridge, and South Mountain framed their experience. But a terrible wind had been forming for two days, deep and broad in its dimensions. It would come with the morning's sun, sweeping across the placid countryside, touching down in a cornfield, among the trees in a pair of woods, over the meetinghouse of pacifists, across a sunken road, and onto a stone-arch bridge. It would be ravenous in its fury, clutching men in numbers beyond those recorded in the past. Wednesday, September 17, 1862, darkened in blood a nation torn apart.

The fire of Union batteries in the early morning heralded an American tragedy. Minutes before six o'clock Hooker's 9,000-man Union corps advanced south along Hagerstown Turnpike. Waiting for them were Jackson's 5,000 Virginians, North Carolinians, Georgians, Alabamians, and Louisianans in six brigades. The cannon blasts and musketry swelled into "a roaring hell of fire." Names would be etched in the country's history: farmer David R. Miller's twenty acres of corn—the Cornfield—East Woods, West Woods, a white-washed brick German Baptist Brethren meetinghouse, known as Dunker Church. Within minutes an explosion of savagery engulfed Yankee and Rebel alike.[80]

Jackson "gloried in battle," declared Harvey Hill. If so, it was there before him in all its grisly magnificence. A Union lieutenant likened the sound of the fury to "a great tumbling together of all heaven and earth." In the Cornfield the cannon and rifle fire leveled stalks and men. West of the field, on Nicodemus Heights, Confederate gun crews under the direction of Major John Pelham of Stuart's horse artillery fired on the charging Federals. Along the southern edge of the Cornfield Lawton's infantrymen clung to a fence, while the Stonewall Division swung out of West Woods, triggering volley after volley into the Federal ranks. "The Rebs fight like mad men," swore a Yankee.[81]

The carnage was staggering, extending from west of the turnpike, through Miller's cornfield, to East Woods. "Men, I can not say fell," wrote Major Rufus Dawes of the 6th Wisconsin, "they were knocked out of the ranks by dozens." Hooker pushed all three of his divisions into the maelstrom. John R. Jones, commanding the Stonewall Division, was stunned by a shell burst and led to the rear. William Starke succeeded him and was soon struck by three bullets, dying an hour later. The Louisianans of Starke's brigade emerged from West Woods and counterattacked along the turnpike toward the Cornfield. The Federals shredded the Louisianans' ranks, killing or wounding three of every five men. Every regimental commander and staff officer fell.[82]

Colonel Andrew Jackson Grigsby of the 27th Virginia replaced Starke and pulled the "shattered columns" back into West Woods. The Stonewall Division appeared to be "no larger than a good regiment": 300 men of about 1,600 gathered around the regimental colors. A major commanded one brigade and a captain another. Jackson's old veterans had "fought with gallantry that has never been surpassed and rarely equaled," boasted Jones in a postwar letter. They had, however, nothing left to give.[83]

East of the turnpike three brigades of Lawton's division were streaming out of the Cornfield and East Woods before the Union onslaught. Like their comrades in the Stonewall Division, these Confederates incurred losses that exceeded 40 percent. Lawton suffered a severe wound, which ended his active field service. Colonel Marcellus Douglass, commanding a brigade, was killed, and Colonel James A. Walker, leading Isaac Trimble's former command, was wounded. Of the twenty-one regimental commanders in the three brigades, nineteen were either killed or wounded. With their retreat Jackson's entire front line had been shattered. Cheering Federals surged across a wedge-shaped pasture between the turnpike and Smoketown Road, heading toward a plateau opposite the whitewashed Dunker Church, the target of the morning's assault.[84]

Emerging from a hollow in front of the plateau came John Hood's division, Colonel William T. Wofford's Texas Brigade on the left, Colonel Evander Law's Alabamians, Mississippians, and North Carolinians on the right. The men had been baking hoecakes on ramrods when ordered into line. They ate the half-baked dough as quickly as they could and then fixed bayonets for the first time in their history. Behind them, on the plateau, four batteries of Colonel Stephen D. Lee's battalion fired on the advancing Union ranks. Lee's gun crews had been taking a hammering from Federal cannon east of Antietam Creek. Lee told Porter Alexander after the battle that Sharpsburg was "Artillery Hell."[85]

Hood's 2,300 officers and men wheeled to the left, facing the Yankees. Combat transfigured Hood; a staff officer maintained that he "would have been named by three-fourths of the army as the finest division commander in the army. His men were devoted to him and believed in him absolutely." A Texan related in his memoirs, "It has always been a question among us whether Hood made the Texas Brigade or the Texas Brigade made Hood."[86]

The Southerners emitted a yell and charged. "It appeared doomsday had come," exclaimed one of them. They unleashed a volley that ripped into the enemy ranks "like a scythe running through our line," declared Rufus Dawes. The Federals lurched to a halt and recoiled. "It is a race for life that each man runs for the corn-field," continued Dawes. The Texas Brigade pursued into the Cornfield; Law's men angled toward East Woods. Hooker's battered ranks rallied and lashed the attacking Rebels. Along the turnpike blue-coated regiments blasted the flank of the Texas Brigade. "It was here that I witnessed the most terrible clash of arms, by far, that has occurred during the war," reported Hood.[87]

In a stunning testament to the courage of men, the 1st Texas swept across leveled stalks—"those corn acres of hell" to a Confederate— toward a Union battery. The regiment's color-bearer carried the flag, which had been crafted from Texas Senator Louis T. Wigfall's wife's wedding dress. From front and flank the Federals decimated the Texans' ranks. The 1st Texas's casualty rate exceeded 80 percent, the highest percentage of loss in a single battle of any regiment in Lee's army. Wofford's and Law's men held on against a three-sided wall of musketry, shellfire, and canister. "Never had I seen men fall as fast and thick," asserted a member of Hampton Legion. "In about an hour's time our whole division was almost annihilated." The survivors retreated to West Woods, except for pockets of Alabamians, Texans, and Georgians standing defiantly in East Woods. When asked later where his command was, Hood answered, "Dead on the field."[88]

In ninety minutes of horrific combat three Confederate divisions had been reduced to remnants. The dead and wounded, Northern and Southern, covered the ground. "It was never my fortune to witness a more bloody, dismal battlefield," reported Hooker, who had suffered a wound and relinquished command of the corps. Jackson had left one unscathed and organized brigade, the Virginians of Jubal Early, who had been supporting the artillery on Nicodemus Heights. Jackson shifted them south into West Woods, and he and Stuart redeployed the cannon onto Hauser's Ridge, behind West Woods. Across the fields, com-

ing out of East Woods, appeared the two divisions of Union Major
General Joseph K. F. Mansfield's Twelfth Corps, 7,900 officers and men.
Jackson asked Harvey Hill for reinforcements.[89]

In this longest of days for the Army of Northern Virginia, sacrifice
measured the hours and the minutes. "The sun seemed almost to go
backwards, and it appeared as if night would never come," confessed
a North Carolinian. So it was now for the troops in the brigades of
Roswell Ripley, Alfred Colquitt, and Samuel Garland, now led by Colonel Duncan K. McRae of the 5th North Carolina. Ordered forward
by Harvey Hill, these Rebels passed the Samuel Mumma farm into a
cauldron framed by the turnpike, Miller's cornfield, and East Woods.[90]

Ripley's and Colquitt's men entered the Cornfield, and there they
bled. Ripley was shot in the throat and carried from the field. Every
field officer in Colquitt's five regiments fell killed or wounded. But their
musketry shattered the ranks of one Twelfth Corps division and cleared
the Cornfield of Hooker's First Corps troops. Behind them McRae's
North Carolinians advanced through the pasture west of Smoketown
Road. When an officer shouted that the Yankees had outflanked them,
McRae's men fled in panic. Their flight exposed Colquitt's flank to the
advance of another Twelfth Corps division, under Brigadier General
George S. Greene. The fire from Greene's troops chased the Southerners rearward. A lull ensued, with the Federals holding the Cornfield and
East Woods. It was only nine o'clock, and Jackson's front was in sham-
bles.[91]

In three hours of combat, in an area of roughly one square mile,
nearly 8,700 Northerners and Southerners had been killed, wounded,
or captured out of approximately 27,000 troops engaged on both sides,
a frightful casualty rate of almost one-third. "The absolute worthless-
ness of human life no where was so evident as here," professed a Union
soldier. Jackson described the carnage as "terrific." Hood's words about
his division being dead on the field could have applied to many units on
both sides.[92]

It was the chosen battlefield of Robert E. Lee, and not until 1864
would he assume more personal conduct of the engagement than he
did on this day. He could ride Traveller again, but an orderly held the
horse's reins. In the Seven Days and at Second Manassas Lee had left

the direction of combat primarily to Jackson, Longstreet, and their sub-ordinates. At Sharpsburg the commanding general was a presence, often close to the fighting and subjected to Union artillery fire. So when Jackson requested additional support, Lee ordered John Walker's two brigades from the army right flank and hurried forward Lafayette McLaws's troops, who had been resting west of town after their daylight arrival on the field.[93]

Walker's and McLaws's infantrymen marched across the fields under Union artillery fire from beyond Antietam Creek. Staff officers pointed the columns toward West Woods. McLaws rode ahead of his troops and met Jackson. While they were speaking, an artillery shell struck the ground in front of their horses but did not explode. The six brigades of Walker and McLaws joined Hood's battered ranks and Early's Virginians, ringing West Woods with thousands of muskets. "The enemy, I could see, were advancing rapidly," reported McLaws.[94]

The Federals seen by McLaws belonged to the leading division of the Second Corps, 5,200 officers and men under Major General John Sedgwick. Ordered across Antietam Creek by McClellan, corps commander Major General Edwin Sumner led his veterans onto the field. When he passed through East Woods, Sumner encountered the wreckage of three hours of combat and a gap between the ranks of the First and Twelfth corps. Convinced he must act swiftly to retain the offensive initiative, Sumner stacked Sedgwick's three brigades into an attack column, with seventy-yard intervals between the lines. The faulty tactical alignment limited the division's firepower to a single brigade and exposed both flanks. No skirmishers fanned out in front of the column, a serious misjudgment.[95]

The Yankees cleared East Woods and wheeled toward Dunker Church and West Woods. A watching Union officer believed "nothing could stop them." Instead, as if blind, they marched into a slaughterhouse. Cannon on Hauser's Ridge unleashed "a seamless wall of canister," and Confederate infantrymen triggered volleys into the disintegrating Union ranks. The Rebel fire, said a Virginian, "was so steady and severe that it looked like a whirlwind was passing through the leaves on the ground and woods." Sedgwick's men staggered before the fury, and then broke to the rear. "It was every man for himself," admitted a Federal. "We all run like a flock of sheep." The Southerners coun-terattacked, advancing into the pasture beyond the turnpike, but were repulsed, primarily by Greene's intact division of the Twelfth Corps. Sedgwick lost 2,200 men killed, wounded, and captured in an action that had lasted all of twenty minutes.[96]

With the bloody repulse of Sedgwick's division, the morning's ill wind shifted south, to the center of the Confederate line, where the inverted L bent west. Here Harvey Hill's last two unscathed brigades— George B. Anderson's North Carolinians and Robert E. Rodes's Ala-bamians, perhaps 2,500 officers and men—held a sunken road, its bed worn away over the years by farmers hauling wagonloads of grain to a grist mill on Antietam Creek. There were few finer troops in Lee's army than these. Earlier, when Lee and Hill had examined the position, Colonel John B. Gordon of the 6th Alabama exclaimed to Lee, "These men are going to stay here, General, till the sun goes down or victory is won."[97]

The initial Union assault against the sunken road, today's Bloody Lane, rolled forth at about ten o'clock, undertaken by Brigadier General William H. French's Second Corps division. French had followed Sedg-wick across Antietam Creek, but without instructions from Sumner he turned his column south, halting in the fields of the William Roulette farm. His command had been organized a week earlier and consisted of ten regiments, seven of which had never been in combat. French had 5,700 men in the ranks, but he negated his numerical advantage and compounded his troops' inexperience by sending in his three brigades one at a time.[98]

When French's leading brigade topped the crest of a ridge north of the worn roadbed, the Confederate ranks erupted in a flash of smoke and flame. The musketry, said a North Carolina colonel, "brought down the enemy as grain falls before the reaper." The Yankees clung to the ridgeline, returning the fire. French ordered in his second brigade, then his third. An Ohioan described the combat as "unabated fury." For an hour it went on in what a Yankee called "a savage continual thunder that cannot compare to any sound I ever heard."[99]

Hill asked for reinforcements. Longstreet, who was nearby, ordered forward the army's final reserve, Richard Anderson's 3,400-man division. Anderson suffered a wound and left the field as his troops deployed in a cornfield and orchard of the Henry Piper farm, directly behind the sunken road. Union cannon pelted the Southerners from east of Antietam Creek. Anderson's successor, Brigadier General Roger Pryor, requested artillery support from Longstreet. "I am sending you the guns, my dear General," the wing commander scribbled in a note. "This is a hard fight and we had all better die than lose it."[100]

As Anderson's men added their firepower to the struggle, French's ranks receded behind the crest, withdrawing to the Roulette farm. His casualties exceeded 1,700. Advancing on their left was the famed Irish Brigade of Brigadier General Israel B. Richardson's Second Corps division. The Irishmen charged down the slope toward the sunken road and met with a killing fire that literally tore gaps in the line. The Federals staggered as if hit by a gale and retired to the crest, leaving behind more than 500 dead and maimed comrades. From the hilltop they returned fire, the roar of musketry mounting to a renewed crescendo.[101]

In the sunken road dead and dying Southerners lay in piles like corded wood. George Anderson was struck in the ankle; the wound subsequently became infected, and he died a month later. Col. Charles C. Tew of the 2nd North Carolina assumed command of the brigade and was mortally wounded within minutes by a bullet to the head. John Gordon suffered five wounds but survived. An artilleryman said of Gordon that he "was the most glorious and inspiring thing I ever looked upon." Amid the carnage Mississippi regiments piled into the roadbed, causing more confusion than assistance. The center of Lee's line at Sharpsburg teetered on collapse.[102]

The disintegration came suddenly, after three hours of an unrelenting struggle. Richardson advanced a second brigade toward the Confederate right when, in the lane, an officer mistakenly withdrew his regiment. The Yankees poured down the slope into the gap, raking the defenders and dissolving their line. The Rebels fled from the deathtrap, sweeping Pryor's men with them to the rear across the Piper farm fields. The enemy dead in the roadbed reminded a Federal of piles of "autumn leaves . . . into which they seemed to have tumbled." Cheering, the victorious Northerners scrambled out of the lane in pursuit, charging through Piper's cornfield.[103]

Before the onrushing Yankees stood four Confederate cannon, James Longstreet, and his staff members. The gunners blasted the enemy with canister. When the Union musketry toppled artillerists, Longstreet's aides worked a gun. The general directed their fire while calmly chewing on a cigar. An officer who rode up with a message later recorded in his diary, "Gen. Longstreet working like a man god in center." Nearby Harvey Hill rallied about 200 infantrymen and led them in a counterattack. Hill wrote afterward to his wife, "My own exertions were almost superhuman on Wednesday and I thank God that I was able to make them." More Confederates assailed the Federal line, raking its flank. Richardson ordered a withdrawal to the ridge above the sunken road.[104]

As Hill's line splintered in the sunken road Longstreet hurried an order to Colonel John R. Cooke of the 27th North Carolina to charge. Cooke's regiment and the 3rd Arkansas had been detached from John Walker's division and posted along Hagerstown Turnpike south of Dunker Church. The brother of Jeb Stuart's wife, Flora, Cooke had led the pair of regiments earlier in an attack that captured an enemy cannon. Now he received instructions to lead them in "a forlorn hope."[105]

Crossing the fields of the Mumma homestead under Union artillery fire, the fewer than 700 North Carolinians and Arkansans slammed into the flank of French's troops west of the Roulette farm. On their right 250 men under Lieutenant Colonel William MacRae advanced in support. The attack caught the Yankees unprepared, but they swung around, and the opposing lines engaged at a distance of 200 yards. More Federal units entered the fight, and, his ammunition expended, Cooke ordered the retreat. The Rebels passed through a gauntlet of artillery fire and musketry before reaching the turnpike. "Cooke stood with his empty guns," reported Longstreet, "and waved his colors to show that his troops were in position." Moxley Sorrel rode up with compliments from Longstreet. "Major," replied Cooke, "thank General Longstreet for the good words, but say . . . we will stay here . . . if we must all go to hell together!" Fewer than half of his men remained around the flags.[106]

This "dreadful day," in Porter Alexander's words, had not ended with the struggle for the sunken road. As the fighting abated into fitful exchanges between skirmishers north of Sharpsburg, it moved toward a climax east of town, where two divisions of Union Major General

Ambrose Burnside's Ninth Corps were advancing, threatening the Confederates' right flank and retreat route to Boteler's Ford. From mid-morning to early afternoon, perched on high bluffs above Rohrbach Bridge (modern-day Burnside's Bridge), Robert Toombs's Georgians thwarted Federal attempts at crossing the span. Finally a pair of Northern regiments raced across the bridge and cleared the way. By then most of the Georgians had abandoned the position as one of Burnside's divisions, having crossed at a downstream ford, closed on Toombs's flank. Another two hours passed, however, before 8,500 Ninth Corps officers and men moved forward at 3:00 P.M.[107]

David R. Jones's 2,800 Southerners met the attackers, resisting stubbornly and slowing the enemy advance. To the south dust clouds marked the approach of Powell Hill's veterans, coming up from Harper's Ferry after a grueling seventeen-mile march in only eight hours. A trailing army chaplain believed that half of Hill's men had fallen out along the route, "The country was literally crowded with stragglers." Maxcy Gregg's South Carolinians spearheaded the counterattack, followed by two more brigades. Lee had witnessed their arrival and met the head of the column, encouraging the men. An eyewitness wrote later that Lee's "worried look left him as he noticed the enthusiasm of Hill's Division."[108]

Gregg's South Carolinians hit the left flank of the Union formation, striking the 16th Connecticut, a novice, untrained regiment. "The devils advanced till our very noses touched theirs," declared a Connecticut sergeant. The untested soldiers broke and fled, taking with them the next regiment in line. Within minutes, as more of Hill's troops joined Gregg's men, the Union ranks unraveled. Officers ordered a retreat, and the Yankees withdrew to the bluffs above Antietam Creek. Sporadic skirmishing and cannon fire ended the fighting. The ill wind died away.[109]

The Battle of Sharpsburg, or Antietam, was the bloodiest single day in American history. Although figures conflict, casualties exceeded 23,000—approximately 10,800 Confederates and 12,500 Federals. More than 3,700 were either killed or mortally wounded, and another 18,300 wounded. On a battlefield of less than a thousand acres the fallen covered perhaps more ground than the survivors. Major Henry Kyd Douglas of Jackson's staff believed that during the night "half of Lee's army were hunting the other half." The next morning, while carrying an order, his fellow staff member Sandie Pendleton thought he had reached the unit. "But he found, to his surprise," recounted Jedediah Hotchkiss, "that it was a whole rank of dead men that the fire of the enemy had mowed down." Pendleton could have been almost anywhere along the Confederate lines.[110]

After nightfall Lee met with a group of generals, including Jackson, Stuart, Harvey and Powell Hill, Hood, David Jones, and Early. The officers reported on the status of their commands. Longstreet arrived late, delayed by seeing to wounded men and assisting a Sharpsburg family whose house was burning. When Lee saw him, he said: "Ah! Here is Longstreet; here's my old *war-horse*! Let us hear what he has to say." Longstreet reported that the situation was "as bad as it can be." Lee announced, however, that the army would remain on the field for another day. The decision surprised the generals. According to a source, Lee asserted, "If McClellan wants to fight in the morning, I will give him battle again." Fortunately for the army, an estimated 6,000 stragglers rejoined their units during the night.[111]

Lee anticipated a renewal of the struggle and compacted his lines overnight. McClellan considered an offensive strike, but his corps commanders warned him about the consequences of a repulse. He explained later that he refused "to hazard another battle with less than an absolute assurance of success." His words would have rung hollow with his audacious opponent across Antietam Creek.[112]

September 18 passed quietly on the scarred landscape around Sharpsburg. "Our army occupies the same line it had held before the battle," Lee stated in a letter to Jefferson Davis. "The enemy I believe do the same. I have again to report the loss of many brave men." During a truce stretcher bearers and burial details gathered the previous day's staggering harvest of the dead and the maimed. Confederate wagons and ambulances rolled to Boteler's Ford and into Virginia. In the afternoon Lee ordered Stuart to march upriver with cavalry, infantry, and artillery and to occupy Williamsport, Maryland. Despite the army's condition and depleted ranks, Lee intended to reenter Maryland, threatening McClellan's supply and communications lines.[113]

After midnight on September 19 Confederate infantry and artillery crossed the Potomac and passed through Shepherdstown. A woman in the town watched the columns march by and asserted, "Never were want and exhaustion more visibly put before my eyes, and that they could march or fight at all seemed incredible." Longstreet admitted privately after the war, "All that we can claim is that we got across the Potomac with an organized army." A Union pursuit followed to the south bank during the evening. The next day Jackson's troops routed the Federals in a clash at Shepherdstown. Upriver Stuart's mission failed when enemy cavalry and two infantry brigades arrived and forced him to withdraw into Virginia. The main army continued south, halting in the lower Shenandoah Valley. The Maryland campaign had ended.[114]

Four days after the battle Walter Taylor of Lee's staff wrote to his sister, "The fight of the 17th has taught us the value of our men, who can even when weary with constant marching & fighting & when on short rations, contend with and resist three times their own number." Echoing his aide's words in his report, Lee professed, "Nothing could surpass the determined valor with which they [officers and men] met the large army of the enemy, fully supplied and equipped, and the result reflects the highest credit on the officers and men engaged."[115]

Indeed the leadership of Jackson, Longstreet, and talented subordinates and the courage and combat prowess of the men in the ranks saved the army from possible destruction. On no other battlefield in the East did the Army of Northern Virginia face such a disparity in numbers in such a vulnerable position. Undoubtedly McClellan, who regarded the battle as his "masterpiece," squandered the opportunity to perhaps destroy Lee's army by fighting corps and divisions in "driblets," as one of his generals put it. He refused to commit William Franklin's troops to an afternoon assault against Jackson's beleaguered line and held the Fifth Corps in reserve throughout the day. In fairness to the Union general, none of his senior officers rivaled Stonewall Jackson and James Longstreet.[116]

Nevertheless Porter Alexander's postwar criticism of Lee's decision to stand at Sharpsburg rings fair. Alexander thought that the commanding general's "overdone" audacity governed his judgment along Antietam Creek. Defeat "would have meant the utter destruction of his army." Alexander concluded, "So he fought where he could have avoided it, & where he had nothing to make & everything to lose—which a general should not do." Lee expected to win, however, and his army held the field.[117]

But on that "exciting amazing day" it had been held by the closest of margins, etched in abiding images: Texas dead in the Cornfield, a shadow of the Stonewall Division left standing, the timely destruction of a Union division in West Woods, "artillery hell" near Dunker Church, a slaughter pit in a sunken road, a major general leading a handful of men in a counterattack, staff officers working cannon, North Carolinians and Arkansans, without ammunition, waving flags in defiance, and the anxiety on an army commander's face until he saw the storied colors of the Light Division. In time Lee regarded Sharpsburg as the army's finest hour. He was right.[118]

General Robert E. Lee, who assumed command of the Army of
Northern Virginia on June 1, 1862, and whose bold operations
changed the war in Virginia.

Lieutenant General Thomas J. "Stonewall" Jackson, commander of the famous "foot cavalry" or the Second Corps. A relentless foe, he fell mortally wounded at Chancellorsville in May 1863.

Lieutenant General James Longstreet, whom Lee called "My Old War Horse." Commander of the First Corps, Longstreet was the army's finest subordinate tactician.

Major General James Ewell Brown "Jeb" Stuart, the army's matchless cavalry commander. Stuart was mortally wounded at Yellow Tavern in May 1864.

Lieutenant General Richard S. Ewell, "Old Bald Head" to his troops. Ewell was one of the army's finest division commanders and combat officers. He succeeded a fallen Jackson as commander of the Second Corps in May 1863.

Major General John Bell Hood, original commander of the famous Texas Brigade. Hood had few peers as a combat officer.

Major General George E. Pickett, "a dapper little fellow." A favorite of Longstreet, Pickett and his division of Virginians achieved enduring fame on the afternoon of July 3, 1863, at Gettysburg.

Colonel Edward Porter Alexander, one of the army's most talented artillerists. Alexander's memoirs are the finest ever written by a member of Lee's army.

Lithograph of leading Confederate generals. Robert E. Lee, with hands on a sword, stands in right center. Generals who served under him and are pictured include John B. Gordon, Wade Hampton, Richard S. Ewell, J. E. B. Stuart, and Thomas J. "Stonewall" Jackson.

Major General George B. McClellan, commander of the Army of the Potomac and Lee's opponent during the Seven Days and Antietam campaigns. Known affectionately as "Little Mac" to his men, McClellan was a cautious general who refused to unleash the fine army that he had created.

Postwar view of ground looking east from Dunker Church to East Woods at Antietam. Smoketown Road angles from left to right.

Dead Confederate soldiers along west side of Hagerstown Pike at Antietam. The men were probably members of Brigadier General William Starke's Louisiana regiments.

A postwar view of the Sunken Road or "Bloody Lane" at Antietam. Before the Federals attacked, Colonel John B. Gordon of the 6th Alabama assured Robert E. Lee, "These men are going to stay here, General, till the sun goes down or victory is won."

Major General Daniel Harvey Hill, brother-in-law of Stonewall Jackson and one of the army's finest combat officers during the 1862 campaigns. Hill' acerbic nature and bluntness evidently irritated Lee, who agreed to Hill's transfer from the army in the winter of 1863.

Major General Joseph Hooker, fourth commander of the Army of the Potomac. Hooker replaced Ambrose Burnside and led the Union army to defeat at Chancellorsville.

Artist's drawing of a charge of Union cavalry on Fleetwood Hill in the Battle of Brandy Station, June 9, 1863. The engagement marked the end of Jeb Stuart's Confederate horsemen's dominance in the East.

The n

Lieutenant General Ambrose Powell Hill, commander of the Light Division and then of the Third Corps. Although Hill feuded with Longstreet and Jackson, Lee regarded the Virginian very highly as a combat commander.

Vie
Wo

Photograph taken days after the Battle of Gettysburg of
Union fieldworks on Culp's Hill.

Postwar view, looking southwest, of Cemetery Ridge and the
ground crossed by George E. Pickett's and J. Johnston Pettigrew's
troops on July 3, 1863.

Postwar painting of the climax of Pickett's Charge at Gettysburg
on the afternoon of July 3, 1863.

Confederate prisoners on Seminary Ridge at Gettysburg in mid-July
1863. Their equipment, uniforms, and slouch hats were typical attire of a
Southern soldier at the time.

Lieutenant General Ulysses S. Grant, whose victories in the West earned him the appointment of General-in-chief of Union armies in March 1864.

Chapter Six

"The Easiest Battle We Ever Fought"

T HE SIGNIFICANCE OF the Battle of Antietam, or Sharpsburg, lay beyond the bloody fields. Three days after the Army of Northern Virginia retreated into Virginia, on September 22, President Abraham Lincoln publicly issued the Preliminary Proclamation of Emancipation, with its promise of freedom to slaves held in Confederate territory after January 1, 1863. The proclamation recast the nature of the conflict and its purposes. It portended as well that a Union victory in the war meant the end of slavery—the economic, social, and political foundation of Southern life.[1]

Lincoln acted as commander-in-chief out of military necessity. The president had informed his Cabinet members of his intention to issue the proclamation at a July 22 meeting. On the advice of Secretary of State William Seward, Lincoln deferred a public announcement until Union military fortunes improved. He used the Confederate withdrawal from Maryland as a victory of Federal arms to issue the Emancipation Proclamation. When the act went into effect, it also authorized the acceptance of blacks into military service.[2]

In his annual message to Congress in December 1861 Lincoln had cautioned that the conflict might become "a violent and remorseless revolutionary struggle." Union victories during the winter of 1862 and the Army of the Potomac's advance to the outskirts of Richmond, Virginia, held the prospects of a swift conclusion to the war before powerful currents of change could be unloosed. Ironically, then, the Confederate victories in the Seven Days and Second Manassas campaigns and the offensive into Maryland assured that the war would not end soon and that those currents of change would alter the country. When Lincoln announced the revolutionary emancipation policy, a Union soldier observed astutely, "I cant see how it even will be settled, the Rebels is bound to fight as long as a man left and we will do the same. We both think we are right."[3]

The achievement of Robert E. Lee and the Army of Northern Virginia in the summer of 1862 must be understood within this broader contest, recognized by Lincoln, that the war had created an unbridgeable divide. Lee and the army had upended the Northern belief in the certainty of Union victory, restored the morale of the Southern populace, and indefinitely lengthened the conflict. Despite the setback in Maryland, Southern civilians approved of Lee's bold offensives as affirmation of their soldiers' bravery and martial heritage. The Richmond newspaper editor Edward A. Pollard, writing after Antietam, declared: "The army which rested again in Virginia had made history that will flash down the tide of time a luster of glory. It had done an amount of marching and fighting that appears almost incredible, even to those minds familiar with the records of great military exertions."[4]

The British historian Frederick Maurice concluded: "Lee's campaign of 1862 is a remarkable example of calculated boldness and imaginative strategy. No other commander has achieved with means so exiguous results more remarkable. And throughout the campaign Fortune had been almost uniformly unkind." As Maurice stated, Lee's use of the strategic offensive and maneuver (turning movements) characterized his generalship and led to tactical victories. In a contest of wills against George McClellan and John Pope, Lee prevailed by accepting risks and daring to act, despite command and organizational flaws and numerical inferiority.[5]

When the army recrossed into Virginia on September 19 it belonged unequivocally to Lee, and he and the army belonged to the Southern people. Reciting a common view at the time, a Georgia officer asserted, "The army almost worships him [Lee] and believe that with Lee, Jackson, and Longstreet at the head, nothing is impossible." The army, wrote Walter Taylor, "was admirably tempered" during the Maryland campaign; Porter Alexander believed that their stand at Sharpsburg on September 18 was an act of defiance that "had given us renewed confidence that we could not be whipped." In a memoir a Virginian maintained, "Of all the battles of the war, the privates in the ranks were proudest of that of Sharpsburg, for it had been essentially their fight . . . a hard stand-up, face-to-face, hand-to-hand affair."[6]

Although the Confederates had been forced to withdraw from Maryland, their presence in the border state enthused the Southern people. Their soldiers had carried the banners of Confederate nationalism beyond its territory, affirming to homefolks the viability of their country. According to the historian Gary Gallagher, "Lee and his army emerged from Maryland as a major rallying point for the Confederacy." After the campaign ended, a Union surgeon gave a telling assessment of his foes that would have been echoed throughout the seceded states, "It is beyond all wonder how such men as the rebel troops can fight as they do; that, filthy, sick, hungry, and miserable, they should prove such heroes in fight, is past explanation."[7]

The army's victories in the Seven Days and at Second Manassas and the tactical draw at Antietam had been achieved at a fearful price. Although casualty figures vary, the Confederates incurred losses of at least 41,000, if not more than 45,000 killed, wounded, and captured. In a letter of September 22 an artillery officer professed, "Death has been *powerfully* busy within the last month." Casualties among the officer corps were even more grievous in the defensive struggle at Antietam. One division commander was killed and three wounded; four brigade commanders killed and twenty wounded. At the regimental level, twenty-eight commanders lost their lives, and more than seventy were either wounded or captured. In the three campaigns the army incurred an average casualty rate of twenty percent. By comparison, the Union casualty rate was slightly more than thirteen percent.[8]

Some historians have been harshly critical of Lee's method of warfare and its concomitant toll in blood. Addressing the campaigns of 1862, Thomas Connelly declared, "Lee's aggressive nature bled the Confederacy of manpower." More specifically Alan Nolan charged that the Maryland campaign "significantly damaged the army in casualties and morale." Louis Manarin maintained that Sharpsburg "momentarily paralyzed" the army, and it "never fully recovered from the battle's losses." Although each criticism has an element of truth, they miss a broader and more significant factor: strategic and tactical circumstances weighed heavily in Lee's conduct of a campaign and a battle.[9]

Unquestionably Lee possessed, in the words of the historian Russell Weigley, "a quality of stubborn pugnacity that impelled him to fight even when his strategic or tactical plans had gone awry," particularly at Antietam. Moxley Sorrel, James Longstreet's chief of staff, said of the Confederate commander, "Blood he did not mind in his general's work." Lee was willing to expend his men's blood, added Sorrel, "when necessary or when strategically advisable." In each of the three campaigns Lee fashioned his strategy on maneuver. Since he took command, roughly half of the army's casualties had been incurred during the Seven Days, when he assailed the Army of the Potomac. The attacks at Mechanicsville, or Beaver Dam Creek, and Malvern Hill resulted from breakdowns in command, and those at Gaines's Mill, the bloodiest of the engagements, and Glendale were necessitated or justified by the situation at hand.[10]

Lee's aggressiveness was calculated, based on the Confederacy's limited resources and manpower. He recognized that time favored the enemy. The longer the conflict lasted, the greater would be the disparity between Confederate and Union forces. Like all great generals, Lee accepted the reality of the soldier's trade, the effusion of blood for a purpose. Within the army the rank and file likewise accepted the costs they bore. There were dissenting voices, typified by a Virginia private, who wrote that fall, "I am getting pretty tried of this mode of wasting lives." Many in both armies undoubtedly shared his sentiment, but sacrifices, even their own, for the cause mattered more. As Sorrel said, Lee spilled blood of necessity and, like his men, for the cause.[11]

The scars of the Seven Days, Second Manassas, and Antietam were unmistakable as the army withdrew into the lower Shenandoah Valley.

In ragged uniforms and barefoot, the "skeleton regiments and brigades" of the Confederacy needed time for healing. "Our Army is badly broken down and scattered," a staff officer wrote in a letter. Jedediah Hotchkiss told his brother, "We must reorganize, though, for many of our regiments have lost all their officers, and some regiments are reduced to mere companies." A Virginia private averred after crossing the Potomac: "If they drag us across the river a few more times we won't have many to fight at all. I hear a great many say they don't intend to cross again."[12]

Within days of entering the Valley, however, Lee considered recrossing the Potomac at Williamsport, Maryland, and advancing toward Hagerstown. "I would not hesitate to make it," Lee informed Jefferson Davis of the offensive on September 25, "even though with our diminished numbers, had the army exhibited its former temper and condition; but, as far as I am able to judge, the hazard would be great and a reverse disastrous. I am, therefore, led to pause." But three days later, with obvious pride, Lee declared to the Confederate president, "History records but few examples of a greater amount of labor and fighting than has been done by this army during the present campaign."[13]

The "pause" that Lee wrote of lasted six weeks. He never quite abandoned the idea of resuming the offensive during that time, but rest for the troops and reorganization overrode a forward movement. The army camps stretched from Winchester north to Bunker Hill. Lee established headquarters near Stephenson's Depot, a few miles from Winchester, where private homes and public buildings served as the army's main hospital. A surgeon estimated that the Valley town held 6,000 wounded and sick men. Roughly ninety miles to the south, Staunton on the Virginia Central Railroad served as the main supply base, with a stream of wagons rolling north and south on the Valley Pike during the weeks.[14]

The wagon trains of supplies hauled critically needed shoes, undergarments, pants, coats, and blankets. The men's letters and diaries at the time described their destitute condition: "Our army is almost without clothes"; "[We] are nearly naked and barefoted"; "We are a dirty, ragged set." At first the clothing items arrived "by degrees," but by mid-October the wagons brought 9,000 garments a week. The demand outstripped the supplies, however. One regiment dubbed their bivouac site "Barefooted Camp." Longstreet ordered beef hides sewn into shoes, which the men called "Longstreet's Moccasins." By November and the approach of cold weather many men still lacked shoes. Despite the shortages, the troops were, claimed one of them, "in very good spirits."[15]

The army had plenty of beef and flour for the men and hay and grain for the horses and mules. "We are consuming provisions that would otherwise fall into the hands of the enemy," Lee wrote. He worked tirelessly at fulfilling the supply and ordnance demands. The troops had, in his words, "an abundance of arms." He reported that since his assignment to command they had captured 66,000 stands of small arms. Officers cautioned the men against wasting ammunition.[16]

Lee instituted daily roll calls at reveille, when each soldier was required to be under arms. The orders resulted from the crippling amount of stragglers and absentees during the recent campaign. "I have taken every means in my power from the beginning to correct this evil," Lee confided to Davis, telling the president that desertion and straggling were "the main cause of its [the army's] retiring from Maryland." Within the rank and file, among those who had been on the field at Antietam, a newspaper reporter expected "a great outcry raised against the stragglers." Dorsey Pender told his wife, "We will have to shoot them before it stops."[17]

During these weeks, however, the army's ranks swelled with the return of stragglers, those who "went home on a French [leave]," and an influx of recruits. The records indicate the extent of straggling in Maryland by the increase of numbers on the rolls. On September 22 the army had 41,520 present. Eight days later the figure had grown to 62,713 present, and on October 10 officers counted an aggregate present of 79,595. Of this last figure, 4,933 officers and 63,100 enlisted men were present for duty.[18]

"In three months I had not seen the army in such a good condition as this morning," Reverend James Sheeran, chaplain of the 14th Louisiana, recorded in his journal on October 18. "The stragglers and those broken down were all up with their commands." Porter Alexander recalled, "We began to feel that again we had an army" and a "renewed confidence that we could not be whipped." Except for the "numerous reveilles and innumerable drills," according to a North Carolinian, the men enjoyed the restful weeks.[19]

Meanwhile the army underwent a major reorganization with the official formation of infantry corps and the promotion of officers. On September 18, President Davis signed into law an act passed by the Confederate Congress that provided for the creation of corps and the appointment of lieutenant generals. Davis wrote then to Lee, asking for his recommendations for the new rank and for promotions of major and brigadier generals. Lee replied on October 2, "confidently" recommending James Longstreet and Stonewall Jackson for corps commanders with the rank of lieutenant general. Both men were soon appointed, Longstreet to rank from October 9; Jackson from October 10.[20]

By date of rank Longstreet became the senior subordinate in the army. Since Lee's accession to command, he had been the most reliable subordinate. With each successive campaign he had matured as a general, demonstrating a tactical acumen on the battlefield unmatched by any other of Lee's lieutenants. John Hood said of him after the war: "Of all the men living, not excepting our incomparable Lee, himself, I would rather follow James Longstreet in a forlorn hope or desperate encounter against heavy odds. He was our hardest hitter."[21]

Harvey Hill wrote to his old friend years later, "You were his [Lee's] confidential friend, more intimate with him than any one else." Lee sought his counsel regularly. Though Longstreet supported Lee's bold strategic movements, he became committed increasingly to the tactical defensive. In the estimation of one officer, he was "thorough and methodical." He approached war dispassionately. Unlike Jackson, no moral imperatives governed his generalship, victory resulted from deliberate, thoughtful preparation. His preference for the tactical defensive lay in his belief in conserving men's lives, risks measured by costs. He favored the counterstrike to the attack. His command was designated the First Corps.[22]

In his letter to Davis, Lee wrote of Jackson: "My opinion of the merits of General Jackson has been greatly enhanced during this expedition. He is true, honest, and brave; has a single eye to the good of the service, and spares no exertion to accomplish his object." His performance in the Second Manassas and Maryland campaigns had removed any lingering doubts Lee had held after the Seven Days. Jackson lacked Longstreet's tactical ability on a battlefield, but he possessed "a relentlessness that bordered on the maniacal," in the judgment of the historian George Rable. Harvey Hill said of Jackson: "Self-denial and self-control explain his wonderful success. He had conquered himself, and was made fit to be a conqueror." William Taliaferro attributed Jackson's success as a general to "the desire to do, to be moving, to make and to embrace opportunity."[23]

Though Jackson's men grumbled and cursed about how he drove them, "the very sight of him was the signal for cheers," claimed one of them. Wherever he went, wrote an officer, Old Jack "instantly aroused the greatest enthusiasm." His actions sometimes seemed beyond understanding, but he invoked great devotion from the troops where it counted the most. "It was in battle that the men showed their great love for, and confidence in, General Jackson," declared Private John Worsham of the 21st Virginia. "His old soldiers had implicit confidence in him." His was the Second Corps.[24]

After Longstreet and Jackson, Lee considered Powell Hill, he informed Davis, "the best commander with me. He fights his troops well, and takes good care of them." According to the historian Frank O'Reilly, Hill's Light Division "had the most brilliant combination of subordinate officers in the army," with such brigadiers as Maxcy Gregg, Dorsey Pender, Edward Thomas, and James Archer. Pender bragged to his wife with good reason: "The fact is, Hill's Division stands first in point of efficiency of any Division of this whole army. . . . It surpasses Jackson's old Division both for fighting and discipline."[25]

During these weeks in the Valley the professional difficulties and personal animosity between Jackson and Powell Hill boiled over, the dispute finally reaching army headquarters. On September 3 Jackson had placed Hill under arrest for neglect of duty for not overseeing the march of the Light Division. When the army returned to Virginia, Hill officially requested a court of inquiry, demanding that Jackson explain the arrest. Lee initially reacted to Hill's request by replying that the circumstances did not justify an inquiry. The prideful Hill responded with a list of charges against Jackson, who restated his charge of "neglect of duty" with eight specifications.[26]

Lee did not settle the matter officially but filed away the papers. Henry Kyd Douglas of Jackson's staff wrote in his memoirs that Lee met with Jackson and Hill in "an interview of some length." A rumor circulated, Douglas stated, that the two generals had a heated verbal exchange before Lee intervened. Major William H. Palmer, Hill's chief of staff, asserted in a postwar letter: "Hill disliked Jackson intensely & never got over it. Lee settled their quarrel at Bunker Hill. Jackson seemed to dismiss it ever after, but Hill never got it out of his mind." In turn one of Jackson's aides, William Allan, confided later to a fellow officer, "Jackson hated Hill."[27]

The creation of the infantry corps and the losses among brigade commanders in the Maryland campaign necessitated removals, transfers, and promotions within the army's leadership. Throughout October and into November Lee's officer corps underwent reorganization and change. Gone from the army permanently because of poor performance, wounds or reassignment were Thomas Drayton, Roswell Ripley, Roger Pryor, Nathan Evans, Robert Toombs, Howell Cobb, and John G. Walker. David R. Jones suffered a heart attack in mid-October and returned to Richmond, where he died on January 15, 1863. Five of the generals—Drayton, Ripley, Pryor, Evans, and Cobb—had been found wanting as combat officers.[28]

Brigadier generals John Bell Hood and George E. Pickett received promotions to major general. Although a rather mediocre administrator as a brigade commander, since Gaines's Mill Hood had been unsurpassed at that level as a combat officer. Captain Thomas G. Goree of Longstreet's staff wrote home when he heard of Hood's impending promotion: "No man deserves it more. He is one of the finest young officers I ever saw." Fellow aide Moxley Sorrel stated, "He might be considered an ideal officer of that rank and command." Although Hood served in Longstreet's wing, it was Jackson who urged his promotion, writing to the War Department of the brigadier's conduct at Antietam: "It gives me pleasure to say that his duties were discharged with such ability and zeal, as to command my admiration. I regard him as one of the most promising officers of the army." Hood's new division consisted of the pair of brigades he had led and two others from David Jones's division, which was divided up.[29]

George Pickett owed his promotion to Longstreet. The two men had served in the same infantry regiment in the Mexican War and remained friends. Pickett had suffered a shoulder wound at Gaines's Mill and did not return to the army until his assignment to division command. He was, remarked an officer, "very foppish in his dress and wore his hair in ringlets. He was what would be called a dapper little fellow but brave as they ever make men." His combat experience paled before that of Hood, and he possessed a volatile temper. Undoubtedly he benefited from Longstreet's endorsement of him and from being a Virginian. His division, which for the most part had been Longstreet's former command, consisted of five brigades, four Virginian and one South Carolinian.[30]

The promotion of Hood and Pickett angered Cadmus Wilcox. He believed, with justification, that he deserved a major generalcy ahead of either of them, who were both junior in rank to him. Wilcox had led more than one brigade capably during the summer campaigns. He asked Lee to be relieved from command and transferred to the west. "I cannot consent to it," answered Lee, "for I require your services here. . . . I know you are too good a soldier not to serve where it is necessary for the benefit of the Confederacy." Lee met with the disgruntled general, and Wilcox remained with the army. A North Carolinian in a corps with only two brigades from that state, Wilcox did not fit into the politics of the reorganization. He blamed Longstreet for his failure to attain higher rank.[31]

Like Wilcox, Isaac Trimble and Jubal Early merited promotion to major general. Both men had been aggressive and skillful in combat. Jackson recommended Trimble, who was still recovering from the wound suffered at Brawner's Farm, for the rank. According to accounts of Jackson's aides, Trimble had declared earlier, "General Jackson, before this war is over, I intend to be a Major General or a corpse!" It would not be until January 17, 1863, that Trimble received the coveted rank.[32]

Jubal Early had been praised by Lee, Jackson, and Jeb Stuart for his conduct at Sharpsburg. Since the battle he had held temporary command of Richard Ewell's division, but until the War Department declared the wounded Ewell incapacitated for field command, no vacancy existed for Early's promotion. A Virginian and an opponent of secession, Early was, said an artillerist, "a bundle of inconsistencies and contradictions." Stoop-shouldered from arthritis, sharp-tongued, irreverent, and profane, Early was personally brave, with few equals on the battlefield. Lee called him affectionately "my bad old man." In time his promotion could not be denied.[33]

At the brigade level ten men received promotion to brigadier general. When the fighting had ended along Antietam Creek, brigadiers led fourteen brigades, while colonels and officers of lower rank, even captains, commanded the remaining twenty-six brigades. The need to fill the units with officers of proper rank was evident, and Lee, Jackson, and Longstreet conferred on the individuals. Lee submitted his recommendations to the War Department on October 27. Political considerations and a candidate's native state factored into the final list, which Lee announced on November 6. Although protests and controversy swirled within the army on some of the appointments, the new brigadiers included talented and deserving men such as George T. Anderson, John R. Cooke, Jerome B. Robertson, Stephen Dodson Ramseur, George Doles, Edward Thomas, and James H. Lane.[34]

Eleven of the new brigadiers were graduates of West Point or VMI and/or had served in the Regular Army or Mexican War. Most of them had acquired combat experience initially at the regimental command level. They had emerged as worthy of promotion because, according to the historian Joseph Glatthaar, "they possessed the right temperament, energy, values, insights, and sound judgment." A veteran described what was expected of them in the confusing, smoke-filled maelstrom of a battle, "Southern generals were up among their men, directing and leading their movements, and encouraging them at critical points." At this time Lee's army retained a pool of capable, if not outstanding, officers who could fulfill those expectations.[35]

The artillery underwent more of a consolidation than a reorganization. At Antietam the artillerists had "a day of glory," in the words of its first historian. Due to a lack of guns, equipment, and horses, Lee directed that batteries be reduced in number and that inefficient officers be removed. William Pendleton remained as chief of artillery, but his panic-stricken conduct at Shepherdstown drew harsh criticism within the ranks of the artillery. One officer asserted: "Pendleton is Lee's weakness. Pn is like the elephant, we have him & we don't know what on earth to do with him, and it costs a devil of a sight to feed him." Lee kept the fellow Virginian in his post for his administrative ability. "It was a notorious fact and generl[l]y remarked," claimed a staff officer of Pendleton, "that he was almost entirely ignored by Genl. Lee" in the tactical control of the artillery. Lee left that to battalion commanders and later to corps chiefs of artillery.[36]

Porter Alexander, the army's chief of ordnance, succeeded Stephen D. Lee as commander of Lee's artillery battalion. Lee had been promoted to brigadier general and assigned to Mississippi. The officers of the battalion requested Alexander's appointment. A West Pointer, the twenty-seven-year-old Georgian had been with the army from its beginnings. A year earlier, a newspaper correspondent had said of him, "He is looked upon as one of the most promising young officers in the army." In the fall of 1861 Alexander had advocated that batteries be organized into battalions, but the idea was not adopted at the time. Longstreet had used his engineering and reconnoitering skills often. An intense man with a keen intellect, Alexander was well liked. Moxley Sorrel wrote that Alexander "was sure of winning in everything he took up." Promoted to colonel, he was assigned to the First Corps.[37]

The reorganization of the army had not been completed when the Federals beyond the Potomac River began stirring. Like their opponents, the Yankees spent the weeks resting and healing. President Abraham Lincoln visited the army at Sharpsburg during the first week of October, conferring with George McClellan and his generals and reviewing the troops. With midterm elections approaching, Lincoln had been urging an offensive into Virginia. The War Department had forwarded dozens of new regiments to the army, whose numbers increased to about 135,000 present for duty. McClellan balked, however, citing shortages of shoes, clothing, and horseshoes. When Lincoln returned to Washington, he directed the army commander on October 6 to "cross the Potomac and give battle to the enemy or drive him south. Your army must move now while the roads are good."[38]

Lincoln warned the general that he would be "a ruined man if [McClellan] did not move forward, moved rapidly and effectively." Still McClellan did not advance, requesting more ammunition, more supplies, and more men. When the army commander complained that the cavalry mounts were "absolutely broken down with fatigue and want of flesh," Lincoln replied, "Will you pardon me for asking what the horses of your army have done since the battle of Antietam that fatigue anything?"[39]

Lincoln's acerbic query came partly in reaction to another embarrassing raid by Jeb Stuart's Confederate horsemen. During the first week of October Stuart discussed with Lee and Jackson a mounted raid into Pennsylvania. Lee approved the expedition, and on October 10 Stuart and 1,800 cavalrymen, drawn from eight Virginia regiments, crossed the Potomac at McCoy's Ford, upriver from the Union army. Riding north, they entered the Keystone State, passing through Mercersburg and reaching Chambersburg that night. Along the route details scoured the countryside for horses and filled wagons with captured revolvers and sabers. Leaving Chambersburg, the troopers rode east, turned south at Cashtown, passed through Maryland villages, and reentered Virginia on October 12, eluding Federal pursuers and without the loss of a man killed or seriously wounded.[40]

Stuart boasted in a letter to his wife that the raid was "the second 'grand rounds' of McClellan's Army." Lee praised the "boldness, judgment and prowess" of Stuart, terming the enterprise "eminently successful." A War Department clerk called it "a most brilliant affair." A dissenting view came from cantankerous Jubal Early, who dubbed it "the greatest horse stealing expedition," which only "annoyed" the Federals. At Sharpsburg Union general George G. Meade predicted that Stuart's raid into Pennsylvania and escape "will be a mortifying affair to McClellan, and will do him, I fear, serious injury."[41]

A fortnight after the Confederate horsemen's return, on October 26, McClellan's Army of the Potomac began crossing the Potomac River at Berlin, Maryland. The Rebels had been awaiting an enemy movement for weeks. An Alabama officer stated, "We had whipped the Yankees several times, but they would not stay whipped; they just 'kept plugging away.'" Several days earlier Harvey Hill had confided to his wife: "Our battles are not over the war, I fear, is just beginning. Few can expect to survive it & all ought to be prepared for the great change." An artillerist noted, "Whatever plan Gen. Lee adopts will, I wholly believe, be the best one."[42]

On the day the Yankees marched, Capt. John W. Carlisle of the

13th South Carolina wrote a letter to a friend about Lee, Jackson, and Stuart: "It is a grand sight—no general creates the enthusiasm he [Jackson] does. . . . When General Lee rides by, the soldiers gaze at him in silent admiration but whenever Jackson is seen every soldier's mouth flies wide open—you can always tell whenever Jackson is coming. General Stuart also creates a considerable enthusiasm. . . . But of all the generals I think General Lee by far the most superior. He has no equal in this continent in my estimation."[43]

Before reacting to McClellan's crossing, Lee waited until additional reports confirmed whether the enemy advance was a major movement or a diversion. Two days later, when scouts indicated that the entire Union army was on the march, Lee ordered Longstreet's First Corps toward Front Royal and through the Blue Ridge. Stuart and two brigades of cavalry followed on October 30. Lee held Jackson's Second Corps in the Shenandoah Valley. By November 5 Longstreet's 32,000 troops had reached Culpeper Court House, where Lee joined them after a brief visit to Richmond and a meeting with Jefferson Davis.[44]

Meanwhile, north of the Rappahannock River and east of the Blue Ridge, Stuart's cavalrymen were clashing with the vanguard of McClellan's army. Stuart was at his best in these operations, slowing enemy movements and gathering intelligence on his foes. "Stuart had excelled every cavalry leader that ever lived, I suppose," asserted a Confederate after the war, "in the work of screening an army from the enemy's observation." At one point Lee commended Stuart, writing to him, "I am glad that you have operated to check the advance of the enemy with your usual skill." Tragically for Stuart during these days he learned that his four-year-old daughter, Flora, named for her mother, had died of typhoid fever. To his staff, with tears on his face, he said, "I will never get over it—never!" Two weeks earlier Lee's twenty-three-year-old daughter, Annie, had also succumbed to typhoid fever.[45]

Duty kept Stuart from consoling his grief-stricken wife. Few men were more devoted to the cause than he; at one time he had told his mother, "I give my life up to God, & my Country, Cheerfully, whenever he pleases to call me & if I were degraded to the Ranks, I would fight there with equal zeal & determination. I fight from a sense of Duty & principles, & *not* for fame or ambition."[46]

Union pressure finally forced Stuart's men south of the Rappahan-nock River. The Federal advanced stalled, however, in the Warrenton area. On November 7, during the season's first snowfall, a War Depart-ment officer delivered an order to Ambrose Burnside. Dated November 5, the dispatch read, "By direction of the President of the United States, it is ordered that Major-General McClellan be relieved of command of the Army of the Potomac, and that Major-General Burnside take command of the army." A close friend of McClellan, Burnside accepted reluctantly. He and the officer traveled to McClellan's headquarters at Rectortown and handed him a copy of the order. McClellan read it and said, "Well, Burnside, I turn command over to you."[47]

The news of McClellan's removal ignited a firestorm of anger and protest among his officers and men, who spoke of a march on the capital to demand his reinstatement. When tempers cooled, most of them con-cluded, in the words of a captain, "that we were fighting for the country, and not for any individual." The bond between the rank and file and Little Mac ran deep, lasting long after he left the army. His cautious and controversial generalship rested on his belief that if the army were destroyed the cause would be lost and on his desire to limit the political and social consequences of the conflict. His men's faith in him, how-ever, transcended his faith in them. Arguably McClellan's greatest fail-ing as a general lay in his unwillingness to unsheathe the weapon he had created.[48]

On November 10, after hosting a party for fellow officers on the pre-vious night and after reviewing troops, McClellan boarded a train that carried him east and out of the war. Lincoln told a group at the White House that the Northern people "have got the idea into their heads that we are going to get out of this fix, somehow by strategy. General McClellan thinks he is going to whip the rebels by strategy; and the army has got the same notion. They have no idea that the war is to be carried on and put through by hard fighting." The president understood that McClellan's concept of limited warfare lay buried in the past amid the war's many graves.[49]

Ambrose Burnside expressed doubts about his ability to command an army, but he understood that the Lincoln administration expected active operations before winter weather limited movement. Burnside organized the infantry corps into wings, assigning two corps to a Grand Division. With Lincoln's approval he started the army toward Falmouth, across the Rappahannock River from Fredericksburg, on November 15. Instead of moving directly against Longstreet's troops south of the river, Burnside chose an advance from Fredericksburg south, toward Richmond.[50]

The vanguard of the Union army reached Falmouth on November 17, having stolen a march on their foes. Burnside had ordered pontoons sent forward from Washington for a crossing of the Rappahannock at Fredericksburg; with the pontoons the Federals could secure the hills west of the historic town. But General-in-chief Henry W. Halleck failed to oversee the prompt execution of the orders, and the pontoon train did not arrive until November 25. By then gray-coated infantry and artillery batteries manned the hills. History, in a terrible form, was to revisit Fredericksburg.[51]

When Robert E. Lee learned of McClellan's removal from command, he wrote to Jeb Stuart: "I am in doubt, whether the change from him to Burnside, is a matter of congratulation or not. I have some acquaintance with McClellan and knew where to place him. Burnside has to be studied." The Confederate commander directed Stuart to "ascertain the position of the enemy." When Stuart confirmed that the entire Union army was on the march east, Lee ordered Longstreet's First Corps to Fredericksburg and instructed Jackson to hasten forward from the Shenandoah Valley.[52]

For the next two weeks the armies gathered across the Rappahannock from each other. Jackson's veterans arrived during the first week of December, extending Confederate lines south until they stretched for thirty miles, from Fredericksburg on the north to Port Royal on the south. East of the river a city of tents rose from the ground, marking the vastness of Burnside's army. A private in the 70th New York wrote to his brother: "Everything seems to be at a standstill. I have been around the troops a good deal and I find that there is a good deal of grumbling and dissatisfaction at the thin way things are going on. The men as a general thing are anxious and willing to move or fight if necessary. They want to finish the war up this winter and get home."[53]

From their camps the Yankees saw the range of hills beyond Fredericksburg, their crests darkened by enemy cannon and infantry. Longstreet's corps held the ground directly west of the town, posted on Taylor's Hill, Marye's Heights, and Telegraph Hill (known today as Lee's Hill). Comprising two hills and a saddle between them, Marye's Heights marked the center of Longstreet's position. Along its base ran a sunken road, its bed edged on the east by a stone wall. From the road an open plain, dotted with a few houses and gardens and bisected by a five-foot-deep and fifteen-foot-wide millrace, stretched several hundred yards to the town. The plain's contour was flush with the top of the stone wall, making the sunken road a natural trench, unseen by the Federals.[54]

Confederate engineers oversaw the placement of artillery pits for cannon, and Longstreet ordered the construction of log and dirt fieldworks along a portion of the line. The batteries of the Washington Artillery, under the direction of Porter Alexander, filled the gun pits on Marye's Heights. While examining the position on the heights, Longstreet noticed cannon held in reserve and suggested to the artillerist that they be brought forward. Alexander replied, "General, we can cover that ground [the plain] now so well that we will comb it as with a fine-tooth comb. A chicken could not live on that field when we open on it." In his memoirs Alexander wrote, "I never conceived for a moment that Burnside would make his main attack right where we were the strongest—at Marye's Hill."[55]

Longstreet's lines extended south from Taylor's Hill six miles to Deep Run. Beyond the stream Jackson had the divisions of Powell Hill and William Taliaferro and artillery batteries holding wooded Prospect Hill for a distance of two miles. The divisions of Jubal Early and Harvey Hill covered possible crossing points on the river toward Port Royal. On Prospect Hill brigades of the Light Division manned Jackson's front along the tracks of the Richmond, Fredericksburg, and Potomac Railroad. Behind Powell Hill's ranks Taliaferro's Stonewall Division provided depth to the defensive position.[56]

The brigades of James Lane and James Archer held the foremost section of Jackson's line. Powell Hill had placed the brigades on opposite sides of an extensive piece of marshy ground, creating a 600-yard gap between them. Batteries unlimbered on both sides of the gap behind the infantry. Lee and Jackson approved of Hill's dispositions. The historian Frank O'Reilly has written in his book on the campaign, "Jackson assumed an organized unit could not penetrate the swampy finger of woods in his front."[57]

According to Harvey Hill, Jackson's "feelings were not kind towards Genl Lee" at this time. Jackson confided to Hill that he thought Lee "had shown partiality to Longstreet in the distribution of guns, clothing, camp & garrison equipage &c" while the army had rested in the Shenandoah Valley after Antietam. Hill claimed further that Jackson "once said that he feared he would be compelled to resign." "I judge however," concluded Hill, "that all this had passed away before his [Jackson's] death."[58]

In the same letter, written in July 1864, Hill recounted a conversation between him and Jackson after the corps had arrived in the Fredericksburg area. "I am opposed to fighting here," Jackson asserted to his brother-in-law, "*we will whip the enemy, but gain no fruits of victory. I have advised the line of the North Anna, but have been over-ruled.*" In Jackson's judgment, if the Federals assailed the Confederate position and were almost certainly defeated, they could recross the Rappahannock, preventing a pursuit by the Rebels. If drawn farther south to the North Anna River, a Federal defeat opened the enemy to a possible piecemeal destruction while in retreat.[59]

In fact Lee had informed Jackson during the Second Corps's march from the Valley, "I do not now anticipate making a determined stand north of the North Anna." Lee's view on the hollowness of a victory at Fredericksburg was similar to Jackson's, but the commanding general altered his plans once he reached Fredericksburg. "My purpose was changed not from any advantage of this position," Lee explained to Secretary of War James Seddon, "but from an unwillingness to open more of our country to depredation than possible, and also with a view of collecting such forage and provisions as could be obtained in the Rappahannock Valley."[60]

Lee's decision to make a stand at Fredericksburg and not farther south, at the North Anna, locked the opponents in place along the Rappahannock. The sense of an impending struggle hung over both armies. "We are in an awful state of suspense," wrote a Virginian, "expecting constant for a great battle to commence." Thousands of Confederates remained shoeless, their feet wrapped in blood-clotted rags. Harvey Hill believed that the barefoot men suffered more than George Washington's Continentals had in the worst of times during the Revolutionary War. Despite the lack of shoes, Lee ordered all of his 78,000 officers and men at their posts.[61]

While Lee's veterans waited, a deeper feeling coursed through their ranks. "Our men are sanguine of success," affirmed a member of the Stonewall Brigade. A soldier in the 8th Georgia predicted that if "Burnside should have the hardihood to attempt to cross the river, we could 'riddle him into dog rags.'" Two soldiers in another Georgia regiment wagered fifty dollars that the Yankees would not attack the Confederates, arguing that the Union commander "would be such a damned fool as to make a real sure-enough attack on 'Mas Bob,' when anybody must know he had the dead wood on him." The 8th Georgia man added, "Many think they see the 'beginning of the end of the war.'"[62]

On December 9 Burnside met with the army's senior leadership. Four days earlier the Federals had attempted a crossing of the Rappahannock at Skinker's Neck, downriver from Falmouth, but encountered resistance and abandoned the effort. Believing that Lee's units were widely scattered, Burnside informed the generals that the army would cross at Fredericksburg, stating that the enemy "did not expect us to cross here." When Burnside heard of opposition to his plan, he summoned the generals to headquarters the next day and reaffirmed his decision. Their duty, he said to the group, was "to aid me loyally." Later that day an officer wrote home: "I have little hope of the plans succeeding. I do not think them good,—there will be a great loss of life and nothing accomplished. I am sure we are to fight against all chances of success."[63]

Union engineers selected three sites for pontoon brigades, one each at the upper and lower ends of the town and a third a mile downstream below Deep Run. Before daylight on December 11, shielded by a heavy fog, the engineers began laying the bridges. Minutes after five o'clock William Barksdale's 1,500 Mississippians, guarding the town, opened fire from rifle pits and barricaded streets and behind buildings. The Federal crews fled to safety. From Stafford Heights on the east side of the river, Union artillerists blasted the Mississippians with solid shot. For seven hours the Rebels foiled repeated attempts to construct the pontoons at the two sites in Fredericksburg.[64]

Frustrated by the enemy's stubborn resistance, Burnside ordered a bombardment of the town. For an hour Union cannon pummeled Fredericksburg's buildings and residents with a storm of solid shot and shells, collapsing walls and igniting fires that spread throughout the town. When the fury subsided, a pair of Union regiments piled into boats and were ferried across the river. More Federal infantrymen followed, and a vicious, street-to-street, house-to-house fight ensued between the Mississippians and the Yankees. Night fell before Barksdale's men retreated, having lost a third of their comrades. Their valiant defense gave "us abundance of time to complete our arrangements for battle," reported Longstreet. "A more gallant and worthy service is rarely accomplished by so small a force."[65]

In unbroken, blue-darkened ranks the Federals filed across the three pontoon bridges throughout December 12. As one regiment passed a group of prisoners, a Southerner drawled to them, "Never mind, Yanks, you chaps will ketch hell over there." Once in the town discipline among the officers and men evaporated in a frenzy of ransacking and destruction. The Yankees looted abandoned houses and businesses, dragged furniture into the streets, smashing the items, and discovered caches of brandy and whiskey. Hundreds of drunken soldiers roamed the streets and alleys. "The whole town was pillaged utterly ripped to pieces," complained a colonel to his wife. The wanton revelry they blamed on their foes for using the town as a defensive position.[66]

West of the town the Confederates finished preparations for the impending battle. Lee, Jackson, and Stuart rode along the lines, attending to final details. Jackson ordered the divisions of Jubal Early and Harvey Hill, posted downriver, to march to Fredericksburg. On Marye's Heights Lafayette McLaws's infantrymen stockpiled ammunition, provisions, and water. By nightfall the Rebels were ready for the enemy, in McLaws's words, "with perfect calmness and with confidence in our ability to repel them."[67]

A heavy fog settled in overnight and clung to the ground before dawn on December 13. At Confederate army headquarters on Telegraph Hill, Longstreet and his staff joined Lee. After a while Jackson rode up. "As he [Jackson] dismounted we broke into astonished smiles," recounted Moxley Sorrel. "He was in a spick and span new overcoat,

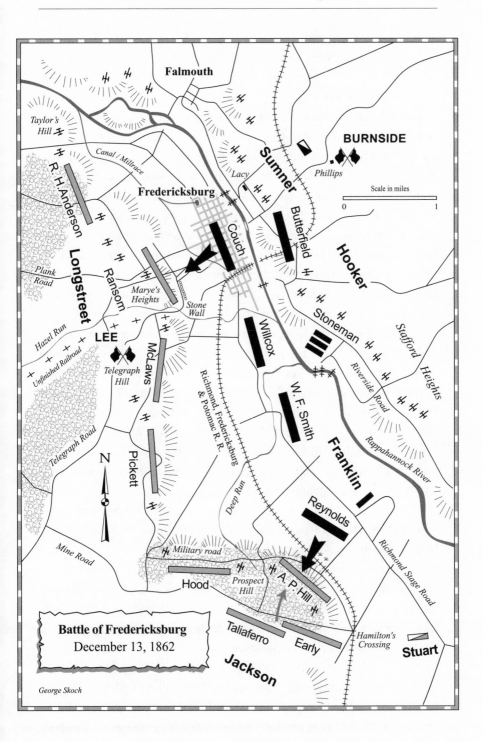

Battle of Fredericksburg
December 13, 1862

George Skoch

new uniform with rank marks, fine black felt hat, and a handsome
sword. We have never seen the like before, and gave him our congratu-
lations on his really fine appearance. Jackson said he 'believed it was
some of friend Stuart's doings.'"[68]

A Richmond tailor had made the uniform coat on instructions from
Stuart, who presented it to Jackson before his Pennsylvania raid. Theirs
was a friendship unique among the army's senior officers. "So dissimilar
in every respect," they shared deep religious convictions and an unquestioned devotion to the cause. "Jackson was more free and familiar with
Stuart than any other officer in the army," asserted Henry Kyd Douglas,
"and Stuart loved Jackson more than he did any living man." Harvey
Hill maintained, "Their meeting after a temporary absence was affectionate and brotherly in the extreme." Stuart particularly enjoyed riding
up to Jackson's headquarters and shouting in a "particularly shrill voice"
to his friend. Jackson called Stuart "my ideal of a cavalry leader."[69]

Lee, Longstreet, Jackson, and the entire Confederate army watched
and waited throughout the morning. Skirmishers plied their work, heralding what a Union officer later called "the saddest hour that the army
of the Potomac ever knew." Burnside planned an attack on Jackson's
front, followed directly by an assault on Longstreet's lines on Marye's
Heights. But Burnside's muddled instructions to William Franklin,
commander of the Left Grand Division, and the subordinate's inability
to decipher them delayed the advance for hours, an ominous precursor
for one of the war's greatest tragedies.[70]

At ten o'clock Major General George G. Meade's 4,500-man division of Pennsylvania Reserves aligned ranks for the attack on Prospect
Hill. Suddenly, at a distance of 400 yards, a solitary Confederate Napoleon cannon, under the command of Major John Pelham, opened fire on
the Pennsylvanians' flank. The initial round stunned the Federals and
brought a fierce response from Union guns with Meade and from Stafford Heights across the river. For an hour Pelham's gunners harassed the
Yankees. Lee watched the action from Prospect Hill and said, "It is glorious to see such courage in one so young." In his initial report he referred
to the twenty-four-year-old Alabamian as "the gallant Pelham."[71]

Meade's Pennsylvanians stepped forth at 1:00 P.M., after two hours
of concentrated Union artillery fire on Jackson's position on Prospect

Hill. "The under taking seemed like madness," thought a lieutenant with Meade, and a sergeant later noted in his diary, "This was a fearful moment." Across the tracks of the Richmond, Fredericksburg, and Potomac Railroad the Federals marched. Confederate cannon on the hill lashed their front, and Stuart rolled out a dozen guns, which tore into their left flank. Weeks earlier a Southerner had written insightfully to his wife, "The feeling of hatred on both sides is becoming intensified and the battles more fierce and desperate." Within minutes the fighting proved his description accurate.[72]

The Pennsylvanians struck the gap between the brigades of James Lane and James Archer, penetrating into the swampy woodland. Several Union regiments drove deeper into the woods, surprising Maxcy Gregg's South Carolinians. Mounted on horseback, Gregg was struck by a bullet in the back. His ranks broke and fled before the onslaught. Archer's men clung to their position against attacks from the front and flank. Two of Archer's regiments fled in disarray, threatening his entire line. The opposing ranks raked each other at close range.[73]

On the right of Meade's troops Brigadier General John Gibbon's division advanced toward Lane's North Carolinians, posted along the railroad tracks. The fighting was indeed "fierce and desperate." Lane's veterans resisted valiantly, but one final surge carried the Yankees across the tracks, driving the North Carolinians rearward. Coming through the trees, however, were the brigades of Jubal Early in a counterattack. On the march from the Valley Early had fallen into disfavor with Jackson over drunken soldiers and stragglers. When Jackson's chief of staff, Sandie Pendleton, sent by the corps commander, questioned Early about the stragglers, the irascible brigadier replied that Jackson had seen stragglers because he had trailed the division.[74]

On this day "Old Jube," as his men called him, acted on his own initiative. Jackson was with Harvey Hill's troops south of Prospect Hill when Early's men plunged into the beleaguered Union ranks. Lane and Archer rallied their regiments and joined the counterthrust. Meade's and Gibbon's Federals debouched from the woods, crossed the tracks, and rushed eastward. Colonel Edmund Atkinson's Georgia brigade pursued past the railroad tracks. Union gunners and infantry reserves decimated the Georgians, whose line appeared to be "melting away like ice under an August sun." The Georgians withdrew into the woods, and the combat subsided. Jackson considered a major counterattack, but thought better of it before the massed enemy batteries on Stafford Heights.[75]

Lee and Longstreet watched the fighting along Jackson's line from Telegraph Hill, also known as Lee's Hill. After Atkinson's Georgians retreated, Lee said to the First Corps commander, "It is well that war is so terrible or we would grow too fond of it." From across the river Union gunners targeted the hill and Marye's Heights to the north. A Confederate artillerist, posted near the generals, wrote a few days later that both men appeared unconcerned by the exploding shells. Lee wore a plain blue overcoat and a wide-brimmed, black felt hat. He was, thought the Rebel, "a fine magnificent looking man." The army commander spoke seldom and only to Longstreet in low tones.[76]

Even as the struggle for Prospect Hill raged, Union assaults against Marye's Heights had begun. It was these attacks that would be seared into the country's memory of Fredericksburg. Lieutenant Abner R. Small, adjutant of the 16th Maine, endeavored later to explain what he had witnessed at this most terrible of places: "I wondered then, and I wonder now equally, at the mystery of bravery. It seemed to me, as I saw men facing death at Fredericksburg, that they were heroes or cowards in spite of themselves."[77]

In succession, from midday on into the evening, six full Union divisions and part of another one, comprising eighteen brigades with eighty-five regiments, between 35,000 and 40,000 Northerners, crossed the plain toward the stone wall and the batteries on Marye's Heights. Behind the wall in the sunken road stood Brigadier General Thomas R. R. Cobb's Georgia regiments. A member of the brigade had a gamecock that had been trained to crow on command; each time the enemy advanced in a new attack, the rooster crowed, and a sheet of flame and musketry exploded along the wall. A Georgian claimed that he "never saw men more cool and more deliberate" than his comrades as they loaded and fired, loaded and fired.[78]

"Charge after charge was made," recounted a Confederate staff officer, "until it looked as if the Gods had made them and that their destruction might surely follow." After one assault Lee asked Longstreet whether his men could hold the line. "General," replied Longstreet, "if you put every man now on the other side of the Potomac in that field to approach me over the same line, and give me plenty of ammunition, I will kill them all before they reach my line."[79]

The words of the survivors of the Union attacks convey the fury that engulfed them before Marye's Heights. A Massachusetts soldier attested that when the enemy cannon fire and musketry hit their line it began "moving *sideways*, as though breasting a 'blizzard' or wind and hail-storm in bluff old New England." A colonel described the plain before the stone wall as "the gates of hell." The Southern fire was so unending and withering that the Federal dead "seemed to be kept constantly in motion from the kick of the rebel bullets striking them." A corporal exclaimed, "Flesh and blood could not face the decimating fire and leave a live man to tell the story, and the line grew thinner and thinner until it practically melted away altogether."[80]

When it ended, thousands of Yankees, the wounded and the unscathed, lay on the long slope before the stone wall. The killed, wounded, and missing exceeded 7,000. Burnside planned on renewing the attacks until his senior generals convinced him of their futility. The troops remained on the plain beneath Marye's Heights for the next two days, with little food and water and under sporadic fire. An informal truce allowed them to attend to the wounded. On the night of December 14–15 the aurora borealis streaked the heavens, which the Confederates believed was an omen, a celestial affirmation of their victory. On the next night, with the darkness serving as a pall, the Army of the Potomac recrossed the Rappahannock River. When Burnside passed a Pennsylvania regiment, no one spoke. "They had no bad words to offer him," stated an officer, "nothing but pity."[81]

The Union army's "saddest hour" cost the Federals 1,284 killed or mortally wounded, 9,600 wounded, and 1,769 captured or missing, for a total of 12,653. Confederate casualties amounted to 595 killed or mortally wounded, 4,061 wounded, and 653 captured or missing, or 5,309 in total. In Lee's army Powell Hill's Light Division sustained nearly 45 percent of the losses in its defense of Prospect Hill.[82]

Among the Confederate fallen were brigadiers Thomas Cobb and Maxcy Gregg. During one of the attacks on his Georgians behind the stone wall, a piece of shell struck Cobb in the thigh, severing his femoral artery. He lived for two hours, dying at 4:00 P.M. on December 13. Cobb had returned from leave after Antietam, was promoted to brigadier, and assumed command of his brother Howell's brigade. The Georgian was a rarity in the army, caring little personally for Lee, whom he described as "haughty and boorish and supercilious in his bearing and is particularly so to me."[83]

Maxcy Gregg lingered in agony and unconsciousness until the morning of December 15, when he died at five o'clock. When he fell wounded, he was taken to Belvoir, the home of the Thomas Yerby family. Jackson and Powell Hill visited Gregg, who lay on a couch in a dimly lit room. The two generals probably thought of the stalwart defense of the army's left flank at Second Manassas by Gregg and his South Carolinians. Hill bent down and kissed his friend's forehead before departing. One of Gregg's men said of him, "He never apprehended failure, he never dreamed of fear." In a letter to the governor of South Carolina, Lee called his death "a costly sacrifice," noting, "He has always been at the post of duty and of danger."[84]

The Union retreat across the Rappahannock disappointed Lee, who had expected a renewal of Union assaults on December 14. Before the Yankees fled he could have counterattacked. Why he did not, he explained in his report: "The attack on the 13th had been so easily repulsed, and by so small a part of our army, that it was not supposed the enemy would limit his efforts to an attempt, which, in view of the magnitude of his preparations and the extent of his force, seemed to be comparatively insignificant. Believing, therefore, that he would attack us, it was not deemed expedient to lose the advantages of our position and expose the troops to the fire of his inaccessible batteries beyond the river, by advancing against him."[85]

Instead Burnside's army escaped further damage, and Lee's frustration with the narrow extent of the victory was evident. When Colonel Bryan Grimes of the 4th North Carolina confirmed the enemy withdrawal to Lee and Jackson on the morning of December 16, both generals reacted, in Grimes's retelling, with "a look of deep chagrin and mortification, very apparent to the observer, on the countenance of each, though nothing of the sort was expressed in words." Later that day Lee confided in a letter to his wife, Mary, that the Federals "suffered heavily as far as the battle went, but it did not go far enough to satisfy me."[86]

Lee addressed the military significance of the battle months later, in July 1863, after the Gettysburg campaign. He said to Major John Seddon, brother of the Confederate secretary of war, "At Fredericksburg we gained a battle, inflicting very serious loss on the enemy in men and material; our people were greatly elated—I was much depressed." His army "had really accomplished nothing" in the engagement. "We had not gained a foot of ground, and I knew the enemy could easily replace the men he had lost; and the loss of material was, if any thing, rather beneficial to him, as it gave an opportunity to contractors to make money."[87]

Lee's dim assessment of Fredericksburg's impact contrasted with the reaction in the North and in the South. Northerners fumed with anger after learning the details of the defeat and reading the casualty lists. A New York City diarist recorded, "The general indignation is fast growing revolutionary." In Washington Republican senators demanded the resignations of Cabinet members. At Falmouth a clique of generals conspired for the removal of Burnside. Abraham Lincoln confessed to a friend, "If there is a worse place than Hell, I am in it." Conversely, Southern newspapers and individuals hailed the victory, believing peace and independence loomed nearer. A typical reaction came from John B. Jones, a Confederate War Department clerk, who wrote in his diary, "Many people regard the disaster of Burnside as the harbinger of peace." A woman diarist exclaimed: "Months do not pass speedily enough for I feel it is that much nearer peace. War's alarm is that much nearer being calmed."[88]

Lee, however, saw the reality before them and the sacrifices that awaited before independence could be attained. In his December 31 congratulatory order to the army, he stated: "The war is not yet ended. The enemy is still numerous and strong, and the country demands of the army a renewal of its heroic efforts in her behalf." Ten days later, in a letter to Secretary of War Seddon, Lee appealed for more men and then wrote, "The country has yet to learn how often advantages, secured at the expense of many valuable lives, have failed to produce their legitimate results by reason of our inability to prosecute them against the reinforcements which the superior numbers of the enemy enable him to interpose between the defeat of an army and its ruin."[89]

Yet Lee did not dismiss his army's accomplishments at Fredericksburg. In his report he praised the troops for their "spirit and courage" and for "the calmness and steadiness with which orders were obeyed and maneuvers executed in the midst of battle." He cited Longstreet, Jackson, and Stuart and praised division and brigade commanders without naming individual officers. Undoubtedly Lafayette McLaws and Jubal Early enhanced their reputations as division commanders. Porter Alexander demonstrated his outstanding skills as an artillerist, and brigade commanders William Barksdale and Joseph Kershaw, who led his regiments and Thomas Cobb's Georgians after Cobb's wounding, performed with distinction.[90]

To be sure, there was little to be criticized in the army's conduct in the battle. Lee, Jackson, and Powell Hill shared the blame for misreading the danger of the gap in Hill's line. A month before the battle Hill wrote a "private" letter to Jeb Stuart, "The Almighty will get tired of helping Jackson after a while, and then he'll get the damndest thrashing—and the shoe pinches, for I shall get my share and probably all the blame, for the people will never blame Stonewall for any disaster." William Franklin's refusal to commit more troops to the attack on Prospect Hill, the stubborn defense of James Archer's and James Lane's troops, and Early's counterattack prevented a possible disaster and spared Jackson and Hill from blame at the time.[91]

Interestingly, Longstreet maintained after the war that he should have brought charges against John Hood for disobedience of orders. Before daylight on December 13, Longstreet rode to Hood, whose division was posted on Jackson's left flank near Deep Run. The corps commander directed that if Jackson's lines were broken, Hood should wheel to the right and counterattack. George Pickett's brigades, lying on Hood's left, would join him in the assault, said Longstreet, who conveyed the orders to Pickett. When the opportunity arose during the action, however, Hood did not act, although Pickett rode to him and suggested a charge. Longstreet stated later that he omitted any reference to this in his report for "it would make official trouble" as Hood was an officer "in high favor with the authorities."[92]

Within the army the victory reaffirmed once again the men's fighting prowess. Porter Alexander called it "the easiest battle of the war." Days after the battle an officer in the 33rd Virginia asserted, "I never saw men in more glorious fighting condition." A Georgian declared: "I feel confident that we can whip any army that they can put in the field, under any leader that they can produce. I consider the Confederate army commanded by Lee, Jackson and Longstreet invincible." The morale in the artillery was described as "superb."[93]

A newspaper correspondent with the army proclaimed: "It were but uttering the simple truth to say, that a better army was never seen than that which Gen. Lee now commands. . . . It is a grand army." Writing to Longstreet after the conflict, Robert Toombs averred, "I had served with the army nearly a year, had an extensive general acquaintance with its general field & company officers and I [do] not believe a finer army or one in better fighting condition ever faced an enemy."[94]

Far beyond the army's camps, across the breadth of the Confederacy, civilians shared with the soldiers the belief in the army's stature as a combat force. After seven months Lee and the rank and file stood preeminent as "a highly visible symbol of Confederate nationalism." Elsewhere across the land, Southern arms had suffered defeats, from Braxton Bragg's Army of Tennessee's failure in its campaign into Kentucky during the autumn to its defeat at year's end at Stone's River or Murfreesboro, Tennessee. Only on the Mississippi River was there success, when the defenders of Vicksburg repulsed a recent Union offensive. But it had been Lee's audacity and his officers' and men's fighting spirit and skill that had seized control of the war in Virginia. With them rested the aspirations of a nation.[95]

With his deep faith in an omnipresent God, Lee attributed the army's success to the workings of the Lord. He wrote to his wife on Christmas: "He has vouchsafed us during the past year. What should have become of us without His crowning help & protection? I have seen His hand in all events of the war. . . . For in Him alone I know is our trust & safety."[96]

Chapter Seven

"The Boldest and Most Daring Strategy of the Whole War"

T HE WINTER CAMPS of the Army of Northern Virginia and the Army of the Potomac sprawled across a blighted land on both sides of the Rappahannock River above and below Fredericksburg, Virginia. Here they would remain for four months, from the aftermath of the battle at Fredericksburg until the warmth of spring dried the roads. The war had brought them here; the war kept them here—Americans divided by something far wider and deeper than the river that flowed between their camps.

With the advent of cold weather, the mood in each army contrasted starkly. The past seven months of campaigning, culminating in the Confederate victory at Fredericksburg, had reversed the conflict's fortunes in Virginia. While men in both armies yearned for peace, Southerners were almost cocksure of the outcome. "Our army is in No 1 condition the men being willing to fight to the last," wrote a Virginian in January 1863. Brigadier General Frank Paxton stated in a letter: "So far as we are concerned here, I feel, perhaps, too confident. We have whipped the army in front of us very often, and I feel sure that we can do it any time." Capt. John Welsh of the 27th Virginia, in Paxton's

Stonewall Brigade, declared, "I never was in better spirits since the war comenced."[1]

President Abraham Lincoln's issuance of the Emancipation Proclamation on January 1, with its provision for the enlistment of African Americans into Union armies, hardened Confederate resolve. Speaking for many officers and men, Captain Welsh asserted to his wife and mother, "I hope how soon we may get out of this dreadful war and all get home with our families again in peace but unless we can maintain our independence peace will do us no good for after Lincoln procklimation any man that wouldent fight to the last ought to be hung as high as haman."[2]

Across the Rappahannock a darkness, deepened by anger and bitterness, stalked the Union army. "One thing is sure," insisted a New York private, "and I would stake my life on it, and that is that another such disaster such as Fredericksburg, and the Army of the Potomac will not fight any more." Since the defeat thousands had deserted. A lieutenant confessed to his wife: "This thing is played out. The whole army is disheartened and want peace on some terms." Despite a deep racial prejudice against blacks, many, if not most, in the army accepted Lincoln's proclamation as a practical act that would weaken the South. But, as a captain put it, the proclamation "precludes the possibility of any settlement except by absolute subjugation, and even that carried to the last extremity." A sergeant expressed a common view. "The south never will give up they are hard boys they fite well."[3]

Morale plummeted even lower in the Federal ranks when army commander Ambrose Burnside undertook an offensive before the end of January. The Yankees marched on January 20, moving upriver to turn the Confederate flank. That night a winter storm blew in, lashing the countryside with downpours. Conditions worsened during the next two days as the army floundered in mud. Finally, Burnside canceled the movement, ending the infamous "Mud March." A New Jersey lieutenant spoke for many: "The Army of the Potomac is no more an army. Its patriotism has oozed out through the pores opened by the imbecility of its leaders, and the fatigues and disappointments of a fruitless winter campaign."[4]

In desperation Burnside ordered several generals, including Joseph

Hooker, dismissed from the service for conspiring against him. The order required Lincoln's approval. When Burnside met with the president, the general demanded that Lincoln either endorse the order or accept his resignation. Lincoln waited a day and then accepted Burnside's resignation and appointed Hooker to command of the army. He did so, Lincoln explained, because of "the unfortunate state of existing circumstances" within the army. A devoted soldier, Burnside relinquished command to Hooker on January 26. Refusing to accept Burnside's resignation of his commission, the president granted the disgraced general a thirty-day leave of absence.[5]

As gifted an organizer as George McClellan, Hooker achieved a remarkable transformation of morale within the army. He disbanded the Grand Division organization and formed the army's mounted units into a long overdue cavalry corps, which had a lasting and important effect. He stanched the flow of deserters, required the issuance of regular provisions of vegetables, built bakeries for providing soft bread, systematized the medical department, and saw to the distribution of four months' back pay. Finally, in an effort to reduce straggling on the march and shirking during a battle, he created distinctive badges for each infantry corps. In time the officers and men took pride in their badges, which gave them a unit identity.[6]

After the "Mud March" and Hooker's appointment, the two armies settled into a period of relative quiet, which extended well into April. A Georgian described life in winter quarters as "very dull," the routine broken only by drills and picket duty along the Rappahannock. Informal truces governed duty on the river banks, and while on picket soldiers in both armies traded goods, mainly southern tobacco for northern coffee. In the Confederate camps the men grumbled about the scarcity of furloughs, the twice-daily ration of biscuits and beef, and the extortionist prices demanded by local civilians for wood and food. Diversions in camp were few, but the troops enjoyed snowball battles, often led by officers and marked by attacks and counterattacks.[7]

As he had after the Seven Days and Maryland campaigns, Robert E. Lee implemented command and organizational changes. The first command decision occurred within weeks of the battle at Fredericksburg, when, on January 1, 1863, Daniel Harvey Hill tendered his resignation, citing health problems. Lee expressed regret at losing "so good & faithful an officer," but there was something about Hill that irritated him. James Longstreet said of his academy classmate and friend, "There was never a more plucky or persistent fighter . . . but he could not resist the temptation when it came to criticise." In fact Hill had put his criticisms in writing in his official campaign reports. He admitted to his wife, "I am so unlike other folks that you could not understand my feelings if I tried to explain them for a week."[8]

In a postwar letter to Longstreet, Hill wrote, "My impression of Genl Lee is not so enthusiastic as that of most men who served under him." But despite suffering constantly from "the most excruciating" pain from his spinal injury and battling mental depression, Hill had rendered Lee and the army outstanding service as a division commander. As Longstreet noted, he had fought from sunrise to sunset at Antietam. His absolute fearlessness, combative spirit, and tactical skill on a battlefield would be missed. At Lee's suggestion the War Department reassigned Hill to command in North Carolina.[9]

Lee replaced Hill with Brigadier General Robert E. Rodes. The officers and men in Hill's division preferred the thirty-two-year-old VMI graduate. Rodes had been an excellent brigade commander under Hill and deserved the appointment. Porter Alexander described the native Virginian as "one of the finest looking & most excellent officers of the army." An Alabamian who served in his brigade stated, "We fear him; but at the same time we respect and love him." In the judgment of the historian Robert K. Krick, Rodes developed into "the very best" division commander in the army.[10]

Lee secured the promotions of other deserving officers. Jubal Early and Isaac Trimble, who was still recovering from his wound, received their overdue major generalcy. Proven colonels Robert F. Hoke, Henry L. Benning, William T. Wofford, and Samuel McGowan were promoted to brigadier general and assigned to brigade command. The capable Robert Ransom and his division left the army for assignment to North Carolina. Within the army some units underwent reorganization with the transfer of regiments. Colonel Isaac Avery of the 6th North Carolina wrote an interesting statement when he learned of his regiment's transfer from John Hood's division to Jubal Early's. "I must say," declared Avery, "I do not care to join 'old Jack's foot cavalry.' . . . General Early may be a very good man, but I would not give Hood for any of them. And beside I think that we all fare much better in Longstreets than in Old Stonewalls Corps."[11]

For some time Lee believed that attaching artillery batteries to infantry brigades and grouping them in divisions had weakened the artillery's efficiency and effectiveness in battle. He instructed Chief of Artillery William Pendleton to formulate a plan of reorganization. Pendleton submitted his initial proposal on February 11, advocating the creation of battalions assigned to each infantry corps. Lee endorsed the plan and forwarded it to Jefferson Davis, with recommendations for promotions of officers. "No class of officers in the army has learned faster or served better than the artillery," he wrote.[12]

Army headquarters announced the official reorganization in special orders on April 16. Each infantry corps had assigned to it four battalions and two reserve battalions, First Corps receiving twenty-six batteries; Second Corps twenty-seven. Two battalions of six batteries formed a general reserve for the army. A corps chief of artillery was appointed, but Longstreet and Jackson retained tactical authority over the battalions. The fourteen battalions contained 264 cannon, with an additional twenty guns in the cavalry's horse artillery.[13]

During the winter months the heaviest burden of command on Lee centered on the chronic scarcity of supplies. He and his staff worked constantly at alleviating the shortages of food for the troops and of forage for the animals. Before the end of January the army commander had confided to President Davis that the want of supplies "causes me the greatest uneasiness," adding that the efficiency of the army could be reduced by the loss of thousands of men. Days later Lee informed Secretary of War James Seddon that his command had only a week's supply of food. "The question of provisioning the army is becoming one of greater difficulty every day," he warned.[14]

The situation became more dire with each successive week. Lee sought supplies from the Shenandoah Valley and southwestern Virginia, but the inefficiency of the railroad system and the bureaucratic incompetence of the Confederate commissary department crippled efforts to meet the demands. On March 27 he informed the administration that the men were on "reduced rations" and added: "I fear they will be unable to endure the hardships of the approaching campaign. Symptoms of scurvy are appearing among them." A month later, with active operations close at hand, he reported that the troops were subsisting on a quarter-pound of meat and sixteen ounces of flour daily, while ten men shared a pound of rice for up to three weeks.[15]

The letters of officers and men conveyed the severity of the hardships. Rejoining his regiment, a Virginia cavalryman related, "I found things in a bad state, men very little to eat & horses starving" and "great dissatisfaction in camp." Regimental officers declared their cavalry units unfit for duty because of the wretched condition of the troopers' mounts. Lee dispersed artillery batteries in attempts to obtain grain for the horses. Forage details searched the countryside for food, but the men ate most of what they had secured before returning to camp. "I find in the army," confessed a Georgian, "that it's root hog or die, and consequently I take care of myself, seldom studying the interests of others."[16]

Camp discipline deteriorated, and desertions increased. Likely accurately, one soldier blamed the breakdown of discipline on incompetent or uncaring company officers. When deserters were apprehended, the "penalties have in some cases been severe," attested a member of the Stonewall Brigade. "The whipping post and hard labor under confinement, and confiscations of wages in others." Shortages of shoes and blankets persisted. As late as mid-April Lee told Davis, "At present we are very much scattered, and I am unable to bring the army together for want of proper subsistence and forage."[17]

A major detachment from the army had transpired in mid-February, when Lee dispatched Longstreet and the divisions of John Hood and George Pickett to Petersburg, twenty miles south of Richmond. Lee sent them as a counter to Union activity in North Carolina. The commanding general and authorities in the capital suspected that the Federal advances were directed toward the vital seaport of Wilmington and the railroad, which connected the Carolinas to Virginia. Longstreet assumed temporary command of 51,000 troops in the Department of Virginia and North Carolina. Begun as a strategic movement, Longstreet's operations evolved into a major supply-gathering mission.[18]

Longstreet directed military operations initially against the Union garrisons at New Bern and Washington, North Carolina. Harvey Hill, who had returned to the state weeks earlier, led the Confederate forces, but both attempts failed before the Federal defenses. But on March 19 Lee wrote to Longstreet that he should "turn all the energies of your department" to "obtaining all the supplies possible of forage and subsistence."[19]

From the beginning of his assignment, Longstreet had wrestled with the duty of acting against the enemy and of keeping Hood's and Pickett's troops readily available for a return to Fredericksburg, if Hooker's army advanced against Lee's lines. When he received Lee's letter, Longstreet answered that he could secure the supplies, "but if the two divisions are to be held in readiness to join you, or even one of them, I can do nothing." After more correspondence passed between the two generals, Lee approved Longstreet's proposal of a movement against the Union garrison at Suffolk, Virginia, west of Norfolk, which would bottle up the Yankees and open up the supply-rich counties along the Virginia–North Carolina border.[20]

The siege of Suffolk lasted from mid-April to month's end. Longstreet refused to assail the defenses, which consisted of eight forts, 17,000 defenders, and gunboats in the Nansemond River. While Hood's and Pickett's men skirmished with the Federals and opposing batteries exchanged periodic fire, commissary trains rolled throughout the region, collecting foodstuffs and grain. "I understand," wrote a Confederate soldier, "we are securing immense supplies from the surrounding country." Citizens gave what they could, and the details amassed tens of thousands of bushels of corn and an estimated million pounds of bacon, enough to feed Lee's men and animals for a least two months.[21]

Longstreet's supply-gathering mission ended on April 29, upon the receipt of a telegram from the War Department, which ordered him and his two divisions to return to Lee's army. On that day the Union Army of the Potomac had crossed the Rappahannock River, upstream from Fredericksburg, in an offensive movement against the Confederates. Weeks of rainy weather had given way to sunny, warm spring days, which dried the roads and brought the long-delayed advance of Hooker's 135,000-man army. Against this formidable force, Lee had barely more than 56,000 officers and men in his ranks.[22]

Prior to the Union army's march, activity along the Rappahannock had been characterized by cavalry raids across the river and mounted clashes. Despite the condition of Confederate horses, Jeb Stuart had been aggressive, keeping scouts in the enemy rear and sending detachments against Federal outposts. On February 25 Fitz Lee and 400 troopers routed Union cavalry at Hartwood Church. When Joseph Hooker learned of the affair, he told his cavalry commander, Major General George Stoneman, "You have got to stop these disgraceful cavalry 'surprises.'"[23]

The major cavalry engagement of the winter occurred at Kelly's Ford, near Culpeper Court House, on March 17. Brigadier General William Averell and 2,100 Union horsemen crossed the Rappahannock at the ford and were met by Fitz Lee and 800 Virginians. Dismounted skirmishing and mounted charges and countercharges marked the fighting. A final attack by Averell's troopers broke Lee's ranks, but Confederate horse artillery stopped the pursuit. Averell withdrew across the river. Casualties on both sides amounted to slightly more than 200. The aggressiveness of the Federal cavalry foretold a new spirit and leadership of the command.[24]

Jeb Stuart and Major John Pelham were in Culpeper Court House on court-martial duty. When the fighting began, they rode to the scene, but Stuart let Fitz Lee direct the action. Pelham joined in an attack and was struck in the head by a piece of shell. Carried into town, the dashing and brilliant artillerist died hours later at the home of a local judge. Stuart's affection for Pelham was that of a brother. When he saw the body, Stuart, with tears in his eyes, bent down, kissed the slain major's head, cut off a lock of hair, and whispered, "Farewell." The next day Stuart wrote his wife, "You must know how his death distressed me." Jennings Cropper Wise, a historian of Lee's artillery, concluded that Pelham's skill in the "management" of horse artillery "amounted to genius." As Stuart asserted, "His loss to the country is irreparable."[25]

At the time of Kelly's Ford or thereabout, Robert E. Lee became seriously ill. Although staff officer Charles Marshall claimed after the war that Lee developed pneumonia, the evidence indicates heart problems, specifically angina pectoris, the inflammation of the membrane around the heart. For days Lee remained bedfast in a farmhouse. Dorsey

Pender told his wife in a letter on April 1: "Gen. Lee has been quite sick but is better. I do not know what we should do if he were taken from us." A week later Lee himself wrote, "My head is ringing with quinine, and I am otherwise [feeling] so poorly I do not seem able to think." As late as October Lee stated that he had "never recovered" from the episode. Undoubtedly the effects of the illness lingered when the Union army began its movement during the final week of April.[26]

Lee had anticipated a forward movement by the Yankees for some time. For weeks northern newspapers had been urging an offensive by "Fighting Joe" Hooker, as the Union commander was nicknamed. Lee's "anxiety" at a Union advance, as he told Davis in mid-April, "arises from the present immobility of the army, owing to the condition of our horses and the scarcity of forage and provisions." Nevertheless if the enemy did not take the initiative, Lee noted, "I think it all-important that we should assume the aggressive by the 1st of May." He broached the idea of moving with the army into the Shenandoah Valley and again crossing the Potomac into Maryland.[27]

But before Lee could assume the offensive, Hooker acted, seizing the strategic initiative. If he had waited, Hooker faced the loss of upward of fifty nine-month and two-year regiments, whose terms of enlistment were to expire in the spring. Their ranks consisted of about 37,000 troops, or roughly one-third of the army's infantrymen. Most important, however, the army's Bureau of Military Intelligence, which Hooker had created, placed Lee's strength at 54,600, a figure just 1,600 less than the actual figure, and had reported that few Confederates guarded the Rappahannock and Rapidan fords beyond the Rebel left flank. Hooker fashioned a broad turning movement, comparable to Lee's strike around John Pope's army in the Second Manassas Campaign.[28]

Hooker committed 43,000 officers and men of the Fifth, Eleventh, and Twelfth corps to the flanking movement, starting them toward the river crossings on April 27. While they marched the First and Sixth corps prepared for a pontoon crossing of the Rappahannock below Fredericksburg and against the center of Lee's lines. Hooker held the Second and Third corps in reserve as reinforcements for either of the two forces. Finally, George Stoneman and six brigades of cavalry rode south in a raid against Lee's railroad connections to Richmond. Hooker reasoned that his opponent would either stand and fight or abandon his works and retreat. In his memoirs Porter Alexander declared of Hooker's offensive, "On the whole I think this plan was decidedly the best strategy conceived in any of the campaigns ever set on foot against us."[29]

The Union offensive proceeded in its early phases as Hooker planned. At Fredericksburg the two corps, under Major General John Sedgwick, secured a lodgment on the west bank south of the town. The flanking column crossed the Rappahannock and Rapidan rivers, encountering only slight opposition, and by midafternoon on April 30 reached Chancellorsville; there a large brick house stood in a seventy-acre clearing, set in a vast swath of trees and underbrush known locally as the Wilderness. Under orders from Hooker, the Federals halted. Fifth Corps commander George Meade urged a further advance east out of the dense, confining forest into open ground, but the senior officer, Major General Henry Slocum, rejected the proposal.[30]

Hooker and his staff rode into Chancellorsville that evening. The commanding general was exuberant at the initial success and prospects, exclaiming, "God Almighty could not prevent me from winning a victory tomorrow." He issued a congratulatory order to the army. The soldiers shared Hooker's optimism, and "the general hilarity in the camps was particularly noticeable," according to an officer. Provost Marshal Marsena Patrick, however, wrote of the Confederates in his diary, "We cannot understand *how* they are so blinded and that is all that makes us afraid some deep plan is laid for us."[31]

Confederate cavalrymen had detected the enemy's march upriver beyond the Southern left flank on April 28. Weeks earlier Jeb Stuart had predicted to an aide, "If there is a spring campaign it will last through the year, and if so, it will go on to the end of Lincoln's time." As the Yankees crossed the river, Stuart kept army headquarters apprised of the Union advance. On April 29 Lee informed Davis, "Their [the enemy's] intention, I presume, is to turn our left, and probably get into our rear." When the Federals arrived at Chancellorsville, Lee ordered Lafayette McLaws's division, without the brigade of William Barksdale, west to join Richard Anderson's division, which was posted at Zoan Church on Orange Turnpike, three miles east of Chancellorsville.[32]

Before McLaws marched, he and Lee had "a long conversation."

According to McLaws, the commanding general "was very confident of his ability to beat back the enemy should our troops behave as well as they have usually done." Lee then added, "General McLaws, let them know that it is a stern reality now, it must be, Victory or Death, for defeat would be ruinous."[33]

Lee clearly understood the gravity of the situation. By a bold movement, his opponent threatened both flanks of Lee's army. Outnumbered better than two-to-one, Lee faced daunting choices: he could either retreat, abandoning ground that he had defended for six months, or split his army, leaving a smaller force at Fredericksburg and confronting the enemy units at Chancellorsville. As he indicated to McLaws, he understood also that the outcome rested with his officers and men, who had passed through a winter of hardship.[34]

Lee's belief in them could not have been otherwise. Despite the past months' privations they possessed a resiliency and a hard-earned confidence in themselves and their leaders. An officer averred during the difficult weeks, "I think that this war had demonstrated that one Division of Confederates is equal to a corps of Yankees, anywhere, on any field, and at anytime." Brigadier General Stephen Dodson Ramseur exclaimed in a letter, "We all feel confident of victory!" Ramseur hoped that Hooker attacked, for he was "willing to leave *all* to Gen'l Lee." A Georgian with McLaws, writing to his wife before they marched toward the Federals, asked, "Do not grieve for me, even if I shall fall, but remember me as one dieing to save his country." With them, Lee chose.[35]

Lee had a recurrence of chest pains on the morning of April 30, but when Stonewall Jackson came to army headquarters later, he and Lee discussed their options. Jackson advocated an attack on the Union force below Fredericksburg and Lee agreed reluctantly, if it could be done. After Jackson spent the afternoon examining the ground and the enemy position, however, he returned to Lee and admitted, "It would be inexpedient to attack here." So instead Lee ordered Jackson and three of his divisions to follow McLaws the next morning, combine with Anderson, and engage the Yankees at Chancellorsville. Jubal Early's division and Barksdale's brigade, 12,400 officers and men, would defend Marye's Heights against Sedgwick's troops. Jackson would confront at least three Union corps with fewer than 44,000 officers and men.[36]

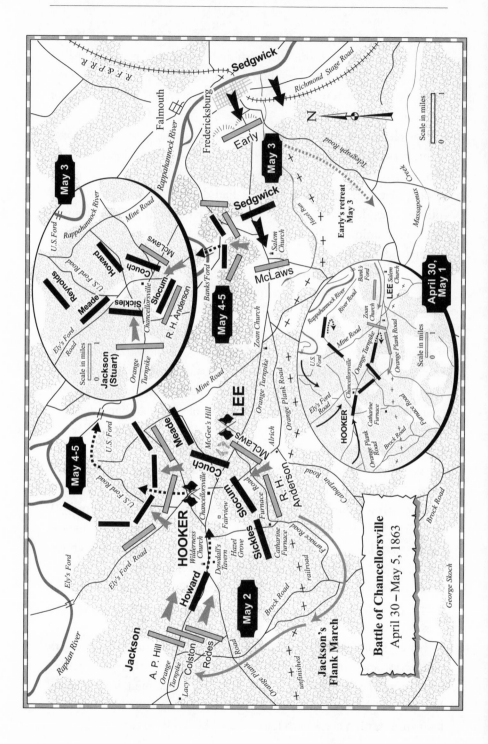

Battle of Chancellorsville
April 30 – May 5, 1863

Jackson's
Flank March

George Skoch

Lee confronted Hooker's boldness with his own, but at far graver risk. He explained his decision in his report: "It was now apparent that the main attack would be made upon our flank and rear. It was, there-fore, determined to leave sufficient troops to hold our lines, and with the main body of the army to give battle to the approaching army."[37]

On May 1 the Southerners marched up Orange Turnpike. Ahead of them, advancing in three columns on separate roads, came the Yan-kees. The collision occurred east of Zoan Church before noon between a division of the Fifth Corps and McLaws's Rebels. The fierce strug-gle stalled the Northerners' movement. To the south of Orange Plank Road members of the Twelfth Corps encountered Anderson's veterans. At Chancellorsville, meanwhile, Hooker received a series of reports of an "apparently large force" of enemy infantry and artillery on the march toward Chancellorsville. Hooker concluded correctly that it had to be Stonewall Jackson's troops. At about 2:00 P.M., the Union commander ordered a withdrawal of the columns into the Wilderness.[38]

Jackson had ridden ahead of his men and watched the action. His friend Jeb Stuart joined him. Stuart's cavalrymen covered the infantry's flanks, reconnoitering and sending back reports. Captain William W. Blackford, an engineer officer on the cavalry general's staff, wrote later: "He [Jackson] and Stuart were the only two men I ever knew whom I thought unconscious of the feeling of fear. There were many as brave, but these two never seemed to feel that danger existed."[39]

At some point Lee arrived at the front and met Jackson, who described the situation. Lee offered no advice, leaving the conduct of the action to his trusted subordinate. The commanding general rode away on a reconnaissance to the right, searching for a possible route beyond the Union left flank that would isolate Hooker from his base across the Rappahannock. Accompanied by Confederate cavalry, Lee found, in his words, "no fit place to attack" in the densely wooded ter-rain. He headed back toward Jackson and the infantry.[40]

When the Yankees retreated, Jackson pressed the pursuit on Orange Turnpike and Plank Road. The Federals resisted in a rearguard action, but the Rebels gained a ridgeline, known as McGee's Hill, slightly more than a mile east of the Chancellorsville clearing. When George Meade saw the enemy on the hill, he allegedly growled, "My God, if we can't hold the top of the hill, we certainly cannot hold the bottom of it." On Jackson's left, on Plank Road, Ambrose Wright's brigade of Georgians reached Catherine Furnace, a mile and a half to the south and rear of Chancellorsville. Stuart, the 1st Virginia Cavalry, and a battery of horse artillery met the infantrymen. Stuart reported that the enemy lay a mile to the north on an open plateau. Wright pushed forward skirmishers into the woods. Stuart brought forward four cannon in support of the Georgians.[41]

The thick woods restricted the Confederates to firing a single gun at a time, but their fire drew counterfire from ten Federal artillery pieces. During the fighting Jackson arrived, and he, Stuart, and some aides walked to the crest of a knoll to survey the enemy lines. When Union shells exploded near the group, Stuart shouted, "General Jackson, we must move from here." As they descended the rise a piece of a shell struck Major R. Channing Price, Stuart's cousin and an adjutant general. Price dismissed the wound as slight, but the shard had severed an artery behind his knee. The twenty-year-old chief of staff died hours later from the loss of blood.[42]

At Chancellorsville Joseph Hooker assured Major General Darius Couch, commander of the Second Corps, "It is all right, Couch, I have got Lee just where I want him; he must fight me on my own ground." Although Hooker's decision to pull back into the Wilderness had merit at the time, he committed his army to an awful battleground. He admitted afterward that when he entered the region on April 30 he "was not prepared to find it an almost impenetrable thicket. It was impossible to maneuver." With the arrival of Couch's corps and the Third Corps, the Union commander had approximately 78,000 infantry and artillery in the Wilderness, with 14,800 officers and men of the First Corps ordered to Chancellorsville. Intelligence reports confirmed that he possessed numerical superiority on the ground.[43]

By his decision to make a defensive stand within the Wilderness and its impenetrable thickets, however, Hooker compromised his manpower advantage, negated his artillery superiority by confining the powerful arm to open spaces, and limited the army's range of sight. With most of the cavalry on the raid with Stoneman, he lacked horsemen for guarding the flanks and detecting enemy movements. Conversely, Stuart's troopers screened the few roads and commanded the edges of the armies. Perhaps most critically Hooker's aggressive opponent held the tactical initiative, controlling the shape of the forthcoming engagement.[44]

By now Lee had entered the Wilderness, establishing temporary headquarters in a stand of pines at the intersection of Orange Plank Road and Furnace Road. There Jackson found the commanding general after dark. Lee asked him if he had located favorable ground for an attack. No, answered Jackson, who said that he believed Hooker would retreat. Lee doubted it. Stuart then arrived with information gathered by Fitz Lee's cavalrymen, that the Union right flank, extending along Orange Turnpike, was unsecured by any dominant terrain and vulnerable to an attack. The army commander asked if a road network existed for a march beyond the enemy flank in a broad turning movement. Stuart did not know but would find out.[45]

When Stuart departed, Lee said to Jackson, "We must attack on our left as soon as practicable." The two generals bedded down for a few hours of sleep before dawn. In a postwar letter Lee wrote to Jackson's widow: "I am misrepresented at the battle of Chancellorsville in proposing an attack in front, the first evening of our arrival. On the contrary I decided against it." In a letter to a former Confederate he affirmed, "There is no question as to who was responsible for the operations of the Confederates, or to whom any failure would have been charged."[46]

That night, after watching Lee and Jackson confer, a member of Lee's staff spoke to Captain Justus Scheibert, an engineer officer in the Prussian army who was with the Confederates as an observer. The aide predicted: "There are going to be great events, and many a mother's son will embrace the grass! When those two men get together, history becomes pregnant and bears bloody for us and hell for the Yankees!"[47]

Jackson's mapmaker, Jedediah Hotchkiss, went to Lee's headquarters at about daylight on May 2. He had spoken earlier with Jeb Stuart and a local citizen, learning from them that a route led to the enemy's right flank and rear along Orange Turnpike. He traced the roads on a map for Lee and Jackson, who were seated on discarded "Yankee Cracker boxes."[48]

The two generals examined the map, and then Lee asked, "General

Jackson, what do you propose to do?" Pointing to the route marked by Hotchkiss, Jackson answered, "Go around here."

"What do you propose to make this movement with?" inquired the commanding general.

"With my whole corps," Jackson replied—three divisions and artillery, 28,000 officers and men.

Jackson's words surprised Lee. "What will you leave me?"

"The divisions of Anderson and McLaws," the subordinate responded.

That left Lee with barely 16,000 troops to demonstrate against the Union center. He hesitated, but then said, "Well, go on." He wanted Stuart's cavalry to lead the march and to rim the column's flank.[49]

With the words "Well, go on," Lee committed the army to one of the war's most daring gambles. He had divided its ranks once against a numerically superior foe; now he did it a second time. The Wilderness offered concealment, but if the Federals discovered Jackson's march and understood its implications, they could assail Anderson's and McLaws's divisions with overwhelming force, threatening the piecemeal destruction of the Confederate army. The audacity of the plan was staggering.[50]

"Whatever the alchemy," the historian Thomas Connelly wrote, "much of Lee's success was due to his character. The Civil War, though altered drastically by the minie bullet and the railroad, was still fought in an era when the moral force of a general could prove decisive." That "moral force," asserted Connelly, "involved the ability to dominate" an opponent. At Chancellorsville, in darkened woods around a campfire, with no certainty of the enemy's dispositions, the fiber of Lee's character was never more evident. A calculated boldness had framed his generalship since he had assumed command of the army. May 2, 1863, epitomized it.[51]

Implicit in Lee's acceptance of the risky movement by nearly two-thirds of his army on the field was his trust in Jackson. During the winter Lee had told Stuart that he "wishes he had a dozen Jacksons for his Lieutenants." Whether the Confederate commander would have entrusted the march and the attack to someone other than Jackson cannot be known. The operation demanded aggressiveness and relentlessness, defining characteristics of Old Jack's generalship. Lee's method of command left the execution entirely with Jackson.[52]

While Lee waited on this long day for the sounds of Jackson's assault, he attended personally to the situation on Anderson's and McLaws's lines. For the plan to succeed, he knew, their troops had to "hold him [the enemy] in check and conceal the movement." He took time to write to Jefferson Davis, telling the president that Hooker "seems determined to make the fight here," and "I am now swinging around to my left to come up in his rear." But, he cautioned, "as far as I can judge, the advantage of numbers and position is greatly in favor of the enemy." He had "no expectations" that Longstreet, who had been ordered north with Hood's and Pickett's divisions, "will join me in time to aid in the contest at this point."[53]

When Jackson rode away from army headquarters, he readied his command for the march. His instructions said a staff officer, were, "ever monosyllabic," Robert Rodes's division to lead, followed by Raleigh Colston's, and then Powell Hill's; only ammunition wagons and ambulances; no bugle calls and no cheering by the men; the pace to be two miles per hour, with a ten-minute rest. Officers were told, "See that the column is kept closed and that there is no straggling." Uncertain of the exact route and destination, Jackson secured two local men as guides. Stuart's cavalrymen rode in the van with the guides and covered the column's flank toward the Federals, sealing off roads.[54]

It was minutes before 7:30 A.M. when the infantry stepped out, four men abreast, down Catherine Furnace Road, past the grove of pine trees where Lee stood by the roadside. Jackson soon appeared on Little Sorrel, his favorite horse, and reined up. The two men spoke briefly, Jackson pointing to the west and Lee nodding. Jackson rejoined the marchers. Ahead for both of them was an impenetrable divide.[55]

An hour into the march the Confederates entered a clearing in the forest near Catherine Furnace and were spotted by Federal lookouts in trees at Hazel Grove, less than a mile to the north. The information was relayed to Union army headquarters, where Hooker notified major generals Oliver Otis Howard and Henry Slocum, commanders of the Eleventh and Twelfth corps, respectively, of the enemy movement to the west. Hooker directed them to take protective measures against an attack and to push forward their pickets. After noon the Third Corps commander, Major General Daniel E. Sickles, advanced troops toward the furnace and captured nearly 300 members of the 23rd Georgia, which had been detached as guards for the Rebel column. "I think it is a retreat," Sickles reported to headquarters. The dispatch contributed to the growing belief by Hooker and his staff that Lee was indeed retreating.[56]

By the time the action began at the furnace, the rear of Jackson's column, Powell Hill's brigades, had passed the location. From Furnace Road the Southerners turned south on Brock Road for a short distance and then angled northwest, following a byroad that paralleled Brock Road and lay farther away from Union observers. "It was through bushes swamps and hills," grumbled Private George W. Slifer of the 2nd Virginia in a letter a week later, "we marched in the heat of the day i thought that he [Jackson] would kill all of us before we would get to the enemy. many laid by bushey rode side." Reentering Brock Road the Confederates marched one mile before turning east onto Orange Turn-pike and the right flank of the Union army. In all they had covered twelve miles.[57]

Jackson rode in the van of the column during most of the march. "Never can I forget the eagerness and intensity of Jackson on that march to Hooker's rear," remembered Dr. Hunter McGuire, the corps's chief surgeon. "His face was pale, his eyes flashing." At times Stuart accompanied his friend, whom he called "a man of *military genius*." At 3:00 P.M., Jackson scribbled a note to Lee: "The enemy has made a stand at Chancellor's which is about 2 miles from Chancellorsville. I hope as soon as practicable to attack. I trust that an Ever Kind Providence will bless us with great success." An hour or so later he wrote again, "The leading division is up & the next two appear to be well closed."[58]

Robert Rodes formed his ranks on a low, wooded ridge about a mile east of the Orange Turnpike–Brock Road intersection, his five brigades aligning on both sides of the turnpike. Two hundred yards to the rear Colston filed the four brigades of the Stonewall Division into line. Another 200 yards to the west the brigades of Dorsey Pender and Henry Heth of Hill's division shifted into the woods north of the turnpike. When completed, the line stretched for a mile and a half, from beyond Orange Turnpike on the north to Orange Plank Road on the south, containing roughly 23,000 of the Confederacy's finest infantrymen.[59]

"Under no circumstances," Jackson emphasized, "was there to be any pause in the advance." When Chief of Staff Sandie Pendleton reported the battle line formed, Jackson rode to the front. "Genl Jackson never & I mean *never*," stressed Henry Kyd Douglas, "indulged in rhetorical heroics on the battlefield." At 5:15 P.M., Jackson turned to his leading division commander and asked, "Are you ready, General Rodes?"

"Yes, sir."

"You can go forward, then."

A single bugle sounded the advance, followed by the notes of a dozen more. With the stride of thousands, the Civil War's most renowned flank attack went forward.[60]

To the east, beyond the thickets and dense trees, members of the Union Eleventh Corps were enjoying their evening meal or relaxing. Their campsites and ranks sprawled along Orange Turnpike, facing south. Earlier in the day, when Hooker's order to be alert arrived, corps commander Howard assured army headquarters, "I am taking measures to resist an attack from the west." But even as reports of enemy troops massing to the west came in from pickets, Howard did nothing, neither refusing nor bending back his right flank nor constructing fieldworks. His corps contained many recent German immigrants and men of German ancestry and were derisively called the "damned Dutch" by soldiers in the other corps. It was not them, but their unpopular one-armed commander, who ignored the signs of an impending whirlwind.[61]

An acoustic shadow deafened the sounds of the Confederate bugles. The first sign of the oncoming fury was the flight of forest creatures out of the woods and into the camps. Behind the animals, voiced by thousands, arose the eerie screech of the "rebel yell"—"the sweetest music I ever heard," Jackson exclaimed once. Volleys swept into the surprised Federal camps and ranks. Regiments at the far end of the line dissolved in a rout of panic-stricken men. Hundreds, even thousands, fled "like a parcele of sheep." Officers rallied troops; regiments shifted into line, facing the attackers, and fought stubbornly until outflanked. A battery of six Napoleons unleashed canister down the turnpike. To the east, on the rise at Fairview, Union gun crews opened fire. A counterattack by a division of the Third Corps further slowed the Confederate onslaught.[62]

Two hours after it had begun, Rodes ordered a halt. "Such was the confusion and darkness that it was not deemed advisable to make a farther advance," he explained in his report. Jackson wanted to press on, but regimental and brigade ranks had become so intermingled that he reluctantly accepted the wisdom of Rodes's order. An Alabamian with Rodes asserted, "Never saw such confus. & scattering." He and his comrades shook hands with each other, thankful for their survival.[63]

The Confederates had inflicted more than 2,400 casualties on the Eleventh Corps, including taking 1,000 prisoners, nine cannon, and a mile and a half of enemy works along the Turnpike and Plank roads. When the attack ended in the darkness, Jackson relieved Rodes's and Colston's disorganized ranks, bringing forward brigades from Hill's division. The nearness of the opposing lines and the shadowy figures in the moonlit woods sparked outbursts of rifle and cannon fire for hours. An effort by Federal units to retake fieldworks along Plank Road ended in "a mess," according to a Union brigadier.[64]

Although Jackson's attack was a stunning success, Lee's army remained vulnerable from the gap between Jackson's command and the divisions of Anderson and McLaws. The advantage gained by the flank assault had to be exploited with a renewal of the struggle in the woods west of Chancellorsville on the next day. After the fighting had subsided Jackson decided to conduct a personal reconnaissance of the enemy's line. Led by Private David Kyle, a cavalryman and former resident of the region, Jackson and an escort followed Plank Road before branching off onto Mountain Road, a narrow trace through the woods and parallel to Plank Road. Passing beyond Southern infantry ranks, Jackson's party halted within a few hundred yards of the Union works, listening to the voices in the darkness for a few minutes. The mounted Confederates then turned back toward their own lines.[65]

For the men lying in the darkened woods, Rebel and Yankee alike, apparitions seemed to come and go. A single rifle shot from a confused or scared soldier could ignite volleys that flashed along the opposing lines, like a forest fire driven by the wind. As Jackson's party proceeded west on Mountain Road, the musketry reflared, spreading to the 18th North Carolina of James Lane's brigade. The North Carolinians lay directly in front of the lieutenant general and his escort and triggered a volley into the night. Three smoothbore balls struck Jackson, one in the right hand and two in the left arm. On Plank Road the North

Carolinians' gunfire hit a group of horsemen with Powell Hill, mortally wounding one of Hill's aides and killing Captain James Keith Boswell of Jackson's staff.[66]

Untouched by the musketry, Powell Hill hurried to the wounded general's aid. The two men's personal animosity and professional difficulties had scabbed over but likely never quite healed. Hill and a few officers collected a litter party, which carried Jackson rearward and lifted him into an ambulance. The vehicle hauled the general to Dowdall's Tavern, where Dr. Hunter McGuire, having learned of the shooting, arrived. McGuire spoke with Jackson, examined the wounds, and proceeded with the ambulance to the Second Corps field hospital at Wilderness Tavern. Assisted by three surgeons, McGuire amputated Jackson's left arm between two and three o'clock on the morning of May 3.[67]

A staff officer delivered the sobering news to Robert E. Lee. The commanding general "was very much distressed and said he would rather a thousand times it had been himself" than Jackson. Lee wrote a message to his wounded lieutenant, congratulating him on the victory and stating, "Could I have directed events, I should have chosen for the good of the country to be disabled in your stead." Later, when Jedediah Hotchkiss went to headquarters with information on Jackson's condition, Lee, said the mapmaker, "did not wish to converse about it."[68]

The staff officer also reported to Lee that Hill had been wounded and that Jeb Stuart had been given temporary command of the Second Corps. The outburst of gunfire that resulted in Jackson's wounds had drawn a response from Union artillery. A piece of shell struck Hill in the leg, disabling the corps's senior subordinate. It was Hill who summoned the cavalry commander to assume direction of the infantry units.[69]

"I did not like Genl Stuart & did not want to see him command that corps," wrote Major William H. Palmer, Hill's chief of staff, after the war. Palmer admitted, however, "I think it was wise in that emergency after Hill to select Stuart for the command. . . . Stuart was well known in our corps." Captain Henry Kyd Douglas of Jackson's staff wrote, "Personally I never liked or admired Stuart & still believe he was vain & pretentious & greatly overrated as a soldier." But, like Palmer, Douglas knew "Genl Stuarts reputation in the corps then was, in some respects

second only to Jacksons. Jackson had great admiration for him as a soldier . . . [and] knew the men of his corps would have more confidence in
him than any man who would take his place." Stuart was "the best man"
under the circumstances.[70]

A captain on Hill's staff located Stuart in a wooded ravine along
Ely's Ford Road. When Jackson's attack had halted in the darkness, Stuart took a cavalry and an infantry regiment with him on the road to
secure a possible Union retreat route. Sometime before midnight Hill's
aide arrived and handed the cavalry general a message. Stuart read it by
candlelight, mounted his horse, and rode away at "topmost speed." The
grave news of his friend's serious wounding must have concerned him
deeply.[71]

The duty before Stuart was daunting. He knew nothing of the dispositions of the infantry units and had no specific orders. Spasms of
gunfire still broke the night's silence, indicating the proximity of the
opposing lines. He met with Sandie Pendleton and sent the talented
staff officer to learn if Jackson had any instructions for him. Stuart
also spoke with Porter Alexander and was told that the corps's chief of
artillery, Colonel Stapleton Crutchfield, also had been wounded. He
appointed Alexander to command of the artillery and directed him to
conduct a reconnaissance. Finally, remounting, Stuart rode to the front
and in the darkness restored some order in the ranks and shifted units
in the lines.[72]

Pendleton and Alexander rejoined Stuart before dawn. Pendleton
had been able to speak briefly with Jackson after he had awakened from
the operation. The chief of staff asked if the general had any orders for
his friend. "I don't know; I can't tell," Jackson replied weakly. "Say to
General Stuart he must do what he thinks best." Alexander described
the tactical importance of Hazel Grove, an elevated, open plateau that
extended for 500 yards. The plateau anchored the southern end of the
Union line astride Orange Plank Road and dominated the surrounding terrain. The artillerist claimed later that he "convinced" Stuart that
Hazel Grove was the key ground on this section of the battlefield.[73]

At about 4:00 A.M., Stuart received the first of two dispatches from
Lee, dated an hour earlier: "It is necessary that the glorious victory thus
far achieved be prosecuted with the utmost vigor, and the enemy be

given no time to rally. As soon, therefore, as it is possible, they must be pressed, so that we can unite the two wings of the army. Endeavor, therefore, to dispossess them of Chancellorsville, which will permit the union of the whole army." The urgency of the situation—the gap in the Confederate front—brought a second message, written thirty minutes later, from Lee: "It is all important that you still continue pressing to the right, turning, if possible, all the fortified points, in order that we can unite both wings of the army."[74]

Stuart and the officers and men of Old Jack's foot cavalry awaited the daylight. Stuart had stacked the divisions in three lines: from front to rear, Powell Hill's Light Division, now under Brigadier General Henry Heth; Raleigh Colston's Stonewall Division; and Robert Rodes's five brigades. Through the woods to the east, from 500 to 700 yards away, stood the Union fieldworks, manned by members of the Third and Twelfth corps. A Georgian remembered that the Rebels "lay all night long listening to the axes hard at work building breastworks for us to charge next morning." The Yankees had piled logs and dirt to a height of three feet, dug a trench in front, and cleared the ground, lacing it with abatis. The Federal position extended north from Hazel Grove to beyond Orange Plank Road. They built additional works farther to the rear.[75]

A New Yorker recalled hearing the "plaintive tones of a whip-poor-will" during the night, thinking the bird's song and the cries of wounded men "produced a strange sensation, like the voice of conscience to the wicked." As dawn neared, recounted a North Carolinian, "it was so still; not a bit of wind, but soft and warm." He thought it "a pity to disturb its hallowed name" of Sabbath. A soldier in the 23rd Virginia asserted that his fellow Southerners were "full of enthusiasm and confidence." To Lieutenant Walter Montgomery of the 12th North Carolina it had become a simple matter, "The assault had to be made."[76]

When it began at sunrise, "we went at it hammer & tongs," according to Porter Alexander. With Stuart's watchword, "Charge, and remember Jackson," the veterans of the Light Division led the attack. Suddenly, said a Yankee of the Rebels, "the whole woods in front of us seemed to be full of them." The Federal volleys blasted back Heth's men, but they charged again, shrieking "like devils." The musketry was "incessant," reported a general. "It is astonishing how these creatures will fight," marveled a Maine private of his foes.[77]

The combat escalated into a grim, bloody slugging match for the possession of the fieldworks. The woods and thick underbrush strained the efforts of the finest Confederate officers to maintain coordination between the attacking units. Colston lost control of the Stonewall Division, and his brigades charged piecemeal into the fearful cauldron of musketry and shellfire. One of his brigadiers, John R. Jones, left the field because of "ulcerated sores on his leg." Within weeks both Colston and Jones were gone from the army.[78]

"The scene was terrific," exclaimed a North Carolinian in James Lane's brigade. "It seemed as if heaven and earth were coming together." The Yankee rifle and artillery fire decimated Lane's ranks, the brigade lost twelve of fifteen field officers either killed or wounded. "Within a space of about forty yards," wrote a member afterward, "the bodies of seventy-six men were found dead."[79]

The Stonewall Brigade incurred the highest number of casualties in any of its battles, losing its commander, Frank Paxton, killed early in the fighting. Captain John Welsh of the 27th Virginia proclaimed in a letter, "It seemed as if nothing but the hand of God could save a man." The 2nd Virginia's Private George Slifer believed that the fighting made "a death noise and death it was to many of our brave boys." In all Jackson's original five regiments suffered 493 casualties.[80]

Along the Confederate lines rode Jeb Stuart. When his horse was killed under him, he borrowed another. He appeared to be everywhere. "In a charge," declared one of his aides, "Stuart seemed on fire." He changed the attack path of James Archer's troops, rallied the Stonewall Brigade, leading it forward with a shout "for the Old Stonewall to follow," and twice personally led the charge of the 28th North Carolina, whose colonel "was perfectly carried away with Stuart."[81]

His leadership in the wooded terrain was of the inestimable kind, personal bravery inspiring the men. He sang, "Old Joe Hooker, won't you come out' the Wilderness—Come Out' the Wilderness." The troops joined him, singing while they loaded and fired. A captain in the Stonewall Brigade said of the cavalryman, "His heroism was beautiful to behold." Porter Alexander asserted, "There can be no doubt that his personal conduct had great influence in sustaining the courage of the men." An officer affirmed, "Jeb impressed himself on the infantry."[82]

In a postwar letter Alexander offered an assessment of Stuart's generalship on this day: "I do not think there was [a] more brilliant thing done in the war than Stuart's extricating that command [Second Corps] from the extremely critical position in which he found it as promptly and boldly as he did. . . . But Stuart never seemed to hesitate or to doubt for one moment that he could crash his way wherever he chose to strike. He decided to attack at daylight, and unlike many planned attacks that I have seen, this one came off promptly on time."[83]

The Yankees fought valiantly, but after two hours of bloody combat the fortunes shifted dramatically in favor of the Southerners. Against objections from Daniel Sickles, Hooker committed a critical mistake, ordering Sickles's Third Corps troops off of Hazel Grove in a consolidation of the Union lines. When Stuart learned of the withdrawal, he ordered Alexander and thirty cannon onto the plateau. Before long Confederate gun crews began "to shake the Federals' lines." The artillerists raked enemy guns on Fairview and poured "a hell of fire" down upon the Chancellorsville clearing. One artillery round struck the porch of the Chancellor house, where Hooker was standing. A pillar was split and knocked Hooker unconscious; he was out for at least thirty minutes.[84]

Stuart ordered Jackson's veterans forward. The Rebels surged over the final line of enemy infantry fieldworks. Stephen Dodson Ramseur's 1,500 or so North Carolinians spearheaded the assault and lost more than half their numbers in the fierce combat. Along another section of the works Dorsey Pender seized a regimental flag and, on horseback, led his brigade into the enemy ranks. "The effect of such examples of daring gallantry at critical moments is incalculable," Powell Hill wrote of Pender's action.[85]

Richard Anderson's division advanced on the right of the Second Corps, and the Confederates swept across the crest of Fairview and toward Chancellorsville. Stuart rode close behind the charging ranks, shouting: "Go forward boys! We have them running, and we'll keep them at it!" Union reserves counterattacked, breaking the Confederate tide. But the wings of Lee's army had been reunited, and the Rebels stood amid the wreckage in the Chancellorsville clearing. The reformed

Union line was shaped like a giant U, with both flanks resting on the Rappahannock River and U.S. Ford secured as a retreat route.[86]

"I never want to git in to another as hard a fight," exclaimed an Alabamian in a letter, "for I can assure you that it was a warm place on Sunday, May the 3rd." Casualties exceeded 17,500 on both sides in the five hours of combat; Southerners' losses amounted to nearly 9,000. The abandonment of Hazel Grove by the Yankees unhinged their line, giving the Rebels a decisive tactical advantage. But as the historian Earl Hess noted, "Whichever side displayed more tenacity would win a contest like this, and the Federals gave way first." The inspired leadership of Stuart, Alexander, and brigade commanders such as Lane, Pender, and Ramseur counted for much. Several days later a Confederate staff officer offered a judgment on the fighting: "How our men ever drove them out of such fortifications as they had is a mystery to me. The Yankee army ought to be ashamed of itself."[87]

Lee and Stuart rode down Orange Plank Road toward the Chancellorsville clearing. Officers and men removed the dead and wounded from the road ahead of the generals. The soldiers removed their hats as the riders passed, and Lee and Stuart returned the salutes. When they reached the Chancellor house, the Confederates cheered, joined by some of the Federal prisoners. A Virginian wrote of Lee, "So grand and majestic was his appearance." Witnessing the men's reaction, Charles Marshall stated, "I thought that it must have been such a scene that men in ancient days rose to the dignity of gods."[88]

The Prussian officer Justus Scheibert observed the Confederate commander during the course of the battle. Lee "was full of calm, quiet, self-possession," he recounted, "feeling that he had done his duty to the utmost, and had brought the army into the most favorable position to defeat the hostile host." The boldness and aggressiveness of Lee's countermoves to Hooker's well-conceived campaign brought him, surrounded by cheering soldiers, on the verge of perhaps his greatest tactical victory.[89]

That victory, however, remained unsecured. The Confederate forces in the Wilderness still confronted a numerically superior foe who could assume the offensive. To the east, at Fredericksburg, Jubal Early's defenders had been driven from Marye's Heights. The Union commander at Fredericksburg, John Sedgwick, had done little since April 29, except undertake weak demonstrations against the outmanned Rebels west of the town. A peremptory order from Hooker to attack finally moved Sedgwick to assail the heights on the morning of May 3. By then only 1,200 Mississippians and eight gun crews held the hill and the stone wall at its base. The Yankees overwhelmed the Rebels, capturing the guns and hundreds of Mississippians.[90]

With the road open to Chancellorsville and the rear of Lee's lines, Sedgwick marched with characteristic caution. Five Confederate brigades, shifted eastward by Lee, met Sedgwick's Sixth Corps troops at Salem Church, three miles from the Chancellorsville clearing. In the afternoon fighting, characterized by charges and countercharges, Paul Semmes's and William Wofford's Georgia brigades and Cadmus Wilcox's Alabama regiments distinguished themselves. A final Southern assault broke the Union ranks, ending the action.[91]

On the morning of May 4 Sedgwick withdrew toward the Rappahannock, anchoring both flanks on the river and covering Banks's Ford. Believing that Hooker would remain behind his fieldworks in the Wilderness, Lee shifted more units against Sedgwick, left Stuart in command at Chancellorsville, and rode east to assume personal direction of operations against the Union Sixth Corps. What the army commander found when he arrived displeased him. "No body knew exactly how or where the enemy's line of battle ran," he said afterward. When angered, Lee "manifested his ill humor," noted Walter Taylor, "by a little nervous twist or jerk of the neck and head, peculiar to himself, accompanied by some harshness of manner." Whether Lee reacted as such at this time is unknown, but evidently he blamed division commander Lafayette McLaws for the loss of "valuable time."[92]

It consequently took the Confederates most of the day to deploy for an assault. Finally, at about 5:30 P.M., Ambrose Wright's brigade of Anderson's division and three of Jubal Early's brigades advanced against the Federal left. The Rebels scattered enemy skirmishers but gained little ground against Union artillery and infantry. For a brief time the fighting was fierce, moving one Yankee to remark, "I no more expected to get out of that place alive than I expected to fly." Darkness ended the combat. Several hours later, early on the morning of May 5, under

instructions from Hooker, Sedgwick began recrossing the Rappahannock at Banks's Ford. Well-liked by fellow officers and his men, Sedgwick failed in his primary mission by not acting aggressively in seizing
Marye's Heights and moving toward Chancellorsville. His caution was
not untypical of many senior leaders in the Union army.[93]

Early on the morning of May 5 at Chancellorsville Jeb Stuart sent a
dispatch to Lee, proposing an assault on the Union line. "I do not know
the circumstances which induce your wish to attack the enemy," replied
Lee at 8:15 A.M. "With your present strength as reported in field returns,
it might be beyond us. If the Enemy is recrossing the Rappk or attempting to do so, or if other circumstances warrant the attack, you can withdraw Heth. If you have to storm entrenchments, unless the Enemy can
be driven from them by cannon, I cannot recommend an attack except
under very favorable circumstances."[94]

Lee followed with a second message during the morning, instructing
Stuart to have the artillery fire on the enemy works for "several hours."
"If you can attack to advantage," he wrote, "you can do so." By then
Lee had been informed of Sedgwick's retreat. Anderson's and McLaws's
divisions started back toward Chancellorsville, and Early's command
reoccupied Marye's Heights. A heavy rain began falling during the
afternoon. At Union army headquarters, over the objections of three of
his five corps commanders, Hooker ordered a retreat after nightfall. The
defeated Army of the Potomac filed across pontoon bridges through the
darkness. A Union captain confessed, "I recrossed with a heavy heart,
and . . . I felt tears rolling down my cheeks."[95]

Confederate skirmishers prowled through the wet woods after daylight on May 6 and confirmed the retreat of the Union army. Lee had
readied his units for an attack on the Federals, and the news evidently
displeased him. In a brief letter to Jefferson Davis he used the word
"escape" to describe the enemy withdrawal. One account contended
that when Dorsey Pender reported the Yankees gone, Lee angrily said
to the brigadier: "This is the way that you young men are always doing.
You have again let these people get away. I can only tell you what to do,
and if you do not do it will not be done."[96]

In the weeks ahead Lee indeed voiced frustration at the "escape" of
the Yankees. He told John Hood, "Had I had the whole army with me,

General Hooker would have been demolished." Later he commented to a Confederate officer, "At Chancellorsville we gained another victory. Our people were wild with delight—I, on the contrary, was more depressed than after Fredericksburg; our loss was severe, and again we had gained not an inch of ground and the enemy could not be pursued."[97]

By Lee's measurement, the Federals had once again eluded a crippling defeat, and the Southerners had paid a dear price for a limited victory. A modern tabulation places Union casualties at 1,575 killed or mortally wounded, 9,594 wounded, and 5,676 captured or missing, a casualty rate of 16 percent. Confederate losses amounted to 1,665 killed or mortally wounded, 9,081 wounded, and 2,018 captured or missing, a casualty rate of 22 percent. Within Lee's army more North Carolinians, nine hundred, lost their lives than soldiers from any other Southern state. In some North Carolina units the casualty rate surpassed two-thirds. In the whole army nearly eighty field officers had fallen or were captured. Only Antietam, with far fewer men in Lee's ranks, had exacted a higher percentage of losses than Chancellorsville.[98]

Chancellorsville stands, however, as a brilliant triumph of Confederate arms and Lee's finest tactical victory. As he had during the Seven Days and at Second Manassas, Lee had imposed his will on an opponent. Unquestionably Hooker's generalship—withdrawing into the Wilderness on May 1, assuming a defensive stand, and ordering the abandonment of Hazel Grove on May 3—contributed significantly to the battle's outcome. The Union commander was also ill-served by subordinates, particularly Oliver Otis Howard and John Sedgwick. At critical points fortune favored the Rebels, but Dorsey Pender put it well in a letter to his wife: "Hooker thought he had us but Lee is too much for him."[99]

Though Lee had fashioned the bold offensive, he was not alone in forging the victory. From the lowliest private in the ranks to generals such as Stonewall Jackson, Jeb Stuart, and Powell Hill, aggressiveness and élan distinguished Lee's army, perhaps more than any other attributes. Chancellorsville starkly demonstrated the different mindsets of the opposing armies. The rank and file of the Army of the Potomac were worthy foes, but since the army's rebirth after First Bull Run they had been cursed by a deeply ingrained caution among their leadership. Whereas Lee and his lieutenants dared to act against daunting odds,

Hooker and his subordinates assumed the defensive behind fieldworks on a haunting landscape that ultimately favored the bold. A Union staff officer grasped the difference: "I am nothing of a General, but why we did not whip them I do not see. . . . We never gave our men a chance."[100]

The Army of Northern Virginia and the Confederacy as a whole hailed Chancellorsville as a remarkable, even stunning victory. Stephen Dodson Ramseur exclaimed about "this glorious army." Writing on May 8, Walter Taylor asserted: "The past week has been a most eventful one. The operations of this army under Genl Lee during that time will compare favorably with the most brilliant ever recorded. When I consider our numerical weakness, our limited resources and the great strength & equipments of the enemy, I am astonished at the result."[101]

Artillerist Ham Chamberlayne proclaimed, "I regard it as by far our greatest victory: there was no straggling; our army was in fighting trim at the end of the engagement, no disorganization, no panic any where." A Virginia officer attested, "Our men fought splendidly . . . and each soldier seemed to feel that he had an important part to act in the grand and bloody drama." Years later Porter Alexander described the victory as "the marvelous story of how luck favored pluck and skill, & how we extricated ourselves by the boldest & most daring strategy of the whole war; combined with some of the most beautiful fighting which it witnessed."[102]

Southern newspapers trumpeted the victory and heralded Lee and the army. Editorials in the Richmond *Daily Dispatch* and *Enquirer* typified the reaction of the press. The *Daily Dispatch* ranked the fighting on May 2 and 3 "amongst the most brilliant in the annals of the Southern Confederacy, already illuminated with triumphs which, for number and magnitude, are not surpassed in history." The *Enquirer* affirmed, "It is no disparagement to other great Generals and gallant forces in our service, to say that General Lee and his Army of Northern Virginia may now be pronounced the most famous Chief and Army on earth at this day."[103]

Chancellorsville culminated an eleven-month record of achievement unsurpassed by any army on either side. The record had been attained at a cost of nearly 60,000 casualties. To be sure, it was a fearful price, but the Army of Northern Virginia had come to symbolize and to embody Confederate nationalism. With each feat of arms, Southern hopes for independence rested increasingly with Lee and his veterans. "Lee's military successes in 1862 and 1863," the historian Gary Gallagher has concluded, "created a belief that independence was possible as long as the Army of Northern Virginia and its celebrated chief remained in the field."[104]

On the morning of May 6, with rain falling and the Union army across the Rappahannock River, Lee ordered his troops into their old camps. As they filed away from the Wilderness, a belief in their invincibility deepened. An artillery officer, Major Willie Pegram, professed a few days later that if the Yankees did not transfer units from the west to the east, "we have very little to fear from the troops opposite." In the estimation of the historian Douglas Southall Freeman, the Army of Northern Virginia "believed it could do anything. Unfortunately, General Lee took the army's estimation of itself." What neither Lee nor his men knew was that they had not defeated the rank and file of the Army of the Potomac, but merely their commander.[105]

Chapter Eight

"I Think We Will Clear the Yankees Out This Summer"

THE AMBULANCE CARRYING the wounded Stonewall Jackson arrived at Fairfield, the residence of Thomas Chandler, at Guiney Station, Virginia, on the night of May 4, 1863. Litter bearers took the general into a small, whitewashed cottage in the yard of the Chandler home. Placed in a bed on the first floor, Jackson requested some bread and tea before sleeping. Dr. Hunter McGuire, two staff officers, Reverend B. Tucker Lacy, and Jim Lewis, the general's black servant, attended to him.[1]

Jackson's condition improved during the next two days. McGuire tended to the stump of the left arm, and Lacy conducted a brief prayer service with the general. Early on the morning of May 7 Jackson awakened with a fever and nausea. McGuire diagnosed the symptoms as pneumonia. The general's wife, Anna Jackson, and their six-month-old daughter, Julia, arrived at noon. When Anna entered the bedroom, she kissed her husband, who smiled and said, "I am very glad to see you looking so bright." At McGuire's request, four physicians joined him for advice and assistance.[2]

The Confederate hero rallied briefly the next day, but during the

night of May 8–9 the painful breathing worsened, with periods of delirium. In the morning the doctors told Anna that her husband would not
recover. Robert E. Lee had been kept informed of his subordinate's condition. When told by Lacy that he would not live, Lee said with deep
emotion: "Surely General Jackson must recover. God will not take him
from us now that we need him so much. Surely he will be spared to us in
answer to the many prayers which are offered for him."[3]

Sunday, May 10, was a warm Virginia spring day. At Guiney Station
Jackson labored against the pneumonia in his lungs. With each passing
hour death neared. As she had during the past few days, Anna went to
his side. Outside of the cottage soldiers and civilians gathered. Shortly
after noon he slipped into a coma. But delirium wracked his mind, and
at times he issued orders aloud as if on a battlefield. Finally he said, "Let
us cross over the river and rest under the shade of the trees." At 3:15
P.M., Thomas Jonathan Jackson died.[4]

"I regret to inform you that the great & good Jackson is no more,"
wrote Lee to Jeb Stuart the next day. He was, said Lee, "calm serene &
happy. May his spirit pervade our whole army. Our country will then
be secure." When Lee spoke of Jackson's death to William Pendleton,
chief of artillery, the Confederate commander wept. To his son Custis,
Lee said, "It is a terrible loss. I do not know how to replace him. Any
victory would be dear at such a cost. But God's will be done."[5]

Lee directed that Jackson's body be taken to Richmond, where a
funeral was held on May 12 and the fallen general lay in state in the
Capitol. From Richmond a railroad train conveyed the remains to
Lynchburg for the journey to Lexington in a canal boat. There, among
former and current VMI students, friends, and hundreds of mourners,
Jackson was buried in the city's cemetery on Friday, May 15. Lexington
had been Jackson's home for a decade before the war. He was buried
beside his first wife, Ellen, their stillborn son, and his and Anna's first
daughter. Trees shaded the gravesite.[6]

The outpouring of grief was nearly universal across the Confederacy. Lee announced Jackson's death to the army in formal orders on
May 11: "Let his name be a watchword to his corps, who have followed
him to victory on so many fields. Let officers and soldiers emulate his
invincible determination to do everything in the defense of our beloved

country." President Jefferson Davis and Jeb Stuart used the same words, a "national calamity," in describing the Confederacy's loss. Stuart called him "the dearest friend I had." In Winchester, Kate Sperry spoke for uncounted Southerners, men and women, when she wrote in her diary, "I . . . feel so miserable—nearly cried my eyes out—poor Jackson—so noble—so brave—so loved by all the people—Oh, how we shall miss him."[7]

In the words of both officers and men, a "gloom" fell upon the army. Their letters were replete with expressions such as "a dreadful blow," "a shock," "a great loss." Major Willie Pegram, an artillerist, confessed, "We never knew how much we all loved him until he died." He noted, however, "Fortunately, with us, the soldiers make the officers, & not the officers the soldiers." An Alabama infantryman declared, with some exaggeration, that Jackson's name "was never spoken in this Army but with adoration. . . . When he rode along the road, if but one soldier saw him he raised a shout. I have never seen him pass a body of soldiers but he raised his cap and bowed his bearded head to them."[8]

"Such an executive officer," Lee said of Jackson, "the sun never shone on." Henry Heth thought him "the most extraordinary man as a soldier that I ever met." Jackson's brilliance lay not as a tactician, but in his single-mindedness of purpose, his unbending devotion to duty, his relentlessness as a foe, and his burning desire, at whatever cost, for victory. His eccentricities infuriated subordinates and endeared him to his men. Independent operations seemed to inflame his soul. He possessed an unmatched ability to impose his will on recalcitrant soldiers and on his enemies. Jedediah Hotchkiss put it well when he wrote that Jackson "stamped a peculiar character upon" the Second Corps. But he was gone, added the mapmaker, "and everything wears an altered and lonely look." He was indeed, as Hotchkiss said, a "singular" man and general.[9]

While Lee mourned the irreparable loss, he worked on plans for a movement without Jackson's presence. His other corps commander and talented subordinate, James Longstreet, had rejoined the main army with the divisions of John Hood and George Pickett. During his return to Fredericksburg, Longstreet stopped in Richmond, where he met with Secretary of War James Seddon. For weeks Seddon had been concerned with the defense of Vicksburg, Mississippi. Recently the Federals, commanded by Major General Ulysses S. Grant, had made a lodgment on the east bank of the Mississippi River south of Vicksburg, increasing the threat to the vital river city and Major General John B. Pemberton's garrison.[10]

Seddon broached the idea to Longstreet of sending Hood's and/or Pickett's division to Pemberton. Longstreet countered by advocating the combining of the detachment from Lee's army with the troops of generals Joseph E. Johnston and Braxton Bragg in an offensive against Major General William Rosecrans's Union army in Tennessee. Once Rosecrans was defeated, argued Longstreet, the Confederate forces could advance into Kentucky, moving toward the Ohio River. Grant's army in Mississippi would be the only Federal command that could meet the Rebel threat. Longstreet had proposed a western concentration as early as the previous February.[11]

Seddon and Longstreet presented their ideas to Jefferson Davis at an evening meeting. The president had been involved in discussions and an exchange of correspondence with Seddon and Lee for the past weeks. He was well aware of Lee's opposition to a detachment from his army and believed that the best solution would be the union of Johnston's command with Pemberton's units. He also ordered Longstreet and the two divisions to Fredericksburg.[12]

When Longstreet arrived at Fredericksburg, he and Lee began a three-day discussion on future operations. From them came the movement into Pennsylvania and a controversy that has endured for a century and a half. After the war, when Longstreet had become a pariah in the South for his political affiliations and the scapegoat for the Confederate defeat at Gettysburg, he devoted pages in various publications, including his memoirs, to a defense of his actions that seemed to distance himself from Lee's plans. In brief Longstreet asserted that he had opposed the offensive across the Potomac River and agreed to it only after Lee assented to fight a defensive battle when the army encountered the enemy on Northern soil.[13]

Contemporary evidence, however, specifically Longstreet's own words, suggests otherwise. When he met with Lee, he repeated the proposal that he had advocated to Seddon and Davis, writing later, "I laid it before him [Lee] with the freedom justified by our close personal and official relations." Lengthy discussions ensued. By the end Lee had per-suaded Longstreet that an offensive in the East held the best prospects for Confederate victory.[14]

When the meetings with Lee concluded, Longstreet wrote a reveal-ing letter to Senator Louis T. Wigfall of Texas, a confidant of the gen-eral and a proponent of the western concentration strategy. Before he penned the body of the letter Longstreet cautioned that "these matters" should not go "beyond Gen. Lee and yourself." He proceeded: "There is a fair prospect of forward movement. That being the case we can spare nothing from this army to re-enforce in the West. On the contrary we should have use of our own and the balance of our Armies if we could get them. If we could cross the Potomac with one hundred & fifty thou-sand men, I think we could demand Lincoln to declare his purpose. If it is a Christian purpose enough of blood has been shed to satisfy any principles. If he intends extermination we should know it at once and play a little at that game whilst we can."

In the matter of sending reinforcements to Mississippi, Longstreet thought that one or two divisions would be insufficient. "Grant seems to be a fighting man," he wrote, "and seems to be determined to fight. Pemberton seems not to be a fighting man." If Pemberton chose not to engage the Federals, "the fewer troops he has the better." If Vicksburg fell, "we would be no worse off than we are now" because the Confeder-ates were already cut off from the states west of the Mississippi River. "In fact, we should make a grand effort against the Yankees this sum-mer, every available man and means should be brought to bear against them."

Longstreet then summarized his views: "When I agreed with the Secy & yourself about sending troops west I was under the impression that we would be obliged to remain on the defensive here. But the pros-pect of an advance changes the aspects of affairs to us entirely. Gen. Lee sent for me when he recd the Secy's letter. I told him that I thought that we could spare the troops unless there was a chance of a forward movement. If we could move of course we should want everything, that we had and all that we could get."[15]

Longstreet's letter is significant not only in its contradiction of his postwar writings but as a reflection of Lee's thinking. In his exchange of views with the administration on the detachment of troops to Mississippi, Lee had argued that the Federals could transfer units more rapidly than the Confederates and that his army was already "greatly outnumbered by the enemy." As a department commander, Lee focused his strategy on his region. He had neither the authority nor the purview to direct operations beyond his department. Furthermore he apparently contended that Pemberton "seems not to be a fighting man," just as Longstreet argued, and that any reinforcements sent to him would only add to Southern losses.[16]

Lee thought, rightfully, that the Confederacy's best hope for independence rested with his army and the best strategy was to carry the war once again beyond the Potomac River. In February he had written to his son Custis that nothing could stop the enemy "except a revolution among their people," and "nothing can produce a revolution except the systematic success on our part." Chancellorsville had given Lee's army an opportunity for further "systematic success." A Rebel advance into Pennsylvania and another battlefield victory might ignite a "revolution" among the Northern citizenry. "Our purpose should have been," asserted Longstreet later, "to impair the *morale* of the Federal army and shake Northern confidence in the Federal leaders." This was Lee's purpose.[17]

The historian Steven Woodworth argued that Lee "seems to have hoped through the combination of decisive battlefield victory on northern soil and cunning manipulation of public opinion by the South's political leaders to achieve that summer the goal for which he had fought so long." Another scholar, Wiley Sword, believed that an urgency impelled Lee to act. The "diminishing assets" in the army, Sword wrote, "made it imperative in his mind that something decisive be done to achieve peace before it was too late."[18]

It would have been uncharacteristic of Lee, however, not to undertake a strategic offensive. When the situation in the East offered the possibility of such a movement, Lee seized it. His secretary, Charles Marshall, contended: "The war in Virginia with all its chances and charges was in fact one campaign. The battles on the Chickahominy and at Manassas, the invasion of Maryland, and the invasion of Pennsylvania, all had a common object": the defense of Richmond and the breaking of Northern civilian will. Ever since the Confederates had retreated into Virginia after Antietam, Lee had sought a propitious time for reentry into Union territory.[19]

"In the opinion of General Lee," added Marshall, "Virginia presented the most favourable theatre of war for this plan of operations." If the Confederates were to win the war, it had to be won there. A victory beyond the Potomac increased the prospects for Southern independence. Most likely urgency factored into Lee's thinking, but calculated boldness drew him northward.[20]

On May 14 Lee traveled to Richmond for conferences with administration officials. A government worker thought the general "looked thinner, and a little pale." Lee spent four days in the capital, sequestered in meetings with Davis and Cabinet members. He presented his plans for an offensive that would shift "the scene of hostilities north of the Potomac," arguing that a movement into Union territory would disrupt Federal operations during the summer, give relief to Virginia, and hold out the prospect for a harvest of badly needed supplies. The enemy would be compelled to move toward the Rebels, which "might offer a fair opportunity to strike a blow at the army."[21]

The proposal sparked considerable debate, with objections from at least one Cabinet officer. Concern remained over the defense of Vicksburg. Although an offensive across the Potomac might offer relief to the Mississippi city, Lee did not stress that factor in his reasons for a movement north. At length, the Cabinet voted five to one in favor of Lee's plan, and Davis approved. Lee's "opinion naturally had great effect in the decisions of the Executive," recounted Secretary of War Seddon. Lee was back with the army on May 18.[22]

Two days later Lee wrote to Jefferson Davis, requesting the president's consideration of a major reorganization of the army's infantry units. "I have for the past year felt that the corps of this army were too large for one commander," stated Lee. "Nothing prevented my proposing to you to reduce their size and increase their number but my inability to recommend commanders." Each of the present two corps consisted of approximately 30,000 officers and men, he explained. "These are more than one man can properly handle and keep under his eye in battle in the country that we have to operate in. They are always beyond the range of his vision, and frequently beyond his reach."[23]

With Jackson's death, this was an opportune time for the expansion of the infantry into three corps. Lee recommended Richard Ewell for command of Jackson's Second Corps and A. P. Hill for the newly formed Third Corps. James Longstreet would retain command of the First Corps. In his recommendation of Ewell and Hill, Lee stated: "The former is an honest, brave soldier, who has always done his duty well. The latter, I think upon the whole, is the best soldier of his grade with me." Davis consented, and Ewell and Hill were promoted to lieutenant general on May 23 and 24, respectively. On May 30, Lee issued the orders of the reorganization, assigning commanders and divisions to the Second and Third corps.[24]

An intriguing choice for a successor to Jackson was his good friend Jeb Stuart. Lee praised the cavalryman for his performance at Chancellorsville in temporary command of the Second Corps. Stuart, said Lee, "exhibited great energy, promptness, and intelligence" and "conducted the operations on the left with distinguished capacity and vigor." In a postwar letter Porter Alexander declared: "I always thought it an injustice to Stuart and a loss to the army he was not from that moment [May 3] *continued in command of Jackson's corps.* He had *won* the right to it. I believe he had all of Jackson's genius and dash and originality." No evidence exists, however, that Lee considered him for the corps command, almost certainly because Lee was unwilling to lose Stuart's leadership of the cavalry.[25]

Instead the forty-six-year-old Ewell, whom Jackson had requested as his successor, assumed command of the corps. The Virginian had not been with the army since his wound at Brawner's Farm on August 28, 1862, which led to the amputation of his left leg. He had been an excellent division commander under Jackson from the Shenandoah Valley Campaign until his crippling wound. Longstreet regarded him as a superior officer in every respect to Hill. Moxley Sorrel called him "one of the strongest of warriors," with "uncommon courage and activity." When Ewell assumed command, Jedediah Hotchkiss exclaimed to his wife, "We have our wishes gratified here in having Gen. Ewell to command the old army of Gen. Jackson."[26]

Some army members thought that "Old Bald Head," as the troops had nicknamed Ewell, possessed more eccentricities than Jackson. An officer claimed that the general held "his head to one-side like a sap-sucker peeping around a tree." He had a renowned reputation for pro-fanity, which he "ingeniously wrought into the whole sentences." A fel-low officer who had served with Ewell in the frontier west before the war averred that he "could swear the scalp off an Apache." But during his months of convalescence Ewell had given up swearing and renewed his religious faith. A recent marriage to a cousin, the widowed Lizinka Campbell Brown, had tempered him even more.[27]

Questions remained about Ewell's physical and mental status after the severe wound and amputation of his leg. Writing after the war, when Ewell's weaknesses as a corps commander had been demonstrated, Longstreet maintained that Ewell had lost much of his efficiency as an officer when he lost his leg. At the time of his appointment doubts lin-gered about his decisiveness and mood swings from "elation to despon-dency." According to a Second Corps staff officer, Lee spoke at length with Ewell about his faults when the subordinate assumed command. There was a belief, whether fair or not, that the new lieutenant general had only "moderate capacity" for a corps commander.[28]

Like Ewell's appointment, Powell Hill's selection placed a familiar figure in command of many of the officers and men in the Third Corps. Of the new corps's thirteen brigades, six had belonged to Hill's Light Division. He had proven to be a competent administrator and had an outstanding record as a combat officer. His fiery temperament and prickly sense of honor had led to clashes with both Longstreet and Jack-son. Yet despite their difficulties, Longstreet called him "a gallant, good soldier," adding, however, "There was a good deal of 'curled darling' and dress-parade about Hill." He seemed to receive almost universal praise among his subordinates. Lee's confidence in both Ewell and Hill was absolute, as he noted in his letter to Davis, "I do not know where to get better men than those I have named."[29]

With the appointments of Ewell and Hill, the army's senior leader-ship, except for Longstreet, was composed of Virginians, though Vir-ginia infantry and cavalry regiments and artillery batteries constituted barely 36 percent of all the units in the army. Longstreet said in his memoirs that there was at the time "no little discontent" because Ewell and Hill were both Virginians. Perceived favoritism toward officers from the Old Dominion had been quietly present since July 1862, when initial promotions and command changes occurred after the Seven Days. Non-Virginians had been particularly incensed over the praise given to Virginians at the expense of others by Richmond newspapers. But the grumbling remained private and among themselves.[30]

The army reorganization and creation of a new corps brought promotions and reassignments. Immediately after Chancellorsville, Robert Rodes received his well-deserved major generalcy and permanent command of Daniel Harvey Hill's former division. "He is a good soldier," Lee said of Rodes, "behaved admirably in the last battles and deserves promotion." At the same time Edward Johnson was assigned to command of Isaac Trimble's former division. Known as "Old Allegheny," Johnson had not held field command since suffering a wound at the Battle of McDowell in May 1862. He had a reputation for bravery, the skillful management of troops in combat, and the use of profanity. He walked with a "very perceptible limp," aided by a "gigantic walking-cane."[31]

The formation of the Third Corps, with the redistribution of brigades, and Hill's promotion created two vacancies in divisional command. Hill recommended Dorsey Pender and Henry Heth for the posts. A particular favorite of Hill, Pender was the senior brigadier in the Light Division and, like Rodes, merited promotion. Never modest, the North Carolinian had boasted to his wife in April, "I believe that I have more reputation than any Brigadier in this Army." Earlier he had told her: "The men seem to think that I am fond of fighting. They say I give them 'hell' out of the fight and the Yankees the same in it." A fellow brigadier in the division, James Archer, loathed Pender. When he heard that Pender had been wounded in the hand at Fredericksburg, he growled, "I wish they had shot him in his damn head."[32]

Henry Heth benefited from Lee's personal regard for him. Heth had served under Lee in western Virginia in the fall of 1861 and had led the Light Division after Hill's wounding in the fighting at Chancellorsville. His new division consisted of two brigades from the Light Division and two brigades recently assigned to the army. The historian Douglas Southall Freeman wrote of Heth that he was "doomed to be one of those good soldiers, unhappily numerous in military history, who consistently have bad luck."[33]

When the reorganization of the infantry was finalized, Longstreet's First Corps consisted of eleven brigades in the divisions of Lafayette McLaws, John Hood, and George Pickett; Ewell's Second Corps contained thirteen brigades in the divisions of Jubal Early, Edward Johnson, and Robert Rodes; and Hill's Third Corps had thirteen brigades under Richard Anderson, Henry Heth, and Dorsey Pender. Two of Pickett's brigades were detached and would not march north with the army. Except for Rodes, a VMI alumnus, all of the division commanders were graduates of West Point. Only McLaws, Hood, Early, and Anderson had led a division in more than one battle.[34]

At brigade level more than one-third of the commanders lacked serious combat experience. Several had been newly promoted to brigadier, a few had joined the army during May, and six held the rank of colonel. Longstreet's First Corps had combat veterans at the head of every brigade. It was in Jackson's old command, now the Second and Third corps, where the inexperience was most telling, with new corps commanders, four division commanders of limited experience, and a dozen brigadiers or colonels also new to their posts.[35]

Lee understood how the diminishing numbers of quality officers impacted the army's effectiveness. On May 21, in response to a letter from Hood, he wrote, "I agree with you in believing that our army would be invincible if it could be properly organized and officered. There never were such men in an army before. They will go anywhere and do anything if properly led. But there is the difficulty—proper commanders. Where can they be obtained?"[36]

In a modern study of the forthcoming campaign, a foremost authority on Lee's army, Robert K. Krick, concluded: "The Confederates' ability to operate as they moved northward was affected by the loss of much mid-level command. The heart of the Confederate Army was starting to feel this difficulty for the first time just before Gettysburg. To the tremendous losses of the successful but costly campaign in the summer of 1862 . . . were added the victims of the dreadful bloodshed at Chancellorsville." From the Seven Days through Chancellorsville, few if any regiments had not lost multiple field-grade officers. Casualties among colonels, lieutenant colonels, and majors surpassed 300 in total in all of the engagements.[37]

It was within the ranks, among the privates and noncommissioned officers, however, where the bedrock of the army lay. Their confidence in themselves and in Lee appeared unbounded. A recruit who joined the 4th Texas professed, "One day's observation has led me to believe that no army on earth can whip these men." A captain in the 1st Virginia averred, "Never before has the army been in such fine condition, so well disciplined and under such complete control." Major Thomas Elder of the 3rd Virginia wrote, "I am glad to know I am serving my country with some degree of usefulness in this her hour of trial. To have served during the war in General Lee's army is indeed . . . a subject of honest pride."[38]

A South Carolinian said of his comrades: "I have little doubt that we had now the finest army ever marshaled on this side of the Atlantic, and one scarcely inferior to any Europe has known. Its numbers were not so imposing. . . . But we were veterans—thoroughly experienced in all that relates to the march or the battle-field, sufficiently drilled to perform any manoeuvre at all likely to be demanded, sufficiently disciplined to obey orders promptly and with energy, yet preserving enough of the proud individuality of Southern men to feel the cause our own, and therefore to be willing to encounter the greatest amount of personal danger and moral responsibility."[39]

"Except in equipment," wrote Porter Alexander, "I think a better army, better nerved up to its work, never marched upon a battle-field." In fact because of the capture of thousands of rifle muskets at Fredericksburg and Chancellorsville, none of Lee's infantrymen carried smoothbore muskets. The Confederates had also seized from the retreating Yankees innumerable sets of accoutrements and more than a half million rounds of musket ammunition. During May some troops received new uniforms, but complained that their cost came out of their pay. The receipt of the uniforms and supplies did not prevent a lieutenant from calling quartermaster and commissary officers "white livered sons of bitches."[40]

A Virginian described his and his comrades' outfits at this time in the war: "Reduced to the minimum, the private soldier consisted of one man, one hat, one jacket, one shirt, one pair of pants, one pair of drawers, one pair of shoes, and one pair of socks. His baggage was one

blanket, one rubber blanket, and one haversack." Unlike Yankees, most
Rebels did not carry a knapsack, but as one of them put it in a letter,
"They roll the blankets and clothes into what we call the horse collar
and throw it around our necks."[41]

By the first week in June Lee had readied the army for the march
north. For weeks he had corresponded with Davis and Seddon in efforts
to transfer four brigades from North Carolina to the army. He argued
that they had been detached from his army and should rejoin it before
the campaign began, but although two brigades were sent to Virginia,
none joined Lee's army. As the army started forth, Lee counted approximately 80,000 officers and men in the infantry, artillery, and cavalry.[42]

On "a beautiful bright" day, June 3, the Army of Northern Virginia
began filing away from its fieldworks, marching up the Rappahannock
River. An officer wrote to his father, "I believe there is a general feeling
of gratification in the army at the prospect of active operations." While
en route Major Eugene Blackford of the 5th Alabama paused on the
Chancellorsville battlefield. "Anything so inexpressibly desolate and
lonesome," he confided in a letter home, "I never saw before, the dreary
ruins, the shattered woods, the half-buried bodies, the swarming buz-
zards tugging at the shallow graves and above all the horrible stillness
& utter loneliness and desolation all combined to create a scene and an
impression never to be forgotten."[43]

Lafayette McLaws's veterans led the movement, followed by their
comrades in the First and Second corps. "The men march remarkably
well," reported a North Carolinian to his hometown newspaper, "not
a straggler is seen, and so much cheerfulness I have never before seen
on a march." By June 8 members of the two corps had halted in Culpeper County, a brief stop in the initial leg. "How far we will go, no
one seems to know," Brigadier General John B. Gordon informed his
wife. "I doubt if Genl Lee himself knows." At Fredericksburg Powell
Hill's Third Corps troops stretched their lines, manning the abandoned
works.[44]

Waiting for the infantry in Culpeper County were five brigades of
Jeb Stuart's cavalry division. The horsemen had passed through a difficult winter, with shortages of forage for their mounts. After the Union
cavalry raid during the Chancellorsville Campaign, Lee had requested

the formation of a second mounted division, even sending Stuart to Richmond to plead the case. When the administration refused the proposal, Lee secured the transfer of two regiments from North Carolina and ordered William E. "Grumble" Jones's regiments from the Shenandoah Valley to join Stuart. By early June Stuart counted more than 10,000 officers and men and five batteries of horse artillery in Culpeper County.[45]

The Confederacy had sought a knight, and since his "ride" around the Union army in June 1862, Jeb Stuart had become that knight. War's pageantry stirred his soul. While waiting for the army's movement northward, Stuart held cavalry reviews near Brandy Station on June 5 and 8. Throngs of civilians attended the first review, watching the troopers charge while cannon roared and bands played music. An onlooker enthused, "It is one of the most sublime scenes I ever witnessed." The second affair was more subdued; it was attended by Lee, Longstreet, Ewell, other generals, and John Hood's veteran infantrymen. When the cavalrymen passed by Hood's soldiers, one of them remarked, "Wouldn't we clean them out, if old Hood would only let us loose on 'em." Afterward Lee wrote to his wife, "Stuart was in all his glory."[46]

While Stuart held the second review, three divisions of Union cavalry, 8,000 troopers, supported by 3,000 infantrymen and four artillery batteries, closed on Beverly Ford and Kelly's Ford on the Rappahannock River. The Federals had been aware of the Confederate cavalry's presence in Culpeper County for some time. On June 7 Union army commander Joseph Hooker ordered Brigadier General Alfred Pleasonton, the acting cavalry commander, "to dispense and destroy the rebel force assembled in the vicinity of Culpeper." Since Hooker's formation of a cavalry corps, the army's mounted units had been acting more aggressively.[47]

At 4:30 A.M., on June 9 blue-jacketed troopers splashed across Beverly Ford, initiating the largest cavalry engagement of the war at Brandy Station. After some delays a second Union column crossed at Kelly's Ford, eight miles downstream. The sudden Yankee attack surprised Stuart and his men. The Rebels scrambled to their horses, charging in counterattacks to save their horse artillery batteries and to slow the enemy onslaught. The opening combat swirled at St. James Church.

Grumble Jones's and Wade Hampton's Southerners fought tenaciously in mounted and dismounted fighting. As he had at Chancellorsville on May 3, Stuart rode close to the action, issuing orders and shifting units.[48]

At about noon the Union column from Kelly's Ford approached the battlefield from the south, advancing on two roads. The Yankees rode toward Fleetwood Hill, the dominant terrain feature in the area, located in the rear of Stuart's ranks at St. James Church. When a courier confirmed reports of the enemy's appearance from the south, Stuart appeared "incredulous" at the news. He ordered Jones's and Hampton's horsemen to withdraw and to "move like lightning on those people in our rear."[49]

The struggle for Fleetwood Hill flowed up and down its slopes and onto its crest. A Virginia cavalryman described the fighting: "On each side, in front, behind, everywhere on top of the hill the Yankees closed in upon us. [W]e fought them single-handed, by twos, fours and by squads, just as the circumstances permitted." A trooper claimed Stuart was "coldly furious" as he directed the action. A final counterattack by the Confederates captured three enemy cannon and secured Fleetwood Hill. On the left of Stuart's lines, on Yew Ridge, Brigadier General William H. F. "Rooney" Lee's regiments repulsed a Federal charge, ending the combat. A son of the army commander, Rooney Lee suffered a serious leg wound and weeks later, while recuperating at his wife's home north of Richmond, was captured by the enemy.[50]

Stuart's horsemen held the field after what one of them called "the hardest cavalry fight that Steward [Stuart] ever witnessed." Union casualties exceeded 850; Confederate losses amounted to more than 425. Within the army and in the southern press Stuart was criticized for being surprised. How much he knew of the grumblings among fellow officers and men is uncertain, but he read the newspaper editorials. He denied being surprised, and the public condemnation of his conduct infuriated him. He jealously guarded his reputation and coveted the acclaim accorded him. "He could never see or acknowledge," wrote his chief of staff, Major Henry McClellan, "that he was worsted in an engagement." Unquestionably Stuart and his horsemen had been caught unprepared, but more important, Brandy Station demonstrated that their dominance over their mounted foes was nearing its end.[51]

The Confederate infantry movement north and west resumed on June 10. Two days earlier Robert E. Lee had written to Secretary of War Seddon: "As far as I can judge, there is nothing to be gained by this army remaining quietly on the defensive, which it must do unless it can be re-enforced. I am aware that there is difficulty and hazard in taking the aggressive with so large an army in its front, intrenched behind a river, where it cannot be advantageously attacked." Lee offered, however, to assume the defensive if the War Department directed, knowing full well that he had the approval of Davis and the Cabinet for an offensive movement. Seddon answered two days later, "I concur entirely in your views of the importance of aggressive movements by your army."[52]

On that same day, June 10, Lee composed a lengthy letter to Jefferson Davis, addressing the disparity in numbers between the two sides and Northern peace efforts. The Confederates must expect, he wrote, that the Federals would make "a vigorous use" of their "superiority" in manpower and resources. "We should not, therefore, conceal from ourselves that our resources in men are constantly diminishing, and the disproportion in this respect between us and our enemies, if they continue united in their efforts to subjugate us, is steadily augmenting." Lee believed that the Davis administration should "give all the encouragement we can, consistently with truth, to the rising peace party of the North." The Confederacy should not distinguish "between those who declare for peace unconditionally and those who advocate it as a means of restoring the Union, however much we may prefer the former." When peace negotiations begin, Lee said, "it will be time enough to discuss its terms."[53]

Lee's assessment of sentiment in the North, gathered from his reading of northern newspapers, reflected in part his strategic thinking at that time. Although he stated afterward in his report that he had not intended "to fight a general battle at such a distance from our base," the significance, militarily and politically, of a Confederate victory on Northern free soil surely factored into his overall thinking for an offensive across the Potomac River. Despite his later disavowal, Lee went north in search of a decisive encounter that would give impetus to Northern civilians' clamor for peace. In Pennsylvania the stakes were to be high.[54]

Richard Ewell's Second Corps, Stonewall Jackson's famed foot cavalry, spearheaded the march on June 10, angling northwest toward the Shenandoah Valley. Rumors in the ranks said the army was headed for Maryland, if true, one of the soldiers speculated, "we will have a good Deal of hard fighting." A member of the Stonewall Brigade wrote, "I think we will clear the Yankees out this summer." A North Carolinian declared that once across the Potomac they should "make this war a war of pillaging plundering, and destroying private citizens' property. I feel like retaliating in the strictest sense. I don't think we would do wrong to take horses; burn houses; and commit every depredation possible upon the men of the North."[55]

Ewell's veterans crossed the Blue Ridge Mountains and entered the Shenandoah Valley on June 12. The one-legged corps commander had prodded the marchers, evoking memories of Jackson riding beside their ranks, saying, "Close up, men. Close up." The next day the Rebels descended on Major General Robert H. Milroy's Union garrison at Winchester, skirmishing with the Federals. Ewell spent much of June 14 skillfully deploying his units for an attack, which went forward at about 5:00 p.m. The Southerners routed the Yankees in the Battle of Second Winchester, capturing twenty-three cannon, 300 wagons loaded with supplies and ammunition, and nearly 4,000 prisoners. Colonel Clement Evans of the 31st Georgia boasted, "As usual our troops are feasting over the Yankee eatables, wearing Yankee shoes, boots, hats, and pants, and underclothing."[56]

On June 15 three brigades of Robert Rodes's division crossed into Maryland, and Brigadier General Albert Jenkins's cavalry regiments rode into Chambersburg, Pennsylvania. East of the Blue Ridge Mountains, Longstreet's First Corps marched out of Culpeper County toward the Shenandoah Valley, while Powell Hill's Third Corps started west from Fredericksburg. Longstreet's men entered the Valley on June 17. On this day the Army of Northern Virginia stretched for more than 100 miles, from Virginia's Piedmont to north of the Maryland-Pennsylvania border.[57]

The Union Army of the Potomac had endured a grueling march in the heat and dust from their campsites around Falmouth. When its commander, Joseph Hooker, learned initially of the Confederate movement toward the Shenandoah Valley, he viewed it as a raid. He proposed to the administration in Washington an overland advance against Richmond. Lincoln rejected the idea. Hooker reiterated the request, and the president denied it again. "I think Lee's army, and not Richmond, is your sure objective point," Lincoln replied. "If he comes toward the Upper Potomac, follow on his flank and on his inside track, shortening your lines while he lengthens his. Fight him, too, when opportunity offers. If he stays where he is, fret him and fret him."[58]

The Yankees marched on June 14. The sun scorched the ranks, water became scarce, and hundreds collapsed from sunstroke. Entire regiments fell out of the ranks. "Strong men wilted down as though blasted by something in the air," professed a sergeant. But by June 17 the army's corps sprawled across northern Virginia, west of the Federal capital. When they halted, a private confessed, "I think I could have slept if I had stood on my head."[59]

Hooker stopped the movement to sift through conflicting reports on the whereabouts of Lee's scattered units. Consequently, on June 17, he ordered Alfred Pleasonton's cavalry toward the gaps of the Blue Ridge in search of better intelligence. To the west, screening the Confederate infantry and artillery beyond the mountains, were Jeb Stuart's horsemen. The first clash occurred on this day at Aldie, followed by engagements at Middleburg on June 19 and at Upperville on June 21. Dismounted skirmishing and mounted attacks and counterattacks characterized the fighting. The Yankees kept pushing the Rebels west, toward the Blue Ridge, but Stuart's men prevented their foes from reaching the gaps. Pleasonton learned, however, from prisoners and local citizens, "The main body of the rebel infantry is in the Shenandoah Valley." He conjectured, without any basis in fact, that the Confederates were moving toward Pittsburgh, Pennsylvania.[60]

During the cavalry engagements Stuart met with Lee and Longstreet in Paris, a small village at the eastern foot of Ashby's Gap, on June 18, while the two generals were passing through to the Shenandoah Valley. The meeting apparently centered on the cavalry operations in the unfolding campaign. Stuart likely proposed at this time according to Lee, that "he could damage the enemy and delay his passage of the river [Potomac] by getting in his rear."[61]

On June 22 and 23 Lee sent letters to Stuart, both written by his military secretary, Charles Marshall. In each one Lee gave Stuart the discretion of either moving west into the Valley, following the army northward, or riding east, passing around the rear of the Union army. The more important letter was the second one, dated 5:00 P.M., June 23, and has formed the basis of the controversy over Stuart's actions in the Gettysburg Campaign. It read in part:

> If General Hooker's army remains inactive, you can leave two brigades to watch him, and withdraw with the three others, but should he not appear to be moving northward, I think you had better withdraw this side of the mountain to-morrow night, cross at Shepherdstown the next day, and move over to Frederick-town [Frederick, Maryland].
>
> You will, however, be able to judge whether you can pass around their army without hindrance, doing them all the damage you can, and cross the river east of the mountains. In either case, after crossing the river, you must move on and feel the right of Ewell's troops, collecting information, provisions, &c.

As a final admonition, Lee ordered, "I think the sooner you cross into Maryland, after to-morrow, the better."[63]

Marshall's wording was confusing. The phrase "should he not appear" contravened the previous words, "If General Hooker's army remains inactive." The secretary might have made an unintended mistake or possibly meant the word "now" instead of "not." The orders were also vague about where the cavalry should cross the Potomac east of the mountains, assigned it multiple duties, and designated no time for Stuart's command to be in Maryland if it passed around the Union army.[64]

Although the instructions were "ambiguous and uncertain," Lee intended for Stuart to cross the Potomac as soon as possible and to join Richard Ewell's corps in Pennsylvania. In his report Lee stated clearly his understanding of Stuart's mission. "It was left to his discretion whether to enter Maryland east or west of the Blue Ridge; but he was instructed to lose no time in placing his command on the right of our column as soon as he should perceive the enemy moving northward."

Marshall and fellow staff officer Armistead L. Long asserted in post-war accounts that that had been Lee's plan. The instruction, "I think the sooner you cross into Maryland, after to-morrow, the better" was unequivocal.[65]

Lee's orders granting Stuart authority to march east and to pass around the enemy forces came with the restriction "without hin-drance." Why the Confederate commander approved such a possible enterprise is difficult to understand. Lee had received reports by June 23, the date of the second letter, that the Federals were laying a pon-toon bridge at Edwards Ferry on the Potomac, indicative of a crossing. He expected, or more likely desired, the Yankees to follow him north, presenting an opportunity for striking units of Hooker's army in detail as they marched. Intelligence on the enemy's movements outweighed any gains derived from an operation in its rear. "When one compares the small beneficial results of raids," Porter Alexander concluded in a fair assessment, "even when successful, with the risks here involved, it is hard to understand how Lee could have given his consent."[66]

The commanding general's regard for and confidence in Stuart's skill and judgment surely factored into his granting the cavalryman such latitude. Stuart had earned it. In Moxley Sorrel's estimation he had become the "true body and soul of Lee." Writing of Stuart in a post-war letter, Longstreet asserted: "I often spoke of him to General Lee, as of the best material for cavalry service, but needing an older head to instruct and regulate him. The General was fond of him, and gave way to him to the disadvantage of both."[67]

Stuart had apparently decided to head east, around the Union army, before he received the June 23 letter. Earlier that day Captain John S. Mosby, commander of a company of partisan rangers, arrived at cavalry headquarters at Rector's Cross Roads (today's Atoka) and reported to Stuart that he and his scouts had discovered a corridor between Hook-er's corps through which the Rebel horsemen could pass en route to the Potomac. "I was present in the room when the plan was adopted to go to Ewell by Hooker's rear," wrote Mosby after the war. If Mosby's memory and account are accurate, Stuart had determined upon another "ride" around the Union army hours before he received the second let-ter from army headquarters.[68]

Stuart spent June 24 readying his command for the march. He chose the brigades of Wade Hampton, Fitz Lee, and Rooney Lee, the last temporarily under the command of Colonel John Chambliss Jr., directing them to a rendezvous site outside of Salem (modern-day Marshall). The mounted force numbered about 5,500 officers and men, with six cannon of the horse artillery. One of the troopers admitted, "Our men and horses were already worn and jaded."[69]

Stuart assigned the brigades of Beverly Robertson and Grumble Jones to guard and scout duty in the gaps of the Blue Ridge, as directed by the army commander. He issued specific instructions to Robertson, the senior officer, to watch the Federals closely and, when they marched away, to follow the Confederate army north into Maryland and Pennsylvania. For months, however, Stuart had known of Robertson's limitations as a cavalry officer. Ultimately neither Robertson nor Jones detected the Union movement. When Lee ordered them north on June 29, the two brigades took four days to reach Cashtown, near Gettysburg. Despite his subsequent disavowals, Robertson failed miserably in his primary duty.[70]

At one o'clock on the morning of June 25 Stuart and his staff rode away from Rector's Cross Roads. They headed west toward the Blue Ridge before turning south and joining the three brigades at Salem. The column marched east through Glascock's Gap in the Bull Run Mountains and approached Haymarket. Before them Union infantry, artillery, and wagons, officers and men of the Second Corps, filled the roadbed, plodding northeast. Stuart brought forward cannon, had the crews fire a few rounds, which drew a response from enemy gunners, and withdrew the cavalry several miles rearward to Buckland. The Confederates dismounted and grazed their horses. Stuart had encountered "hindrance."[71]

Jeb Stuart stood at a critical junction in his career as a Confederate horse soldier and in history's judgment of him. "It was now clearly impossible for Stuart to follow the route originally intended," admitted Chief of Staff Henry McClellan in his memoir. He either must retrace his route and cross the Blue Ridge into the Shenandoah Valley or make "a wider *detour*." Conferring with no one, he decided to ride around the Union army. The historian Douglas Southall Freeman concluded,

"Stuart almost certainly was prompted to undertake a long ride in order to restore the reputation he felt had been impaired in the Battle of Brandy Station." The road ahead, not the one behind, beckoned with the possibilities of silencing his critics and recapturing his status as a Confederate hero. It was to be a costly misjudgment.[72]

To Robert E. Lee, Stuart and his 5,500-man cavalry command disappeared from the campaign for a week. In his report Lee stated, "The movements of the army preceding the battle of Gettysburg had been much embarrassed [adversely affected] by the absence of the cavalry." Coming from Lee, this was pointed criticism. When asked in a postwar interview about the reasons for the Confederate defeat in Pennsylvania, Lee attributed one of them to "Stuart's failure to carry out his instructions." The commanding general might have meant that when Stuart found his route blocked, he should have turned around and ridden toward the Valley, crossing the Potomac west of the mountains. His chosen route was not "without hindrance."[73]

On the day Stuart encountered the Union Second Corps column, June 25, the campaign increased in activity. Joseph Hooker's entire army resumed the march, with three infantry corps crossing the Potomac into Maryland. West of the mountains, Longstreet's First Corps and Hill's Third Corps were also across the river, moving toward the Mason-Dixon Line. In Pennsylvania Ewell's veterans were spreading across the south-central section of the state, moving along two main roads toward the Susquehanna River. Ewell had orders from Lee to capture Harrisburg, the state capital.[74]

Like a plague the Southerners descended upon the fertile lands of the Cumberland Valley in the Keystone State. "We passed through the most beautiful and highly cultivated country that I ever saw," exclaimed a North Carolinian in a typical letter. "It was literally a land of plenty." They were not impressed with the residents, though, who were mostly of German descent, the so-called "Dutch." A surgeon claimed, "The people all look very *sour* at us." A private noted that the folks "treated us very kindly but I think it was only from their teeth out."[75]

Lee issued orders on the men's conduct while in the state, enjoining "the troops to abstain with the most scrupulous care from unnecessary or wanton injury to private property." When it came to foraging, however, the men, asserted a South Carolinian, "paid no more attention to them [the orders] than they would to the cries of a screech owl." Quartermaster and commissary details, acting under official instructions, filled wagons with supplies and foodstuffs. The men in the ranks roamed through the countryside, getting "every thing to eat that hart could wish," bragged one of them, who added, "Every thing was cheap all it cost us was to go after it." Writing of the civilians, a Rebel declared, "I guess they thought we were all hungry Methodist preachers." "Never did soldiers appear more buoyant and cheerful than Lee's army," proclaimed a Louisianan.[76]

Some of the Confederates rejoiced in the gray-coated scourge upon the fertile land. When Major Eugene Blackford of the 5th Alabama entered Pennsylvania, he averred, "I had it as the proudest day of my life, the day for which I have been looking so long, when Confederate infantry would invade this state." He noted that when they reached the state line a band played "Bonnie Blue Flag," accompanied by cheers from the soldiers. Before the army crossed the Potomac Colonel Clement Evans of the 31st Georgia wrote home: "The rascals [Federals] are afraid we are going to overrun Pennsylvania. That would indeed be glorious, if we could ravage that state making her desolate like Virginia. It would be a just punishment." Once in Pennsylvania a Virginian declared, "I could rather fight them a hundred years than to be Subjugated by Such a worthless race."[77]

Members of the First and Third corps joined Ewell's troops in Pennsylvania throughout June 26 and 27. Lee, Longstreet, and Hill arrived in Chambersburg on the evening of June 27, establishing their headquarters on the city's eastern edge. A staff officer saw Lee and Longstreet ride through a town, removing their hats to local folks. "The beautiful majesty of Lee's whole person," recounted the aide, "and the lion-like serenity of Longstreet, seemed to produce a profound impression."[78]

Lieutenant Colonel James Arthur Lyon Fremantle of the British Coldstream Guards overtook the Confederate army at Chambersburg. Sent to America as an observer, Fremantle had traveled through the Confederacy before following Lee's army north into Pennsylvania. Lee and Longstreet welcomed him at their headquarters. "General Lee is, almost without exception," the British officer recorded in his diary, "the handsomest man of his age I ever saw. . . . The relations between him and Longstreet are quite touching—they are almost always together." During the march north the two generals had conferred nearly every day. One of Longstreet's aides said of Lee, "I think he relied very much on Longstreet." In a postwar letter the First Corps commander wrote of Lee and himself, "Our talks and letters were almost always of severe thought and study."[79]

Lee appeared sanguine about his army's prospects in Pennsylvania. On the march into northern territory Colonel Eppa Hunton of the 8th Virginia spoke with Lee, expressing his "disinclination to the movement in Pennsylvania." According to Hunton's later account, "General Lee replied that the movement was a necessity; that our provisions and supplies of every kind were very nearly exhausted in Virginia, and that we had to go into Pennsylvania for supplies. He believed that the invasion of Pennsylvania would be a great success, and if so, it would end the war, or we would have rest for sometime to come." Hunton added, "General Lee was so enthusiastic about the movement that I threw away my doubts and became as enthusiastic as he was."[80]

While at Chambersburg John Hood visited army headquarters and found the commanding general in "buoyant spirits." Lee remarked to the fine combat officer, "Ah! General, the enemy is a long time finding us; if he does not succeed soon, we must go in search of him." Hood assured Lee, "I was never so well prepared or more willing." What concerned Lee, however, was the lack of intelligence on Union movements. "I heard General Lee express this apprehension more than once while we lay at Chambersburg," contended Charles Marshall, "and the apprehension was due entirely to his hearing nothing from General Stuart."[81]

The initial report of the location of Hooker's Union corps came to Lee not from Stuart, but from Henry Harrison, a Confederate spy. Longstreet had used the services of Harrison, an erstwhile actor, in southeastern Virginia during the winter. Longstreet hired him before the campaign began, gave him gold coins for expenses, and sent him to Washington, D.C., to gather intelligence. "Where shall I find you, General, to make this report?" asked the spy.

"With the army," replied Longstreet. "I shall be sure to be with it."[82]

"Dirt-stained, travel-worn, and very much broken down," Harrison arrived in Chambersburg on the night of June 28 and was escorted under guard to Longstreet's headquarters. There he reported that the entire Union army was in Maryland, having crossed the Potomac River during June 25 and 26. The army's leading units had reached Frederick. Moxley Sorrel recalled that Longstreet was "immediately on fire at such news." The general directed Major John W. Fairfax of his staff to take the spy at once to Lee's headquarters.[83]

While Harrison waited with the guards, Fairfax entered Lee's tent and repeated the spy's report. According to the aide, Lee "was very reluctant to make a move without confirmation by his cavalry." Distrustful of spies, Lee asked Fairfax if Harrison was reliable. Longstreet had confidence in him, replied Fairfax. With that said, Fairfax departed, taking Harrison with him to Longstreet's headquarters. "Excitement," recalled an officer, prevailed at army headquarters.[84]

Harrison's news forced Lee to act. He suspended Ewell's advance on Harrisburg and ordered the Second Corps commander to concentrate his scattered divisions at either Cashtown or Gettysburg. He also instructed Hill to take the Third Corps across South Mountain to Cashtown the next day, followed by Lafayette McLaws's and John Hood's divisions of Longstreet's First Corps on June 30. George Pickett's brigades would remain in Chambersburg with the army's wagon trains. "In the absence of the cavalry," Lee reported, "it was impossible to ascertain his [Hooker's] intentions; but to deter him from advancing farther west, and intercepting our communication with Virginia, it was determined to concentrate the army east of the mountains."[85]

Lee should not have been surprised at Harrison's information; he had known for a week of the Federals' construction of a pontoon bridge across the Potomac. He had wanted the enemy to abandon Virginia and to follow him north. If the Yankees could not find him, as he told Hood, he would find them. His surprise must have rested in part from having heard nothing from Stuart that the Union army was approaching South Mountain and the Pennsylvania border.[86]

Lee reacted to the spy's news, however, not by concentrating west of South Mountain, but to the east, where an encounter with the Federals seemed most likely. Porter Alexander argued, "The concentration which was ordered at Gettysburg was intended as an offer of battle to him [the enemy]." Henry Heth thought similarly that Lee's "intention was to strike the enemy the very first available opportunity that offered—believing he could, when such an opportunity offered, crush him." Chief of Staff Walter Taylor wrote of Lee, "He sought an encounter with his opponent, but upon his own terms as to time and place."[87]

The Confederates marched on June 30. Ewell's units resumed their retrograde movement; Hill's troops crossed South Mountain to Cashtown; and, Lee, Longstreet, their staffs, and the divisions of McLaws and Hood left Chambersburg for Greenwood, at the mountain's western base. The advance, wrote Lee, was "conducted more slowly than it would have been had the movements of the Federal Army been known." Also unknown to Lee on this day, Jeb Stuart's errant three brigades clashed with Union cavalry at Hanover, a dozen or so miles east of Gettysburg. The engagement forced Stuart to swing farther east, farther away from the main Confederate army.[88]

Late on the morning of June 30 Brigadier General J. Johnston Pettigrew's brigade of North Carolinians of Heth's division encountered Union cavalry west of Gettysburg. Pettigrew had been sent to the town to secure a reported cache of shoes and supplies. Instructed "not to precipitate a fight," Pettigrew halted when he met the Federal horsemen and sent back for further orders from Heth. The division commander thought the foes were only militia troops, but he repeated his earlier orders. Pettigrew retired toward Cashtown.[89]

Heth reported the incident to Hill, who informed Lee and Ewell of it. From the reports of scouts, Hill too believed that Pettigrew had encountered only Federal horsemen and that the infantry of the Army of the Potomac was miles away from Gettysburg. In his message to Ewell he wrote, "I intended to advance the next morning and discover what was in my front." Heth told Hill, "If there is no objection, I will take my division to-morrow and go to Gettysburg and get those shoes!"

"None in the world," answered the Third Corps commander.[90]

That night at army headquarters at Greenwood the "conversation [was] unusually careless & jolly" among Lee's aides, recalled Porter Alexander. They had learned during the day that Major General George G. Meade had replaced Joseph Hooker as commander of the Army of the Potomac. Upon hearing of the change, Lee allegedly remarked that Meade "was not only a soldier of intelligence and ability, but that he was also a conscientious, careful, thorough and painstaking man; that he would make no such mistake in his [Lee's] front as some of his predecessors had made, and if he [Lee] made any mistake in Meade's front he [Meade] would be certain to take advantage of it."[91]

Early on the morning of June 28, outside of Frederick, Meade was awakened by a general from the War Department. Hooker had tendered his resignation the day before over a dispute between him and General-in-chief Henry W. Halleck. Hooker wanted Harper's Ferry abandoned and the 10,000-man garrison sent to his army; Halleck wanted the place held. Evidently Hooker thought he could force the issue, but President Lincoln accepted the resignation and appointed Meade. With the army's senior leadership wracked with dissension since Chancellorsville, Lincoln had learned indirectly that if Hooker were to be replaced, Meade was acceptable to fellow corps commanders. The order from the War Department offered Meade little recourse: he could accept the duty or resign his commission. He accepted command of the army.[92]

A West Pointer, the forty-seven-year-old Meade had been a professional soldier for nearly three decades. He had risen from brigade and divisional command in the Pennsylvania Reserve Division to head of the Fifth Corps. An admirer of George McClellan, he had avoided the army's politics and intrigue. He possessed a volcanic temper, but was a thorough and competent soldier. None of his predecessors, however, had assumed command of the army under more difficult and possibly momentous circumstances. He had been instructed to cover Washington and Baltimore and to give battle to the Confederates. Perhaps no army commander in American history faced such a critical duty and burden.[93]

Throughout June 29 and 30 Meade advanced his seven infantry corps and cavalry divisions across a broad front in Maryland, covering Baltimore and the Union capital. Brigadier General John Buford's mounted brigades reached Gettysburg on June 30 and halted Pettigrew's march toward the town. At nightfall the Union First Corps encamped several miles south of Gettysburg along Emmitsburg Road, with five other infantry corps either in Pennsylvania or a few miles from the state line. "But the Army of the Potomac was no band of school girls," declared a staff officer at this time. "They were not the men likely to be crushed or utterly discouraged by any mere circumstances in which they might find themselves placed."[94]

To the north and west, around the campfires of the Yankees' foes, a deep-seated confidence, a sense of invincibility had sunk into the marrow of the army and its members. "An overweening confidence possessed us all," admitted Walter Taylor. "I am sure," professed Porter Alexander, "there can never have been an army with more supreme confidence in its commander than that army had in Gen. Lee. We looked forward to victory under him as confidently as to successive sunrises." A South Carolinian proclaimed that his comrades "looked upon themselves as invincible." On July 1, 1863, Fremantle recorded in his diary, "The universal feeling in the army was one of profound contempt for an enemy whom they have beaten so constantly, and under so many disadvantages."[95]

During the afternoon of June 30 Lee talked with a group of officers. According to one of them, the Confederate commander said, "Tomorrow, gentlemen, we will not move to Harrisburg as we expected, but will go over to Gettysburg and see what General Meade is after."[96]

Chapter Nine

"The Enemy Is There and I Am Going to Strike Him"

T HE SOUND ROLLED ACROSS the countryside, a low, indistinct rumble like that of a distant summer's storm. To veteran soldiers marching on roads toward Gettysburg, Pennsylvania, on the morning of Wednesday, July 1, 1863, it had the familiar bellow of artillery fire. Men's steps quickened and officers closed up ranks as the rumble swelled and deepened. It heralded a warning, like the growl of an enraged giant.

Robert E. Lee heard the gunfire as he rode with James Longstreet up the western slope of South Mountain. The Confederate commander had greeted his subordinate that morning "in his usual cheerful spirits." When they reached the crest, the sound from the east was unmistakable and incessant. Lee left Longstreet behind to expedite the march of trailing infantry divisions and artillery batteries and hurried forward to Cashtown, where he met Powell Hill. Lee inquired about the artillery fire. Hill, who was feeling "very unwell," replied that he knew little more than that the divisions of Henry Heth and Dorsey Pender had gone toward Gettysburg in a reconnaissance-in-force.[1]

Not since his assignment to command of the army thirteen months earlier to the day had Lee heard such ominous cannon fire. According

to Armistead L. Long of the general's staff, Lee "had previously considered the possibility of engaging the enemy in the vicinity of Gettysburg,
but the time and position were to have been of his own selection." The
clamor of a battle was unexpected and disquieting. While at Cashtown
Lee reportedly told Richard Anderson, one of Hill's division commanders, that without any dispatches from Jeb Stuart he was "ignorant as to
what we have in front of us here. It may be the whole Federal army, or
it may be only a detachment. If it is the whole Federal force we must
fight a battle here; if we do not gain a victory, those defiles and gorges
through which we passed this morning will shelter us from disaster."[2]

Leaving Cashtown, Lee rode east on Chambersburg Pike toward a
billowing and unwanted battle. By his own admission Henry Heth had
"*stumbled* into this fight" earlier in the morning. His instructions had
been "to ascertain what force was at Gettysburg, and, if he found infantry opposed to him, to report the fact immediately, without forcing an
engagement." Instead an encounter with Union cavalry ended in a collision with Union infantry.[3]

Heth's Confederates met John Buford's blue-clad division of horse
soldiers in the fields and on the ridges west of Gettysburg at about 7:30
A.M. Armed with breech-loading carbines, Buford's troopers slowed
Heth's march, forcing the Rebels to deploy skirmishers. The Federal
cavalryman resisted the enemy advance for two hours, holding on
until blue-coated infantry, coming from the south, reached the battlefield. Major General John F. Reynolds, commander of the First Corps
and acting wing commander, preceded his veteran troops, spoke with
Buford, and urged the cavalry general to hang on. At about 9:30 A.M.,
Heth deployed the brigades of Joseph Davis and James Archer on both
sides of Chambersburg Pike and ordered them forward. Southern artillerists unlimbered cannon on Herr Ridge and opened fire.[4]

Advancing south of the pike, Archer's Tennesseans and Alabamians crossed Willoughly Run, passed over the western crest of McPherson's Ridge, and entered Herbst Woods. As the Southerners neared the
ridge's eastern crest "those damned black hats" of the Union Iron Brigade appeared, and volleys of musketry erupted. John Reynolds trailed
the Iron Brigade; as he turned in the saddle, shouting, "Forward men,
forward, for God's sake, and drive those fellows out of the woods," a bul-

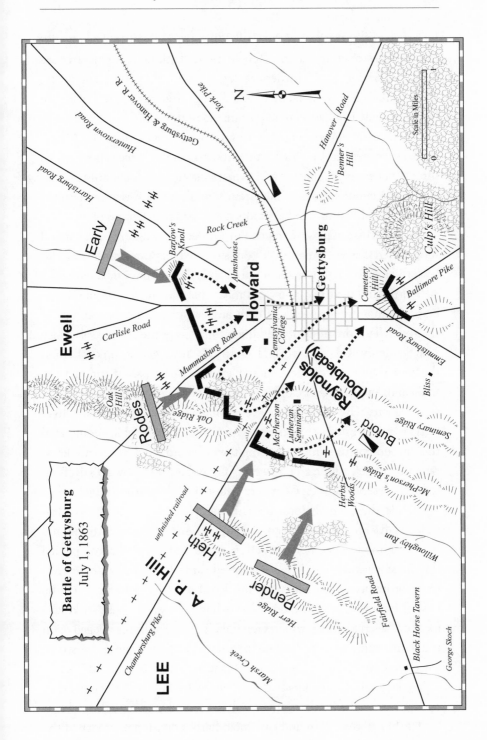

Battle of Gettysburg
July 1, 1863

let struck him at the base of the skull, killing him instantly. The oncoming Yankees overlapped the Rebels' right flank, splintered Archer's
ranks, and drove the Confederates across Willoughby Run. The Federals captured 200 prisoners, including Archer, the first general officer to
be taken since Lee had assumed command of the army.[5]

North of Chambersburg Pike Davis's North Carolinians and Mississippians, officers and men of limited or no combat experience, routed
three other enemy regiments and swung south toward an unfinished railroad cut. A counterattack by men from New York and Wisconsin resulted
in a frenzied, hand-to-hand fight along the road bed. Dozens of members
of the 2nd Mississippi were trapped in the deepest section of the cut and
surrendered. Davis's remaining troops streamed rearward across the fields
back to Herr Ridge. It was about noon, and a lull in the combat ensued.[6]

During the next two hours, on roads that radiated out from Gettysburg, the infantry vanguards of both armies gathered north and west of
the town. Two divisions of the Union First Corps filed onto Oak Ridge
and Seminary Ridge, north and south of Chambersburg Pike. Behind
them two divisions of the Union Eleventh Corps passed through the
town and deployed on the open fields about a mile north of Gettysburg's
town square. The Eleventh Corps commander, Major General Oliver
Otis Howard, posted a third division on Cemetery Hill, which dominated
the surrounding terrain south of the town. Buford's and Reynold's determination to defend the ground west of Gettysburg and Howard's decision
to hold a reserve force on Cemetery Hill shaped the forthcoming battle.[7]

While the Federals formed their lines, Robert E. Rodes's five brigades of Richard Ewell's Second Corps veered off Carlisle Road and
halted on the wooded northern crest of Oak Ridge. Ewell accompanied
the division, and he and Rodes went ahead to Oak Hill, an eminence
that lay just north of Mummasburg Road and the right flank of the
Union First Corps. Rodes described what he saw. "I could strike the
force of the enemy with which General Hill's troops were engaged upon
the flank, and that, besides moving under cover, whenever we struck
the enemy we could engage him with the advantage in ground." Rodes
ordered forward an artillery battalion onto Oak Hill, and the gun crews
opened fire on the Yankees along Oak Ridge and Seminary Ridge.[8]

Farther to the north and east Jubal Early's division approached the battlefield on Harrisburg Road. When Early's four brigades arrived, the Confederates had a numerical advantage of 28,000 to 22,000. "The god of battles appeared to be smiling upon the Confederacy," the historian Stephen Sears wrote in his campaign study. "Beginning the day knowing virtually nothing about the Federals' whereabouts, the two wings of the Army of Northern Virginia had stumbled blindly into positions to smite the Yankees in front and flank simultaneously. It was as if they planned it that way."[9]

Earlier in the morning Ewell had received instructions from Lee; these were, in Ewell's words, "In case we found the enemy's force very large, he did not want a general engagement brought on till the rest of the army came up." Now, however, as the Second Corps commander assessed the situation in front of him, he concluded, "It was too late to avoid an engagement without abandoning the position already taken up, and I determined to push the attack vigorously." Rodes deployed three brigades into line and ordered them forward. It was minutes after 2:00 P.M., and Lee's unwanted battle spiraled into a major clash of arms.[10]

As Rodes's veterans moved to the attack, Lee reached the battlefield. Uncertainty gnawed at him. Where were Stuart and his cavalry? Where was the main body of the Union army? At Cashtown he had said to Richard Anderson: "I cannot think what has become of Stuart; I ought to have heard from him long before now. He may have met with disaster, but I hope not." Later, while riding east, he met Ewell's chief of staff and stepson, Major G. Campbell Brown, who had been sent to inform Lee that Rodes's and Early's divisions were en route to Gettysburg. In Brown's retelling, the commanding general "asked me with a peculiar searching, almost querulous impatience" whether Ewell had heard from Stuart. Lee's demeanor and tone surprised the aide. "I now appreciate," wrote Brown, "that he was really uneasy & irritated by Stuart's conduct."[11]

When Lee arrived, Powell Hill joined him. Soon Henry Heth reined up and requested permission to advance his remaining two brigades, supported by Dorsey Pender's troops. "I do not wish to bring on a general engagement today," responded Lee. "Longstreet is not up." Before long Major Andrew R. Venable of Stuart's staff appeared and reported that the long-absent cavalry was at Carlisle, roughly twenty-five miles to the north. Lee directed Venable to inform Stuart that the mounted command should march to Gettysburg "at once."[12]

The outburst of cannon fire and musketry signaled Rodes's attack. Heth returned to Lee, seeking permission once more for a forward movement. "Wait awhile," Lee told him, "and I will send you word when to go in." A powerful, unseen current had been undammed that day, gathering strength and drawing in two old foes as it swept across the fields, woodlots, and ridges. Soon Lee could no longer breast its force, and he committed Heth to an attack. A grim, bloodthirsty specter had settled over Gettysburg.[13]

Rodes's initial assault ended in a bloody debacle. On the left flank Colonel Edward A. O'Neal's Alabamians suffered a repulse and recoiled. To their right Brigadier General Alfred Iverson Jr.'s North Carolinians swung into pastures south of Oak Hill, angling toward Sheads's Woods on Oak Ridge. Moving deeper into the fields the North Carolinians approached a stone wall along the ridge. Unseen by the Rebels, Yankee infantrymen waited behind the wall. When the Southerners closed to within one hundred yards, the Federals rose and triggered volleys into the stunned North Carolinians' line.[14]

Entire ranks of Iverson's men dropped, mowed down by the gunfire. Trapped in the field, the Confederates "fought like Tigers," claimed a survivor, but they were being slaughtered. The Northerners rushed into the field, and more than 300 North Carolinians surrendered. Iverson, who had remained in the rear, lost slightly more than 900 officers and men out of 1,350 in the brigade. When the brigadier saw his diminished ranks, he "went to pieces and became unfit for further command." He was gone from the army after the campaign.[15]

The next morning Confederate artillerist Private Henry Berkeley walked into the field where Iverson's men had fallen. He counted seventy-nine North Carolinians "laying dead in a straight line." Berkeley recorded afterward in his diary: "I stood on the right and looked down their line. It was perfectly dressed. Three had fallen to the front, the rest had fallen backward; yet the feet of all these dead men were in a perfectly straight line."[16]

The decimation of Iverson's regiments presaged a mounting fury. While Rodes's third brigade, Brigadier General Junius Daniel's North

Carolinians, engaged the Yankees on Oak Ridge, Johnston Pettigrew's and John Brockenbrough's brigades of Heth's division assailed Herbst Woods and McPherson's Ridge, south of Chambersburg Pike. The 2,500 Confederates marched with ranks dressed "in perfect alignment." In their front waited Pennsylvanians, New Yorkers, and the Westerners of the Iron Brigade, roughly 3,500 northerners. A Pennsylvania officer called the oncoming enemy "grey treason."[17]

Within Pettigrew's ranks marched the 26th North Carolina, nearly 850 officers and men, the largest regiment in the Confederate army. Their attack path took them directly toward Herbst Woods and the 24th Michigan of the Iron Brigade. When the Rebels neared Willoughby Run, barely fifty yards or so from the Michiganders, the black-hatted veterans fired a volley, opening the doors of hell for both sides. For the next twenty minutes, in fighting that staggered belief, the opponents ravaged each other, unleashing volleys from distances of forty yards or less. Seven of every ten men on each side fell killed or wounded. The North Carolinians pressed the Michiganders through the woods to a second, third, and fourth line.[18]

A final push by the North Carolinians cleared the woods, and the survivors of the 24th Michigan retreated to Seminary Ridge. On the flanks of the 26th North Carolina Pettigrew's other regiments and Brockenbrough's Virginians wrenched McPherson's Ridge from the Yankees, who joined their comrades on Seminary Ridge. In Herbst Woods the carnage covered the ground. The 24th Michigan's losses exceeded 360 killed, wounded, or missing, more than 70 percent of its numbers. The casualties in the 26th North Carolina amounted to 86 killed and 502 wounded, a casualty rate of 70 percent. The North Carolinians lost their colonel, twenty-one-year-old Henry Burgwyn, and fourteen color-bearers. At Gettysburg these two sustained more casualties than any other regiment in their respective armies.[19]

Behind Pettigrew's and Brockenbrough's men came three brigades of Dorsey Pender's division. Brigadier General Alfred Scales's 1,350 North Carolinians spearheaded the assault, passing over the eastern crest of McPherson's Ridge into the low ground before Seminary Ridge. From the heights of Seminary Ridge Union cannon and infantrymen shredded the Confederate ranks, which "went down like grass before the scythe," according to a Federal officer. Scales suffered a wound, and every field officer except one in his five regiments was killed or wounded. More than 700 North Carolinians fell in the failed charge.[20]

To the south Colonel Abner Perrins's nearly 1,900 South Carolinians, who had stood with Maxcy Gregg at Second Manassas and Fredericksburg, endured a withering fire from the Federals but crossed the fields and plunged into a gap in the Union line on Seminary Ridge. With their flank exposed, the Northerners' line unraveled. Individual regiments hung on until nearly surrounded. The Yankees streamed off the ridge toward town, with the Confederates "so close that we could hear them yelling at us to halt and surrender," exclaimed a soldier in the 7th Wisconsin.[21]

North of Chambersburg Pike Rodes's units renewed the attacks on Oak Ridge, led by Dodson Ramseur's North Carolinians. "Ramseur," wrote Colonel A. M. Parker of the 30th North Carolina, "could handle troops under fire with more ease than any officer I ever saw." The North Carolinians struck the end of the Federal line on Oak Ridge, unhinging the entire line. The Yankees poured off the high ground toward Gettysburg. When members of the Union First Corps reached the town's houses and streets, all order disintegrated. "There was no more discipline or semblance of ranks," confessed one of them, "than would be found in a herd of cattle."[32]

On the plain east of Oak Ridge and north of town the luckless "damned Dutch" of the Union Eleventh Corps were caught in a scissors of Confederate attackers. Brigadier General John B. Gordon's brigade of Early's division collapsed the Federal line, shredding the ranks of enemy regiments on Blocher's Knoll. One of Gordon's veterans said of him later, "He dressed for a battle as others would dress for a ball, and when the boys saw his clear gauntlets and his shining epaulets on him, they ate all their rations, lest they should die before they had a chance to finish them." More Southerners—Georgians, Louisianans, and North Carolinians—hit the beleaguered Eleventh Corps's ranks in front and on the flank, driving them toward Gettysburg. Some Northerners resisted until engulfed. A Pennsylvanian admitted: "It seemed to me the rebels were bound to get to town. They shot a hole through the line where we were."[23]

The members of the Union First and Eleventh corps fled south through the streets and alleys of Gettysburg toward Cemetery Hill. Behind them came the Rebels, who fired at the fleeing enemy and shouted, "Halt, you Yankee sons of bitches." When the Federal survivors reached Cemetery Hill, a staff officer described them as "a miserable remnant" and a "pitiable sight." In all the Confederates captured between 4,000 and 5,000 prisoners and killed or wounded about 5,000 more. In the town the Southerners celebrated the victory with "joy and exultation" and began stripping enemy dead of their uniforms, shoes, and accoutrements.[24]

From Seminary Ridge Robert E. Lee had watched the flight of the Federals through the town and up Cemetery Hill. The commanding general "then directed me to go to General Ewell," recounted Chief of Staff Walter Taylor, "and say to him that, from the position which he occupied, he could see the enemy retreating over those hills, without organization and in great confusion; that it was only necessary to press 'those people' in order to secure possession of the heights, and that, if possible, he wished him to do this." Taylor found Ewell in town and delivered the orders. "General Ewell did not express any objection," continued Taylor, "or indicate the existence of any impediment, to the execution of the order conveyed to him, but left the impression upon my mind that it would be executed."[25]

After Taylor rode away, Ewell conferred with Jubal Early and Robert Rodes, who urged an attack on the heights if supported by Powell Hill's troops on the right. Ewell directed Lieutenant James Power Smith, a staff officer, to convey Early's and Rodes's views to Lee. Ewell and Early then proceeded south on Baltimore Street to reconnoiter the Union position on Cemetery Hill. They saw on the heights rallied Federal infantry and dozens of cannon, which commanded the approaches to the hill.[26]

It was after 5:00 P.M. when Smith returned from delivering the message to Lee. The Confederate commander had no units available to support an assault, reported Smith, but Lee wished Ewell "to carry the hill occupied by the enemy, if he found it practicable, but to avoid a general engagement until the arrival of the other divisions of the army." In the judgment of the historian Stephen Sears, "The decision was left entirely in Ewell's hands, and he was urged to start a fight but not to start a battle."[27]

Ewell's indecisiveness, a source of subsequent heated controversy, is understandable. Lee's instructions were discretionary, but also contradictory. His best division commanders, Early and Rodes, opposed an attack without assistance. Early's units had become disorganized during the pursuit, and Rodes's brigades had suffered costly losses in their attacks. Furthermore Brigadier General William Smith reported that an unknown enemy force threatened Ewell's left flank on York Road. In response Ewell sent Gordon's brigade east on the road, following it with Early and Rodes on a personal reconnaissance. The report could not be verified, but Ewell left Smith and Gordon as protection for his flank. All of this consumed more time.[28]

At about six o'clock Edward Johnson met Ewell and reported that his division would arrive in an hour or so. By then Ewell had shifted his attention to Culp's Hill, a wooded, higher elevation east of Cemetery Hill. He had sent two aides to the heights to investigate whether Union troops occupied it. When Johnson arrived, Ewell directed him to place his division in line next to Rodes's brigades while Early advanced to seize Culp's Hill. Early objected at once to the proposal, claiming that his men were "not in condition to make the move." Early and Johnson exchanged heated words, laced with profanities, but Ewell acceded to Early's protests, ordered his troops into camp, and directed Johnson to bring forward his division and to await further instructions.[29]

Then and thereafter, to fellow Confederates and future historians, Ewell allowed a splendid opportunity to slip away and consequently to reshape the battle at Gettysburg. In a private postwar letter Porter Alexander described Ewell's conduct as "*abominable.*" After the war, in a veiled criticism of Ewell's actions on July 1, Lee said, that he "could not get [Ewell] to act with decision." In other postwar accounts, written by former aides of Stonewall Jackson, they argued that if their former commander had been there, he would have pressed the attack and secured the heights. One of them quoted Major Sandie Pendleton, Ewell's chief of staff, saying at the time, "Oh, for the presence and inspiration of 'Old Jack' for just one hour!"[30]

Yet a success in an assault on Cemetery Hill was doubtful. Burdened with enemy prisoners and disorganized by the attacks and pursuit into town, Second Corps units would have required time to prepare for an advance. An attack could not have gone forward before five o'clock at best, if not later. By then roughly 12,000 men of the two Union corps had regrouped on Cemetery Hill, and upwards of forty cannon swept the approaches to the heights. John Buford's cavalry division lay to the south, near the Peach Orchard, and could have threatened the flank of Hill's units had they joined in an assault. Additionally the 9,000-man Twelfth Corps was coming up on Baltimore Pike when the Federal lines north and west of town collapsed.[31]

Union Major General Winfield Scott Hancock had been sent by army commander George G. Meade to assume overall command at Gettysburg. Hancock arrived on Cemetery Hill before four o'clock. With the death of John Reynolds, Hancock was unquestionably the army's finest corps commander and a redoubtable fighter. He believed that after the survivors of the First and Eleventh corps had been rallied, the Confederates could not have taken the hill. Similarly Armistead Long of Lee's staff conducted a reconnaissance of the Union position and stated later: "I found Cemetery Hill occupied by a considerable force, a part strongly posted behind a stone fence near its crest, and the rest on a reverse slope. In my opinion an attack at that time, with the troops at hand, would have been hazardous and of very doubtful success."[32]

"Ewell's mistake on July 1 was not that he failed to attack Cemetery Hill," wrote Donald Pfanz, a biographer of the general, "but that he did not take Culp's Hill." He bowed to Early's opposition against using his troops in a movement against Culp's Hill and subsequently assigned the duty to Johnson's division. By the time Ewell issued specific orders to Johnson to seize the hill if unoccupied and for the troops to move into position, it was, in Johnson's words, "late on the night of July 1." By early morning on July 2, the Federal Twelfth Corps manned the hill. Presciently, when Ewell hesitated to attempt the capture of the hill by Johnson, Early warned the corps commander, "If you do not go up there tonight, it will cost you 10,000 lives to get up there tomorrow."[33]

Ultimately, however, primary responsibility for the Confederates not pressing the offensive after four o'clock rested with Lee. Typically he had granted Ewell discretion, but when the subordinate requested support for an assault on Cemetery Hill, Lee withheld it. He must have concurred in Powell Hill's judgment that the divisions of Henry Heth and Dorsey Pender were "exhausted by some six hours' hard fighting." But in fact the brigades of James Lane and Edward Thomas of Pender's division had incurred few casualties and could have been used in an assault. Lee also had at hand Richard Anderson's five brigades, which had been halted on Lee's orders two miles west of Gettysburg along Chambersburg Pike.[34]

The evidence describes a reluctant Lee. With sounds of battle clearly audible to the east, Anderson rode forward, seeking clarification about the order to halt his division. "General Lee replied that there was no mistake made," Anderson related, "and explained that his army was not all up, that he was in ignorance as to the force of the enemy in front, that . . . [Anderson's] alone of the troops present, had not been engaged, and that a reserve in case of disaster, was necessary." In his report Lee stated that without knowledge of the enemy's strength and location, he was concerned about "exposing the four divisions present, already weakened and exhausted by a long and bloody struggle, to over-whelming numbers of fresh troops."[35]

Although the army had routed two Union corps, inflicted heavy casualties, and captured thousands of prisoners, the uncertainty that had plagued Lee for days remained. He dispatched four officers south of Seminary Ridge in a reconnaissance. The party studied the Union position on Cemetery Hill, as related by Armistead Long. One of the officers, Captain Samuel Johnston, thought, however, that the mission's purpose "was to be ready for a flank movement on the part of the enemy." If it were so, the reconnaissance might explain, in part, Lee's retention of Anderson's division as a reserve. From sunrise to sunset on July 1 Confederate operations had been hampered by the lack of solid intelligence on the main body of Meade's army. Uncharacteristic caution, not aggressiveness, governed Lee's decisions.[36]

While Ewell wrestled with command problems in Gettysburg, James Longstreet joined Lee on Seminary Ridge. The British observer Arthur Fremantle noted in his diary that the First Corps commander was "invariably spoken of as 'the best fighter in the whole army.'" Fremantle added that as Longstreet passed a column of troops en route to the battlefield one of the soldiers shouted to his comrades, "Look out for work, now, boys, for here's the old bulldog again." Longstreet arrived after five o'clock and found that Lee "was engaged at the moment." He examined the terrain south of town through field glasses and did not like what he saw. Where the Yankees were regrouping, the ground appeared naturally strong.[37]

When Lee had finished, Longstreet turned to him and spoke up: "We could not call the enemy to position better suited to our plans. All we have to do is file around his left and secure good ground between him and his capital." But Lee did not like the idea of a flank or broad turning movement, and his "impatience" with the proposal surprised Longstreet. Jabbing a fist at Cemetery Hill, Lee exclaimed, "If the enemy is there tomorrow, we must attack him."

"If he is there," rebutted Longstreet, "it will be because he is anxious that we should attack him—a good reason, in my judgment, for not doing so."[38]

The exchange between Lee and his finest officer underlay subsequent events during the next two days and ignited one of the most enduring controversies about the Confederate defeat at Gettysburg. At that moment, in the waning hours of daylight on July 1, Longstreet's proposal was impractical. Lee neither knew the location of Meade's other five infantry corps nor had Stuart's cavalry to screen such movement of perhaps fifteen or twenty miles. Besides, Lee had won a decisive victory and refused to relinquish the initiative to his opponent. He had not sought or wanted a battle on this day, but now he reacted to the circumstances on the battlefield.[39]

The disagreement between the two soldiers extended beyond the immediate present, lying rooted in conflicting views on tactics and in past understandings. "Longstreet did not wish to take the offensive," argued Porter Alexander. "His objection to it was not based at all upon the peculiar strength of the enemy's position for that was not yet recognized, but solely on general principles." By the conflict's third summer, Longstreet had concluded, "the time had come when it was imperative that the skill of generals and the strategy and tactics of war should take the place of muscle against muscle." In a private postwar letter he explained further, "Our losses were so heavy when we attacked that our army must soon be depleted to such extent that we should not be able to hold a force in the field sufficient to meet our adversary."[40]

While on the march to Pennsylvania, Lee and Longstreet had conferred almost daily. They discussed the army's previous campaigns and, in Longstreet's words, "had concluded even victories such as these were consuming us, and would eventually destroy us." From the meetings, according to Longstreet, "the ruling idea of the campaign" had emerged: "Under no circumstances were we to give battle, but exhaust our skill in trying to force the enemy to do so in a position of our own choosing. The 1st Corps to receive the attack and fight the battle. The other Corps, to then fall upon and try to destroy the Army of the Potomac."[41]

Longstreet maintained that his support for an offensive movement into the North was predicated on "the understanding that we were not to deliver an *offensive* battle." He reportedly stated after the war that Lee promised not to fight a general engagement in Pennsylvania. When Lee learned of this, he doubted whether Longstreet had ever said that and dismissed the idea as "absurd." To be sure, some of Longstreet's postwar statements, given in reply to his critics, lacked credibility. It was understood at army headquarters, however, that the Confederates expected to wage a defensive battle. Lee's design, wrote Walter Taylor, was to select "a favorable time and place in which to receive the attack which his adversary would be compelled to make on him, to take the reasonable chances of defeating him in a pitched battle."[42]

July 1 unraveled the design. Lee had witnessed a signal victory, another affirmation of his army's incomparable prowess. "It had not been intended to fight a general battle at such a distance from our base, unless attacked by the enemy," he wrote in his report, agreeing with Longstreet's claim. But the fighting had been joined, Lee explained, and "a battle thus became, in a measure, unavoidable. Encouraged by the successful issue of the engagement of the first day, and in view of the valuable results that would ensue from the defeat of the army of General Meade, it was thought advisable to renew the attack."[43]

Lee had led the army north toward a reckoning. It had come unexpectedly and unwanted on this day, but there could be no turning back from it. He could have disengaged, waited for all of his divisions to arrive, and maneuvered the enemy into assailing his army. Evidently he never considered adopting a defensive stand, and, at Antietam Creek, he would not abandon a battlefield until the issue was settled.[44]

Above all else Lee was a warrior. Porter Alexander said of him, "He had the combative instinct in him as strongly developed as any man living." As for the outcome of July 1, Longstreet wrote, "The sharp battle fought by Hill and Ewell on that day had given him a taste of victory." A biographer of the Confederate commander, Emory Thomas, argued insightfully that Lee "confronted the moment of truth at Gettysburg and never flinched."[45]

When Longstreet rode away from Seminary Ridge at seven o'clock, he was convinced that his commander would renew the offensive on the next day. The lieutenant general came to his temporary headquarters along Chambersburg Pike a few miles west of town, near the bivouac sites of Lafayette McLaws's and John Hood's troops. Over a meal with staff members and guests Longstreet described the Federal position as "very formidable." He believed it would require the "whole army" to take the heights, and "then at a great sacrifice." He shook "his head gravely over the advantages conferred by this position," recalled a listener.[46]

Before Lee slept he went to Ewell's headquarters, located north of town, near the Adams County almshouse. The commanding general met with Ewell, Early, and Rodes on the porch of a house. Lee wanted to attack the Federals early the next morning and suggested that the Second Corps shift to the right, abandoning the town, and join Longstreet's troops in the assault. All three of the subordinates opposed the idea, arguing that such a movement would demoralize the troops after their victory and leave behind in Gettysburg seriously wounded men. Lee agreed reluctantly to keep the Second Corps on the army's left and departed.[47]

Hours later Lee changed his mind, directing that Ewell bring his corps to the west side of town. The order brought Ewell to Lee's tent, erected in a field behind Seminary Ridge, beside Chambersburg Pike. Under the mistaken belief that Johnson's division had either seized Culp's Hill or would soon do so, Ewell reiterated his argument against the move, and Lee again relented. In an unpublished account Porter Alexander addressed the consequences of leaving the Second Corps where it was, "The ground [Culp's Hill] is there still for any military engineer to pronounce whether or not Ewell's Corps & all its artillery, was not practically paralyzed and useless by its position during the last two days of the battle."[48]

During the night, on dusty, dark roads, in ranks stretching for miles, thousands of officers and men of the Army of the Potomac trudged toward Gettysburg. George Meade sent Winfield Hancock to the battlefield with these directions: "If you think the ground and position there a better one to fight a battle under existing circumstances, you will so advise the general [Meade], and he will order all the troops up." Earlier Meade had issued a contingency plan for the army to assume a defensive position behind Pipe Creek, miles south of Gettysburg, but, like Lee, he found himself drawn into a battle. When a message from Hancock reached headquarters at Taneytown, Maryland, at about 6:00 P.M., Meade ordered a concentration of the army at Gettysburg.[49]

The Union commander and his staff started for Gettysburg, arriving before midnight on Cemetery Hill. Met by a coterie of generals, Meade inquired about the terrain. Informed that it was good ground for a fight, he replied that he was pleased to hear it, because "it was too late to leave it." Accompanied by Oliver Howard and the army's chief of artillery, Henry J. Hunt, Meade rode over the ground and had a staff officer sketch a map for the posting of the infantry corps as they arrived on the field.[50]

The terrain studied by Meade possessed natural strength and a concave character, which could expedite the movement of units from one section of the line to another. In time it would be described as a fishhook. Cemetery Hill rose sixty to eighty feet above its base and formed the hinge or bend of the line. Rising 140 feet high east of Cemetery Hill, wooded Culp's Hill anchored the Federal right flank, the barb of the fishhook. Cemetery Ridge extended south from Cemetery Hill nearly a mile and a half, descending in elevation into a bottomland at the base of Little Round Top. Although wooded Big Round Top towered more than 100 feet above the lower hill, Little Round Top, with its western face cleared of trees, dominated the ground on the left flank. Orchards, pastures, and fields of corn and wheat, dotted with farmhouses and barns, patterned the land to Seminary Ridge, less than a mile away to the west.[51]

By midmorning on July 2 all of Meade's infantry corps except the Sixth had arrived on the battlefield. Like their foes, these veteran infantrymen and artillerists sought a reckoning with their old nemesis. When they had crossed into Pennsylvania, civilians cheered for them. A New Yorker expressed a common sentiment to his wife. "If I ever felt I wanted to fight the enemy, it was here where those ladies were calling us to drive the Rebels back into Virginia where they belonged." This was their land, free soil, where the cause must be sustained. For this army, cursed by bad luck and bad leadership, Gettysburg offered redemption for the past. So as they filed into line on the finest ground they had ever defended, something immeasurable, beyond duty, honor, and the salvation of a country, steeled them. "The Army of the Potomac," asserted a staff officer, "would do as it was told, always."[52]

While the Federals gathered, Lee, Longstreet, and countless fellow Southerners rose before sunrise. This second day at Gettysburg, Thursday, July 2, would come to haunt Confederate history. Within weeks of the campaign's conclusion and for nearly a century and a half since, enticing possibilities, speculative what-ifs, and strident controversy have characterized the study of this most critical day at Gettysburg and the reasons for the Confederate defeat. July 2, 1863, has lingered in the memory of generations of Americans. For Northerners and Southerners on the battlefield that day, it was the reality that mattered, the fearful combat and the staggering carnage. If Gettysburg marked a divide in the Civil War, the second day constituted the passage through it.[53]

Robert E. Lee had not fashioned a specific plan for the day except to resume the offensive when Longstreet joined him on Seminary Ridge. When the two generals conferred, Lee indicated that he needed the First Corps divisions of Lafayette McLaws and John Hood for an attack on the Union position. Longstreet repeated his idea of a broad flanking movement beyond the Federals' left flank, which would place the Confederates between Meade's army and Washington, D.C. The Yankees, argued Longstreet, would have to assail the entrenched Southerners. "I consider it part of my duty," he explained in a letter a few weeks later, "to express my views to the commanding general." For a second time Lee rejected the proposal.[54]

Lee rightfully dismissed Longstreet's plan as still impractical, espe-

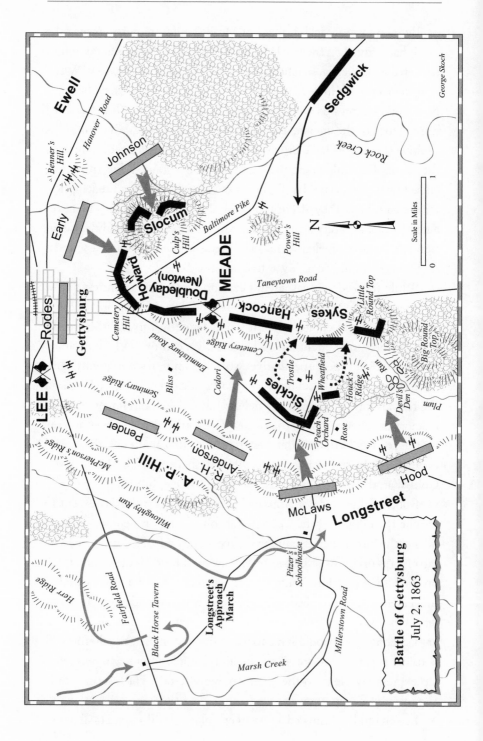

Battle of Gettysburg
July 2, 1863

George Skoch

cially with the enemy nearby. The Confederate commander could have, however, assumed a defensive stand. It might have been prudent of him to do so, for the military and political burden of driving the Rebels out of Pennsylvania rested with Meade. But the "prevailing idea" at army headquarters was, according to Lee's aide Walter Taylor, to press the Federals and to follow up the tactical initiative gained on the first day.[55]

When asked about Gettysburg a few years later, Lee answered, in the words of the questioner: "Everything was risky in our war. He knew oftentimes that he was playing a very bold game, but it was the only *possible* one." General Henry Heth contended about the resumption of the offensive, "The fact is, General Lee believed the Army of Northern Virginia, as it then existed, could accomplish anything." Although Porter Alexander thought Lee was "forcing the game at Gettysburg," he agreed with Heth, "I surely think that Gen Lee never paid his soldiers a higher compliment than in what he gave them to do on this occasion [July 2]." Justus Scheibert, the Prussian army engineer with the army, attributed Lee's decision to "excessive disdain for the enemy."[56]

At about daybreak Lee sent Charles Venable of his staff to seek Richard Ewell's opinion of an attack along the Second Corps's lines and detailed Captain Samuel Johnston, an engineer officer, on a reconnaissance of the enemy's left flank south of Gettysburg. The commanding general needed intelligence on Federal strength and dispositions before crafting an offensive strike. While he and Longstreet waited near the Lutheran Seminary for the aides' return, members of their staffs and generals Powell Hill, Henry Heth, and John Hood joined them. Later the foreign observers with the army and Francis Lawley, a correspondent for the London *Times*, came in at various times during the morning. Often Lee, Longstreet, and Hill sat on a log or fallen tree turnk.[57]

Accounts of those present with Lee conflict on the general's demeanor. Lawley thought that Lee appeared "more anxious and ruffled than I had ever seen him before, though it required close observation to detect it." Scheibert observed that during July 2 and 3 Lee was "not at his ease," looked "care-worn," and lacked the "quiet self-possessed calmness" that he had had at Chancellorsville. Conversely, Lafayette McLaws, who joined the group, stated that the commanding general "was as calm and cool as I ever saw him." In two different accounts Hood described him as "full of hope" and "seemingly anxious" for an attack. When Hood inquired about the Yankees' position, Lee responded, "The enemy is here, and if we do not whip him, he will whip us."[58]

Captain Johnston returned between seven and eight o'clock. Accompanied by Major John J. Clarke, Longstreet's engineer, he had ridden onto the western slope of Little Round Top, "where I had a commanding view" of the area. He traced his route on a map for Lee, who asked him, "Did you get there?," indicating Little Round Top. Johnston assured him that he had proceeded that far, reporting that he had seen only three or four Union cavalrymen as they rode on Emmitsburg Road. Lee, wrote Johnston later, "showed clearly that I had given him valuable information."[59]

Johnston was a capable officer who refrained from the postwar controversies on events of the second day. But his destination on the reconnaissance has puzzled historians. If he had ascended Little Round Top, as he claimed in later private correspondence, how had he not detected the presence of men of the Union Third Corps, who were in the fields at the base of the hill? "It must be concluded," wrote the historian Harry W. Pfanz in his excellent study of the second day, "that when Captain Johnston's reconnaissance party failed to detect Federal units in the area between the Peach Orchard and the Round Tops and on the lower end of Cemetery Ridge, it was somehow the victim of grave misfortune. As a result of this failure, Captain Johnston made an incorrect report to his commanding general that was to have serious consequences later in the day."[60]

Johnston's report settled the matter for Lee. Longstreet's divisions of McLaws and Hood would undertake the primary attack, an oblique assault north of the Round Tops toward the lower end of Cemetery Ridge, sweeping up the ridge and collapsing the Union left flank. Lee showed McLaws on a map that he wanted the subordinate's division aligned perpendicular to the Emmitsburg Road in the area of the Peach Orchard. Lee then asked McLaws if he could "get there if possible without being seen by the enemy." McLaws replied that he knew of "nothing to prevent me." At this point Longstreet interceded, saying that he wanted the division posted parallel to the road. Lee said no, and assigned Johnston as a guide for the march.[61]

It was nine o'clock, and Longstreet knew that his two divisions would lead the Confederate offensive. At about this time he instructed Porter Alexander to bring up his artillery battalion and to examine the ground opposite the Round Tops. Longstreet's opposition to an assault remained, however. Chief of Staff Moxley Sorrel admitted that the general "failed to conceal some anger." While on Seminary Ridge Longstreet said to Hood: "The General [Lee] is a little nervous this morning; he wishes me to attack; I do not wish to do so without Pickett. I never like to go into battle with one boot off." At the time George Pickett's three brigades of Virginians were on the march from Chambersburg and would not approach the battlefield until late afternoon.[62]

Lee left at about this time for a conference with Ewell. For the next two hours, until Lee's return, Longstreet apparently did little in preparation for the movement of his divisions. Although duty required him to attend to matters with the thoroughness that had marked his generalship on previous battlefields, he allowed his disagreement with the commanding general to affect his conduct. Sorrel wrote of Longstreet, "There was apparent apathy in his movements." He had earned Lee's trust, and despite his strong reservations about the wisdom of an offensive, he owed Lee and his veteran soldiers his finest efforts.[63]

From history's perspective, Longstreet's judgment was sound. No member of Lee's army offered more astute, even harsh postwar criticisms of Confederate operations at Gettysburg than Porter Alexander. The writings of the talented artillerist bristled with sharp observations. The Yankees, he contended, held a "wonderfully strong position," which "could never have been successfully assaulted." The ground possessed natural advantages, with interior lines for troop movements. By contrast, once established the Confederate line extended in an exterior or convex arc for nearly five miles. He described it as "the *utter absurdity* of our position. It was simply preposterous to *hope* to win a battle when so strung out & separated that cooperation between the three corps was impossible by a miracle. And comparatively little pains was exercised to bring it about either."[64]

History, however, would have to wait. For the present the vaunted Army of Northern Virginia assumed the offensive at the direction of its commanding general. Lee arrived back on Seminary Ridge at about eleven o'clock. He and Ewell had examined the Federal line on Culp's Hill and Cemetery Hill. According to Jedediah Hotchkiss, Lee "feared we would only take it at a great sacrifice of life." Then on rejoining Longstreet, he issued the orders for the advance of the two First Corps divisions. Longstreet requested a delay until Brigadier General Evander Law's brigade of Hood's command, known to be en route, arrived from New Guilford, where it had been stationed. Lee consented.[65]

As finalized, the offensive demanded timeliness, coordination, and aggressive leadership—elusive attainments on a battlefield. Assuming that the Union army was in fact where Lee believed it to be, McLaws's and Hood's troops would march by a concealed route beyond the Union left flank, deploy, and charge north along Emmitsburg Road, rolling up the enemy's line on Cemetery Ridge. When they attacked, Richard Anderson's Third Corps brigades, posted in the Confederate center on Seminary Ridge, would continue the assault. Powell Hill's other divisions would "threaten the enemy's center," preventing Federal reinforcements from opposing Longstreet's attackers. On the Confederate army's left, Ewell's Second Corps units would make "a simultaneous demonstration" that might "be converted into a real attack should the opportunity offer."[66]

On one occasion Lee explained his method of command to the Prussian officer, Scheibert. Various versions of his words have been printed, but one account has him saying, "Captain, I do everything in my power to make my plans as perfect as possible, and to bring my troops upon the field of battle; the rest must be done by my generals and their troops, trusting to Providence for the victory." In the absence of Stonewall Jackson, this method was to be tested more than it ever had been in the past.[67]

Longstreet's 14,500 officers and infantrymen, with two artillery battalions, began the march between noon and 12:30 P.M. When the head of the column reached a rise east of Black Horse Tavern, it came into view of a Union signal station on Little Round Top. Forced to backtrack, the countermarch further delayed the opening of Longstreet's assault. The Confederates followed a farm lane to Fairfield Road, marched north a short distance before striking a road along Willoughby Run, and angled southeast, shielded by Seminary Ridge. At Pitzer's Schoolhouse they struck Millerstown Road, turned east, and approached the ridge's crest. Across the fields, barely 600 yards away, Union infantry and artillery manned the Peach Orchard, their lines extending southeast toward Little Round Top and north along Emmitsburg Road.[68]

The Yankees belonged to Major General Daniel E. Sickles's Third Corps, numbering about 10,700 officers and men. Sickles's two divisions had been posted during the morning on the low ground at the southern end of Cemetery Ridge. As the hours passed, the colorful Sickles, whom Meade could barely abide personally, became more concerned about the ridge in his front along Emmitsburg Road. Perhaps he thought of his ordered abandonment of Hazel Grove at Chancellorsville and the grievous results. Without orders and without Meade's knowledge, he advanced his command to the high ground, jeopardizing the army's entire line. He had too few men to cover the distance from Devil's Den to the Peach Orchard and north up Emmitsburg Road. The new deployment formed a salient at the orchard, making it vulnerable to an attack on three sides. Longstreet remarked later that Sickles's line "was, in military language, built in the air."[69]

When McLaws saw the Federals in his front, he admitted, "The view presented astonished me." During the march Longstreet had assured him, "There is nothing in your front; you will be entirely on the flank of the enemy." Instead they confronted an entirely unexpected tactical situation. Had Sickles remained on Cemetery Ridge and covered Little Round Top, as instructed, Lee's plan of an assault along Emmitsburg Road would have exposed the Confederates' flank. By his unauthorized action Sickles not only endangered the Union army's position but presented the Southerners with an exposed target.[70]

Porter Alexander maintained that had Longstreet attacked two or three hours earlier the chance of success would have "immensely increased." His argument, however, lacks merit. Since midmorning Meade's army had manned the length of Cemetery Ridge, with the Fifth Corps in reserve, east of the ridge's southern end and Little Round Top. The historian Douglas Southall Freeman concluded that Cemetery Ridge "was held by strong, well-placed troops" hours before Lee issued the orders for Longstreet's march. "In that fact," wrote Freeman, "which is historically verifiable, much of the criticism of Longstreet [for delays] evaporates." The arrival of the Confederates on the southern end of the battlefield between three and four o'clock favored them.[71]

Skirmish and artillery fire announced the Confederates' presence. McLaws shifted his four brigades into line, two brigades in front and two directly behind. Riding south on Seminary Ridge, Lee joined Longstreet and "was impatient that the charge was delayed." Faced now with the Third Corps in their front, Lee either directed Longstreet or approved Longstreet's decision to alter the attack path. Unable to advance up Emmitsburg Road, the Rebels would charge ahead in a line roughly parallel to the road. Longstreet posted Hood's four brigades, aligned like McLaws's, lengthening the line southward across Emmitsburg Road. A South Carolinian with McLaws thought that Longstreet "had more the look of gloom than I had ever noticed before." Skirmishers and artillerists continued their work.[72]

Before Longstreet ordered the advance he received a request from Hood for permission to turn the Union flank by marching around Big Round Top. Hood had sent several Texans on a scout, and they reported that they had gone into the enemy's rear and found only a park of wagons. Longstreet denied the request, though Hood asked a second and third time. Longstreet rightly rejected the idea, for it would have dangerously separated his two divisions, and by the time Hood passed behind the hill, the Union Sixth Corps was in the area. Longstreet told Hood, "It is General Lee's order—the time is up—attack at once."[73]

Their time had come, these Alabamians, Texans, Arkansans, Georgians, South Carolinians, and Mississippians. "Never was a body of soldiers fuller of the spirit of fight, and the confidence of victory," claimed a Mississippian. A South Carolinian boasted in his unit history, "There was a kind of intuition, an apparent settled fact, among the soldiers of Longstreet's corps, . . . when the hard, stubborn, decisive blow was to be struck, the troops of the first corps were called upon to strike it." Before them, in the words of the historian Bruce Catton, "was a test of what men can nerve themselves to attempt and what they can compel themselves to endure, and at shattering cost it proved that the possibilities in both directions are limitless."[74]

Hood's veterans stepped out at four o'clock. When they cleared the trees, Union gunners opened on them. "Then was fairly commenced," wrote Longstreet after the war, "what I do not hesitate to pronounce the best three hours' fighting ever done by any troops on any battle-field." Twenty minutes into the charge, however, a piece of shell struck Hood in the arm as he sat on his horse in the orchard of the Michael Bushman farm, knocking him to the ground and rendering his left hand useless for the rest of his life. A Georgian wrote a few weeks before that Hood "knows more about the management of volunteers, than any officer I have ever seen." But he was carried to the rear, and aides went in search of Evander Law, the division's senior brigadier general, to replace him.[75]

The coordination between the brigades soon dissolved. Regiments in Law's Alabama brigade veered apart, and a gap formed in the center of Jerome Robertson's Texas Brigade. While these units angled toward the Round Tops, behind them, moving toward Rose's Woods and Devil's Den, came the pair of Georgia brigades under Henry Benning and George T. Anderson. A Georgia lieutenant said afterward that the Yankees held "the strongest position I ever saw."[76]

Union artillery fired on them. "I could hear bones crash like glass in a hail storm," asserted a Georgian. Colonel Dudley M. DuBose of the 15th Georgia avowed, "I never saw troops move more steadily & in better order than these did on that occasion." When they closed on Sickles's infantry ranks, the combat escalated into a howling fury. A Rebel insisted, "It seemed to me that my life was not worth a straw." "The Confederates appeared to have the devil in them," thought Colonel P. Regis de Trobriand, a Third Corps brigade commander. Watching from Cemetery Ridge, a Union staff officer exclaimed, "What a hell is there down that valley."[77]

The Alabamians, Texans, and Georgians charged against a wall of musketry and artillery. Through Rose's Woods, across a triangular-shaped field, along the lower slope of Big Round Top, known as the "Devil's Kitchen," across Houck's Ridge, and into Devil's Den, the Rebels drove, shattering enemy ranks and capturing cannon. On the far right end of the line the 15th and 47th Alabama surged toward the southeastern slope of Little Round Top. On the hill the 20th Maine and 83rd Pennsylvania of Colonel Strong Vincent's Fifth Corps brigade blasted the Confederates. The Alabamians regrouped and came again. The Mainers fired a volley, and the line of the 15th Alabama "wavered like a man trying to walk into a strong wind." Colonel William Oates rallied his Alabamians, and once more they ascended the bloody slope. The opposing ranks ravaged each other at distances of ten yards. With their ammunition nearly exhausted, the Mainers charged down the hillside and scattered the Alabamians.[78]

To the left of the Alabamians, the 4th and 5th Texas and 48th Alabama, swinging past Devil's Den, assailed the open, western face of Little Round Top. A soldier in the 4th Texas wrote later, "We had to fight the Yankees on a mountain where it was very steep and rocks as large as a meeting house." The Southerners scrambled up the slope in a struggle another Texan likened to "a devil's carnival." The Confederates broke through the ranks of one Union regiment and neared the crest. One Texan admitted, "Confusion reigned supreme everywhere." A counterattack by more troops of the Union Fifth Corps repulsed the Texans and Alabamians, securing Little Round Top.[79]

The killing and maiming continued. Casualties among the Alabamians, Texans, and Georgians approached or exceeded 2,000. In the Texas Brigade commander Robertson had been wounded, three regimental commanders had fallen killed or wounded, and nearly all of the field officers lay on the ground. Late in the war, when a remnant of the brigade remained, Lee told Texas Senator Louis Wigfall, "These I have are the very best in my army." Henry Benning described the conduct of his Georgians on July 2 as "magnificent."[80]

It was five o'clock or a few minutes past when Longstreet ordered forward Joseph Kershaw's South Carolinians and Paul Semmes's Georgians of McLaws's division. Longstreet had assumed uncharacteristic personal direction of McLaws's units, infuriating McLaws. In a letter to his wife four days after the battle he described Longstreet as "exceedingly overbearing . . . a humbug, a man of small capacity, very obstinate, not at all chivalrous, exceedingly conceited, and totally selfish." In a postwar letter to McLaws, Longstreet explained that Lee had been dissatisfied with his performance at Chancellorsville, "I thus became responsible for anything that was not entirely satisfactory in your command from that day," he wrote, "and was repeatedly told of that fact." Longstreet's commitment of McLaws's brigades to the attack lends credence to his subsequent assertion.[81]

When the South Carolinians and Georgians appeared, the twenty-seven Union cannon in the Peach Orchard and along Wheatfield Road opened fire on them. "Hell broke loose," swore a Georgian, and "it was Malvern Hill all over again, but on a grander scale." Kershaw wheeled three of his regiments toward the guns along Wheatfield Road, while Semmes's veterans marched straight ahead across the Rose family fields. A shell fragment struck Semmes in the leg, severing the femoral artery, he applied a tourniquet and rallied his men. (The wound eventually proved to be fatal. Semmes died on July 10.) A 10th Georgia soldier wrote of the brigadier, "When a battle was imminent, General Semmes dressed with extraordinary care, carefully polished boots, spotless linen, elegant uniform, a brilliant sash around his waist and shoulders and a red turban on his head." Porter Alexander believed Semmes to be "the most promising Major general among all the excellent brigadiers in the whole army."[82]

Three of Kershaw's regiments charged toward Stony Hill and the Wheatfield, where Anderson's Georgians had been engaged with Federals of the Third Corps. The struggle for Stony Hill, the six acres of wheat, and a stone wall along the field's southern edge epitomized the fighting on this day on the southern end of the battle. Confederate attackers met Union reserves in vicious charges and countercharges. Four Southern brigades and a few regiments opposed seven Northern brigades, more than 5,000 Rebels fighting nearly 9,000 Yankees. As more enemy soldiers appeared, a Confederate exclaimed: "Great God! Have we got the Universe to whip?"[83]

Two Union Fifth Corps brigades entered the Wheatfield initially in support of the hard-pressed men of the Third Corps. Behind them came Brigadier General John Caldwell's Second Corps division. Caldwell's four brigades, including the famed Irish Brigade, were among the finest combat soldiers in the army. When they swept into the Wheatfield, the ground became a cauldron of hell. For nearly two hours the opponents fought on Stony Hill and in the field of trampled grain. The stone wall along the field's southern edge changed hands six times. A Federal officer professed: "The men were firing as fast as they could load. The din was almost deafening." A South Carolina officer recalled that the opposing lines were so close and the combat "so desperate I took two shots with my pistol at men scarcely thirty steps from me."[84]

To the west Longstreet committed to the attack McLaws's final two brigades, William Barksdale's Mississippians and William Wofford's Georgians. Barksdale had been chafing to enter the struggle. He "had a very thirst for battlefield glory," said one of his men, "to lead his brigade in the charge." The Mississippians went forward with a yell and crushed the Union salient at the Peach Orchard. They met fierce resistance but shattered the ranks of two Federal brigades, captured a general, and overran two batteries. A watching Confederate called it "the most magnificent charge I witnessed during the war."[85]

Barksdale wheeled three regiments north along Emmitsburg Road and sent a fourth regiment down Wheatfield Road. With Barksdale leading them, the three regiments drove across the fields of the Abraham Trostle farm, forcing a Union battery to retreat. More Federal Second Corps troops met them, laced the Mississippians with volleys, and broke their attack. Bullets struck Barksdale in the chest, puncturing a lung, and his left leg, fracturing a bone. Enemy soldiers carried the former congressman to a field hospital, where he died the next morning. Writing of July 2, a member of the brigade averred, "Miss. has lost many of her best & bravest sons."[86]

Wofford's Georgians swept down Wheatfield Road toward Stony Hill and Trostle's Woods, north of the roadbed. The Georgians cleared the woods of Yankees, and on their right, Kershaw's, Semmes's, and Anderson's troops plunged into the Wheatfield. A recently arrived division of the Fifth Corps was caught in the Confederate onslaught and driven east across Plum Run. The victorious Rebels crossed Houck's Ridge into the valley before Little Round Top. Coming at them in a counterattack was a brigade of Pennsylvania Reserve troops. The Yankees pushed the Southerners back across the ridge and into the Wheatfield. To the north Wofford's Georgians were retreating, and the fighting on that section of the battlefield abated into deadly sharpshooting.[87]

Longstreet had ordered the withdrawal of Wofford's brigade. "We felt at every step the heavy stroke of fresh troops," he explained later, "the sturdy regular blow that tells a soldier instantly that he has encountered reserves or reinforcements. We received no support at all, and there was no evidence of co-operation on any side. To urge my men forward under these circumstances would have been madness." They had little left to give. Casualties in the two First Corps divisions had reached 4,700 in killed and wounded, with Hood seriously wounded, brigade commanders Semmes and Barksdale mortally wounded, and dozens of regimental field officers fallen.[88]

Longstreet's assault had been disjointed, as brigades became isolated, regiments veered away from their commands, and units broke under the heavy artillery fire and musketry. But the officers' and men's combat prowess and bravery wrecked one Union corps, shattered the ranks of several brigades, and nearly reached the crest of Little Round Top. The natural strength of the Federal position, the advantage of interior lines, the tenacity of the Federal rank and file, the availability of reserves, and capable leadership saved Meade's army from a possible disaster. McLaws's words ring true. "It can be with justice claimed that no troops in the Army of Northern Virginia better sustained their high reputation than did those of Longstreet's corps during the battle of Gettysburg."[89]

When the brigades of Barksdale and Wofford had advanced, Richard Anderson ordered forward his Third Corps division. A crucial time had come in Lee's offensive, a continuation of the assault by units in the center of the army's line, opposite Cemetery Ridge and Cemetery Hill. At that moment, however, Confederate command broke down. Although present on Seminary Ridge, Lee apparently neither oversaw nor intervened in the execution of his orders. Powell Hill seemed to have disappeared. "Hill's role in the battle of Gettysburg is an enigma," concluded the historian Harry Pfanz, "and none of his actions are more enigmatic than those of the late afternoon of 2 July." While Longstreet, in the words of one of his men, "stayed on the firing line from its inception to its finish, and by his presence encouraged his men to their bravest efforts," Hill remained a passive witness to the valor in front of him.[90]

The lack of active leadership by either Lee or Hill resulted in a charge of only three of Anderson's five brigades: Cadmus Wilcox's Alabamians, Colonel David Lang's Floridians, and Ambrose "Rans" Wright's Georgians. On Anderson's left the highly capable Dorsey Pender readied his division for an advance when a piece of shell struck him in the thigh, causing a grievous wound. Without his leadership his troops never joined in the assault. On Pender's flank Robert Rodes had explicit orders "to cooperate with the attacking force as soon as any opportunity of doing so with good effect was offered." Rodes advanced two of his brigades toward Cemetery Hill but never ordered an attack.[91]

Like Longstreet's troops, Wilcox's and Lang's men drove back an initial Federal line along Emmitsburg Road and descended into the low ground along Plum Run. Once again, however, Union reserves and rallied units repulsed the gray-coated attackers. To the north Wright's Georgians charged through a gale of enemy artillery fire and musketry onto the crest of Cemetery Ridge, south of a copse of trees. Federal artillerists and infantrymen raked the Georgians' flanks. With losses of nearly 700, half their numbers, the Georgians retreated. It was approximately 6:30 P.M., and Meade's army still held Little Round Top, Cemetery Ridge, and Cemetery Hill.[92]

Yet the second day's bloody work had not ended. When Longstreet's attack began, Richard Ewell opened fire with artillery on Culp's Hill and Cemetery Hill. Union gun crews responded, pounding the Confederate batteries and silencing them. Ewell ordered Edward Johnson to attack Culp's Hill and directed Jubal Early and Robert Rodes to advance. In the darkening woods three of Johnson's brigades crossed Rock Creek and ascended Culp's Hill. Since morning the Federals had been at work constructing three-foot-high log-and-dirt breastworks. Johnson's movement came at an opportune time, as only one Twelfth Corps brigade, Brigadier General George S. Greene's five New York regiments, remained on the hill. The other units had been pulled off and hurried in support of the army's beleaguered center.[93]

When Johnson's veterans appeared through the trees, Greene's New Yorkers laced the ranks with volleys. His comrades "did as hard fighting as I ever saw men do," asserted a New Yorker. The Rebels wrested from the Federals a section of the fieldworks on the lower part of the hill. But the steepness of the hill, the protection accorded the defenders by the earthworks, and reinforcements stopped the attackers. The fighting continued until 10:00 P.M., before ending "by degrees and by common consent." The foes remained in close proximity. During the night the rest of the Twelfth Corps brigades returned to the hill.[94]

While the struggle for Culp's Hill flamed in the woods, Early sent Brigadier General Harry Hays's Louisianans and Colonel Isaac Avery's North Carolinians against Union infantry and artillery on

East Cemetery Hill. In a day steeped in courage, these 2,400 Southerners summoned forth all that could be asked of men. Passing through open fields they descended into a ravine, climbed the opposite slope, scaled a stone wall, and ascended the hillside. Enemy infantrymen fled before them as they closed on Federal gun crews. In a wild melee the Rebels seized cannon, prisoners, and flags. But what had been taken could not be held. Through the evening's deepening shadows bluecoated infantrymen rushed toward them, followed by more troops. The Confederates retreated, abandoning the captured guns. Their losses amounted to roughly 700, including a mortally wounded Avery. They had expected support from behind and from the west by Rodes's command. When Rodes did not advance, Early wisely held back John Gordon's brigade.[95]

Wednesday, July 2, proved to be the critical day at Gettysburg. The Confederates had battered and stretched the Union line until it nearly snapped. But the valor and skill of Lee's officers and men could not overcome the advantages of their foes' position and their own command failings. "Our only hope was to make our attacks simultaneous," thought Porter Alexander. "But that is the thing which always looks beforehand very simple & easy, & always proves afterward to be impossible, from one of a hundred possible causes." Chief of Staff Walter Taylor wrote similarly afterward: "The whole affair was disjointed. There was an utter absence of accord in the movements of the several commands, and no decisive result attended the operations of the second day."[96]

There was more to it, however, for Southern valor had met Northern bravery no longer crippled by the army's leadership. Sickles's blunder had been rectified at a fearful cost by scores of brigade, regimental, and company commanders. The words of a Union sergeant, written in his diary during the morning, explained much, "This AM say this is to be the Battle of the war and every man must stand." They had stood and were willing to do so again.[97]

Meade met with his senior officers at his headquarters in the small, whitewashed home of Mrs. Lydia Leister beside Taneytown Road. Before the generals gathered, Meade telegraphed the War Department in Washington, "[I] shall remain in my present position to-morrow." At the meeting he learned that morale was good, and they had about

58,000 men still in the ranks. The generals decided by a vote that the army should stay on the defensive for at least another day. When the council ended at midnight Meade told John Gibbon, whose Second Corps division manned the center of the line on Cemetery Ridge, "If Lee attacks tomorrow, it will be in *your front*." Gibbon inquired why he thought so, and Meade replied, "Because he had made attacks on both our flanks and failed and if he concluded to try it again, it will be on our centre." Afterward Meade approved an attack to recapture the lost fieldworks on Culp's Hill.[98]

According to the existing accounts, Lee conferred personally with none of his corps commanders. The day's offensive had not gone as he expected or planned. Consequently, as he wrote in his report: "the result of this day's operations induced the belief that, with proper concert of action, and with the increased support that the positions gained on the right would enable the artillery to render the assaulting columns, we should ultimately succeed, and it was accordingly determined to continue the attack. The general plan was unchanged." In brief, Ewell's troops would resume their assault on Culp's Hill, while Longstreet's two divisions, reinforced by George Pickett's three brigades, which had reached the battlefield during the afternoon of July 2, would again attack the enemy's left flank on the southern end of Cemetery Ridge.[99]

For the next day's operations Lee had with him, finally, Jeb Stuart and three cavalry brigades. Stuart had preceded his troopers from Carlisle, arriving between noon and 1:00 P.M. on July 2. When he reported to Lee, the army commander purportedly said, "Well, General Stuart, you are here at last." No record exists of their conversation, but Stuart's chief of staff, Major Henry McClellan, claimed the meeting was "painful beyond description." That night Lee assigned Stuart's horsemen to the army's left flank, east of Gettysburg, but their duty remains ill-defined to this day. No evidence exists that Stuart was ordered to strike the Union rear when the Confederates assaulted Cemetery Ridge in the afternoon.[100]

When Lee's orders for a daylight attack on Culp's Hill reached Ewell's headquarters, staff members voiced opposition to the plan. Neither Lee nor Ewell had personally examined the ground on Culp's Hill. But the seizure of the enemy's works on the lower section of the heights convinced Ewell that "he knew it could be done." He augmented John-son's force by bringing forward Johnson's fourth brigade and drawing two brigades from Rodes's division and one from Early's. At daylight 9,000 Southerners waited in the woods on Culp's Hill below the works of roughly the same number of Northerners. All the advantages of ter-rain rested with the Yankees.[101]

At the opposite end of the Confederate line Porter Alexander came to Longstreet's headquarters for instructions. He learned that the news from elsewhere on the battlefield was "indefinite." Longstreet informed him that McLaws's, Hood's, and Pickett's divisions "would assault the enemy's line." "My impression is the exact point for it had not been designated," recounted Alexander, "but I was told it would be to our left of the Peach Orchard." Longstreet instructed the artillerist to bring for-ward more batteries and to post them. Alexander slept two hours that night.[102]

Robert E. Lee rose before daylight and rode Traveller south on Seminary Ridge to Longstreet's bivouac site. He found neither Pickett's division on the field nor preparations under way for an attack. For rea-sons not altogether clear, Longstreet had failed to order Pickett's three brigades to be on the field before daylight. Consequently, Pickett's Vir-ginians did not begin arriving until about eight o'clock. More impor-tant, without Pickett, Lee's plans for an early offensive strike had to be abandoned. In the estimation of William Piston, a historian favorably disposed to Longstreet, the corps commander's neglect constituted "a shocking mishandling of Pickett's division."[103]

Instead, when Lee joined him, Longstreet proposed a flanking move-ment around Big Round Top, based on the report of scouts. "With some impatience," according to Longstreet, Lee rejected the idea. "The rela-tions existing between us were affectionate, confidential, and even ten-der, from first to last," maintained Longstreet. "There was never a harsh word between us." That might have been so, but now Lee pointed at either Cemetery Ridge or Cemetery Hill and stated firmly, "The enemy is there, and I am going to strike him." When Pickett arrived, continued Lee, his division, reinforced by units from the Third Corps, would make the assault.[104]

"I felt then that it was my duty to express my convictions," wrote

Longstreet. Then, in words that have resonated throughout Civil War history, he said: "General, I have been a soldier all my life. I have been with soldiers engaged in fights by couples, by squads, companies, regiments, divisions, and armies, and should know, as well as any one, what soldiers can do. It is my opinion that no fifteen thousand men ever arranged for battle can take that position." He explained after the war, "I should not have been so urgent had I not foreseen the hopelessness of the proposed assault. I felt that I must say a word against the sacrifice of my men." Lee was undeterred, he and Longstreet began preparations.[105]

While the two generals met, the sounds of combat boiled up from Culp's Hill. At 4:30 A.M., Union artillery opened fire on the Confederates on the hillside. After fifteen minutes the cannon fire ceased, but before the Federals could advance as planned, "defiant yells" rolled up the slope, emitted by oncoming Rebels. Suddenly, as if an unseen being had shouted an order, "the whole hillside seemed enveloped in a blaze," declared a Southerner. For the next six hours, without respite, the fighting raged. During that time Johnson launched three major assaults, each one failing to dislodge the defenders. The gunfire stripped bark from trees, and gore and blood pooled in the trenches behind the breastworks and saturated the ground on the hillside.[106]

Union commanders shuttled regiments in and out of the works, allowing the men to rest and to replenish their cartridges. The Confederates never had a chance of seizing the hill. The roar of musketry was so deafening that officers had to shout orders into their men's ears. A veteran Alabama soldier professed, "I thought I had been in hot places before—I thought I had heard Minnie balls; but that day capped the climax." An Ohioan attested, "If a man exposed himself, he was sure to get shot." When the combat ended with the withdrawal of the Southerners, an estimated 2,400 of them had been killed, wounded, or captured. Federal casualties amounted to 950. A New York enlisted man put it well after he had walked across the scarred ground. "None but Demons can delight in war."[107]

Throughout the morning, with the fury on Culp's Hill rising up from the wooded heights, Lee and Longstreet planned the attack. No decision of Lee's generalship has been more controversial than what became known generally as Pickett's Charge. The commanding general committed nine brigades from three divisions, between 12,500 and 13,000 officers and men, to the main attack force. He assigned the brigades of Cadmus Wilcox and David Long, about 2,000 troops, as flank support, and designated Richard Anderson's other three brigades, an additional 3,000 men, as a reserve. Longstreet stated later that among officers on the field it was thought that 30,000 infantrymen would be required for a successful assault.[108]

The plan was to send the attackers across 1,400 yards of open, undulating ground, criss-crossed by fences, in a front a mile long against an array of Union cannon and about 5,300 waiting infantrymen, Second Corps veterans, with thousands more in nearby support. To reach Cemetery Ridge while maintaining unit cohesiveness, the Confederates would have to march at "common time," or seventy yards per minute. They needed twenty minutes to cover the distance, all of the time subjected to solid shot, shellfire, or canister from enemy batteries. Before the Southern infantry advanced, the Union artillery would have to be silenced or seriously crippled. This could be accomplished only by a sustained cannonade prior to the assault. Then it would be left to the infantry to carry out a bayonet charge or shock tactics by withholding its fire until close to the enemy. In the view of the historian Paddy Griffith, shock tactics demanded, "exceptional leadership, or exceptionally high-quality soldiers to make the system work."[109]

In his fine study of the Gettysburg campaign, Edwin Coddington addressed the July 3 assault. "For basic simplicity and audacity of concept his [Lee's] plan evokes admiration, though it could work only if an almost infinite number of pieces in its pattern fell into the right place at the right time." The plan rested, however, on Confederate batteries inflicting enough damage on their counterparts to spare their infantry comrades from a firestorm of Union guns. But Lee's ably manned cannon lacked sufficient long-range ammunition and were plagued with notoriously poor gunpowder and fuses for shells. In fact before the campaign began the army had received fuses from Charleston, South Carolina, because of an explosion at a factory in Virginia, the usual source of fuses. Unknown to the artillery officers and men, the new fuses burned slower, resulting in late explosions and missed targets.[110]

Against the outspoken opposition of his finest subordinate and contrary to his own training and experience, Lee committed upwards of 15,000 and possibly more officers and men to what in hindsight was a forlorn hope. He must have believed the assault could succeed, for no other explanation is rational. "The formidable character of the Union position never awed him," Coddington said of Lee. Staff officer William Allan, who interviewed the former Confederate commander after the war, contended that Lee thought "this great prize," the defeat of Meade's army, was "within his grasp." Moxley Sorrel wrote that Lee "believed his troops could do what he asked of them; never yet had they failed him." In the end it must have been his belief in his men and their belief in themselves, forged at places whose names adorned their battleflags that convinced Lee his plan was sound.[111]

As preparations proceeded, the infantry filed into position. George Pickett's three brigades—Virginians all, under James Kemper, Richard Garnett, and Lewis Armistead—deployed in a broad swale behind the Henry Spangler farm and in adjacent woods. These troops had not been engaged in heavy combat since Antietam, before Pickett had assumed command of the division. Described as "a singular figure indeed" and "a very dashing officer," Pickett was one of Longstreet's favorite subordinates. "He was what would be called a dapper little fellow," stated an aide, "but brave as they ever make men."[112]

To the north, on the reverse or southern slope of Seminary Ridge, Henry Heth's four brigades of North Carolinians, Alabamians, Tennesseans, Mississippians, and Virginians formed ranks. Johnston Pettigrew led the division as Heth recovered from a bullet wound to his head suffered on July 1. Heth's life was spared by the wadded paper with which he had lined the inside of the too-large hat he had acquired at some point during the campaign. Two North Carolina brigades from Dorsey Pender's division completed the formation, posted behind Pettigrew's right center and right flank units. Lee had assigned Major General Isaac R. Trimble to temporary command of the North Carolinians. Recovered from his wound at Brawner's Farm in August 1862, Trimble had rejoined the army during the march north but without a command assignment.[113]

With the infantry in place and instructions given to commanders, Longstreet and Lee rode twice along the lines "to see that everything was arranged according to his [Lee's] wishes." Problems remained, however. Neither Lee nor Powell Hill appeared to realize the casualty toll that had been exacted from the Pettigrew division on July 1. Its assignment to the attack force evidently resulted from its position on Seminary Ridge. Furthermore a gap existed between Pettigrew's right and Pickett's left. Once the attack began, Pickett's troops would have to execute a left oblique maneuver as they crossed the fields, exposing the length of their line to a Union battery on Little Round Top. Finally, no one seemed to have considered how fences, particularly the sturdy post-and-rail fences along both sides of Emmitsburg Road, could disrupt attack formations. If the attack were to work, as noted by Coddington, many pieces needed to fit together into a pattern. They did not.[114]

Minutes past one o'clock in the afternoon Confederate gun crews near the Peach Orchard fired successive shots from a pair of cannon. Stillness across the battlefield ended as more than 160 Southern cannon roared, their shells and solid shots arcing toward Union artillerists and guns on Cemetery Ridge and Cemetery Hill. As instructed, the Rebels worked the guns "slowly and deliberately." Blue-coated infantrymen hugged the ground amid the falling shards of metal. "The air seethed with old iron," proclaimed a Maine private. "We hardly knew what it meant." Before long, Yankee gun crews responded, and "a mighty hurricane" of artillery fire blew across the fields. Nothing in the veterans' experience compared to it. A Rebel told his wife a few days later, "If the crash of worlds and all things combustible had been coming in collision with each other, it could not have surpassed it."[115]

Although many men on both sides remembered the cannonade lasting more than one or two hours, Confederate guns began falling silent after forty-five minutes or so. At 1:40 P.M., Porter Alexander scribbled a hasty note to George Pickett: "The 18 guns have been driven off. For God's sake come on quick or we cannot support you ammunition nearly out." The enemy cannon referred to had not been driven off but had ceased firing; the Confederate cannonade had failed in its primary mission. Too many rounds had overshot their targets, bursting in the air behind Cemetery Ridge. Thirty-four Union guns had been either disabled or withdrawn, but Union Chief of Artillery Henry Hunt replaced them with forty-one cannon. From Cemetery Hill to Little Round Top,

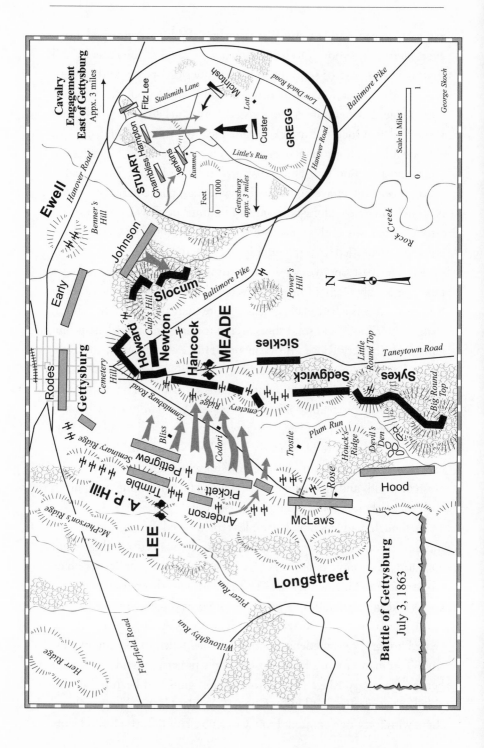

Battle of Gettysburg
July 3, 1863

nearly 120 Federal gun crews awaited the appearance of the Southern infantry.[116]

During the worst of the maelstrom Longstreet rode his horse slowly in front of Pickett's men, who lay upon the ground. Brigadier General James Kemper declared afterward of the corps commander: "His bearing was to me the grandest moral spectacle of the war. I expected to see him fall every instant." Longstreet then returned to Spangler's Woods, where Pickett found him and asked, "General, shall I advance?" Longstreet nodded. "Sir, I shall lead my division forward," replied Pickett. Longstreet joined Alexander on the rise in front of the woods. The general looked at the Union position through field glasses one more time and, turning to Alexander, said, "I don't want to make this attack—I believe it will fail—I do not see how it can succeed—I would not make it even now, but that General Lee has ordered and expects it."[117]

Up and down the mile-long line men stood and formed ranks, officers went to their posts, and color-bearers and guards stepped forward with flags unfurled in a pageantry that belied what lay ahead. Pettigrew's men passed the crest of Seminary Ridge and strode down the slope, while Pickett's Virginians emerged from the swale as if risen from the ground. Across the 1,400 yards of fertile Pennsylvania land, Union artillerists rammed in charges and infantrymen gazed at the "rising tide of armed men rolling towards us in steel crested billows," according to a soldier in the 1st Minnesota. A Pennsylvania captain declared, "Onward they came, and it would seem as if no power could hold them in check." Then began a shriek of shells and the hum of solid shot in the air.[118]

A newspaperman watching from the Union lines reported that the initial artillery fire "seemed to smite the column of attack as if it had been struck by some unseen power, some great physical body, causing the column to waver, reel, and for a moment halt." "Deep gaps" appeared in the Confederate ranks, only to be immediately closed. A soldier in the 14th Virginia told his wife, "Now & then a man's hand or arm or leg would fly like feathers before the wind." As Kemper's and Garnett's lines obliqued left, Union batteries on lower Cemetery Ridge and Little Round Top scoured the ranks with enfilading fire. Although the Southerners could not hear the words, some of their foes on the ridge shouted, "Fredericksburg! Fredericksburg!" and "Come on, Come on; come to Death!"[119]

When the Confederates reached Emmitsburg Road, Union gunners switched to canister and infantrymen triggered waves of musketry. Along Pettigrew's front his men struggled to get across the post-and-rail fence, exposing themselves to the merciless gunfire. Once in the roadbed hundreds refused or lacked the courage to go farther. More of their comrades kept going, up the slope toward a zigzagging line of stone walls. These men carried with them a legacy forged on the slopes of Gaines's Mill and Malvern Hill, behind a railroad bed at Second Manassas, in a cornfield and sunken road at Antietam, and among underbrush and woods at Chancellorsville. Before Cemetery Ridge they enriched this legacy by their valor and sacrifice.[120]

The Rebels cheered and, in Kemper's description, entered a "vortex of death." Some of his and Garnett's Virginians reached the outer stone wall. On their left North Carolinians and Mississippians braved the galling musketry to within feet of the inner stone wall. On both ends of the Confederate line Union infantry spilled off the ridge, wheeled toward the enemy ranks, and trapped them in a three-sided box of hellfire. "It looked like murder," said a Yankee.[121]

This American tragedy demanded a climax, and it came with a surge of several hundred Confederates across the outer stone wall. Led by Lewis Armistead, the attackers fought the defenders in a hand-to-hand melee for minutes in the shadow of a clump of trees, before being overwhelmed by more Federals. By then a river of survivors and walking wounded flowed back west toward Seminary Ridge. Only one of Trimble's two brigades crossed Emmitsburg Road before retreating. Union infantrymen pursued, capturing hundreds and seizing twenty-eight battleflags. In a final, needless sacrifice, on orders from Longstreet, Cadmus Wilcox's Alabamians and David Lang's Floridians recrossed the ground of the previous day and were caught in a "death trap." Union artillery and infantry shredded their ranks. The Rebels fled rearward.[122]

George Pickett had watched the decimation of his command from somewhere along Emmitsburg Road. He had fulfilled his duty, requesting support. Longstreet had belatedly sent forward Wilcox and Lang but countermanded orders for the advance of Richard Anderson's other three brigades. Evidently Lee expected all of Anderson's troops and perhaps Robert Rodes's remaining units to move in support of the main attack. That night Lee told Brigadier General John Imboden that if the attackers "had been supported as they were to have been . . . we would have held the position and the day would have been ours." Despite Lee's belief, had the Confederates breached the Union position they would have encountered thousands of oncoming reserves. There is compelling truth in the words Meade had written to his wife that morning, "Army in fine spirits & they are determined to do or die."[123]

Lee rode out and met the survivors of the charge, saying to officers and men, "It is my fault." Casualties among the nine brigades in the main force reached 50 percent or more. Garnett died with his men on the slope, his body never identified. Armistead fell yards away from the clump of trees, was carried to the rear by his foes, and died two days later. Kemper and Trimble suffered severe wounds and were left behind at Gettysburg when the army retreated. "Poor Virginia bleeds again at every pore," asserted a staff officer in a letter four days later. He could have said the same for North Carolina, Tennessee, Alabama, and Mississippi.[124]

Since midmorning Jeb Stuart's cavalrymen had been involved in an inconclusive, dismounted engagement with Brigadier General David McM. Gregg's Union troopers on farmland four miles east of Gettysburg. As Confederate infantrymen retreated toward Seminary Ridge after the repulse of Pickett's Charge, a frustrated Stuart ordered a mounted charge at about 3:00 p.m. During the next hour the Rebels rode forth in two attacks, only to be met by Yankee counterattacks. In fighting reminiscent of the struggle for Fleetwood Hill at Brandy Station, the opponents clashed in a series of saber-to-saber and revolver-to-revolver encounters that toppled horses and killed and wounded men. The Federals—primarily Michiganders led by recently promoted Brigadier General George A. Custer—prevailed, forcing their foes rearward. After nightfall Stuart withdrew to the north.[125]

After sundown on July 3 Lee met with his corps commanders. If Meade did not attack tomorrow, he told them, the army would begin the return march to Virginia. In his initial campaign report the Confederate commander wrote: "The conduct of the troops was all that I could desire or expect, and they deserve success so far as it can be deserved by heroic valor and fortitude. More may have been required of them than they were able to perform." In simpler words, with more truth than he could have known, a Union soldier offered an assessment of Gettysburg in a letter written two weeks later. Lee "supposed he could walk right over the Army of the Potomac."[126]

Chapter Ten

"A Glorious Army"

PRIVATE HENRY BERKELEY, a Confederate artillerist, visited farmhouses outside of Gettysburg in search of water on the morning of July 4, 1863. When he had finished walking across the fields, he recorded in his diary: "Blood everywhere. Dead and dying men everywhere." The carnage smothered the ground. A Union officer wrote to his wife, "My very clothes smell of death." A fellow Northerner professed, "I have seen many a big battle, most of the big ones of the war, and I never saw the like." A survivor compared July 4 to "a funeral."[1]

A captain in the 38th Virginia of Lewis Armistead's brigade confided in his diary, "I do not know who is living." A Confederate infantryman exclaimed to his sister, "The slaughter on both sides was terrible & exceeds any thing of the war." Although he could not have known the figures, no single battle of the war matched "the appalling slaughter of Gettysburg." The three days exacted a total of 51,000 killed, wounded, and missing or captured. More than 9,600 had been slain or mortally wounded. Union losses amounted to 23,049; Confederate, 28,063.[2]

In the three-day engagement 92,000 Federals had opposed 72,000 Confederates on the firing lines. While the Army of the Potomac sustained a casualty rate of 25 percent, the Army of Northern Virginia incurred a staggering casualty rate of nearly 39 percent. Jennings Cropper Wise declared in his history of the Confederate army's artillery: "Gettysburg was more than a defeat. It was a disaster from which no army, in fact, no belligerent state, could soon recover."[3]

The battle decimated Robert E. Lee's officer ranks. Division commander Dorsey Pender's leg wound became infected, and after surgeons amputated the limb he died on July 18. Brigade commanders Lewis Armistead, William Barksdale, Richard Garnett, and Paul Semmes were dead, all of them capable and experienced officers. John Hood and Wade Hampton, Jeb Stuart's finest subordinate, suffered serious wounds and were incapacitated for months. Isaac Trimble, James Kemper, and James Archer had been captured; none of them would hold active field command again.[4]

At the regimental level approximately 150 colonels, lieutenant colonels, and majors had been killed, wounded, or captured. Of that number, nineteen colonels had been slain, the most in any single battle in which the army had engaged. Captains now led many regiments. The impact of the casualties among the army's veteran officers and men can hardly be overstated. A graphic example of service in the army was that of the Liberty Hall Volunteers or Company I, 4th Virginia. In April 1861 seventy-three volunteers had enlisted in the company, but when it marched away from Gettysburg, three members stood in the ranks.[5]

Lee's crippled army slipped away from Gettysburg in a drenching rainstorm during the night of July 4–5. Miles of ambulances and wagons carrying wounded men preceded the columns of infantry and artillery. An estimated 5,000 wounded Rebels were left behind in the care of their enemy. Jeb Stuart's cavalrymen screened the marchers. Through the troughs of mud the Confederates reached the swollen Potomac River by July 7. The river's swift, rising current, fed by the heavy rains, prevented a crossing, and the army dug in, erecting fieldworks along a front of nine miles from Hagerstown, Maryland, on the north to Falling Waters on the south.[6]

Clashes occurred daily between Stuart's horsemen and Union troopers. On July 10 George Meade's infantry and artillery crossed South Mountain and deployed before the Confederate lines. Meade conferred with his corps commanders on the night of July 12, proposing either a reconnaissance-in-force or an attack the next day. A majority of the generals voted against the plan, and Meade postponed it until he could conduct a personal reconnaissance of the enemy works. After an examination of the Rebel position, the Federal commander issued orders for an advance on July 14. It was, however, too late.[7]

By July 13 the Potomac River had subsided enough to be forded at Williamsport, and Confederate engineers had completed a pontoon bridge at Falling Waters. After dark that night Lee's army began the crossing into Virginia, the sounds of the passage muffled by a heavy rainstorm. In the campaign's final action Union cavalry attacked a contingent of Southern infantry before the Rebels had reached the river at Falling Waters. During the brief encounter Johnston Pettigrew suffered a mortal wound, the sixth general officer in the army to be fatally wounded.[8]

The return of the Confederates to Virginia profoundly disappointed Abraham Lincoln. The president believed—wrongly—that Lee's army, having been routed at Gettysburg, was during its retreat within "easy grasp" of Meade, who had failed to act on the opportunity. General-in-chief Henry Halleck informed the Union commander of the "great dissatisfaction in the mind of the President" over the enemy's escape. An angry Meade asked to be relieved of command. Halleck replied that his message "was not intended as a censure" and that Meade's inaction was "not deemed as sufficient cause for your application to be relieved." The affair, however, left both Lincoln and Meade bitter.[9]

In the camps of the Army of the Potomac some members shared Lincoln's frustration with the Rebels' crossing of the Potomac without a fight. "The hog has got away & we the whippet run up to the fence and bark," as one soldier put it. The prevailing mood, however, was expressed by another enlisted man, who wrote that he and his comrades "gave the rebels one of the damdest lickens they have ever had." At Gettysburg the Yankees confronted their past, a record of defeats unmatched by an American army since the American Revolution, and redeemed it. Unlike in previous campaigns, Meade and the army's leadership proved to be worthy of the rank and file. An artillery lieutenant boasted in a letter to his mother immediately after the battle, "It is now *an honor* indeed to belong to the Amy of the Potomac." Writing a week after the Confederate crossing, a staff officer asserted, "I really believe that we are learning to outfight the rebels on even fields, in spite of their dash and fanatical desperation."[10]

South of the Potomac, in the camps of the Army of Northern Virginia, members offered conflicting views on the army's condition and on the significance of and reasons for the defeat. "Our old army is badly cut up," argued a soldier, though a staff officer declared, "Our army is in good health and perfect in its organization. Now, as ever, it is invincible on Virga [Virginia] soil." Some men used the words "dark and gloomy," "depressed," "most disastrous," "broken harted," and "desperation." Others admitted that they and their fellow soldiers were "broken down & completely worn out" from the campaign's rigors. Thousands had straggled, moving a North Carolinian to assert, "It seemed that only a skeleton of an army had returned."[11]

Lee's men retained their stubborn resilience and firm confidence, which was also evident in their correspondence. Before they crossed the river, an Alabamian wrote, "Our army was buoyant and full of life and the repulse wholly unexpected by men & officers." Jedediah Hotchkiss proclaimed to his wife, "The Army of Northern Virginia stands, as it has always stood, the sure defence of the heart of the Confederacy," and then added, "Our army is in fine spirits, and ready to meet the foe any where in the open field." A Georgian noted much the same: "Lee's army is now the great hope of the South. There is a terrible band of veterans here yet." Within weeks, according to Lafayette McLaws, the officers and men had "all our old spirit and self confidence."[12]

Like Southern civilians, they regarded the surrender of Vicksburg and Port Hudson, Mississippi, as more disastrous to the cause than the defeat at Gettysburg. "The news of the fall of Vicksburg and Port Hudson has startled us like a clap of thunder on a cloudless day," exclaimed a North Carolinian. "We were not prepared for such intelligence." A fellow North Carolinian admitted to his brother, "Our whole army were very much depressed by the news from the west. The fall of Vicksburg took us all by surprise." A Virginian claimed that the news "has had a very depressing effect on us all & some seem to be almost in despair."[13]

Ultimately Lee's officers and men addressed the reasons for the defeat at Gettysburg. An enlisted man admitted, "I think we got *the* worst end of the bargain this time . . . menny a pore soldier killed in

Mayerland and Pensilvany." Almost universally they believed, as a member of the 57th North Carolina stated, "it was the hardest fite I was ever in." A Georgian in Henry Benning's brigade wrote similarly: "It was I think the hardest fought battle of the war. It was terrible." A private in the 41st Virginia put it plainly. "Had a good time till we got to Gettysburg."[14]

Many of them attributed the outcome to the Union position and their opponents' defense of it. Brigadier General Dodson Ramseur called it "a Gibraltar of a position." A Georgian averred, "The Yankees were impregnably posted and on their own soil they fought undoubtedly well." A captain stated, "It was a second Fredericksburg affair, only the wrong way." Artillery Captain William W. Parker noted, "We had forgotten the power of the spade and the immense advantages which position may give."[15]

In their search for answers some of the Confederates blamed Lee and his generals. A South Carolinian argued that the Yankees had not defeated them, but "our Generals failed to carry the position." A quartermaster officer confessed to his wife, "Now, I know, we should not have attacked him [the enemy] on high hills and mountains, but we did so." Major Eugene Blackford of the 5th Alabama denounced the high command for its "insanity" in attacking the Federals and then proclaimed: "Yankees. They are as mere chaff before the wind when they come out in an open country, but this makes the policy of attacking them when entrenched the more criminal." A Texan wrote, "We are not such hero-worshippers as to believe even Lee infallible."[16]

Lee accepted responsibility for the defeat at Gettysburg. On July 31 he wrote a revealing letter to Jefferson Davis in response to a critical article in the Charleston *Mercury*: "No blame can be attached to the army for its failure to accomplish what was projected by me, nor should it be censured for unreasonable expectations of the public—I am alone to blame, in perhaps expecting too much of its prowess & valour. . . . I still think if all things could have worked together it [victory] would have been accomplished. But with the knowledge I then had, & in the circumstances I was then placed, I do not know what better course I could have pursued. With my present knowledge, & could I have foreseen that the attack on the last day would have failed to drive the enemy from his position, I should certainly have tried some other course. What the ultimate result would have been is not so clear to me."[17]

In his report and in postwar interviews and correspondence Lee offered reasons for the army's defeat. He gave a general explanation in a letter written a few days after the army's surrender at Appomattox: "Its loss was occasioned by a combination of circumstances. It was commenced in the absence of correct intelligence. It was continued in the effort to overcome the difficulties by which we were surrounded, and would have been gained could one determined and united blow have been delivered by our whole line." Elsewhere he also attributed defeat to Jeb Stuart's absence prior to the battle, to Richard Ewell's indecisiveness on July 1 and 2, and to James Longstreet's and Powell Hill's failure "to act in concert."[18]

As it was with the Army of the Potomac, the past haunted the Army of Northern Virginia at Gettysburg. Lee's method of command, granting his senior commanders discretion in the execution of orders, faltered and broke down. He accused Stuart of disobeying his instructions, acting injudiciously, and so failing him and the army. Longstreet's opposition to offensive strikes on July 2 and 3 affected his performance, and Ewell's and Hill's inexperience at corps command had been exposed. "No commander of an army does his whole duty who simply gives orders, however well considered," declared Porter Alexander. "He should *supervise their executions*, in person or by staff officers, constantly, day & night, so that if the machine balks at any point he may be most promptly informed & may most promptly start it to work." At Gettysburg Lee's army was a clanging machine at command levels.[19]

The singular fact remains that more than any other individual Lee shaped the battle at Gettysburg. Drawn into an unwanted and untimely engagement on July 1, he was forced by circumstances, as he said, to wage a fight on that battlefield. In doing so he exploited the tactical initiative on the first day by assuming the offensive. He can hardly be faulted for attacking on the second day, but his decision to undertake a frontal assault against the Union center on July 3 stands as a tragic mistake. Perhaps it was as the historian Frank Vandiver concluded: "I think that he failed to accept reality at Gettysburg. He simply wanted to go on and attack because he wanted to attack." Another historian,

Wiley Sword, believed that "Lee wanted a devastating, army-destroying victory. . . . To do this Lee was willing to make certain concessions and take serious risks."[20]

In a sense, the past loomed before Lee. Russell Weigley argued in his study of war, "Confederate defeat at Gettysburg was also the logical outcome of Lee's own generalship." His adoption of the strategic, or operational, offensive since his assumption of command impelled him after Chancellorsville to carry the conflict beyond the Potomac in search of a decisive victory that would secure Confederate independence. With him went an army suffused with confidence, with a belief in its invincibility, that Lee understood and shared. The army's epitaph at Gettysburg belonged to Lee: "I thought the army was invincible; I expected too much of it."[21]

Lee wrote to Jefferson Davis on August 8, proposing "to Your Excellency the propriety of selecting another commander" for the Army of Northern Virginia. "I have seen and heard of expression of discontent in the public journals at the result of the expedition," he continued. "I do not know how far this feeling extends in the army. My brother officers have been too kind to report it, and so far the troops have been too generous to exhibit it." Lee cited also "the growing failure of my bodily strength" since his illness in the spring. "Everything, therefore," he submitted, "points to the advantages to be derived from a new commander, and I more anxiously urge the matter upon Your Excellency from my belief that a younger and abler man than myself can readily be attained."[22]

Davis replied three days later. After expressing concern about the lingering effects of Lee's illness, the president inquired, "Where am I to find that new commander who is to possess the greater ability which you believe to be required?" Then he stated, "To ask me to substitute you by some one in my judgment more fit to command, or who would possess more of the confidence of the army, or of the reflecting men of the country, is to demand an impossibility." Davis hoped that Lee would "take all possible care of yourself," for the country required his services in the struggle "for the independence which we have engaged in war to maintain."[23]

The struggle for independence would last another twenty-one

months. During that time the conflict slid deeper into the abyss. Casualties mounted in unprecedented numbers; paths of destruction scarred Virginia, Georgia, and South Carolina, and wretched prison camps stained both sides' honor. Within the Confederacy the suffering of civilians intensified from the ravages of inflation and the scarcity of food and other necessities. And across the Southern lands Union armies moved as night descended across the Confederacy.

Following the Confederate retreat into Virginia, Lee met with an officer sent from Richmond. During their conversation Lee asserted that his men had bloodied the enemy so badly at Gettysburg that the Union "army will be as quiet as a sucking dove" for the next six months. His prediction became essentially true, as both armies needed a period of healing after the three days of bloodletting and the rigors of the campaign. An interlude characterized operations in Virginia, extending through the fall of 1863 and into the spring of 1864.[24]

Before winter settled in, both Lee and Meade undertook separate offensive movements. In early September, at the request of the Davis administration, Lee detached Longstreet, with two infantry divisions and an artillery battalion, to General Braxton Bragg's army in the west. Longstreet's command arrived in time to be instrumental in the Confederate victory at Chickamauga, Georgia, on September 19–20. When the Union War Department sent the Eleventh and Twelfth corps from Meade's army west in reaction to the defeat at Chickamauga, Lee advanced against the Federals in the Bristoe Campaign of mid-October. The only significant action of the operation occurred at Bristoe Station, Virginia, on October 14, when Powell Hill bungled attacks, resulting in a bloody repulse. Then, during the final week of November, the Yankees crossed the Rapidan River in the indecisive Mine Run Campaign. When Meade retreated, the opponents occupied a front along the Rappahannock and Rapidan rivers for the next five months.[25]

The winter of 1864 proved to be even more difficult for the Confederates than the winter of the previous year. The scarcity of rations for the men and forage for the animals stalked the camps, and desertions bled more soldiers from the ranks. At one point during the winter Lee told Henry Heth, "The question of *food for this army* gives me more trouble and uneasiness *than every thing else combined.*" Despite the grievous casualties incurred and the tactical defeat at Gettysburg, Lee also confided to Heth that he would invade Pennsylvania again if he could. "I believe it to be our true policy," said the Confederate commander. A movement across the Potomac, he explained, would spare Virginia and thwart Union plans, and a victory in the Keystone State was more important than one in the Old Dominion.[26]

But Lee's desire for another thrust into the North was unrealistic. Chancellorsville and Gettysburg, with their staggering casualties, had blunted his army's ability to win a victory of annihilation. Though Lee evidently clung to his belief in a strategic offensive, the war's landscape had shifted by the spring of 1864, preventing such a movement. Circumstances and his enemy's operations forced him to adopt a defensive strategy, which held the possibility of intensifying the war-weariness of the Northern populace and of causing the defeat of Abraham Lincoln in the forthcoming presidential election.[27]

Lee's veterans endured the hardships with stoic resolve and awaited the advent of spring. The "profound bond" between them and the commanding general remained unbroken. Colonel Clement Evans wrote of Lee: "He is the only man living in whom they would unreservedly trust all power for the preservation of their independence. They had enthusiasm for [Stonewall] Jackson, but their love and reverence for Lee is far deeper and more general feeling." A Virginia cavalryman swore, "No army ever had such a leader as General Lee."[28]

Public affirmation of Lee's attachment to his men came when Longstreet's troops returned from Tennessee. On April 29, 1864, Lee reviewed the First Corps infantrymen and artillerists. With cannon booming and ranks formed, Lee removed his hat, returning the salute. Longstreet's veterans shouted and color-bearers waved their scarred flags in response. "Sudden as a wind, a wave of sentiment, such as can only come to large crowds in full sympathy . . . seemed to sweep the field," recounted Porter Alexander. "Each man seemed to feel the bond which held us all to Lee. There was no speaking, but the effect was that of a military sacrament, in which we pledged anew our lives."[29]

Lee, Longstreet, and their staffs rode the length of the line, passing by so closely that they could see each man's face. A chaplain asked Charles Venable of Lee's staff, "Does it not make the general proud to see how these men love him?" "Not proud," replied Venable, "it awes him." When they had finished the ride, Lee, Longstreet, and the aides halted on a knoll. The infantrymen and gun crews formed into columns and marched past. "All were certainly glad to see General Lee," professed a Georgian. "And I expect he was glad to have us again under his Banner."[30]

The return of the First Corps's two infantry divisions and artillery battalion proved timely, as the anticipated Federal offensive began within a week of the review. During the winter the Army of the Potomac had undergone reorganization with the disbandment of the First and Third corps. Most important, however, the Lincoln administration had appointed Ulysses S. Grant as general-in-chief of all Union forces, with the newly authorized rank of lieutenant general. Grant had fashioned a succession of victories in the west, culminating with the capture of Vicksburg in July 1863 and the defeat of Bragg's army at Chattanooga that November. Instead of remaining in Washington, Grant joined Meade's army in the field. As an opponent, Grant was a relentless warrior, a man unbowed by setbacks and battlefield defeats. His friend and fellow general William T. Sherman said of Grant: "I'll tell you where he beats me and where he beats the world. He don't care a damn for what he can't see the enemy doing, and it scares me like hell!"[31]

The Yankees came on May 4, a "lovely spring day," fording the Rapidan River. With their crossing Grant seized the strategic initiative in Virginia and, unlike his predecessors, never relinquished the grip on Lee's army. For the next forty days 119,000 Northerners and 75,000 Southerners passed through the nightmare of the Wilderness, Spotsylvania, North Anna, and Cold Harbor. Nothing that had come before compared to it. Death wrapped both armies in a shroud that could not be removed. Grant's casualties exceeded 55,000; Lee's, nearly 32,000. A Yankee likened the Overland Campaign to "a funeral procession."[32]

Throughout the campaign Lee's veterans fought on the defensive behind fieldworks and won tactical victories on each battlefield. Still the costs mounted. On May 6 Longstreet suffered a crippling wound at the Wilderness, accidentally shot by his own men. Five days later, at Yellow Tavern, a few miles north of Richmond, Jeb Stuart fell with a mortal wound, dying the next day in the capital. Twice, at the Wilderness and at Spotsylvania, Lee rode so close to the firing lines that his own men ordered him to the rear. Near the end of May he relieved Richard Ewell of command of the Second Corps and assigned Jubal Early to the post.[33]

While the armies lay at Cold Harbor on the Peninsula east of Richmond, Lee dispatched Early and the Second Corps west to Lynchburg, Virginia, a vital railroad center. A Union army under Major General David Hunter had advanced south up the Shenandoah Valley, threatening the city. When Early's troops arrived, they chased Hunter's force into the Allegheny Mountains, then marched north and, in the first week of July, entered Maryland. Lee had given Early discretionary orders for a movement across the Potomac. It was, once again, a daring gamble by Lee to retake the strategic initiative from Grant. Early's men reached the defenses of Washington before retreating into Virginia.[34]

Early's raid into Maryland embarrassed the Lincoln administration. Military operations in the spring and summer of 1864 unfolded against the backdrop of the Northern presidential election in November. Lincoln's reelection hopes were closely tied to Union military fortunes. By the time Early appeared before the Federal capital, Lincoln's prospects looked doubtful. The horrific casualties of the Overland Campaign stunned Northern civilians, and in the west William Sherman's campaign against Atlanta, proceeded with disheartening slowness. Lee and the Davis administration closely watched the political situation in the North. In their judgment an electoral defeat of Lincoln held the possibility of a negotiated settlement to the war and Confederate independence.[35]

In Virginia meanwhile the struggle between Grant and Lee had shifted across the James River to Petersburg, located twenty miles south of Richmond. When Federal assaults failed to capture the railroad center, Grant besieged Petersburg, where the countryside was laced with networks of formidable earthworks. Several Union offensives against Lee's lines and the defenses of Richmond failed, but the operations had an inexorableness to them, slowly draining away the life of the Confederate defenders. Before Early left for Lynchburg, Lee had said to him: "We must destroy this army of Grant's before he gets to the James River. If he gets there, it will become a siege, and then it will be a mere question of time."[36]

In September Union victories foretold the inevitability of the Confederate defeat. On September 2 Sherman captured Atlanta. Seventeen days later the Army of the Shenandoah, led by Major General Philip H. Sheridan, routed Early's Army of the Valley in the Battle of Third Winchester. Sheridan's troops defeated the Rebels a second time three days later, at Fisher's Hill. The Federals penetrated deeper into the Shenandoah Valley. When Sheridan withdrew north, his cavalry left behind charred barns, mills, and houses in what became known as "The Burning." Finally, on October 19, the Yankees inflicted the third defeat on Early's forces at Cedar Creek, effectively securing Federal control of the region.[37]

The drumroll of victories assured Lincoln's reelection on November 8. At month's end Sherman began his "March to the Sea"; from a burning Atlanta to Savannah the path of destruction through Georgia embraced hundreds of square miles. After Sherman captured Savannah he marched his veterans into South Carolina, where more fires and smoke marked the army's passage. By March 1865 the Yankees had entered North Carolina, opposed by a patchwork Confederate army under General Joseph E. Johnston.[38]

At Petersburg, meanwhile, attrition and desertion eroded away the vaunted Army of Northern Virginia. Grant applied increasing pressure, moving against the railroads that supplied Petersburg and Richmond and stretching Lee's lines even thinner. The end came swiftly. On April 1 the Federals, led by Sheridan, routed Rebel defenders at Five Forks, shredding the right flank of Lee's army. The next day a massive Union assault broke through the Southern works at Petersburg. During the fighting Powell Hill was killed. Lee ordered the abandonment of the Petersburg and Richmond defenses. Through the night of April 2–3 the Confederates marched away, angling west. In Richmond flames consumed blocks of the city, a symbol of a dying nation.[39]

The Confederate retreat and Union pursuit ended on April 8, when Federal cavalrymen overtook the van of Lee's army and closed the roads to the west at Appomattox Court House. The next morning, Palm Sunday, April 9, with flags raised, officers and men of the Army of Northern Virginia stepped out in a final charge. There were not many of them, but the majority were veterans of Stonewall Jackson's "foot cavalry."

Union infantry repulsed the attack. When Lee was informed of the failure of the breakthrough, he reportedly said, "Then there is nothing left me but to go and see General Grant, and I would rather die a thousand deaths." Longstreet, who had returned to duty months earlier, assured Lee that his close West Point and antebellum friend Grant would be fair in his surrender terms. If he were not, Lee's "old war-horse" said, "come back and let us fight it out."[40]

Dressed in full uniform, with sash and sword, Lee met Grant in the home of Wilmer McLean in Appomattox Court House. As Longstreet thought, Grant was generous, insisting only that the Confederates surrender their arms in a formal ceremony. On April 12 Lee departed for Richmond. He did not watch as his veterans formed ranks, filed into a column, and marched together for the last time, passing before lines of their foes and laying down their arms and flags. From there they went home.[41]

Before Lee left he had Charles Marshall compose a farewell address to the army. General Orders No. 9 began with these words. "After four years of arduous service, marked by unsurpassed courage and fortitude, the Army of Northern Virginia has been compelled to yield to overwhelming numbers and resources." It ended thus: "You will take with you the satisfaction that proceeds from the consciousness of duty faithfully performed, and I earnestly pray that a Merciful God will extend to you His blessing and protection. With our increasing admiration of your constancy and devotion to your country, and a grateful remembrance of your kind and generous considerations for myself, I bid you all an affectionate farewell."[42]

Even before the war ended, Lee and the Army of Northern Virginia had become the icons of Confederate history. In the years and decades that followed Appomattox they emerged as the central figures in the "Lost Cause" interpretation of the war, an army of unrivaled prowess that nearly won Southern independence against the vast material and manpower resources of the North. Today, a century and a half later, monuments of and memorials to Lee, Stonewall Jackson, Jeb Stuart, and their fellow generals attest to their historic fame. In courthouse squares across the former Confederacy private soldiers in stone stand defiantly. None symbolize the Confederate past more perfectly than Lee and his lieutenants.

In their own time Lee and his men forged a record of military achievement that stands perhaps preeminent in American history. From the Seven Days to Gettysburg they reshaped the conflict in the East. "Lee's campaigns of 1862," concluded the British historian Frederick Maurice, "are supreme in conception, and have not been surpassed, as examples of strategy by any other achievement of their kind by any other commander in history." The historian Joseph Harsh stated, "In Lee's hands, the Army of Northern Virginia would come close, perhaps as near as it could come, to achieving protracted stalemate against the imbalanced odds it faced."[43]

The victories in the Seven Days Campaign and at Second Manassas, Fredericksburg, and Chancellorsville raised Southern civilians' hopes for independence. "By the midpoint of the conflict," wrote the historian Gary Gallagher, "Lee and his men had become the preeminent symbol of the Confederate struggle for independence and liberty." Southern civilians placed their faith in Lee's army, which endured through most of the dark days in 1864 and 1865. In Gallagher's words, Lee's "admittedly bloody battles of 1862–63 created an aura of invincibility that offset gloomy events in the West; that aura clung to him and his army through the defensive struggles of 1864–65. Lee's initial eighteen months as commander of the Army of Northern Virginia had built credibility on which he drew for the rest of the war to sustain civilian morale."[44]

Lee's audacity and adoption of the strategic offensive formed the core of the army's operations. From his initial days in command he committed the army to aggressive and daring movements. He based the strategy on a reasoned assessment of how the Confederacy could achieve victory over a numerically superior opponent with nearly unlimited resources. In Lee's judgment, a passive defensive policy meant a slow wearing-away before the North's industrial and human might overwhelmed the South. Necessity demanded that he strike his foes or the shadow of defeat would not be stayed. His aggressiveness fulfilled the expectations of Jefferson Davis's administration and the Southern populace.[45]

"Lee never had an even chance tactically," argued the historian Douglas Southall Freeman. Almost always outnumbered on the battlefield, Lee preferred a broad turning movement strategically and a flanking maneuver tactically. The Seven Days, Second Manassas, Antietam,

Chancellorsville, and even Gettysburg in its earlier phases exemplified his utilization of maneuver, either strategically or tactically. Unlike the third day at Gettysburg, circumstances on the field at Gaines's Mill, Glendale, Second Manassas, and Chancellorsville governed his decisions to attack. The tragedy of Malvern Hill lay more in a combination of command failures and misunderstandings than in Lee's penchant for assaults.[46]

Longstreet believed that his commander's "characteristic fault was headlong combativeness"; he called Lee "too pugnacious." Unquestionably, when Lee encountered the Federals on a battlefield, he sought a battle of annihilation. In his reports and correspondence he used words such as "destroy," "crush," "ruin," and "wipe out" when discussing the desired fate of Union forces. The barren results of the victories at Fredericksburg and Chancellorsville frustrated Lee, who wanted a killing blow. But such a victory was beyond the capability of his and any other Civil War army. "As long as there was a willingness on both sides to fight to the bitter end," the historian Earl Hess maintained, "there would be no decisive battle that quickly led to an end of the war."[47]

To be sure, Lee prevailed against George McClellan, John Pope, Ambrose Burnside, and Joseph Hooker, Union generals notable for either their caution or their incompetence. Joseph Harsh described the campaigns in the East as "a remarkable contest of wills between Lee and a series of Federal commanders to determine whose offensives would dominate." From the Seven Days to Gettysburg Lee shaped the contours of the theater and the battlefields. Except for the initial movements in the Fredericksburg and Chancellorsville campaigns, he either held or regained the strategic initiative in Virginia from the beginning of the Seven Days, on June 26, 1862, until May 4, 1864, when Grant led the Army of the Potomac across the Rapidan River. Against Grant, the finest of all Union generals, Lee waged a defensive struggle that inflicted fearful casualties on his opponent, producing a grinding stalemate that might have prevented Lincoln's reelection if not for Federal victories elsewhere. At the end too few of Lee's troops manned the trenches at Petersburg.[48]

"By 1864," the historian Russell Weigley contended, "Lee was to discover that his army had lost the power to conduct effective offensive maneuver; but it was his own expensive mode of war that did most to bring it to that plight." Had Lee, as Weigley and other historians have charged, taken the bloodiest road? Had his string of victories been too dearly purchased at the cost of Confederate independence? The casualties sustained by his army from June 1862 through July 1863 were staggering. Although exact figures conflict, Lee lost in those thirteen months nearly 90,000 officers and men, killed, wounded, or missing. Of that number, more than 10,000 men had been killed, mortally wounded, or permanently disabled. In that time the Union Army of the Potomac incurred losses of 97,000. Except at Fredericksburg, the Southern casualty rate, with fewer troops, exceeded the Northern rate.[49]

The rate of officers' casualties in Lee's army was the highest for any Confederate army. Among colonels, the casualty rate amounted to 50 percent, although fewer than half of all officers of that rank in Confederate service belonged to Lee's army. The historian Robert K. Krick calculated that 422 colonels, lieutenant colonels, and majors were killed or mortally wounded under Lee, nearly one-fourth of all field officers in the army. These figures reflect the expectation that Southern officers lead their men in combat and might reflect the aggressiveness Lee demanded of officers at all levels.[50]

Among general officers, those who led brigades, divisions, and corps from the Seven Days through Gettysburg, the slain included Stonewall Jackson, William Dorsey Pender, Lawrence O'Bryan Branch, Maxcy Gregg, Samuel Garland, George B. Anderson, Charles Winder, Lewis Armistead, Richard Garnett, Paul Semmes, William Barksdale, J. Johnston Pettigrew, William Starke, and Thomas Cobb. The conflict's final year took the lives of Ambrose Powell Hill, Jeb Stuart, Robert Rodes, and Stephen Dodson Ramseur. Of the division commanders with Lee when he assumed command on June 1, 1862, only James Longstreet, crippled by wounds, remained with him at Appomattox Court House.[51]

Had Lee's generalship bled his army to the bone? "The aggressiveness of Robert E. Lee, the greatest Yankee killer of all time," declared the historian Grady McWhiney, "cost the Confederacy dearly." The depleted ranks and the attrition in officers was, according to Weigley, "another product of Lee's own mode of war." Harsh concluded, "The fatal flaw in his [Lee's] thinking is the confusion between strategic and tactical operations. Without doubt, the tactical defense is superior to the tactical offense under certain conditions."[52]

The historic image of Lee's needless expenditure of his men's blood rests in part on the second and third days at Gettysburg. But that battle, in the view of the historian Archer Jones, was "an aberration" in Lee's generalship when compared to Second Manassas, Antietam, Fredericksburg, and Chancellorsville. In three of those engagements Lee's army fought either primarily or entirely on the defensive. At Chancellorsville, confronted by twice his numbers, Lee attacked an exposed flank of the Union army, a decision that led to eventual victory. He ordered the assaults on May 3 to unite the wings of his army, a critical need. Although very costly, Lee's "forcing the game" at Gettysburg, as Porter Alexander put it, held the prospects, in Lee's mind, of a victory of significant consequence. It was what he had strived for since assigned command of the army.[53]

The historian Alan Nolan argued, "The South's true grand strategy of the defensive could have kept its armies in the field long enough to wear down the North's willingness to carry on the war." In Nolan's view, "true" is what the strategy should have been. The Confederate government, however, witnessed the consequences of a passive defensive strategy during the fall of 1861 and the winter of 1862, when Union armies scored victories and penetrated into Southern territory. By the time Lee took command of the army, prospects for Confederate independence appeared doubtful at best. As Weigley observed, "The Confederacy lacked strategic options."[54]

A singular fact stands foremost: Lee and the Army of Northern Virginia recast the war's direction. The victories in 1862 and 1863, according to Gary Gallagher, "undoubtedly advanced the Confederate cause." By maneuver and daring, Lee led his army on what must be regarded as the Confederacy's best route to a victory against formidable odds. To await a Federal onslaught was to accept defeat. "Lee was so deadly an opponent on the tactical level," asserted Weigley, "that he merits his place in the pantheon of great generals whatever his flaws."[55]

Lee's imprint on the army was undeniable; its imprint on him forged an enduring military legacy. His method of command allowed for the emergence of a group of talented subordinates perhaps unequaled in any Civil War army. Stonewall Jackson and James Longstreet rank among the finest, if not as the finest corps commanders on either side. From June 1862 to July 1863 Ambrose Powell Hill, Richard Ewell, Daniel Harvey Hill, John Bell Hood, Jubal Early, and Robert Rodes led infantry divisions, all men with distinguished combat records. In Jeb Stuart Lee had the premier light cavalry commander in the war. Casualties reduced the quality of leadership, but during the conflict's final year gifted brigade commanders such as John B. Gordon, Stephen Dodson Ramseur, Cadmus Wilcox, Joseph Kershaw, William Mahone, Charles Field, and Wade Hampton filled the voids. Jackson's loss was irreparable.

Behind Lee, Jackson, Longstreet, and the others marched men whose fighting spirit and prowess resound through history. "I never had any doubt that our people would make good fighters," said Longstreet in a postwar interview. The record attests to the veracity of Lee's words to John Hood in May 1863, "There never were such men in an army before." Lee never quite bent them fully to his will, in camp or on the march. But when the time came, when courage was to be tested in the hellish confines of combat, they answered. As Sergeant William B. Robertson of the 14th Virginia wrote to his wife after Gettysburg, "I am always up when Old Mars Bob wants me to fight for him but I tell you Mat that he puts me in some tight places sometimes." Elizabeth Pryor, a recent biographer of the general, wrote, "Lee's sway over his troops is unsurpassed in military annals."[56]

One of the finest tributes paid to Lee's officers and men came not from a comrade or a historian, but from an enemy, Joseph Hooker. In testimony before a congressional committee, the former commander of the Army of the Potomac stated: "With a rank and file vastly inferior to our own, intellectually and physically, [Lee's] army has, by discipline alone, acquired a character for steadiness and efficiency unsurpassed, in my judgment, in ancient or modern times. We have not been able to rival it, nor has there been any near approximation of it in the other Rebel armies."[57]

When William Pitt Ballinger, an attorney in Galveston, Texas, heard the news of the Confederate victory at Chancellorsville, he exclaimed, "What a glorious army that of Lee is." Chancellorsville marked the culmination of achievement for Lee's "glorious army" that remains indelibly etched in the nation's history. No American army, against such odds and in less than a year, compiled such a record as that of the Army of Northern Virginia, and none altered the direction of a conflict more.[58]

Abbreviations

Works cited by the author and short titles will be found in full in the bibliography. The following abbreviations are used in the notes.

ADAH   Alabama Department of Archives and History

AHC   Atlanta History Center

ANB   Antietam National Battlefield

B&L   *Battles and Leaders of the Civil War*

CV   *Confederate Veteran Magazine*

CWTI   *Civil War Times Illustrated*

DU   Duke University

EU   Emory University

FSNMP   Fredericksburg-Spotsylvania National Military Park

GAHS   Georgia Historical Society

GDAH   Georgia Department of Archives and History

GNMP   Gettysburg National Military Park

HL   Huntington Library

HU   Harvard University

IHS   Indiana Historical Society

LC   Library of Congress

LSU   Louisiana State University

LVA   Library of Virginia

MC   Museum of the Confederacy

MNBP   Manassas National Battlefield Park

N&S   *North & South Magazine*

NC	Navarro College
NYHS	New-York Historical Society
NYPL	New York Public Library
NCDAH	North Carolina Division of Archives and History
OR	*U.S. War Department, War of the Rebellion: A Compilation of the Official Records of the Union and Confederate Armies*
SHSP	*Southern Historical Society Papers*
SOR	*Supplement to the Official Records of the Union and Confederate Armies*
UGA	University of Georgia
UM	University of Michigan
UNC	University of North Carolina
USAMHI	United States Army Military History Institute
UPS	Union Presbyterian Seminary
UVA	University of Virginia
VATU	Virginia Tech University
VHS	Virginia Historical Society
VMI	Virginia Military Institute
WLU	Washington and Lee University
WRHS	Western Reserve Historical Society

Notes

Prologue

1. Edward Dix-Sally, June 7, 1862, Dix Letters, WLU; Gordon, *Reminiscences*, p. 56.
2. Wert, *General James Longstreet*, pp. 113–21.
3. Ibid., pp. 120–21.
4. Ibid., pp. 121, 122; Furgurson, *Ashes*, p. 139.
5. W. C. Davis, ed. *Confederate General*, vol. 5, pp. 173, 175.
6. Harsh, *Confederate Tide Rising*, pp. 47–49; Woodworth, *Davis and Lee*, p. 148; E. M. Thomas, *Robert E. Lee*, p. 225.
7. E. M. Thomas, *Robert E. Lee*, pp. 210, 225.
8. Ibid., p.225; Wert, *General James Longstreet*, p. 126.

Chapter One

1. Reid, *History*, p. 91; Gallagher, ed., *Fighting*, p. 90; McClellan, *I Rode*, p. 427n.
2. Wert, *General James Longstreet*, p. 125; E. M. Thomas, *Robert E. Lee*, pp. 198, 199.
3. E. M. Thomas, *Robert E. Lee*, pp. 199, 201–12; Wert, *General James Longstreet*, p. 125.
4. Harsh, *Confederate Tide Rising*, p. 74; Freeman, *R. E. Lee*, vol. 4, pp. 175–76; Alexander, *Memoirs*, p. 111.
5. Freeman, *R. E. Lee*, vol. 4, p. 175; Chesnut, *Diary*, pp. 94, 95; Sorrel, *Recollections*, p. 89; Worsham, *One of Jackson's Foot Cavalry*, p. 15; John Daniel to T. Z. Rosser, April 16, 1901, Gordon and Rosser Family Papers, UVA; Pryor, *Reading the Man*, p. 323.
6. W. Taylor, *Four Years*, p. 77; Wert, *General James Longstreet*, p. 128.
7. Pryor, *Reading the Man*, p. 332; Lee, ed., *Recollections*, p. 89; Maurice, *Robert E. Lee*, p. 139; Tucker, *High Tide*, p. 53; *Confederate History Symposium*, p. 62; Wert, *General James Longstreet*, p. 128.

8. W. Taylor, *Four Years*, p. 77; Wert, *General James Longstreet*, p. 129; Harsh, *Confederate Tide Rising*, p. 50.

9. Harsh, *Confederate Tide Rising*, p. 50; Freeman, *R. E. Lee*, vol. 4, p. 170.

10. Freeman, *R. E. Lee*, vol. 4, p. 170, 171, 173; Harsh, *Confederate Tide Rising*, p. 50; Wert, *General James Longstreet*, p. 128; Roland, *Reflections*, pp. 99, 100.

11. Gallagher, ed., *Richmond Campaign*, p. 11.

12. T. L. Jones, ed., *Campbell Brown's Civil War*, p. 141; Wert, *General James Longstreet*, pp. 98–109.

13. Gallagher, *Confederate War*, p. 134.

14. Wert, *General James Longstreet*, p. 108.

15. Maurice, ed., *Aide-De-Camp*, p. 73.

16. Ibid., p. 74; Gallagher, *Lee and His Army*, pp. 163, 172, 173; Harsh, *Confederate Tide Rising*, p. 58; Roland, "Lee's Invasion Strategy," *N&S*, v. 1, no. 6, p. 36.

17. Harsh, *Confederate Tide Rising*, p. 56; Carmichael, ed., *Audacity*, p. 2; Gallagher and Glatthaar, eds., *Leaders*, pp. 9, 35.

18. Gallagher, *Lee and His Army*, pp. 173, 178; Harsh, *Confederate Tide Rising*, pp. 56, 57, 58; Roland, *Reflections*, pp. 89, 90, 97, 99; Dowdey and Manarin, eds., *Wartime Papers*, p. 816.

19. E. P. Alexander to Frederick Colston, February 9, 1904, Campbell-Colston Family Papers, UNC; Gallagher, ed., *Fighting*, p. 91.

20. Polley, *Hood's Texas Brigade*, p. 153; Wert, *Gettysburg*, p. 43; Gallagher, ed., *Fighting*, p. 265; Harsh, *Taken at the Flood*, pp. 20, 490, 492.

21. Harsh, *Confederate Tide Rising*, pp. 57–59; Gallagher and Glatthaar, eds., *Leaders*, pp. 11, 35; Freeman, *R. E. Lee*, vol. 4, p. 174; *Confederate History Symposium*, p. 9; Roland, *Reflections*, p. 99.

22. Freeman, *R. E. Lee*, vol. 4, pp. 173, 174; Roland, *Reflections*, pp. 90, 97; Glatthaar, *General Lee's Army*, p. 124; Maurice, ed., *Aide-De-Camp*, p. 74; Harsh, *Confederate Tide Rising*, pp. 58, 59.

23. W. Taylor, *Four Years*, p. 90; Gallagher, *Confederate War*, pp. 127–30; Harsh, *Confederate Tide Rising*, pp. 59, 74.

24. Harsh, *Confederate Tide Rising*, pp. 50, 51; Woodworth, *Davis and Lee*, p. 150; Gallagher, ed., *Fighting*, p. 90; J. B. Jones, *Rebel War Clerk's Diary*, vol. 1, p. 133.

25. W. C. Davis, ed., *Confederate General*, vol. 5, pp. 173, 175; Woodworth, *Davis and Lee*, pp. 150, 151; Dowdey and Manarin, eds., *Wartime Papers*, p. 182.

26. Harsh, *Confederate Tide Rising*, pp. 52, 83, 84; Dowdey and Manarin, eds., *Wartime Papers*, p. 181.

27. *OR*, vol. 5, p. 913; Dowdey and Manarin, eds., *Wartime Papers*, pp. 181–82.

28. *OR*, vol. 11, pt. 1, p. 81; Livermore, *Numbers and Losses*, p. 81; Sorrel, *Recollections*, p. 66; William W. Bentley to My Dear Mother, June 13, 1862, Bentley Letter, VMI.

29. S. W. Smith, ed., *Freeman on Leadership*, pp. 62, 66, 84, 86; Gallagher, ed., *Fighting*, p. 48; Ratchford, *Some Reminiscences*, p. 40; Glatthaar, *General Lee's Army*, pp. 128, 129; D. H. Hill to My Dear Wife, June 10, 1862, Hill Papers, USAMHI; Reid, *History*, p. 93.

30. Harsh, *Confederate Tide Rising*, p. 86; New York *Times*, July 29, 1879.

31. S. W. Smith, ed., *Freeman on Leadership*, pp. 62, 63, 64; Allardice, *Confederate Colonels*, p. 17n; Krick, *Lee's Colonels*, p. xiii; *SHSP*, vol. 10, p. 37.

32. S. W. Smith, ed., *Freeman on Leadership*, p. 63; McCarthy, *Detailed Minutiae*, p. 39; Casler, *Four Years*, p. 12; Eggleston, *Rebel's Recollections*, pp. 71, 80.

33. Sword, *Southern Invincibility*, pp. 11, 12; Phillips, *Diehard Rebels*, pp. 2, 4; McPherson, *For Cause*, pp. 91, 95, 98; Sheehan-Dean, *Why Confederates Fought*, pp. 3, 4, 61.

34. Sorrel, *Recollections*, p. 87; Gallagher, *Confederate War*, pp. 66–67; Carmichael, *Lee's Young Artillerist*, p. 35; Lowe and Hodges, eds., *Letters to Amanda*, p. 11; Samuel J. C. Moore to My Dearest Ellen, May 29, 1861, Moore Papers, UNC; Wiley, *Life*, pp. 309, 310; Phillips, *Diehard Rebels*, pp. 2, 6, 9, 182, 188.

35. Samuel J. C. Moore to My Dear Little Boy, May 16, 1861, Moore Papers, UNC; Glatthaar, *General Lee's Army*, p. 33.

36. J. B. Jones, *Rebel War Clerk's Diary*, vol. 1, pp. 132–33.

37. McCarthy, *Detailed Minutiae*, pp. 8, 9; Mast, *State Troops*, p. 92; New York *Times*, July 29, 1879.

38. Allardice, *Confederate Colonels*, pp. 19–22; Krick, *Lee's Colonels*, pp. xiii, 26–384; McMurry, *Virginia Military Institute*, pp. v, vi, 58, 59, 64; Sword, *Southern Invincibility*, pp. 151, 152.

39. Gallagher, *Confederate War*, pp. 96, 98; Krick, *Lee's Colonels*, pp. xiii, 11; Wise, *Long Arm*, p. 101; McMurry, *Virginia Military Institute*, pp. 4, 65.

40. *OR*, vol. 11, pt. 2, pp. 483–89; Allardice, *Confederate Colonels*, p. 13.

41. Freeman, *Lee's Lieutenants*, vol. 1, p. 518; *OR*, vol. 11, pt. 2, pp. 483–89; Warner, *Generals in Gray*, *passim*.

42. *OR*, vol. 11, pt. 2, pp. 483–89; Warner, *Generals in Gray*, *passim*; Allardice, *Confederate Colonels*, p. 14.

43. Warner, *Generals in Gray*, *passim*.

44. Ibid.; E. M. Thomas, *Robert E. Lee*, pp. 220–23; Wert, *General James Longstreet*, pp. 102, 103, 129, 130.

45. Warner, *Generals in Gray*, p. 234; Wise, *Long Arm*, p. 198.

46. Wert, *Cavalryman*, pp. 18, 37–39, 46, 62, 64.

47. Early, *Lieutenant General*, p. 90; Glatthaar, *General Lee's Army*, p. 128.

Chapter Two

1. Wert, *Sword*, pp. 81, 90.

2. Ibid., pp. 81–84.

3. Ibid., pp. 83, 93, 94.

4. J. E. Johnston to R. E. Lee, April 30, 1862, Lee Papers, WRHS.

5. D. H. Hill to My Dear Genl, May 5, 1876, Hill Papers, NC; Carmichael, ed., *Audacity*, p. 9; Dowdey and Manarin, eds., *Wartime Papers*, p. 184.

6. S. W. Smith, ed., *Freeman on Leadership*, pp. 66–68; Glatthaar, *General Lee's Army*, pp. 127–31; Wise, *Long Arm*, pp. 198, 199; *OR*, vol. 11, pt. 3, pp. 572, 576, 585; D. H. Hill to Wife, June 10, 1862, Hill Papers, USAMHI.

7. Carmichael, ed., *Audacity*, pp. 84, 87, 88, 97; Venable, "Personal Reminiscences," UVA; W. Taylor, *General Lee*, p. 157.

8. Carmichael, ed., *Audacity*, pp. 87, 88, 89, 90; W. Taylor, *General Lee*, p. 56; R. H. Chilton to D. H. Hill, January 1, 1868, Hill Papers, LVA.

9. *OR*, vol. 11, pt. 3, pp. 571–72.

10. Ibid., pp. 572, 573; Wert, *General James Longstreet*, p. 131; Dowdey and Manarin, eds., *Wartime Papers*, p. 184; Diary, January 29, 1863, Cooke Papers, DU.

11. Harsh, *Confederate Tide Rising*, pp. 53, 54; Woodworth, *Davis and Lee*, p. 153; Robert Toombs to General, February 5, 1879, Longstreet Papers, GAHS; Wert, *General James Longstreet*, pp. 129–30.

12. Wert, *General James Longstreet*, pp. 130, 131; Sorrel, *Recollections*, p. 67; James Longstreet to Robert N. Johnson, September 6, 1888, Law Papers, NYPL; Charles Marshall to A. L. Long, April 6, 1880, Long Papers, UNC; Harsh, *Confederate Tide Rising*, p. 53; Woodworth, *Davis and Lee*, pp. 153, 154; James Longstreet to General, May 13, 1875, Hill Papers, LVA; A. Z. Long to James Longstreet, February 27, 1870, Longstreet Papers, DU.

13. D. H. Hill to My Dear Genl, May 5, 1876, Hill Papers, NC.

14. Harsh, *Confederate Tide Rising*, pp. 54, 55, 56.

15. Glatthaar, *General Lee's Army*, p. 132; Dowdey and Manarin, eds., *Wartime Papers*, pp. 183–84, 188; Woodworth, *Davis and Lee*, pp. 159–60.

16. Wert, *General James Longstreet*, p. 131; Longstreet, *From Manassas to Appomattox*, p. 112.

17. Wert, *General James Longstreet*, pp. 115–17, 123; *OR*, vol. 11, pt. 3, p. 580; Joseph E. Johnston to My dear General, February 3, 1879, Longstreet Papers, GAHS.

18. Wert, *General James Longstreet*, pp. 22, 97; Cutrer, ed., *Longstreet's Aide*, pp. 60, 72; Houghton and Houghton, *Two Boys*, p. 53; W. W. Blackford, *War Years*, p. 47; Tucker, *High Tide*, pp. 4, 6.

19. Long, *Memoirs*, p. 166; D. H. Hill to My Dear Genl, May 5, 1876, Hill Papers, NC; Longstreet, *From Manassas to Appomattox*, p. 114; Freeman, ed., *Lee's Dispatches*, p. 11.

20. J. E. B. Stuart to R. E. Lee, June 4, 1862, Stuart Papers, HL.

21. *OR*, vol. 11, pt. 2, p. 490.

22. Hattaway and Jones, *How the North Won*, pp. 14, 15; Harsh, *Confederate Tide Rising*, pp. 66, 71, 72.

23. Harsh, *Confederate Tide Rising*, pp. 68, 69, 70; Nolan, *Lee Considered*, pp. 77, 78, 79; Conversations with Dr. W. S. Buckler, 1870, McIntosh Papers, VHS; *OR*, vol. 29, pt. 2, p. 819; Wert, *Gettysburg*, pp. 43, 44.

24. *OR*, vol. 11, pt. 2, p. 490.

25. Ibid., pt. 3, pp. 590–91; Wert, *Cavalryman*, p. 96.

26. Wert, *Cavalryman*, pp. 94–100.

27. Ibid., pp. 100, 101; *OR*, vol. 11, pt. 2, p. 490.

28. *OR*, vol. 11, pt. 2, pp. 589–90; Robertson, *Stonewall Jackson*, p. 458; Harsh, *Confederate Tide Rising*, p. 181.

29. *B&L*, vol. 2, p. 347; Longstreet, *From Manassas to Appomattox*, p. 121.

30. Harsh, *Confederate Tide Rising*, pp. 180, 181; Carmichael, ed., *Audacity*, pp. 35–37; Robertson, *Stonewall Jackson*, p. 464; *OR*, vol. 11, pt. 3, p. 238; Dowdey and Manarin, eds., *Wartime Papers*, pp. 198–200.

31. Carmichael, ed., *Audacity*, pp. 35, 37; Harsh, *Confederate Tide Rising*, p. 77; Dowdey and Manarin, eds., *Wartime Papers*, pp. 198–200.

32. James Longstreet to My Dear General, November 5, 1877, Hill Papers, LVA; D. H. Hill to My Dear Genl, May 5, 1876, Hill Papers, NC; Longstreet, *From Manassas to Appomattox*, pp. 121, 122; *B&L*, vol. 2, p. 347; Robertson, *Stonewall Jackson*, p. 466.

33. Robertson, *Stonewall Jackson*, pp. 448–50; Gallagher, ed., *Fighting*, p. 94.

34. Eggleston, *Rebel's Recollections*, p. 132; Lyle, "Stonewall Jackson's Guard," p. 10, WLU; Charles C. Wright Memoirs, Wright Family Papers, VHS; Smith, *With Stonewall Jackson*, p. 64.

35. Dabney, *Life*, p. 736; R. Taylor, *Destruction*, p. 89; Greene, *Whatever You Resolve to Be*, pp. 15, 16; Douglas, *I Rode*, p. 214; Boyd, *Reminiscences*, p. 9; Gallagher, ed., *Fighting*, p. 157; Glatthaar, *General Lee's Army*, p. 135; Cozzens, *Shenandoah 1862*, p. 511.

36. Greene, *Whatever You Resolve to Be*, p. 17; Jedediah Hotchkiss to My Dr. Wife, April 14, 1862, Hotchkiss Papers, LC; R. Taylor, *Destruction*, p. 52; *Annals*, p. 647; W. Taylor, *General Lee*, p. 61.

37. Runge, ed., *Four Years*, p. 20; Stevens, *Reminiscences*, p. 45; English Combatant, *Battle-Fields*, p. 141; Sorrel, *Recollections*, p. 22.

38. Harsh, *Confederate Tide Rising*, pp. 180, 181; *Confederate History Symposium*, p. 11; Harsh, *Sounding the Shallows*, pp. 104, 106; Wise, *Long Arm*, p. 206; Wert, *Sword*, p. 95.

39. A. B. Simms to Mother, June 6, 1862, Simms Family Papers, AHC; Hassler, ed., *General to His Lady*, p. 158; J. B. Jones, *Rebel War Clerk's Diary*, vol. 1, p. 134.

40. Dowdey and Manarin, eds., *Wartime Papers*, pp. 198–99.

41. Longstreet, *From Manassas to Appomattox*, p. 121; Robertson, *Stonewall Jackson*, pp. 458–61, 467–68; A. B. Butner to Sir, July 8, 1862, Butner Papers, NC.

42. Robertson, *Stonewall Jackson*, pp. 470–72; Greene, *Whatever You Resolve to Be*, p. 46; Hotchkiss, ed., *Confederate Military History*, vol. 3, p. 285.

43. Greene, *Whatever You Resolve to Be*, p. 48; Robertson, *Stonewall Jackson*, pp. 472, 473; *OR*, vol. 11, pt. 2, pp. 491, 552–53.

44. Carmichael, ed., *Audacity*, p. 30; Wert, *Sword*, pp. 98–99; Gallagher, ed., *Lee: The Soldier*, p. 16; *OR*, vol. 11, pt. 2, p. 756.

45. Carmichael, ed., *Audacity*, pp. 39, 40; Gallagher, ed., *Lee: The Soldier*, p. 16; *OR*, vol. 11, pt. 2, p. 835.

46. Robertson, *General A. P. Hill*, pp. 7, 38, 48, 62, 64, 80, 85; Freeman, *Lee's Lieutenants*, vol. 1, p. 218; W. C. Davis, ed., *Confederate General*, vol. 3, p. 96; Warner, *Generals in Gray*, p. 134; Tucker, *High Tide*, pp. 11, 12, 13; Schenck, *Up Came Hill*, pp. 17, 19.

47. Wert, *Sword*, pp. 99–102; Gallagher, ed., *Fighting*, pp. 95, 100.

48. *OR*, vol. 11, pt. 2, pp. 491, 835, 841; Burton, *Extraordinary Circumstances*, pp. 67–75.

49. *OR*, vol. 11, pt. 2, pp. 835, 841; John M. Fullerton to Honored Parents, Brother, Sister, July 4, 1862, Miller Family Letters, USAMHI; Wert, *Sword*, p. 102; Burton, *Extraordinary Circumstances*, pp. 74, 75.

50. *B&L*, vol. 2, p. 361.

51. Maurice, ed., *Aide-de-Camp*, p. 96; *OR*, vol. 11, pt. 2, pp. 491, 835.

52. *OR*, vol. 11, pt. 2, pp. 222, 223, 272, 386; Wert, *Sword*, pp. 102, 103.

53. Maurice, ed., *Aide-de-Camp*, p. 96; Longstreet, *From Manassas to Appomattox*, p. 125; Robertson, *Stonewall Jackson*, pp. 475, 476.

54. *OR*, vol. 11, pt. 2, pp. 491, 492, 553, 554; Longstreet, *From Manassas to Appomattox*, p. 125; Robertson, *Stonewall Jackson*, pp. 475–76; Carmichael, ed., *Audacity*, pp. 40, 41, 42.

55. *OR*, vol. 11, pt. 2, pp. 492, 836, 837; Carmichael, ed., *Audacity*, p. 42; Wert, *Sword*, p. 104.

56. Burton, *Extraordinary Circumstances*, pp. 91, 92; Caldwell, *History*, p. 64; W. C. Davis, ed., *Confederate General*, vol. 3, pp. 41, 42; Krick, *Smoothbore Volley*, pp. 156, 157.

57. Burton, *Extraordinary Circumstances*, pp. 94–102; *OR*, vol. 11, pt. 2, p. 487; M. Warrenton to Parents, July 4, 1862, Warrenton Papers, NC; Wert, *Sword*, pp. 103–5.

58. *OR*, vol. 11, pt. 2, p. 492; Gallagher, ed., *Fighting*, pp. 101–2.

59. *OR*, vol. 11, pt. 2, p. 492; Longstreet, *From Manassas to Appomattox*, pp. 126, 127; Venable, "Personal Reminiscences," UVA; Robertson, *Stonewall Jackson*, pp. 478–81.

60. *OR*, vol. 11, pt. 2, p. 493; Longstreet, *From Manassas to Appomattox*, p. 127; Carmichael, ed., *Audacity*, p. 43; Burton, *Extraordinary Circumstances*, pp. 100–102, 104, 106, 107, 115, 126.

61. *OR*, vol. 11, pt. 2, pp. 483–87, 757; Burton, *Extraordinary Circumstances*, pp. 119, 126.

62. Wert, *General James Longstreet*, p. 138; *OR*, vol. 11, pt. 2, p. 493; Simpson, *Hood's Texas Brigade*, p. 117.

63. Warner, *Generals in Gray*, pp. 142, 143; Lasswell, ed., *Rags and Hope*, p. 151; Haskell, ed., *Haskell Memoirs*, p. 16; Everett, ed., *Chaplain Davis*, p. 149; Lord, ed., *Fremantle Diary*, p. 193; Ratchford, *Some Reminiscences*, p. 56; Chesnut, *Diary*, p. 297; Polley, *Hood's Texas Brigade*, p. 204.

64. *OR*, vol. 11, pt. 2, p. 492; Wert, *Sword*, pp. 105–6; Burton, *Extraordinary Circumstances*, p. 136.

65. W. Taylor, *General Lee*, p. 69; OR, vol. 11, pt. 2, pp. 758, 773.

66. Burton, *Extraordinary Circumstances*, pp. 135–37; Freeman, *Lee's Lieutenants*, vol. 1, p. 536; Dyer, *Gallant Hood*, p. 93; OR, vol. 11, pt. 2, pp. 569, 855; SOR, v. 2, p. 431; Gallagher, ed., *Richmond Campaign*, pp. 205, 207; Ratchford, *Some Reminiscences*, p. 25.

67. Wert, *Sword*, pp. 106–7.

68. Ibid., pp. 107, 108.

69. OR, vol. 11, pt. 2, pp. 493, 494; Wert, *General James Longstreet*, pp. 139–40.

70. Longstreet, *From Manassas to Appomattox*, pp. 130, 131; Freeman, ed., *Lee's Dispatches*, p. 21.

71. OR, vol. 11, pt. 2, p. 494; B&L, vol. 2, pp. 383, 386; Gallagher, ed., *Richmond Campaign*, p. 108.

72. Gallagher, ed., *Richmond Campaign*, p. 108; Carmichael, ed., *Audacity*, pp. 48, 49; Burton, *Extraordinary Circumstances*, pp. 182, 184, 192.

73. Burton, *Extraordinary Circumstances*, pp. 214–21; Wert, *Sword*, pp. 110–12; W. C. Davis, ed., *Confederate General*, vol. 3, p. 45; Dinkins, *1861–1865*, p. 44.

74. Robertson, *Stonewall Jackson*, pp. 487, 488; OR, vol. 11, pt. 2, p. 675.

75. OR, vol. 11, pt. 2, p. 687; Wert, *Cavalryman*, p. 109; R. H. Chilton to J. E. B. Stuart, June 29, 1862, Stuart Papers, HL.

76. Robertson, *Stonewall Jackson*, pp. 488–90; OR, vol. 11, pt. 2, pp. 680, 687; Wert, *General James Longstreet*, p. 141.

77. Wert, *Sword*, pp. 112, 113.

78. Allan, *Army*, p. 120; Gallagher, ed., *Fighting*, p. 109.

79. Wert, *General James Longstreet*, p. 141; OR, vol. 11, pt. 2, pp. 495, 759, 906, 907; Longstreet, *From Manassas to Appomattox*, p. 134.

80. OR, vol. 11, pt. 2, p. 759; Longstreet, *From Manassas to Appomattox*, pp. 134, 135; Cutrer, ed., *Longstreet's Aide*, p. 95; SOR, vol. 2, p. 444.

81. OR, vol. 11, pt. 2, p. 759; C. M. Wilcox to E. P. Alexander, July 6, 1869, Alexander Papers, UNC; Burton, *Extraordinary Circumstances*, pp. 276–83; Wert, *Sword*, p. 114.

82. Wert, *General James Longstreet*, pp. 143–44; OR, vol. 11, pt. 2, pp. 838, 839; Burton, *Extraordinary Circumstances*, pp. 288–97, 300; Gallagher, ed., *Fighting*, p. 107.

83. OR, vol. 11, pt. 2, p. 759; Burton, *Extraordinary Circumstances*, p. 298; Wert, *General James Longstreet*, p. 144; W. C. Davis, ed., *Confederate General*, vol. 2, p. 119.

84. Burton, *Extraordinary Circumstances*, p. 299; Allan, *Army*, p. 121; Gallagher, ed., *Fighting*, pp. 109, 110.

85. Wert, *General James Longstreet*, p. 145; Robertson, *Stonewall Jackson*, pp. 493, 494; Freeman, *Lee's Lieutenants*, vol. 1, p. 576.

86. Wert, *General James Longstreet*, p. 145; Robertson, *Stonewall Jackson*, pp. 495–97; Maurice, ed., *Aide-de-Camp*, pp. 111, 112; Wade Hampton to E. P. Alexander, March 1901; Thomas T. Munford to My dear General, March 23, 1901, Alexander Papers, UNC.

87. Gallagher, ed., *Richmond Campaign*, pp. 79, 82; Burton, *Extraordinary Circumstances*, p. 394; Greene, *Whatever You Resolve to Be*, pp. 73, 74; Vandiver, *Mighty Stonewall*, p. 317; Robertson, *Stonewall Jackson*, chapter 16, p. 394.

88. Gallagher, ed., *Richmond Campaign*, p. 83; Robertson, *Stonewall Jackson*, pp. 496, 497; OR, vol. 11, pt. 2, p. 495.

89. Robertson, *Stonewall Jackson*, p. 497; Greene, *Whatever You Resolve to Be*, pp. 65, 66; Carmichael, ed., *Audacity*, p. 52; Burton, *Extraordinary Circumstances*, p. 300; Gallagher, ed., *Fighting*, p. 110.

90. Freeman, *R. E. Lee*, vol. 2, p. 199; Wert, *Sword*, p. 117.

91. Wert, *Sword*, p. 119.

92. Longstreet, *From Manassas to Appomattox*, p. 142; Freeman, *R. E. Lee*, vol. 2, p. 200; A. Jones, *Civil War Command*, p. 69; Carmichael, ed., *Audacity*, p. 53; Harsh, *Confederate Tide Rising*, p. 70; Bridges, *Lee's Maverick General*, p. 77; Allan, *Army*, p. 136.

93. *B&L*, vol. 2, pp. 390, 391; W. A. Smith, *Anson Guards*, p. 120; Warner, *Generals in Gray*, p. 136.

94. OR, vol. 11, pt. 2, p. 496; Lafayette McLaws to James Longstreet, November 30, 1885, Longstreet Papers, EU; Burton, *Extraordinary Circumstances*, pp. 314–16; Longstreet, *From Manassas to Appomattox*, pp. 142, 143.

95. Longstreet, *From Manassas to Appomattox*, pp. 143, 144; OR, vol. 11, pt. 2, p. 677.

96. Burton, *Extraordinary Circumstances*, pp. 325, 326; Greene, *Whatever You Resolve to Be*, p. 69; Carmichael, ed., *Audacity*, p. 102.

97. Wert, *General James Longstreet*, p. 147; Burton, *Extraordinary Circumstances*, pp. 316–20; OR, vol. 11, pt. 2, p. 496.

98. OR, vol. 11, pt. 2, pp. 489, 496, 536; Wert, *General James Longstreet*, p. 147; Wise, *Long Arm*, pp. 223, 230, 231.

99. Longstreet, *From Manassas to Appomattox*, p. 144; OR, vol. 11, pt. 2, p. 760; *B&L*, vol. 2, p. 403.

100. Wert, *General James Longstreet*, p. 148; OR, vol. 11, pt. 2, p. 819; Todd, "Reminiscences," p. 21, UNC; Turner, ed., *Captain Greenlee Davidson*, p. 71.

101. OR, vol. 11, pt. 2, pp. 677–78; Harsh, *Confederate Tide Rising*, p. 96.

102. OR, vol. 11, pt. 2, pp. 496, 819; Wert, *Sword*, p. 120.

103. Undated and untitled manuscript, McLaws Papers, DU; *B&L*, vol. 2, p. 394; OR, vol. 11, pt. 2, p. 749.

104. Theodore Fogel to Father and Mother, August 8, 1862, Fogel Papers, EU; John Cocke to Parents, Sister and All, July 14, 1862, Cocke Family Papers, VHS; Brown, *Reminiscences*, p. 20; Gallagher, ed., *Fighting*, p. 113; Todd, "Reminiscences," p. 24, UNC.

105. Undated and untitled manuscript, McLaws Papers, DU; Lafayette McLaws to General, November 30, 1885, Longstreet Papers, EU; D. H. Hill to R. L. Dabney, July 21, 1864, Dabney Papers, UPS; *B&L*, vol. 2, p. 394.

106. OR, vol. 11, pt. 2, pp. 496, 629, 680; Douglas, *I Rode*, p. 107; Houghton and Houghton, *Two Boys*, p. 78; Sorrel, *Recollections*, p. 75; Stiles, *Four Years*, p. 101.

107. Burton, *Extraordinary Circumstances*, pp. 357, 358.

108. Wert, *Sword*, p. 121; Douglas, *I Rode*, p. 110; Freeman, *R. E. Lee*, vol. 2, pp. 222, 223.

109. Douglas, *I Rode*, p. 109; Wert, *Cavalryman*, p. 111.

110. OR, vol. 11, pt. 2, p. 519; Wert, *Cavalryman*, pp. 111–12; R. E. Lee to General, July 3, 1862, Stuart Papers, HL.

111. Venable, "Personal Reminiscences," UVA; Wert, *Cavalryman*, p. 112; W. Taylor, *Four Years*, p. 41.

112. Venable, "Personal Reminiscences," UVA; R. E. Lee to My dear Mrs. Jackson, January 25, 1866, Lee Papers, WLU; OR, vol. 11, pt. 2, p. 497.

113. Wert, *Sword*, pp. 113, 118, 122–25.

114. Ibid., p. 96.

Chapter Three

1. OR, vol. 11, pt. 2, p. 500.

2. Ibid., pp. 500–501.

3. McPherson, *Crossroads*, pp. 46, 47.

4. Ibid., p. 47; Gallagher, *Confederate War*, p. 5; Harsh, *Confederate Tide Rising*, p. 63.

5. Harsh, *Confederate Tide Rising*, pp. 99, 100; Sears, ed., *On Campaign*, p. 44; Joinville, *Army*, p. 97.

6. Gallagher, ed., *Fighting*, p. 96; Styple, ed., *Writing and Fighting Confederate War*, pp. 119, 121; Gallagher, ed., *Richmond Campaign*, pp. 13, 17.

7. A. Jones, *Civil War Command*, p. 70; OR, vol. 29, pt. 2, p. 819; Rafuse, *Robert E. Lee*, p. 17; E. P. Alexander to Colston, February 9, 1904, Campbell-Colston Family Papers, UNC.

8. Griffith, *Battle Tactics*, p. 35; Weigley, *Great Civil War*, pp. 133, 134.

9. Gallagher, ed., *Fighting*, p. 96; Dowdey and Manarin, eds., *Wartime Papers*, p. 230.

10. OR, vol. 11, pt. 2, p. 497; W. Taylor, *General Lee*, p. 74.

11. Maurice, ed., *Aide-De-Camp*, pp. 165–66; OR, vol. 11, pt. 2, pp. 497, 537; W. Taylor, *General Lee*, p. 65; Glatthaar, *General Lee's Army*, pp. 145, 146; Burton, *Extraordinary Circumstances*, pp. 395, 396; Wise, *Long Arm*, pp. 236–40.

12. Carmichael, ed., *Audacity*, pp. 101, 104.

13. B&L, vol. 2, p. 403; Gallagher, ed., *Fighting*, p. 105.

14. OR, vol. 11, pt. 2, pp. 498, 511; Sears, *To the Gates*, p. 345.

15. Burton, *Extraordinary Circumstances*, p. 386; OR, vol. 11, pt. 2, pp. 502–10; Sears, *To the Gates*, pp. 343–45; Weigley, *Great Civil War*, p. 134.

16. Burton, *Extraordinary Circumstances*, p. 387; OR, vol. 11, pt. 2, pp. 839, 840; SOR, vol. 2, p. 435; Schenck, *Up Came Hill*, pp. 106, 107; Freeman, *Lee's*

Lieutenants, vol. 1, pp. 605, 605n; Allen and Bohannon, eds., *Campaigning*, p. 114.

17. Krick, *Lee's Colonels* (5th edition), *passim*; Gallagher, *Confederate War*, p. 115.

18. *B&L*, vol. 2, pp. 352, 395.

19. Maurice, *Robert E. Lee*, p. 119; Allan, *Army*, pp. 136, 137; Carmichael, ed., *Audacity*, pp. 53, 54; Harsh, *Confederate Tide Rising*, p. 70.

20. Allan, *Army*, p. 137.

21. Frank O. Robinson to Friend Frank, July 12, 1862, Robinson Letter, USAMHI; Gramm, ed., *Battle*, p. 129; Hess, *Rifle Musket*, pp. 4, 5, 108; Todd, Reminiscences, p. 21, UNC; Wise, *Long Arm*, p. 240.

22. Wilkinson and Woodworth, *Scythe of Fire*, p. 152; Jensen, *32nd Virginia Infantry*, p. 82; Tower, ed., *Lee's Adjutant*, p. 68; J. H. Bayol to My Own Dear Parents, November 21, 1861, Bayol Papers, VHS; Samuel J. C. Moore to My Dearest Ellen, July 20, 1862, Moore Papers, UNC; Glatthaar, *General Lee's Army*, p. 153; Pryor, *Reading the Man*, p. 323.

23. Jensen, *32nd Virginia Infantry*, p. 82; T. L. Jones, ed., *Campbell Brown's Civil War*, p. 133; Reid, *History*, p. 103; Stiles, *Four Years*, p. 105.

24. Jensen, *32nd Virginia Infantry*, p. 80; McPherson, *For Cause*, p. 8; Glatthaar, *General Lee's Army*, pp. 141–42; J. B. Jones, *Rebel War Clerk's Diary*, vol. 1, p. 144.

25. Harsh, *Confederate Tide Rising*, p. 103; OR, vol. 11, pt. 2, p. 497; Dowdey and Manarin, eds., *Wartime Papers*, p. 229.

26. OR, vol. 11, pt. 3, p. 639; Styple, ed., *Writing and Fighting Confederate War*, p. 119; Harsh, *Confederate Tide Rising*, pp. 100, 101, 103, 104; Jedediah Hotchkiss to My Dr. Wife, August 3, 1862, Hotchkiss Papers, LC; J.B. Jones, *Rebel War Clerk's Diary*, vol. 1, p. 142.

27. Freeman, *Lee's Lieutenants*, vol. 2, p. xiv; Connelly, *Marble Man*, pp. 196, 199.

28. Freeman, *Lee's Lieutenants*, vol. 1, pp. 606, 607, 611, 613; Vandiver, *Rebel Brass*, p. 31; Styple, ed., *Writing and Fighting Confederate War*, p. 118; J. W. Smith, ed., *Freeman on Leadership*, pp. 99, 100; W. C. Davis, ed., *Confederate General*, vol. 3, p. 116; vol. 4, p. 140; Gallagher, ed., *Richmond Campaign*, pp. 97, 105, 114, 115, 117.

29. OR, vol. 51, pt. 2, p. 596; Glatthaar, *General Lee's Army*, p. 157.

30. Freeman, *Lee's Lieutenants*, p. 663; Sorrel, *Recollections*, pp. 26, 69, 79, 92; Long, *Memoirs*, p. 178; Cutrer, ed., *Longstreet's Aide*, p. 98.

31. A. Jones, *Civil War Command*, p. 70; Connelly, *Marble Man*, p. 197; Gallagher, ed., *Fighting*, p. 96; SOR, vol. 4, p. 500; E. P. Alexander to Colston, April 7, 1898, August 19, 1906; Frederick Colston, "Campaign of Gettysburg," Campbell-Colston Family Papers, UNC.

32. Allen and Bohannon, eds., *Campaigning*, pp. 131, 145; W. W. Blackford, *War Years*, p. 85; Robertson, *Stonewall Jackson*, p. 511.

33. D. C. Pfanz, *Richard S. Ewell*, p. 236; Eggleston, *Rebel's Recollections*, p. 136;

Allen and Bohannon, eds., *Campaigning*, p. 114; Thomas Munford to Jedediah Hotchkiss, August 19, 1896, Hotchkiss Papers, LC.

34. Sorrel, *Recollections*, p. 54; Freeman, *Lee's Lieutenants*, vol. 1, p. xxxvi; Boyd, *Reminiscences*, p. 29.

35. Stiles, *Four Years*, p. 65; Burton, *Extraordinary Circumstances*, p. 392; Warner, *Generals in Gray*, p. 136; Sorrel, *Recollections*, p. 54.

36. Sorrel, *Recollections*, p. 54; Freeman, *Lee's Lieutenants*, vol. 1, pp. 630, 631; *OR*, vol. 11, pt. 3, p. 646.

37. Freeman, *Lee's Lieutenants*, vol. 1, pp. 664–65; Wert, *General James Longstreet*, pp. 153–54.

38. Wert, *General James Longstreet*, pp. 153–54; Sorrel, *Recollections*, pp. 79, 80; Cutrer, ed., *Longstreet's Aide*, p. 170.

39. Sorrel, *Recollections*, pp. 80, 81; *OR*, vol. 51, pt. 2, p. 590; Freeman, *Lee's Lieutenants*, vol. 1, pp. 667, 668; Freeman, ed., *Lee's Dispatches*, pp. 38, 39.

40. Freeman, *Lee's Lieutenants*, vol. 1, pp. 671–73; vol. 2, p. 64; Sorrel, *Recollections*, p. 128.

41. Early, *Lieutenant General*, pp. 70, 77; Sorrel, *Recollections*, pp. 43, 50; S. W. Smith, ed., *Freeman on Leadership*, p. 98; Haskell, *Haskell Memoirs*, p. 18.

42. Commission, Major General, July 25, 1862; R. E. Lee to J. E. B. Stuart, July 27, 1862; T. J. Jackson to My dear General, July 31, 1862, Stuart Papers, VHS.

43. R. E. Lee to J. E. B. Stuart, July 27, 1862; A. L. Long to Major Genl. J. E. B. Stuart, July 27, 1862; T. J. Jackson to My dear General, July 31, 1862, Stuart Papers, VHS; *OR*, vol. 12, pt. 3, p. 920.

44. *OR*, vol. 12, pt. 3, 920; *Annals*, p. 669; Wert, *Cavalryman*, pp. 115–17; William G. Deloney to My Dear Rosa, July 21, 1862, Deloney Family Papers, UGA.

45. Wise, *Long Arm*, pp. 241, 243; Burton, *Extraordinary Circumstances*, p. 393; Freeman, *Lee's Lieutenants*, vol. 1, p. 673.

46. Reidenbaugh, *27th Virginia Infantry*, p. 61; Boulware, Diary, LVA; Sorrel, *Recollections*, p. 86.

47. A. B. Simms to Sister, July 16, 1862, Simms Family Papers, AHC; J. W. Jackson to My Dear Wife Mother Father and Sisters, July 6, 1862, Jackson Letters, MNBP; Fletcher, *Rebel Private*, p. 44.

48. Wert, *Sword*, p. 129.

49. Ibid., pp. 129, 130.

50. Ibid., p. 130; Hennessy, *Return*, pp. 10, 11; Harsh, *Confederate Tide Rising*, pp. 108, 109.

51. Robertson, *Stonewall Jackson*, p. 513; A. B. Butner to Sir, July 8, 1862, Butner Papers, NC.

52. Dowdey and Manarin, eds., *Wartime Papers*, pp. 232–33; Harsh, *Confederate Tide Rising*, p. 109.

53. Dowdey and Manarin, eds., *Wartime Papers*, pp. 232–39; *OR*, vol. 12, pt. 3, pp. 916–17; Harsh, *Confederate Tide Rising*, pp. 110–13.

54. OR, vol. 12, pt. 3, pp. 916–17, 918, 919.

55. Ibid., p. 919; Harsh, *Confederate Tide Rising*, p. 113.

56. OR, vol. 12, pt. 3, p. 924; Harsh, *Confederate Tide Rising*, pp. 115, 116; Wert, *Sword*, p. 133.

57. Dowdey and Manarin, eds., *Wartime Papers*, pp. 246–47, 250; Wert, *Sword*, p. 133.

58. Wert, *Sword*, pp. 132, 133.

59. Hattaway and Jones, *How the North Won*, p. 222; Maurice, ed., *Aide-De-Camp*, p. 67.

60. Hattaway and Jones, *How the North Won*, pp. 222, 232; Rafuse, *Robert E. Lee*, p. 23; Maurice, ed., *Aide-De-Camp*, pp. 67, 71, 73, 74; Dowdey and Manarin, eds., *Wartime Papers*, pp. 182–83.

61. Harsh, *Confederate Tide Rising*, pp. 119, 120, 121; OR, vol. 11, pt. 3, p. 675; Dowdey and Manarin, eds., *Wartime Papers*, p. 262.

62. Dowdey and Manarin, eds., *Wartime Papers*, p. 248; Robertson, *Stonewall Jackson*, pp. 523, 525–27.

63. Robertson, *Stonewall Jackson*, pp. 527–34. The most detailed and finest account of the battle is Krick, *Stonewall Jackson at Cedar Mountain*, chapters 4–13.

64. Robertson, *Stonewall Jackson*, pp. 535, 538; Samuel J. C. Moore to My Dear Sir, August 12, 1862, Moore Papers, UNC.

65. Ivy W. Duggan to [Editor], July 15, 1862, Duggan Papers, UGA; OR, vol. 12, pt. 2, p. 185; Wert, *General James Longstreet*, p. 157; Hennessy, *Return*, pp. 28, 29; Allan, *Army*, p. 180.

66. Robertson, *Stonewall Jackson*, p. 539; Latrobe, Diary, VHS; Wert, *General James Longstreet*, p. 157; OR, vol. 12, pt. 3, p. 929.

67. Robertson, *Stonewall Jackson*, pp. 539, 540; Wert, *General James Longstreet*, chapter 20.

68. Sorrel, *Recollections*, p. xvii; Cutrer, ed., *Longstreet's Aide*, pp. 84, 97; Douglas, *I Rode*, p. 129; Wert, *Cavalryman*, pp. 163–65; S. L. Blackford, ed., *Letters*, p. 115.

69. Wert, *General James Longstreet*, pp. 205–6.

70. Freeman, *R. E. Lee*, vol. 2, pp. 273, 274; Harsh, *Confederate Tide Rising*, p. 122; Dowdey and Manarin, eds., *Wartime Papers*, p. 258.

71. OR, vol. 12, pt. 3, p. 929; Maurice, ed., *Aide-De-Camp*, p. 124; Freeman, *R. E. Lee*, vol. 2, pp. 279, 280; Grinman, "General Lee's Movement," FSNMP; Longstreet, *From Manassas to Appomattox*, p. 159.

72. Dowdey and Manarin, eds., *Wartime Papers*, pp. 259–60; Maurice, ed., *Aide-De-Camp*, p. 125; Greene, *Whatever You Resolve to Be*, p. 76.

73. Longstreet, *From Manassas to Appomattox*, p. 159; Freeman, *R. E. Lee*, vol. 2, pp. 279, 280; Maurice, ed., *Aide-De-Camp*, p. 125.

74. Wert, *General James Longstreet*, p. 158; Harsh, *Confederate Tide Rising*, p. 127; Tower, ed., *Lee's Adjutant*, p. 39; Hennessy, *Return*, p. 50; Scott, *History of Orange County*, p. 115.

75. Wert, *Cavalryman*, p. 124.
76. Ibid., p. 125.
77. Ibid.; Sorrel, *Recollections*, p. 53; Thompson, *Robert Toombs*, pp. 196, 197; Moses, "Autobiography," UNC; Haskell, *Haskell Memoirs*, p. 17.
78. Wert, *Cavalryman*, p. 125.
79. Venable, "Personal Reminiscences," UVA; *OR*, vol. 12, pt. 2, pp. 552, 726; pt. 3, p. 934; Maurice, ed., *Aide-De-Camp*, p. 125; Alexander, *Military Memoirs*, p. 187; James Longstreet to My Dear General Munford, November 13, 1891, Munford-Ellis Family Papers, DU.
80. *OR*, vol. 12, pt. 3, p. 934; Hennessy, *Return*, p. 50; Cooling, *Counter-Thrust*, p. 73; Longstreet, *From Manassas to Appomattox*, pp. 161, 162.
81. S. L. Blackford, ed., *Letters*, p. 115; John S. Mosby to General Fitzhugh Lee, December 28, 1895, Coleman Papers, VHS.
82. James Power Smith to My dearest Sister, August 19, 1862, Schenck Collection, NC.

Chapter Four

1. Sutherland, *Seasons*, p. 7.
2. Cozzens and Girardi, eds., *New Annals*, p. 113.
3. *OR*, vol. 12, pt. 2, pp. 564, 564; Notations, Second Bull Run Report, Wilcox Papers, LC; Wert, *General James Longstreet*, pp. 160–61.
4. Wert, *General James Longstreet*, p. 161; Mooney, Memoir, VHS; Hennessy, *Return*, pp. 87–90.
5. Wert, *Cavalryman*, p. 127.
6. Ibid., pp. 127–28; Chiswell Dabney to Father, September 10, 1862, Saunders Family Papers, VHS; *OR*, vol. 12, pt. 2, p. 731.
7. Wert, *Cavalryman*, p. 128; Neese, *Three Years*, p. 102; Dowdey and Manarin, eds., *Wartime Papers*, p. 262.
8. *OR*, vol. 12, pt. 3, pp. 603, 942.
9. Longstreet, *From Manassas to Appomattox*, p. 198; Freeman, *R. E. Lee*, vol. 2, pp. 298, 299; *OR*, vol. 12, pt. 3, p. 941; Maurice, ed., *Aide-De-Camp*, p. 130.
10. Harsh, *Confederate Tide Rising*, pp. 68, 69; *OR*, vol. 29, pt. 2, p. 809.
11. Maurice, ed., *Aide-De-Camp*, p. 130; *OR*, vol. 12, pt. 3, p. 943.
12. *OR*, vol. 12, pt. 3, p. 942.
13. Driver and Howard, *2nd Virginia Cavalry*, p. 55; Cozzens and Girardi, eds., *New Annals*, p. 113; *B&L*, vol. 2, p. 522.
14. *SOR*, vol. 4, pp. 499, 500.
15. *OR*, vol. 12, pt. 2, p. 554; Longstreet, *From Manassas to Appomattox*, pp. 197, 198; Wert, *General James Longstreet*, p. 162.
16. Longstreet, *From Manassas to Appomattox*, p. 198; Harsh, *Confederate Tide Rising*, pp. 41, 137, 138; Undated note, Taylor Papers, LVA; Robertson, *Stonewall Jackson*, p. 547.

17. Freeman, *R. E. Lee*, vol. 2, p. 302; Longstreet, *From Manassas to Appomattox*, p. 198.
18. Gallagher, ed., *Fighting*, p. 130; Robertson, *Stonewall Jackson*, pp. 548, 549; Hassler, ed., *General to His Lady*, p. 164.
19. Gallagher, ed., *Fighting*, p. 130; Stiles, *Four Years*, p. 169; Beard, Diary, FSNMP; Rable, *Fredericksburg!*, p. 22; Anna M. Jackson to My dear Sir, August 4, 1862, McGuire Papers, VHS.
20. Gallagher, ed., *Fighting*, p. 130; Beard, Diary, FSNMP; Robertson, *Stonewall Jackson*, pp. 549, 550; Harsh, *Confederate Tide Rising*, p. 182.
21. Gallagher, ed., *Fighting*, p. 130; Bland, Diary, FSNMP; Roper, ed., *Repairing*, p. 383; Robertson, *Stonewall Jackson*, pp. 550, 551; Wert, *Cavalryman*, p. 131.
22. OR, vol. 12, p. 643; Hennessy, *Return*, pp. 111–12; Robertson, *Stonewall Jackson*, pp. 551–52.
23. Robertson, *Stonewall Jackson*, p. 553; Hassler, ed., *General to His Lady*, p. 171.
24. Chesnut, *Diary*, pp. 330, 331.
25. Chamberlayne, ed., *Ham Chamberlayne*, p. 99; Sorrel, *Recollections*, p. 90; OR, vol. 12, pt. 2, p. 643.
26. OR, vol. 12, pt. 2, pp. 643, 734; Hennessy, *Return*, p. 113.
27. OR, vol. 12, pt. 2, pp. 643, 720, 721, 734, 741.
28. Hennessy, *Return*, pp. 130–34.
29. Robertson, *Stonewall Jackson*, p. 557; Wert, *Cavalryman*, p. 133.
30. Wert, *Brotherhood*, p. 141; Hennessy, *Return*, pp. 125–27.
31. OR, vol. 12, pt. 2, pp. 644, 645, 734; Hennessy, *Return*, pp. 143–46; Harsh, *Confederate Tide Rising*, pp. 148, 149.
32. Hennessy, *Return*, pp. 144, 145, 146; OR, vol. 12, pt. 2, p. 644; Freeman, *Lee's Lieutenants*, vol. 2, pp. 105–6.
33. Hennessy, *Return*, p. 144; Harsh, *Confederate Tide Rising*, pp. 148, 152, 154; Freeman, ed., *Lee's Dispatches*, p. 56.
34. Hennessy, *Return*, pp. 103, 116, 117.
35. Wert, *Brotherhood*, pp. 142, 143; Hennessy, *Return*, p. 140.
36. Harsh, *Confederate Tide Rising*, p. 153; Hennessy, *Return*, pp. 139, 141, 147.
37. Wert, *Brotherhood*, pp. 144–48.
38. Ibid., pp. 148–52.
39. Ibid., pp. 100, 101, 153; Hennessy, *Return*, p. 188.
40. Robertson, *Stonewall Jackson*, p. 562; Wert, *Brotherhood*, pp. 154, 155; Surgeon's Report, Participant Accounts, Ewell File, GNMP.
41. Harsh, *Confederate Tide Rising*, p. 154; Hennessy, *Return*, pp. 194–99.
42. Wert, *General James Longstreet*, p. 164.
43. Freeman, *R. E. Lee*, vol. 2, pp. 309, 312; Longstreet, *From Manassas to Appomattox*, pp. 90, 173; Hennessy, *Return*, p. 153; Latrobe, Diary, VHS; Granville W. Belcher to Wife, September 5, 1862, Belcher Papers, DU.
44. Sorrel, *Recollections*, p. 50; Haskell, *Haskell Memoirs*, p. 28; Young, "History," MNBP; Latrobe, Diary, VHS; Hennessy, *Return*, pp. 154–57.
45. Longstreet, *From Manassas to Appomattox*, pp. 174, 175; Hennessy, *Return*, pp. 157–60; Todd, "Reminiscences," p. 36, UNC; Latrobe, Diary, VHS.

46. Latrobe, Diary, VHS; Longstreet, *From Manassas to Appomattox*, p. 180; OR, vol. 12, pt. 2, p. 736; Wert, *Cavalryman*, pp. 134, 135.

47. Venable, "Personal Reminiscences," pp. 55, 56, UVA.

48. Berkeley, "War Reminiscences," pp. 47–49, MNBP.

49. Durkin, ed., *John Dooley*, p. 17; Wert, *General James Longstreet*, pp. 167, 168; Lewis, "Account," MNBP.

50. Walter H. Taylor to Sister, August 30, 1862, Taylor Papers, LVA; Allan, *Army*, p. 320.

51. *Confederate History Symposium*, p. 65; B&L, vol. 2, p. 405; James Longstreet to F. J. Porter, September 23, 1866, Daniel Papers, UVA.

52. Longstreet, *From Manassas to Appomattox*, pp. 158, 181; R. E. Lee to Sir, October 31, 1867, Lee Papers, NYHS.

53. Longstreet, *From Manassas to Appomattox*, pp. 182, 183; R. E. Lee to Sir, October 31, 1867, Lee Papers, NYHS.

54. OR, vol. 12, pt. 2, pp. 565, 736; W. W. Blackford, *War Years*, pp. 126–27; Longstreet, *From Manassas to Appomattox*, p. 183; R. E. Lee to Sir, October 31, 1867, Lee Papers, NYHS.

55. Hennessy, *Return*, chapters 11–15; Parrish, *Wiregrass*, p. 25.

56. Hennessy, *Return*, chapters 12, 14, 15; Hess, *Rifle Musket*, p. 108; Robertson, *Stonewall Jackson*, p. 568.

57. Hennessy, *Return*, pp. 247–51.

58. Ibid., pp. 251–57; Krick, *Smoothbore Volley*, pp. 145, 146, 155.

59. Hennessy, *Return*, pp. 260–66.

60. Ibid., pp. 272, 274; Krick, *Smoothbore Volley*, p. 161.

61. Cozzens and Girardi, eds., *New Annals*, pp. 116–18; Randolph Barton to A. C. Hamlin, February 6, 1893, Hamlin Papers, HU; Robertson, *Stonewall Jackson*, p. 567.

62. Hennessy, *Return*, pp. 270–86, quote on p. 278; Cozzens and Girardi, eds., *New Annals*, p. 118; OR, vol. 12, pt. 2, p. 556.

63. Harsh, *Confederate Tide Rising*, p. 157; B&L, vol. 2, p. 519; Longstreet, *From Manassas to Appomattox*, p. 183.

64. OR, vol. 12, pt. 2, pp. 367, 565, 598, 605; Longstreet, *From Manassas to Appomattox*, p. 184; Fletcher, *Rebel Private*, p. 37.

65. Notations, Second Manassas Report, Wilcox Papers, LC; B&L, vol. 2, p. 520.

66. Hennessy, *Return*, pp. 235–37, 306–7, 465–66; C. M. Wilcox to F. J. Porter, June [?], 1870, Daniel Papers, UVA.

67. SHSP, vol. 5, pp. 274–79; Wert, *General James Longstreet*, p. 172; Freeman, *R. E. Lee*, vol. 2, p. 325.

68. *Annals*, pp. 628–31; Fitz John Porter to James Longstreet, October 30, 1862, Longstreet Papers, GDAH; Harsh, *Confederate Tide Rising*, p. 157; Hennessy, *Return*, pp. 460, 461.

69. Hennessy, *Return*, p. 460; Longstreet, *From Manassas to Appomattox*, p. 158.

70. Wood, *Reminiscences*, p. 31; Wert, *General James Longstreet*, p. 175; Harsh, *Confederate Tide Rising*, p. 159.

71. Freeman, *R. E. Lee*, vol. 2, pp. 328–30; Longstreet, *From Manassas to Appomattox*, p. 186; Hennessy, *Return*, pp. 314, 315.
72. Freeman, ed., *Lee's Dispatches*, pp. 56–58.
73. *SHSP*, vol. 6, pp. 62–64; Gallagher, ed., *Fighting*, p. 134; Wert, *General James Longstreet*, p. 175.
74. Hennessy, *Return*, pp. 310, 311, 332; Harsh, *Confederate Tide Rising*, p. 161.
75. OR, vol. 12, pt. 2, p. 41; *B&L*, vol. 2, pp. 486, 487; Hennessy, *Return*, pp. 324, 328, 333.
76. OR, vol. 12, pt. 2, pp. 368, 646, 647; Wert, *General James Longstreet*, p. 176; Hennessy, *Return*, pp. 340, 341, 343.
77. Hennessy, *Return*, pp. 340, 343; Wert, *Brotherhood*, pp. 146, 158; Jedediah Hotchkiss to Wife, September 21, 1862, Hotchkiss Papers, LC.
78. Hennessy, *Return*, chapter 19, quote on p. 347; William G. McAdoo Diary, Floyd-McAdoo Family Papers, LC; T. L. Jones, *Lee's Tigers*, p. 124.
79. OR, vol. 12, pt. 2, p. 607; Douglas, *I Rode*, p. 140; Longstreet, *From Manassas to Appomattox*, pp. 186, 187, 188; *Annals*, pp. 629, 630.
80. James Longstreet to General, July 25, 1873, McLaws Papers, UNC; Longstreet, *From Manassas to Appomattox*, p. 188; Hood, *Advance and Retreat*, p. 36; James Longstreet to My Dear General, July 17, 1869, Alexander Papers, UNC; CV, vol. 33, p. 221.
81. CV, vol. 22, p. 231; George W. Dickenson to Wash, September 7, 1862, Dickenson Papers, DU; *B&L*, vol. 2, p. 523.
82. OR, vol. 12, pt. 2, p. 565; Hennessy, *Return*, pp. 366–70; Polley, *Soldier's Letters*, p. 76.
83. Hennessy, *Return*, pp. 366–72, 373; Polley, *Soldier's Letters*, pp. 75, 76; Todd, "Reminiscences," p. 41, UNC.
84. Hennessy, *Return*, pp. 375–80, 384–85.
85. Ibid., pp. 392–400, 401; Henry H. Pearson to Friend, September 5, 1862, Pearson Letter and Map, USAMHI.
86. Hennessy, *Return*, pp. 401–6; Warner, *Generals in Gray*, p. 155; Henry H. Pearson to Friend, September 5, 1862, Pearson Letter and Map, USAMHI.
87. Wert, *General James Longstreet*, p. 177; Tower, ed., *Lee's Adjutant*, p. 41; Hennessy, *Return*, pp. 411, 412.
88. OR, vol. 12, pt. 2, p. 563; Cooling, *Counter-Thrust*, p. 132; Hennessy, *Return*, pp. 382, 383.
89. OR, vol. 12, pt. 2, p. 647; Cooling, *Counter-Thrust*, p. 134; Harsh, *Confederate Tide Rising*, p. 162; Hennessy, *Return*, pp. 426–29, quote on p. 427; Robertson, *Stonewall Jackson*, p. 574.
90. James Power Smith to My dearest Sister, August 31, 1862, Schenck Collection, NC; Hennessy, *Return*, pp. 411–15.
91. Hennessy, *Return*, pp. 416–24; William Mahone to James Longstreet, March 15, 1887, Longstreet Papers, EU; Latrobe, Diary, VHS; Wert, *Cavalryman*, p. 136.
92. Longstreet, *From Manassas to Appomattox*, p. 191; Long, *Memoirs*, p. 206; Sorrel, *Recollections*, p. 96; Harsh, *Confederate Tide Rising*, pp. 165–66.

93. Longstreet, *From Manassas to Appomattox*, pp. 191–94; OR, vol. 12, pt. 2, pp. 557, 558, 647; Harsh, *Confederate Tide Rising*, pp. 166, 168, 171; Hennessy, *Return*, p. 446.

94. Harsh, *Confederate Tide Rising*, pp. 171, 172; Wert, *Sword*, p. 137; Hassler, ed., *General to His Lady*, p. 170.

95. OR, vol. 12, pt. 2, pp. 560–62; Weigley, *Great Civil War*, p. 143; Harsh, *Confederate Tide Rising*, pp. 182, 183; McMullen, ed., *Surgeon*, p. 39.

96. Krick, *Lee's Colonels* (5th edition), *passim*; Latrobe, Diary, VHS; Oates, *War*, p. 147; Caldwell, *History*, p. 37; A. M. Erskine to My Dear Bettie, September 2, 1862, Erskine Papers, NC; Simpson, *Hood's Texas Brigade*, p. 157; OR, vol. 12, pt. 2, pp. 560–62, 595.

97. Freeman, *Lee's Lieutenants*, vol. 2, pp. 142, 143; Harsh, *Taken at the Flood*, p. 42.

98. Styple, ed., *Writing and Fighting the Confederate War*, p. 98; Hassler, ed., *General to His Lady*, pp. 171, 173; Gallagher, ed., *Fighting*, p. 128.

99. Boritt, ed., *Why the Confederacy Lost*, p. 76; Dowdey and Manarin, eds., *Wartime Papers*, p. 268; Harsh, *Confederate Tide Rising*, p. 68; Hennessy, *Return*, p. 457.

100. OR, vol. 12, pt. 2, p. 558; Gallagher, ed., *Fighting*, p. 139.

101. Harsh, *Taken at the Flood*, p. 41; Hennessy, *Return*, pp. 457, 459.

102. Hennessy, *Return*, pp. 458, 459, 461; Sorrel, *Recollections*, p. 92; *B&L*, vol. 2, p. 522; Washington *Post*, June 11, 1893.

103. Freeman, *Lee's Lieutenants*, vol. 2, pp. 138, 139, 140; Hennessy, *Return*, pp. 461, 462; Worsham, *One of Jackson's Foot Cavalry*, p. 80; W. C. Davis, ed., *Confederate General*, vol. 2, p. 119.

104. Wert, *Cavalryman*, pp. 132, 135, 138; Wise, *Long Arm*, pp. 274, 275, 276, 278; Hennessy, *Return*, p. 462.

105. Hennessy, *Return*, p. 463; Gramm, ed., *Battle*, p. 133.

106. Wert, *Sword*, pp. 135, 136, 138.

107. Ibid., pp. 138, 139.

Chapter Five

1. OR, vol. 19, pt. 1, p. 144; pt. 2, p. 590.

2. Ibid., pt. 2, p. 590.

3. Ibid., pp. 590–91.

4. Maurice, ed., *Aide-De-Camp*, p. 148; Harsh, *Confederate Tide Rising*, pp. 60, 61, 62; Glatthaar, *General Lee's Army*, p. 157; Gallagher, *Confederate War*, p. 10.

5. Maurice, ed., *Aide-De-Camp*, p. 148; OR, vol. 19, pt. 1, p. 145; Pryor, *Reading the Man*, p. 327.

6. OR, vol. 19, pt. 1, p. 144; Harsh, *Sounding the Shallows*, pp. 146, 147; Pryor, *Reading the Man*, p. 329.

7. Caldwell, *History*, p. 30; McPherson, *Crossroads*, p. 88; Harsh, *Taken at the Flood*, pp. 43, 44; Henry C. Conner to Ellen, September 5, 1862, Conner

Papers, USC; Parrish, *Wiregrass*, p. 35; S. B. Davis, *History*, p. 46; Theodore T. Fogel to Father and Mother, October 4, 1862, Fogel Papers, EU; Oeffinger, ed., *Soldier's General*, p. 154; Coffman and Graham, *To Honor These Men*, pp. 88, 89; Wert, *Brotherhood*, p. 164.

8. Turner, ed., *Captain Greenlee Davidson*, pp. 47, 49, 50; Harsh, *Taken at the Flood*, pp. 43, 44, 45; Gallagher, ed., *Antietam*, p. 36; OR, vol. 51, pt. 2, p. 613; Longstreet, *From Manassas to Appomattox*, p. 284.

9. Sturkey, *Hampton Legion*, p. 30: Harsh, *Taken at the Flood*, p. 45.

10. A. M. Erskine to My dear Bettie, September 2, 1862, Erskine Papers; J. B. Polley to Mother, September 3, 1862, Polley Papers, NC; Allan, *Army*, p. 326; McDonald, ed., *Make Me a Map*, p. 78; Krick, *4th Virginia Infantry*, p. 17; Harsh, *Taken at the Flood*, p. 45.

11. OR, vol. 19, pt. 1, pp. 803–9; Harsh, *Taken at the Flood*, pp. 39, 40, 42.

12. Harsh, *Sounding the Shallows*, p. 139; A. B. Simms to Sister, September 4, 1862, Simms Family Papers, AHS; J. G. Montgomery to Brother Arthur and Sister Bettie, January 1, 1863, Montgomery Letter, FSNMP; Freeman, *Lee's Lieutenants*, vol. 2, p. 145; *B&L*, vol. 2, p. 605.

13. OR, vol. 19, pt. 1, pp. 803–10; pt. 2, pp. 592–93; Wise, *Long Arm*, pp. 278, 279, 280–83; Runge, ed., *Four Years*, p. 27.

14. Harsh, *Sounding the Shallows*, p. 154; OR, vol. 19, pt. 2, p. 593; Moseley, ed., *Stilwell Letters*, p. 39; Thomas G. Pollock to Father, September 7, 1862, Pollock Papers, UVA.

15. Jedediah Hotchkiss to My Dr. Wife, September 8, 1862, Hotchkiss Papers, LC; Thomas C. Elder to Wife, September 4, 1862, Elder Papers, VHS.

16. Harsh, *Taken at the Flood*, pp. 71, 85; OR, vol. 19, pt. 2, p. 593.

17. Snell, ed., *Maryland Campaign*, p. 30; Styple, ed., *Writing and Fighting the Confederate War*, p. 147; Ivy W. Duggan to [Editor], October 1, 1862, Duggan Papers, UGA; Longstreet, *From Manassas to Appomattox*, p. 284.

18. Wert, *Cavalryman*, pp. 141, 144.

19. OR, vol. 19, pt. 2, pp. 601–2; Paul Semmes to My Dear Wife, September 8, 1862, Semmes Letters, USAMHI; John B. Magruder to Papa, December 4, 1862, Magruder Papers, DU; Harsh, *Sounding the Shallows*, p. 158.

20. Harsh, *Taken at the Flood*, pp. 145, 147; Wert, *General James Longstreet*, pp. 181, 182; *B&L*, vol. 2, p. 620.

21. OR, vol. 19, pt. 1, p. 145; Harsh, *Taken at the Flood*, pp. 146, 147; Wert, *Sword*, p. 148; Pierro, ed., *Maryland Campaign*, p. 109.

22. Wert, *General James Longstreet*, p. 183; D. H. Hill to My Dear Sir, July 21, 1864; J. Chamblin to Sir, May 25, 1885, Hill Papers, LVA; Harsh, *Taken at the Flood*, p. 147.

23. OR, vol. 19, pt. 1, p. 145; pt. 2, pp. 603–4.

24. James Longstreet to D. H. Hill, February 22, 1883, Hill Papers, LVA; Cutrer, ed., *Longstreet's Aide*, p. 183.

25. James Longstreet to D. H. Hill, June 6, 1883, Hill Papers, LVA; *B&L*, vol. 2, p. 663.

26. OR, vol. 19, pt. 2, pp. 603–4; Wert, *Cavalryman*, p. 143.

27. *B&L*, vol. 2, p. 664; Gettysburg Clipping Books, vol. 6, p. 82, GNMP; Harsh, *Taken at the Flood*, p. 167.

28. OR, vol. 19, pt. 1, p. 145; Wert, *General James Longstreet*, p. 184; Harsh, *Taken at the Flood*, pp. 168–75.

29. OR, vol. 19, pt. 1, p. 953; Harsh, *Taken at the Flood*, pp. 176, 178, 179, 181–203.

30. OR, vol. 19, pt. 1, p. 145; R. E. Lee to J. E. B. Stuart, September 12, 1862, Stuart Papers, HL; Wert, *Cavalryman*, pp. 144, 145; Latrobe, Diary, VHS; Freeman, *Lee's Lieutenants*, vol. 2, p. 721.

31. OR, vol. 19, pt. 2, p. 597.

32. Gallagher, ed., *Fighting*, pp. 141, 142; Sorrel, *Recollections*, p. 103; Andrew B. Wardlaw to Wife, September 24, 1862, Wardlaw Letters and Diary, ANB; Robertson, "Memoirs," p. 19, DU; Loehr, *War History*, p. 31; Wood, *Reminiscences*, p. 33; Clark, ed., *Histories*, vol. 1, p. 627.

33. McDonald, ed., *Make Me a Map*, p. 78; Krick, *Smoothbore Volley*, p. 137; *SHSP*, vol. 10, p. 243; Gallagher, *Lee and His Army*, p. 11; John C. Winsmith to My Dear Mother, September 21, 1862, Winsmith Letters, LVA; Durkin, ed., *John Dooley*, p. 55; R. W. Martin to Ellen Johnson, September 8, 1862, Martin Papers, DU; J. W. Jackson to My Dear Wife, September 21, 1862, Jackson Letters, MNBP.

34. Harsh, *Taken at the Flood*, pp. 223–28.

35. Wert, *Sword*, pp. 142–48.

36. Ibid., p. 149; OR, vol. 19, pt. 2, p. 281.

37. Wert, *Sword*, pp. 149, 150.

38. Ibid., p. 150; Harsh, *Taken at the Flood*, pp. 241, 252.

39. Wert, *Cavalryman*, p. 146.

40. Gallagher, ed., *Lee: The Soldier*, p. 26; OR, vol. 19, pt. 2, p. 606; Charles Marshall to General, November 18, 1867, Hill Papers, LVA.

41. James Longstreet to My Dear General, June 6, 1883, Hill Papers, LVA; *B&L*, vol. 2, pp. 665, 666.

42. Wert, *Cavalryman*, p. 148; Harsh, *Taken at the Flood*, p. 252.

43. R. E. Lee to J. E. B. Stuart, September 14, 1862, Stuart Papers, HL; Wert, *Cavalryman*, pp. 148, 149; Alexander, *Military Memoirs*, p. 80.

44. OR, vol. 19, pt. 1, pp. 808, 809, 1022; D. H. Hill to James Longstreet, February 11, 1885, Longstreet Papers, DU.

45. Clark, ed., *Histories*, vol. 1, p. 166; Clarence C. Buel to Sir, June 6, 1885, Hill Papers, LVA.

46. OR, vol. 19, pt. 1, pp. 1019–20, 1026; SOR, vol. 60, p. 587; D. H. Hill to James Longstreet, February 14, 1885, Longstreet Papers, DU.

47. OR, vol. 19, pt. 1, p. 1020; Freeman, *Lee's Lieutenants*, vol. 2, pp. 178–80; Wert, *Sword*, p. 152.

48. OR, vol. 19, pt. 1, p. 1020; D. H. Hill to James Longstreet, February 14, 1885, June 5, 1885, Longstreet Papers, DU.

49. OR, vol. 19, pt. 1, pp. 1020, 1021; Freeman, *Lee's Lieutenants*, vol. 2, pp. 180, 181; Allan, *Army*, p. 360; Coffman and Graham, *To Honor These Men*,

p. 98; D. H. Hill to James Longstreet, February 14, 1885, Longstreet Papers, DU; William J. Russet to My Dear Sir, June 18, 1885, Hill Papers, LVA.

50. Wert, *General James Longstreet*, pp. 188–89.

51. Freeman, *Lee's Lieutenants*, vol. 2, pp. 182, 183; Wert, *Brotherhood*, pp. 169, 171; OR, vol. 19, pt. 1, p. 839; Longstreet, *From Manassas to Appomattox*, pp. 227, 228; Sorrel, *Recollections*, p. 101.

52. Wert, *Sword*, p. 153; Pierro, ed., *Maryland Campaign*, p. 445; OR, vol. 19, pt. 1, p. 1021.

53. Hood, *Advance and Retreat*, p. 41; Wert, *General James Longstreet*, p. 190; Harsh, *Sounding the Shallows*, pp. 181, 182; Pierro, ed., *Maryland Campaign*, p. 169; OR, vol. 51, pt. 2, pp. 618–19.

54. OR, vol. 19, pt. 1, pp. 818, 824, 826; Wert, *Cavalryman*, p. 149.

55. Wert, *Sword*, pp. 153, 154.

56. Wert, *Cavalryman*, pp. 149, 150.

57. OR, vol. 19, pt. 2, p. 608; Harsh, *Taken at the Flood*, pp. 292–94.

58. OR, vol. 19, pt. 1, pp. 147, 951; Wert, *General James Longstreet*, p. 190; Harsh, *Taken at the Flood*, pp. 294, 295.

59. Wert, *General James Longstreet*, pp. 190, 191; Longstreet, *From Manassas to Appomattox*, pp. 233, 234; Gallagher, ed., *Antietam*, p. 55; OR, vol. 19, pt. 1, p. 148; Latrobe, Diary, VHS.

60. Harsh, *Taken at the Flood*, p. 307; OR, vol. 19, pt. 1, p. 951; Wert, *General James Longstreet*, p. 190.

61. OR, vol. 19, pt. 1, pp. 148, 951.

62. Charles H. Eager to My Dear Wife, September 16, 1862, Eager Letters, USAMHI; Wert, *Cavalryman*, p. 145.

63. Wert, *Cavalryman*, p. 151.

64. Wert, *Sword*, pp. 155, 156.

65. Turner, ed., *Captain Greenlee Davidson*, p. 50.

66. Pierro, ed., *Maryland Campaign*, p. 187; Longstreet, *From Manassas to Appomattox*, p. 288; B&L, vol. 2, p. 666.

67. Gallagher, ed., *Fighting*, pp. 145, 146.

68. Maurice, *Robert E. Lee*, p. 152; Gallagher, ed., *Antietam*, p. 55; Harsh, *Taken at the Flood*, p. 55.

69. Gallagher, ed., *Lee: The Soldier*, p. 13; R. E. Lee to My dear Mrs. Jackson, January 25, 1866, Hotchkiss Papers, LC.

70. Gallagher, ed., *Lee: The Soldier*, p. 8; OR, vol. 19, pt. 1, p. 151; pt. 2, p. 606; Freeman, *R. E. Lee*, vol. 2, p. 383.

71. Pierro, ed., *Maryland Campaign*, p. 465; Harsh, *Sounding the Shallows*, p. 201; Priest, *Antietam*, pp. 318–30; OR, vol. 19, pt. 1, pp. 898, 901, 905, 1013, 1022, 1037; CV, vol. 6, p. 27; SOR, vol. 13, p. 369; Mast, *State Troops*, pp. 339, 360; Wyckoff, *History*, p. 105; Wood, *Reminiscences*, p. 40; Iowa M. Royster to Ma, June 29, 1863, Royster Papers, UNC; Nichols, *Soldier's Story*, p. 53; Clary, *History*, p. 58.

72. Durkin, ed., *John Dooley*, p. 49; Gallagher, ed., *Antietam*, pp. 103, 105; C. Johnson and Anderson, *Artillery Hell*, pp. 39, 47.

73. Wert, *Sword*, p. 156.
74. Harsh, *Taken at the Flood*, pp. 330–44; Wert, *Cavalryman*, pp. 152, 153.
75. Wert, *Cavalryman*, p. 152; Gallagher, ed., *Fighting*, p. 148; Andrews, "Johnny Reb," ANB.
76. Wert, *Sword*, pp. 156, 157.
77. Ibid., p. 157.
78. Styple, ed., *Writing and Fighting Confederate War*, pp. 104–5.
79. Durkin, ed., *John Dooley*, p. 99.
80. Wert, *Sword*, pp. 158, 159.
81. Ibid., pp. 159, 160; Cozzens, ed., *B&L*, vol. 5, p. 134; Hugh C. Perkins to Friend, September 21, 1862, Perkins Letters, USAMHI.
82. John R. Jones to My dear Sir, February 25, 1896, Carman Papers, ANB; *OR*, vol. 19, pt. 1, p. 1017; J. W. Jackson to My Dear Wife, September 21, 1862, Jackson Letters, MNBP; T. L. Jones, *Lee's Tigers*, p. 130.
83. Wert, *Brotherhood*, pp. 181, 182; *OR*, vol. 19, pt. 1, p. 808; John R. Jones to My Dear Sir, February 25, 1896, Carman Papers; H. J. Williams to Jedediah Hotchkiss, January 30, 1897, 5th Virginia Infantry File, ANB.
84. *OR*, vol. 19, pt. 1, pp. 806, 956, 978, 979; W. C. Davis, *Confederate General*, vol. 4, p. 27; Wert, *Brotherhood*, p. 182.
85. *OR*, vol. 19, pt. 1, p. 804; Sears, *Landscape*, p. 197; Schipke, *We Can Hear*, p. 143; E. P. Alexander to My dear Colston, April 7, 1898, Campbell-Colston Family papers, UNC.
86. Sturkey, *Hampton Legion*, p. 37; Chestnut, *Diary*, p. 297; Haskell, *Haskell Memoirs*, p. 16; Lasswell, ed., *Rags and Hood*, p. 43.
87. Keller, *Crossroads*, p. 123; Stevens, *War Reminiscences*, p. 75; Wert, *Brotherhood*, pp. 183, 184; *OR*, vol. 19, pt. 1, p. 923.
88. Wert, *Brotherhood*, pp. 183, 184, 185; Stevens, *War Reminiscences*, p. 75; *OR* vol. 19, pt. 1, pp. 923, 924; McPherson, *Crossroads*, p. 119; Sturkey, *Hampton Legion*, p. 38; Keller, *Crossroads*, p. 121; John B. Hood to Major Genl. McLaws, May 24, 1863, McLaws Papers, UNC.
89. *OR*, vol. 19, pt. 1, pp. 218, 219, 956; Wert, *Cavalryman*, p. 156.
90. Clark, ed., *Histories*, vol. 2, p. 437; Sears, *Landscape*, pp. 204–8; *OR*, vol. 19, pt. 1, p. 1033; William J. DeRusset to My dear Sir, June 18, 1885, Hill Papers, LVA.
91. Sears, *Landscape*, pp. 208–13; Clark, ed., *Histories*, vol. 1, pp. 185, 189, 226; William J. DeRusset to My dear Sir, June 18, 1885, Hill Papers, LVA; W. C. Davis, ed., *Confederate General*, vol. 2, p. 9.
92. Wert, *Sword*, p. 160; *OR*, vol. 19, pt. 1, p. 956.
93. Harsh, *Taken at the Flood*, p. 377; *B&L*, vol. 2, pp. 675, 676; *OR*, vol. 19, pt. 1, pp. 857, 858; Snell, ed., *Maryland Campaign*, p. 37; Lafayette McLaws to Henry Heth, November 13, 1894, Carman Papers, ANB.
94. *OR*, vol. 19, pt. 1, pp. 857, 858; *B&L*, vol. 2, pp. 676, 677, 678; *SOR*, vol. 3, p. 569; Snell, ed., *Maryland Campaign*, p. 37.
95. Wert, *Sword*, pp. 161, 162.
96. Ibid., pp. 162, 163; Jensen, *32nd Virginia Infantry*, p. 90; John C. Winsmith

to My Dear Mother, September 21, 1862, Winsmith Letters, LVA; Constantine A. Hege to Parents, September 20, 1862, Hege Letters, USAMHI; Wert, *Cavalryman*, p. 156.

97. Wert, *General James Longstreet*, p. 196; Gordon, *Reminiscences*, p. 84.

98. Wert, *Sword*, p. 164.

99. Ibid., pp. 164–65; Sears, *Landscape*, pp. 236–40, 241.

100. Wert, *General James Longstreet*, p. 197.

101. Wert, *Sword*, pp. 164, 165.

102. OR, vol. 19, pt. 1, pp. 1047, 1048; Clark, ed., *Histories*, vol. 1, pp. 167, 168, 216; W. C. Davis, ed., *Confederate General*, vol. 1, p. 19; SOR, vol. 60, p. 299; Mast, *State Troops*, p. 359; Stiles, *Four Years*, p. 210; Sears, *Landscape*, p. 244.

103. Wert, *Sword*, p. 165.

104. Sears, *Landscape*, pp. 245–47; *B&L*, vol. 2, p. 669; Cutrer, ed., *Longstreet's Aide*, p. 26; Latrobe, Diary, VHS; George T. Anderson to Henry Heth, May 19, 1893, Carman Papers, ANB; Bridges, *Lee's Maverick General*, p. 146; Ratchford, *Some Reminiscences*, p. 66.

105. OR, vol. 19, pt. 1, p. 915; *B&L*, vol. 2, p. 679; Clark, ed., *Histories*, vol. 2, p. 434; Sears, *Landscape*, pp. 249, 250.

106. Sears, *Landscape*, p. 250; OR, vol. 19, pt. 1, pp. 840, 915; Sloan, *Reminiscences*, p. 45; Sorrel, *Recollections*, pp. 106, 107; Clark, ed., *Histories*, vol. 2, pp. 435, 436, 437.

107. Wert, *Sword*, pp. 168–69.

108. Wert, *General James Longstreet*, p. 199; Durkin, ed., *Confederate Chaplain*, p. 31; Pryor, *Reading the Man*, p. 330.

109. Wert, *Sword*, p. 169.

110. Ibid.; Douglas, *I Rode*, p. 174; McDonald, ed., *Make Me a Map*, pp. 130, 131.

111. Harsh, *Sounding the Shallows*, pp. 208, 209, 212, 213; Wert, *Cavalryman*, p. 159; Sorrel, *Recollections*, p. 108; Clark, ed., *Histories*, vol. 1, p. 626.

112. Wert, *Sword*, p. 170.

113. [R. E. Lee to Jefferson Davis, September 18, 1862], Marshall, Substance of a letter, NYHS; Wert, *Cavalryman*, p. 159.

114. Gallagher, ed., *Antietam*, pp. 42, 43; James Longstreet to J. E. Jones, February 6, 1896, Jones Papers, DU; R. E. Lee to My dear Mrs. Jackson, January 25, 1866, Hotchkiss Papers, LC; McGrath, *Shepherdstown*, chapter 5; Wert, *Cavalryman*, pp. 160, 161.

115. Tower, ed., *Lee's Adjutant*, p. 44; OR, vol. 19, pt. 1, p. 151.

116. Wert, *Sword*, pp. 166, 167, 171, 172.

117. Gallagher, ed., *Fighting*, p. 92.

118. Latrobe, Diary, VHS.

Chapter Six

1. Weigley, *Great Civil War*, p. 176; Wert, *Sword*, pp. 173, 209.
2. Weigley, *Great Civil War*, pp. 174, 176; Wert, *Sword*, pp. 208, 209.
3. Wert, *Sword*, p. 173.
4. Maurice, *Robert E. Lee*, pp. 154, 155; Gallagher, *Lee and His Army*, p. 8.
5. Maurice, *Robert E. Lee*, p. 155; Harsh, *Confederate Tide Rising*, p. 68.
6. Gallagher, *Lee and His Army*, p. 33; W. Taylor, *Four Years*, p. 73; Gallagher, ed., *Fighting*, p. 155; Reidenbaugh, *27th Virginia Infantry*, p. 71.
7. Gallagher, ed., *Antietam*, pp. 5, 6, 11, 27; McPherson, *Crossroads*, p. 99.
8. Harsh, *Sounding the Shallows*, pp. 33–50, 201; McPherson, *Crossroads*, pp. 129, 133; Weigley, *Great Civil War*, pp. 154, 255; Chamberlayne, ed., *Ham Chamberlayne*, p. 112; Krick, *Lee's Colonels* (5th edition), *passim*; McWhiney and Jamieson, *Attack and Die*, p. 8; Hess, *Rifle Musket*, p. 199.
9. Connelly, *Marble Man*, p. 208; Gallagher, ed., *Fredericksburg Campaign*, p. 26; Nolan, *Lee Considered*, p. 83.
10. Weigley, *Great Civil War*, p. 152; Sorrel, *Recollections*, p. 73.
11. Sheehan-Dean, *Why Confederates Fought*, p. 98; B. B. Weirman to My Dear Kate, October 25, [1862], Weirman Letters, FSNMP; Casler, *Four Years*, p. 89.
12. Reidenbaugh, *27th Virginia Infantry*, p. 71; SOR, vol. 3, p. 577; Jedediah Hotchkiss to My dear Brother, September 28, 1862, Hotchkiss Papers, LC; J. R. Shaffner to C. T. Pfohl, October 3, 1862, Pfohl Papers, UNC; John Bolling to Sir, September 24, 1862, Armistead-Blanton Family Papers, VHS; Driver, *52nd Virginia Infantry*, p. 28.
13. OR, vol. 19, pt. 2, pp. 626, 627, 633; Tower, ed., *Lee's Adjutant*, pp. 45–46.
14. McDonald, ed., *Make Me a Map*, p. 87; Ordnance Journal, Alexander Papers, UNC; Gallagher, ed., *Fighting*, p. 155; Clayton G. Coleman Jr. to My dear Lucy, September 20, 1862, Coleman Papers, VMI.
15. OR, vol. 19, pt. 2, p. 614; Moseley, ed., *Stilwell Letters*, p. 60; Schipke, *We Can Hear*, p. 144; Theodore Fogel to Father and Mother, October 13, 1862, Fogel Papers, EU; James P. Charlton to Oliver, November 11, 1862, Charlton Family Papers, VATU; Piston, "Lee's Tarnished Lieutenant," p. 190; Styple, ed., *Writing and Fighting Confederate War*, p. 113; McMullen, ed., *Surgeon*, p. 40; William Cocke to Parents and Sisters, October 7, 1862, Cocke Family Papers, VHS.
16. OR, vol. 19, pt. 2, pp. 622, 623, 663; Glatthaar, *General Lee's Army*, p. 214; Wiley, *Life*, p. 289; Gallagher, ed., *Fighting*, p. 60.
17. OR, vol. 19, pt. 1, p. 143; pt. 2, pp. 617, 618, 619, 622; Styple, ed., *Writing and Fighting Confederate War*, p. 109; Hassler, ed., *General to His Lady*, p. 179.
18. John Garibaldi to Wife, October 24, 1862, Garibaldi Letters, VMI; Loehr, *War History*, p. 31; OR, vol. 19, pt. 2, pp. 621, 639, 660, 674.
19. Durkin, ed., *Confederate Chaplain*, p. 33; Gallagher, ed., *Fighting*, p. 155; Paxton, ed., *Civil War Letters*, p. 57; SOR, vol. 61, p. 51.

20. Wert, *General James Longstreet*, pp. 204, 205; *OR*, vol. 19, pt. 2, p. 643.

21. Fitzgerald, *Judge Longstreet*, p. 19.

22. D. H. Hill to James Longstreet, May 21, 1885, Longstreet Papers, DU; Walter H. Taylor to [Jedediah Hotchkiss], June 23, 1896, McGuire Papers, VHS; J. S. McNeely to John Daniel, December [?], 1904, Daniel Papers, UVA; Cutrer, ed., *Longstreet's Aide*, p. 60; Wert, *General James Longstreet*, pp. 205–6.

23. *OR*, vol. 19, pt. 2, p. 643; Weigley, *Great Civil War*, p. 139; Rable, *Fredericksburg!*, p. 22; Cozzens, ed., *B&L*, vol. 5, p. 134; Jackson, *Memoirs*, p. 510.

24. Worsham, *One of Jackson's Foot Cavalry*, pp. 102, 103; McKim, *Soldier's Recollections*, p. 92; Jackson, *Memoirs*, p. 535; Hamlin, *Battle of Chancellorsville*, p. 117.

25. *OR*, vol. 19, pt. 2, p. 643; Hassler, *General to His Lady*, pp. 176, 178.

26. Freeman, *Lee's Lieutenants*, vol. 2, pp. 147–48, 243–46.

27. Ibid., p. 246; Douglas, *I Rode*, pp. 195, 196; Undated fragment of a letter by W. H. Palmer, "Confederate Letters & notes on Battle of Chancellorsville"; Randolph Barton to A. C. Hamlin, February 6, 1893, Hamlin Papers, HU.

28. *OR*, vol. 19, p. 2, pp. 703, 712; vol. 21, p. 1030; W. C. Davis, ed., *Confederate General*, vol. 3, p. 201; vol. 5, p. 65; Coffman and Graham, *To Honor These Men*, p. 106; Stone, ed., *Wandering to Glory*, p. 82; Harsh, *Sounding the Shallows*, p. 142.

29. Moses, "Autobiography," UNC; Cutrer, ed., *Longstreet's Aide*, p. 100; Sorrel, *Recollections*, p. 127; Dyer, *Gallant Hood*, p. 144.

30. Moses, "Autobiography," UNC; James Dearing to Uncle, April 28, 1862, Dearing Papers, VHS; Freeman, *Lee's Lieutenants*, vol. 2, p. 257; Wert, *General James Longstreet*, pp. 210, 211.

31. Notation, Fredericksburg Report, Wilcox Papers, LC; R. E. Lee to Cadmus Wilcox, November 12, 1862, Lee Family Papers, VHS; Wert, *General James Longstreet*, pp. 210, 211.

32. Freeman, *Lee's Lieutenants*, vol. 2, pp. 256, 257; W. C. Davis, ed., *Confederate General*, vol. 6, p. 61.

33. Freeman, *Lee's Lieutenants*, vol. 2, p. 260; *OR*, vol. 19, pt. 1, pp. 149, 821, 956; Stiles, *Four Years*, p. 189; W. C. Davis, ed., *Confederate General*, vol. 2, p. 89.

34. *OR*, vol. 19, pt. 2, pp. 683–84, 698–99; James Longstreet to R. H. Chilton, June 2, 1875, Longstreet Papers, MC; Freeman, *Lee's Lieutenants*, vol. 2, pp. 253, 266.

35. *OR*, vol. 19, pt. 2, pp. 698, 699; Warner, *Generals in Gray*, pp. 6, 56, 61, 63, 74, 148, 172, 224, 229, 244, 251, 305; Glatthaar, *General Lee's Army*, p. 194; Robson, *How a One-Legged Rebel Lives*, p. 111.

36. *OR*, vol. 19, pt. 2, pp. 632, 647–54; Wise, *Long Arm*, pp. 310, 332, 343, 345; Chamberlayne, ed., *Ham Chamberlayne*, p. 134; Cutrer, ed., *Longstreet's Aide*, p. 159.

37. Gallagher, ed., *Fighting*, pp. 159, 160, 165; Warner, *Generals in Gray*, p. 3;

Wise, *Long Arm*, p. 141; Styple, ed., *Writing and Fighting Confederate War*, p. 41; Sorrel, *Recollections*, pp. 70, 119.

38. Wert, *Sword*, pp. 175, 176, 177.

39. Ibid., p. 177.

40. Wert, *Cavalryman*, pp. 167–75.

41. Ibid., pp. 175, 176, 177; Wert, *Sword*, p. 178.

42. Wert, *Sword*, p. 179; Oates, *War*, p. 162; D. H. Hill to My Dear Wife, October 8, 1862, Hill Papers, USAHMI; Chamberlayne, ed., *Ham Chamberlayne*, p. 121.

43. John W. Carlisle to Col. B. B. Foster, October 26, 1862, Carlisle Letter, Krick Collection.

44. Wert, *General James Longstreet*, p. 213; OR, vol. 19, pt. 2, pp. 696, 701, 710, 713; Latrobe, Diary; R. E. Lee to Mary Lee, November 6, 1862, Lee Family Papers, VHS.

45. CV, vol. 35, p. 261; Wert, *Cavalryman*, pp. 179–80, 181, 182; Lee, *Recollections*, p. 81.

46. Wert, *Cavalryman*, p. 182; Elizabeth L. Stuart to Dear Miss Mary, May 24, 1870, Maury Papers, VHS.

47. Wert, *Sword*, pp. 174, 175; OR, vol. 19, pt. 2, p. 545.

48. Wert, *Sword*, p. 182.

49. Ibid., pp. 179, 181, 183.

50. Ibid., pp. 184–86.

51. Ibid., p. 186.

52. Robert E. Lee to J. E. B. Stuart, November 13, 1862, Stuart Papers, HL; Wert, *Cavalryman*, pp. 184, 185.

53. Wert, *Sword*, pp. 187, 188.

54. O'Reilly, *Fredericksburg Campaign*, pp. 102, 249; Wert, *General James Longstreet*, pp. 216, 218.

55. OR, vol. 21, p. 569; Moore, *Life*, p. 124; B&L, vol. 3, pp. 72, 79, 89, 91; Gallagher, ed., *Fighting*, pp. 167, 168, 169.

56. O'Reilly, *Fredericksburg Campaign*, pp. 104, 132.

57. Ibid., pp. 131, 499, 500; Schenck, *Up Came Hill*, p. 233; OR, vol. 21, p. 553.

58. D. H. Hill to My Dear Sir, July 21, 1864, Hill Papers, LVA.

59. Ibid.

60. OR, vol. 21, pp. 549, 1021.

61. R. W. Martin to Nellie, November 25, 1862, Martin Papers, DU; OR, vol. 19, pt. 2, p. 718; vol. 21, p. 1057; John P. Welsh to Becca, December 7, 1862, Welsh Family Papers, WLU; Lowe and Hodges, eds., *Letters to Amanda*, p. 33; Paxton, ed., *Civil War Letters*, p. 65; Durkin, ed., *John Dooley*, p. 71; Jubal A. Early to D. H. Hill, August 2, 1885, Hill Papers, LVA; W. H. Andrews, *Footprints*, pp. 93, 95.

62. Roper, *Repairing*, p. 323; Wilkinson and Woodworth, *Scythe of Fire*, p. 199; Cozzens, ed., *B&L*, vol. 5, pp. 212, 213.

63. Wert, *Sword*, pp. 188, 189; O'Reilly, *Fredericksburg Campaign*, p. 53.

64. Wert, *Sword*, p. 189; O'Reilly, *Fredericksburg Campaign*, chapter 3.
65. Wert, *Sword*, pp. 189, 190; *OR*, vol. 21, pp. 552, 571.
66. Wert, *Sword*, pp. 191, 192; O'Reilly, *Fredericksburg Campaign*, pp. 118–26.
67. McDonald, ed., *Make Me a Map*, p. 99; *B&L*, vol. 3, pp. 89, 91.
68. Sorrel, *Recollections*, p. 131; *OR*, vol. 21, pp. 630, 663.
69. Wert, *Cavalryman*, pp. 163, 164; Douglas, *I Rode*, p. 193; Cozzens, ed., *B&L*, vol. 5, p. 135; Richmond *Southern Opinion*, January 9, 1869.
70. Wert, *Sword*, pp. 194, 195, 204; O'Reilly, *Fredericksburg Campaign*, pp. 127, 128.
71. Wert, *Cavalryman*, pp. 190–91; *OR*, vol. 21, p. 547.
72. O'Reilly, *Fredericksburg Campaign*, pp. 139, 140; Taggart, Diary; Heffelfinger, Diary, USAMHI; Richard H. Watkins to [Wife], September 22, 1862, Watkins Papers, VHS.
73. O'Reilly, *Fredericksburg Campaign*, pp. 166–86; Krick, *Smoothbore Volley*, p. 168; Schenck, *Up Came Hill*, p. 232.
74. O'Reilly, *Fredericksburg Campaign*, pp. 40, 41, 187–97.
75. Ibid., chapter 8, quote on p. 231; Rable, *Fredericksburg!*, p. 252; Early, *Lieutenant General*, p. 178.
76. O'Reilly, *Fredericksburg Campaign*, p. 237; Freeman, *R. E. Lee*, vol. 2, p. 462; Sorrel, *Recollections*, p. 131; William B. Pettit to Wife, December 16, 1862, Pettit Papers, UNC.
77. Wert, *Sword*, p. 197; Small, ed., *Road*, p. 70.
78. Wert, *Sword*, pp. 199, 200, 201, 202; Macon *Telegraph*, December 25, 1862; Woods, "Reminiscences," FSNMP.
79. W. W. Blackford, *War Years*, p. 147; *B&L*, vol. 3, p. 81.
80. Wert, *Sword*, pp. 201, 202.
81. Ibid., pp. 203, 204.
82. *OR*, vol. 21, pp. 142, 562; Rable, *Fredericksburg!*, pp. 254, 288.
83. *OR*, vol. 21, pp. 554, 555; *CV*, vol. 22, p. 501; Coffman and Graham, *To Honor These Men*, p. 119; W. C. Davis, ed., *Confederate General*, vol. 2, p. 3.
84. Krick, *Smoothbore Volley*, pp. 169, 170, 171; McIntosh, "Ride," pp. 32, 33, UNC; Hamilton, Diary, FSNMP; Caldwell, *History*, p. 63; *OR*, vol. 21. p. 1067.
85. *OR*, vol. 21, p. 555.
86. Ibid.; O'Reilly, *Fredericksburg Campaign*, pp. 432, 433, 452, 453; Dowdey and Manarin, eds., *Wartime Letters*, p. 365.
87. Gallagher, ed., *Fredericksburg Campaign*, p. 131.
88. Ibid., pp. 117–19, 120, 121; Wert, *Sword*, pp. 205, 206; J. B. Jones, *Rebel War Clerk's Diary*, vol. 1, p. 218.
89. *OR*, vol. 21, pp. 549, 550, 1085, 1086.
90. Ibid., pp. 556, 571, 582; Gallagher, ed., *Fighting*, p. 176; O'Reilly, *Fredericksburg Campaign*, pp. 212, 500, 501.
91. A. P. Hill to My dear Stuart, November 14, [1862], Stuart Papers, VHS.
92. *B&L*, vol. 3, pp. 75, 76; O'Reilly, *Fredericksburg Campaign*, p. 362; James

Longstreet to E. P. Alexander, January 19, 1868, Longstreet Papers, DU; Longstreet, *From Manassas to Appomattox*, p. 317.

93. Gallagher, ed., *Fighting*, p. 185; George R. Bedinger to My dear Ma, December 23, 1862, Bedinger-Dandridge Family Papers, DU; Wilkinson and Woodworth, *Scythe of Fire*, p. 202; Wise, *Long Arm*, p. 406.

94. Styple, ed., *Writing and Fighting Confederate War*, p. 125; Robert Toombs to James Longstreet, February 5, 1879, Longstreet Papers, GDAH.

95. Gallagher, *Confederate War*, pp. 10, 140, 141; Pryor, *Reading the Man*, p. 337.

96. Dowdey and Manarin, eds., *Wartime Papers*, pp. 379–80.

Chapter Seven

1. John F. Sale to Uncle, January 22, 1863, Sale Papers, LVA; Paxton, ed., *Civil War Letters*, p. 71; John P. Welsh to Mother and Wife, January 19, 1863, Welsh Family Papers, WLU.

2. John F. Sale to Uncle, January 22, 1863, Sale Papers, LVA; John P. Welsh to Mother and Wife, January 30, 1863, Welsh Family Papers, WLU.

3. Wert, *Sword*, pp. 210, 211, 212.

4. Ibid., pp. 213, 214.

5. Ibid., pp. 215, 216, 217.

6. Ibid., pp. 220–26.

7. Wert, *General James Longstreet*, pp. 225–26.

8. W. C. Davis, ed., *Confederate General*, vol. 3, p. 104; James Longstreet to General Alexander, August 26, 1902, Alexander Papers, UNC; Bridges, *Lee's Maverick General*, pp. 147, 148, 149, 162, 163; Younger, ed., *Inside*, p. 81.

9. D. H. Hill to James Longstreet, August 29, 1879, Longstreet Papers, DU; Bridges, *Lee's Maverick General*, p. 149; W. C. Davis, ed., *Confederate General*, vol. 3, p. 104; James Longstreet to E. P. Alexander, August 26, 1902, Alexander Papers, UNC.

10. Eugene Blackford to My dear Father, n.d., Blackford Letters, USAMHI; Gallagher, ed., *Fighting*, p. 202; Hubbs, ed., *Voices*, p. 90; Krick, *Smoothbore Volley*, p. 134; Gallagher, ed., *First Day at Gettysburg*, p. 115.

11. OR, vol. 21, pp. 1099, 1100; W. C. Davis, ed., *Confederate General*, vol. 5, p. 81; Schipke, *We Can Hear*, pp. 158, 159.

12. OR, vol. 25, pt. 2, pp. 614–19, 625–26, 651; Wise, *Long Arm*, pp. 412, 414, 419.

13. OR, vol. 25, pt. 2, pp. 728, 729, 730; Wise, *Long Arm*, pp. 419, 420.

14. OR, vol. 21, p. 1110; vol. 25, pt. 2, p. 597.

15. Ibid., vol. 25, pt. 2, p. 598; Wells J. Hawks to Col., March 17, 1863, Hawks Letter, USAMHI; Dowdey and Manarin, eds., *Wartime Papers*, p. 418; J. B. Jones, *Rebel War Clerk's Diary*, vol. 1, p. 297.

16. Robert Brooke Jones to My Dear and Sweet Wife, n.d., Jones Family Papers;

John O. Collins to Wife, March 16, 1863, Collins Papers, VHS; Wert, *General James Longstreet*, p. 231; Moseley, ed., *Stilwell Letters*, p. 134.

17. Scheibert, *Seven Months*, p. 36; Hassler, ed., *General to His Lady*, p. 227; A. Baldwin to Cousin, April 12, [1863], Holliday Papers, DU; Roper, *Repairing*, p. 383; *OR*, vol. 21, pp. 1097, 1099; vol. 25, pt. 2, p. 725.

18. Wert, *General James Longstreet*, pp. 228–29.

19. Ibid., pp. 232, 233; *OR*, vol. 18, p. 927.

20. *OR*, vol. 18, pp. 926, 927, 933, 934, 937, 942, 943.

21. Wert, *General James Longstreet*, pp. 236–38; E. P. Reeve to Wife, April 21, 1863, Reeve Papers, UNC; Henricks, Civil War Account, MNBP.

22. *OR*, vol. 25, pt. 2, p. 758; Wert, *Sword*, pp. 230, 232, 234.

23. Wert, *Cavalryman*, pp. 203, 205, 207.

24. Ibid., pp. 207–8.

25. Ibid., pp. 208, 209; Wise, *Long Arm*, pp. 302, 349; Blackford, Annotations, UVA.

26. "A Reunion of Confederate Officers and Their Ladies," McIntosh Papers, USAMHI; E. M. Thomas, *Robert E. Lee*, pp. 277, 278; Scheibert, *Seven Months*, p. 35; Hassler, ed., *General to His Lady*, pp. 215, 221, 227; *SOR*, vol. 95, p. 166.

27. R. E. Lee to J. E. B. Stuart, April 21, 1863, Stuart Papers, HL; *OR*, vol. 25, pt. 2, pp. 713, 720, 725.

28. Wert, *Sword*, pp. 229, 230, 232, 234.

29. Ibid., p. 232; Gallagher, ed., *Fighting*, p. 195.

30. Wert, *Sword*, pp. 231–33, 246.

31. Ibid., p. 234; Sears, *Chancellorsville*, p. 191; *B&L*, vol. 3, p. 157; *OR*, vol. 25, pt. 1, p. 171.

32. Wert, *Cavalryman*, pp. 214–15; *OR*, vol. 25, pt. 1, pp. 796, 797; pt. 2, p. 756; R. E. Lee to J. E. B. Stuart, April 29, 30, 1863, Stuart Papers, HL; Bigelow, *Campaign*, p. 210.

33. Oeffinger, ed., *Soldier's General*, p. 179.

34. *OR*, vol. 25, pt. 1, p. 797.

35. Samuel J. C. Moore to My Dearest wife, February 17, 1863, Moore Papers; Stephen D. Ramseur to Dearest Nellie, April 5, 1863, Ramseur Papers, UNC; Lowe and Hodges, eds., *Letters to Amanda*, p. 67.

36. Sears, *Chancellorsville*, p. 174; Robertson, *Stonewall Jackson*, pp. 702, 703; *OR*, vol. 25, pt. 1, p. 797; Wert, *Sword*, p. 235.

37. *OR*, vol. 25, pt. 1, p. 797.

38. Sears, *Chancellorsville*, pp. 202–9, 210, 211.

39. Wert, *Cavalryman*, p. 219; W. W. Blackford, *War Years*, p. 79.

40. Sears, *Chancellorsville*, p. 230; Gallagher, ed., *Lee: The Soldier*, p. 9.

41. Wert, *Sword*, pp. 236, 237; Sears, *Chancellorsville*, p. 221.

42. Wert, *Cavalryman*, pp. 219, 220.

43. *B&L*, vol. 3, p. 161; Wert, *Sword*, p. 237; *OR*, vol. 25, pt. 2, p. 320.

44. Wert, *Sword*, pp. 237, 238.

45. Gallagher, ed., *Lee: The Soldier*, p. 9; Wert, *Cavalryman*, pp. 220, 221; Robertson, *Stonewall Jackson*, pp. 709, 710.

46. R. E. Lee to My dear Mrs. Jackson, January 25, 1866, Lee Letter, WLU; OR, vol. 25, pt. 1, p. 798; Maurice, ed., *Aide-De-Camp*, p. 166.

47. Scheibert, *Seven Months*, p. 62.

48. McDonald, ed., *Make Me a Map*, p. 137; Robertson, *Stonewall Jackson*, pp. 712–14.

49. Wert, *Brotherhood*, p. 227; Robertson, *Stonewall Jackson*, p. 714, OR, vol. 25, pt. 1, p. 798.

50. OR, vol. 25, pt. 1, p. 798.

51. Connelly, *Marble Man*, p. 195.

52. Diary, Cooke Papers, DU.

53. OR, vol. 18, pp. 1032, 1037; vol. 25, pt. 1, p. 798; pt. 2, p. 765; Sears, *Chancellorsville*, p. 251.

54. S. L. Blackford, ed., *Letters*, p. 115; Robertson, *Stonewall Jackson*, p. 715; Sears, *Chancellorsville*, pp. 241, 242.

55. Robertson, *Stonewall Jackson*, p. 715; Sears, *Chancellorsville*, p. 240.

56. Sears, *Chancellorsville*, pp. 244–45, 255–57; Wert, *Sword*, p. 239.

57. Sears, *Chancellorsville*, p. 246; George W. Slifer to Unkle, May 9, 1863, Slifer Letters, FSNMP.

58. Clark, ed., *Histories*, vol. 1, p. 191; Hotchkiss, ed., *Confederate Military History*, vol. 3, p. 383; Diary, Cooke Papers, DU; Robertson, *Stonewall Jackson*, p. 720.

59. Robertson, *Stonewall Jackson*, pp. 720–22; Sears, *Chancellorsville*, p. 272; OR, vol. 25, pt. 1, pp. 798, 890, 935, 940; pt. 2, p. 846.

60. Robertson, *Stonewall Jackson*, pp. 721, 722; Marginal notes in Mary Anna Jackson, *Life and Letters of General Thomas J. Jackson*, p. 325, Douglas, Personal Library, ANB.

61. Wert, *Sword*, pp. 239, 240.

62. Ibid., pp. 240, 241; Robertson, *Stonewall Jackson*, pp. 722–24; Sears, *Chancellorsville*, pp. 272–87.

63. OR, vol. 25, pt. 1, p. 941; Robertson, *Stonewall Jackson*, p. 724; Hubbs, ed., *Voices*, p. 162.

64. Wert, *Sword*, p. 241; Sears, *Chancellorsville*, p. 295; OR, vol. 25, pp. 941, 942.

65. CV, vol. 4, p. 308; OR, vol. 25, p. 2, p. 769. An excellent and thorough description of Jackson's reconnaissance is in Krick, *Smoothbore Volley*, chapter 1.

66. Krick, *Smoothbore Volley*, pp. 17, 18, 20, 28, 29; Wert, *Cavalryman*, p. 224.

67. Wert, *Cavalryman*, p. 224; Robertson, *Stonewall Jackson*, pp. 734, 735, 736, 737.

68. Wert, *Cavalryman*, p. 227; OR, vol. 25, pt. 2, p. 769; SOR, vol. 4, p. 518.

69. Randolph Barton to A. C. Hamlin, February 6, 1893, Hamlin Papers, HU; Freeman, *Lee's Lieutenants*, vol. 2, p. 571; OR, vol. 25, pt. 1, p. 942.

70. Undated fragment of a letter, "Confederate Letters & Notes on Battle of Chancellorsville"; Henry K. Douglas to A. C. Hamlin, April 21, 1893, Hamlin Papers, HU.

71. *OR*, vol. 25, pt. 1, pp. 885, 886, 887; Wert, *Cavalryman*, p. 223.

72. *SHSP*, vol. 14, p. 157; Bigelow, *Campaign*, p. 340; E. P. Alexander to Father, May 11, 1863, Alexander Papers, NC; Gallagher, ed., *Fighting*, p. 206; Jedediah Hotchkiss to My Dear Wife, May 20, 1863, Hotchkiss Papers, LC; Wise, *Long Arm*, p. 497.

73. Robertson, *Stonewall Jackson*, pp. 735, 737, 738; *SHSP*, vol. 14, p. 157; Bigelow, *Campaign*, map 23, plan 3; Alexander, *Military Memoirs*, p. 342.

74. *OR*, vol. 25, pt. 2, p. 769; R. E. Lee to J. E. B. Stuart, May 3, 1863, Stuart Papers, HL.

75. *OR*, vol. 25, pt. 1, p. 890; Bigelow, *Campaign*, p. 342; Sears, *Chancellorsville*, p. 314; Fox, *Red Clay*, p. 160; Hess, *Field Armies*, pp. 175, 180, 182, 312.

76. Wert, *Sword*, p. 243; Clark, ed., vol. 1, *Histories*, pp. 629, 669; Charles Anderson Raine Memoir, p. 6, 23rd Virginia Infantry File, FSNMP.

77. E. P. Alexander to Father, May 11, 1863, Alexander Papers, NC; CV, vol. 1, p. 235; *OR*, vol. 25, pt. 1, p. 891; Wert, *Sword*, p. 244.

78. Hess, *Field Armies*, p. 182; Sears, *Chancellorsville*, pp. 316–46; Samuel J. C. Moore to My Dearest wife, May 4, 1863, Moore Papers, UNC; W. C. Davis, ed., *Confederate General*, vol. 2, p. 13; vol. 3, p. 207.

79. Charlotte *Western Democrat*, May 19, June 9, 1863.

80. Colt, *Defend the Valley*, p. 242; John P. Welsh to Mother and Wife, May 8, 1863, Welsh Family Papers, WLU; George W. Slifer to Unkle, [May 9, 1863], Slifer Letters, FSNMP; Thomas Smiley to Sister, May 9, 1863, Smiley Correspondence, UVA; Hess, *Field Armies*, p. 182.

81. *OR*, vol. 25, pt. 1, pp. 908, 911, 921, 968, 987, 996, 997, 1014, 1017, 1018; *SHSP*, vol. 8, p. 491; Sears, *Chancellorsville*, p. 324; Wert, *Cavalryman*, pp. 228, 229; Tumilty, "Filling Jackson's Shoes," p. 31.

82. Samuel J. C. Moore to My Dearest wife, May 4, 1863, Moore Papers, UNC; Alexander, *Military Memoirs*, p. 347; CV, vol. 5, p. 289.

83. Tumilty, "Filling Jackson's Shoes," p. 31.

84. *OR*, vol. 25, pt. 1, pp. 823, 888; Wert, *Sword*, p. 244; E. P. Alexander to Father, May 11, 1863, Alexander Papers, NC; Hess, *Field Armies*, p. 185; Alexander, *Military Memoirs*, p. 347.

85. *OR*, vol. 25, pt. 1, p. 930; Sears, *Chancellorsville*, pp. 335–36; A. P. Hill to R. E. Lee, May 24, 1863, Hill Letter, NYHS.

86. *OR*, vol. 25, pt. 1, p. 930; Clark, ed., *Histories*, vol. 1, pp. 146, 193; Sears, *Chancellorsville*, p. 346; Wert, *Sword*, pp. 244–45.

87. Jeremiah Tate to Sister Mary, May 10, 1863, Tate Papers, NYHS; Sears, *Chancellorsville*, p. 366; Hess, *Field Armies*, pp. 182–83; M. M. Andrews, ed., *Scraps of Paper*, p. 114.

88. Scheibert, *Seven Months*, p. 70; Fox, *Red Clay*, p. 168, 169; Pryor, *Reading the Man*, p. 344; E. M. Thomas, *Robert E. Lee*, pp. 285, 286.

89. *SHSP*, vol. 5, p. 92.

90. Wert, *Sword*, pp. 246, 147.

91. Ibid., p. 247; Sears, *Chancellorsville*, pp. 376–85; *OR*, vol. 25, pt. 1, p. 858; Styple, ed., *Writing and Fighting Confederate War*, p. 147; Coffman and Graham, *To Honor These Men*, p. 145.

92. Wert, *Sword*, p. 248; W. C. Davis, ed., *Confederate General*, vol. 4, p. 130; W. Taylor, *General Lee*, p. 156.

93. Sears, *Chancellorsville*, pp. 410–17; Wert, *Sword*, pp. 248, 249.

94. R. E. Lee to Gen'l, 8:15 AM, May 5, 1863, Stuart Papers, HL.

95. R. E. Lee to Gen'l, AM, May 5, 1863, Stuart Papers, HL; Wert, *Sword*, pp. 250, 251, 252.

96. *SOR*, vol. 4, p. 671; McDonald, ed., *Make Me a Map*, p. 141; Sears, *Chancellorsville*, p. 430.

97. Sears, *Chancellorsville*, p. 449; *SHSP*, vol. 4, p. 154.

98. Weigley, *Great Civil War*, p. 229; *OR*, vol. 25, pt. 1, p. 809; Mast, *State Troops*, p. 186; *SOR*, vol. 60, pp. 300, 394, 395, 475; vol. 61, p. 37; vol. 95, p. 200; Pryor, *Reading the Man*, p. 346; Krick, *Lee's Colonels* (5th edition), *passim*.

99. Hassler, ed., *General to His Lady*, p. 235.

100. Wert, *Sword*, pp. 254, 255.

101. Stephen D. Ramseur to My Precious Nellie, May 25, 1863, Ramseur Papers, UNC; Tower, ed., *Lee's Adjutant*, p. 53.

102. Chamberlayne, ed., *Ham Chamberlayne*, p. 176; Sword, *Southern Invincibility*, p. 153; Gallagher, ed., *Fighting*, p. 195.

103. Sears, *Chancellorsville*, pp. 443, 444; Richmond *Enquirer*, May 8, 1863.

104. Weigley, *Great Civil War*, pp. 229, 255; McWhiney and Jamieson, *Attack and Die*, p. 8; Hess, *Rifle Musket*, p. 199; Gallagher, *Confederate War*, pp. 10, 139, 140.

105. McDonald, ed., *Make Me a Map*, pp. 141, 142; Carmichael, *Lee's Young Artillerist*, p. 92; S. W. Smith, ed., *Freeman on Leadership*, p. 72.

Chapter Eight

1. Robertson, *Stonewall Jackson*, pp. 741–43.

2. Ibid., pp. 747, 748.

3. Ibid., pp. 748, 749; Hotchkiss, ed., *Confederate Military History*, vol. 3, p. 393.

4. Robertson, *Stonewall Jackson*, pp. 751, 752, 753; R. E. Lee to J. E. B. Stuart, May 11, 1863, Stuart Papers, HL.

5. R. E. Lee to J. E. B. Stuart, May 11, 1863, Stuart Papers, HL; Robertson, *Stonewall Jackson*, p. 754; Downey and Manarin, eds., *Wartime Papers*, p. 484.

6. *OR*, vol. 25, pt. 2, p. 791; Robertson, *Stonewall Jackson*, pp. 756–61.

7. *OR*, vol. 25, pt. 2, pp. 791, 793; *Annals*, p. 674; Thomason, *Jeb Stuart*, p. 412; Robertson, *Stonewall Jackson*, p. 755.

8. Armstrong, Diary, VHS; Lowe and Hodges, eds., *Letters to Amanda*, p. 69;

Turner, ed., *Ted Barclay*, p. 83; Herndon, Reminiscences, p. 14, MC; Abraham Fulkerson to My dear Wife, May 18, 1863, Fulkerson Family Papers; Henry H. Dedrick to Father, May 10, 1863, Dedrick Civil War Papers, VMI; Theodore Fogel to Father and Mother, May 11, 1863, Fogel Papers, EU; Carmichael, *Lee's Young Artillerist*, pp. 92, 93; R. F. Crenshaw to My Dear Cousin Sallie, May 12, 1863, Crenshaw Letter, USAMHI.

9. Freeman, *Lee's Lieutenants*, vol. 2, p. 687; Jackson, *Memoirs*, p. 576; Jedediah Hotchkiss to My Dear Wife, May 20, 1863, Hotchkiss Papers, LC.

10. *B&L*, vol. 3, p. 244; Latrobe, Diary, VHS; Longstreet, *From Manassas to Appomattox*, p. 327; *OR*, vol. 51, pt. 2, p. 704.

11. J. B. Jones, *Rebel War Clerk's Diary*, vol. 1, p. 311; *Annals*, pp. 415, 416; James A. Seddon to James Longstreet, April 16, 1875, Longstreet Papers, DU; James Longstreet to Lafayette McLaws, July 25, 1873, McLaws Papers, UNC; Wert, *General James Longstreet*, pp. 239, 240.

12. Longstreet, *From Manassas to Appomattox*, pp. 327, 328.

13. Ibid., p. 331; *B&L*, vol. 3, pp. 246, 247; *Annals*, p. 416; James Longstreet to Lafayette McLaws, July 25, 1873, McLaws Papers, UNC; Wert, *General James Longstreet*, p. 243.

14. James Longstreet to Louis T. Wigfall, May 13, 1863, Wigfall Papers, LC; *Annals*, p. 416.

15. James Longstreet to Louis T. Wigfall, May 13, 1863, Wigfall Papers, LC.

16. *OR*, vol. 25, pt. 2, p. 790; James Longstreet to Lafayette McLaws, July 25, 1873, McLaws Papers, UNC; *Annals*, p. 416.

17. Dowdey and Manarin, eds., *Wartime Papers*, p. 411; *B&L*, vol. 3, p. 247.

18. Woodworth, *Davis and Lee*, p. 243; Sword, *Courage under Fire*, p. 226.

19. Maurice, ed., *Aide-De-Camp*, pp. 67, 71, 74; Gallagher, ed., *First Day at Gettysburg*, pp. 7, 10.

20. Maurice, ed., *Aide-De-Camp*, p. 75; *Annals*, pp. 305, 306.

21. Freeman, *R. E. Lee*, vol. 2, p. 19; James Longstreet to John R. Cooke, May 16, 1863, Cooke Family Papers, VHS; J. B. Jones, *Rebel War Clerk's Diary*, vol. 1, p. 325; *OR*, vol. 27, p. 2, p. 305.

22. Freeman, *R. E. Lee*, vol. 2, pp. 19–20; James A. Seddon to James Longstreet, April 16, 1875, Longstreet Papers, DU.

23. *OR*, vol. 25, pt. 2, p. 810.

24. Ibid., pp. 810, 840; Warner, *Generals in Gray*, pp. 84, 135.

25. *OR*, vol. 25, pt. 1, p. 803; J. E. B. Stuart to My Darling One, May 20, 1863, Stuart Papers, VHS; McClellan, *I Rode*, p. 256.

26. D. C. Pfanz, *Richard S. Ewell*, p. 273; Warner, *Generals in Gray*, p. 84; Washington *Post*, June 11, 1893; Sorrel, *Recollections*, p. 47; Jedediah Hotchkiss to My Darling Wife, May 31, 1863, Hotchkiss Papers, LC.

27. *SHSP*, vol. 7, p. 523; Boyd, *Reminiscences*, p. 12; Eggleston, *Rebel's Recollections*, p. 136; D. C. Pfanz, *Richard S. Ewell*, pp. 82, 84, 266, 268.

28. Washington *Post*, June 11, 1893; Gallagher, ed., *Lee: The Soldier*, p. 11; Boyd, *Reminiscences*, p. 22; Haskell, *Haskell Memoirs*, p. 18.

29. OR, vol. 25, pt. 2, p. 810; vol. 27, pt. 2, pp. 288–90; Haskell, *Haskell Memoirs*, p. 16; Washington *Post*, June 11, 1893.

30. OR, vol. 27, pt. 2, pp. 283–91; Longstreet, *From Manassas to Appomattox*, p. 332; Lafayette McLaws to Miss Lizzie, February 18, 1863, Ewell Papers, LC.

31. OR, vol. 25, pt. 2, pp. 774, 787; Freeman, ed., *Lee's Dispatches*, p. 88; W. C. Davis, ed., *Confederate General*, vol. 3, p. 187; Samuel J. C. Moore to My Dearest Wife, January 30, 1863, Moore Papers, UNC; Stiles, *Four Years*, p. 218.

32. OR, vol. 25, pt. 2, p. 827; A. P. Hill to R. E. Lee, May 24, 1863, Hill Letter, NYHS; Hassler, ed., *General to His Lady*, pp. 191, 225; W. A. Montgomery, *Life*, pp. 9, 10; CV, vol. 3, p. 18; W. C. Davis, ed., *Confederate General*, vol. 5, p. 11.

33. Morrison, ed., *Memoirs*, p. 156; Gallagher, ed., *First Day at Gettysburg*, p. 96; Warner, *Generals in Gray*, p. 133; Freeman, *Lee's Lieutenants*, vol. 2, p. xliv.

34. OR, vol. 27, pt. 2, pp. 283–91; Freeman, *Lee's Lieutenants*, vol. 2, p. 712.

35. OR, vol. 27, pt. 2, pp. 283–91; Freeman, *Lee's Lieutenants*, vol. 2, pp. 710–12; Clark, ed., vol. 1, *Histories*, p. 523; W.C. Davis, ed., *Confederate General*, vol. 3, p. 203; vol. 5, p. 128; vol. 6, p. 87.

36. Dowdey and Manarin, eds., *Wartime Papers*, p. 490.

37. Gallagher, ed., *First Day at Gettysburg*, pp. 7–8; Krick, *Lee's Colonels* (5th edition), *passim*.

38. Raymer, *Confederate Correspondent*, p. 77; Gottfried, *Brigades of Gettysburg*, p. 404; West, *Texan*, p. 53; Durkin, ed., *John Dooley*, p. 97; Sword, *Southern Invincibility*, pp. 145, 153.

39. Caldwell, *History*, p. 95.

40. B&L, vol. 3, p. 358; OR, vol. 21, p. 568; vol. 25, pt. 1, pp. 818, 819; Gallagher, ed., *Fighting*, pp. 60, 61, 122; Hess, *Rifle Musket*, p. 45; Moseley, ed., *Stilwell Letters*, p. 161; Nanzig, ed., *Civil War Memoirs*, p. 118.

41. McCarthy, *Detailed Minutiae*, p. 26; John F. Sale to Aunt, April 19, 1863, Sale Papers, LVA.

42. OR, vol. 18, pp. 1063, 1071, 1085, 1088; vol. 25, pt. 2, pp. 814, 833, 848, 849, 851, 852; Busey and Martin, *Regimental Strengths*, p. 322.

43. Gallagher, ed., *Fighting*, p. 221; OR, vol. 27, pt. 2, p. 293; John W. Daniel to Father, June 4, 1863, Daniel Papers, UVA; Eugene Blackford to Father, June 8, 1863, Blackford Letters, USAMHI.

44. OR, vol. 27, pt. 2, p. 293; Raymer, *Confederate Correspondent*, p. 84; John B. Gordon to My Darling Wife, June 7, 1863, Gordon Family Papers, UGA.

45. OR, vol. 25, pt. 2, p. 782; R. E. Lee to J. E. B. Stuart, May 11, 1863, Stuart Papers, HL; Wert, *Cavalryman*, pp. 202, 203, 238, 239.

46. Wert, *Cavalryman*, pp. 238, 239.

47. Ibid., pp. 240, 241.

48. Ibid., pp. 241–45.

49. Ibid., pp. 244, 245.

50. Ibid., pp. 245–48; quotes on p. 247.

51. Ibid., pp. 249–52; J. E. B. Stuart to My Darling Wife, June 12, 1863, Stuart

Papers, VHS; *SHSP*, vol. 8, p. 453; Freeman, *Lee's Lieutenants*, vol. 3, p. 18; McClellan, *I Rode*, p. 294; W. W. Blackford, *War Years*, p. 233; Savannah *Republican*, June 20, 1863; Richmond *Sentinel*, June 11, 1863; Mobile *Advertiser and Register*, June 30, 1863.

52. OR, vol. 27, pt. 3, pp. 868, 869, 882.

53. Ibid., p. 881.

54. Ibid., pt. 2, p. 308; pt. 3, p. 881.

55. Ibid., pt. 2, p. 295; Henry M. Talley to My Dear Mother, June 11, 1863, Brown Papers, NCDAH; Ferdinand J. Dunlap to Sister, June 22, 1863, Dunlap Letters, USAMHI; H. C. Kendrick to Mother, June 6, 1863, Kendrick Papers, UNC.

56. OR, vol. 27, pt. 2, pp. 440–42; Stephens, ed., *Intrepid Warrior*, p. 196.

57. OR, vol. 27, pt. 2, pp. 357, 442, 610, 613; Latrobe, Diary, VHS; Diary, Alexander Papers, UNC.

58. Wert, *Sword*, p. 263; OR, vol. 27, pt. 1, pp. 34–35.

59. Wert, *Sword*, p. 263.

60. Wert, *Cavalryman*, pp. 254–56, 257.

61. Latrobe, Diary; H. B. McClellan to A. L. Long, March 14, 1887, Stuart Papers, VHS; OR, vol. 27, pt. 2, pt. 316.

62. OR, vol. 27, pt. 3, pp. 913, 914, 915, 923; R. E. Lee to J. E. B. Stuart, June 23, 1863, pp. 23–24, Lee Letterbook, VHS.

63. OR, vol. 27, pt. 3, p. 923; R. E. Lee to J. E. B. Stuart, June 23, 1863, pp. 23–24, Lee Letterbook, VHS.

64. Gallagher, ed., *First Day at Gettysburg*, pp. 16, 145n; Trudeau, *Gettysburg*, p. 69n; R. E. Lee to J. E. B. Stuart, June 23, 1863, pp. 23–24, Lee Letterbook, VHS.

65. Gallagher, ed., *First Day at Gettysburg*, pp. 17, 19; OR, vol. 27, pt. 2, p. 316; Maurice, ed., *Aide-De-Camp*, pp. 201, 207, 208n; A. L. Long to H. B. McClellan, March 11, 1887, McClellan Papers, VHS.

66. Sears, *Gettysburg*, p. 105; Gallagher, ed., *First Day at Gettysburg*, pp. 14, 17, 20; Freeman, *Lee's Lieutenants*, vol. 3, p. 57; SOR, vol. 5, p. 83; OR, vol. 27, pt. 2, p. 297; Gallagher, ed., *Lee: The Soldier*, p. 14; Alexander, *Military Memoirs*, p. 374.

67. Coddington, *Gettysburg Campaign*, p. 108; Sorrel, *Recollections*, p. 114; James Longstreet to My Dear General Munford, November 8, 1891, Munford-Ellis Family Papers, DU.

68. OR, vol. 27, p. 3, p. 923; Freeman, *Lee's Lieutenants*, vol. 3, p. 57; Coddington, *Gettysburg Campaign*, p. 109; McClellan, *I Rode*, p. 315; Wert, *Cavalryman*, p. 262.

69. OR, vol. 27, pt. 2, p. 692; Wert, *Cavalryman*, pp. 263–64.

70. OR, vol. 27, pt. 3, p. 927; Wert, *Cavalryman*, pp. 291–92.

71. Wert, *Cavalryman*, pp. 264–65.

72. Ibid., pp. 267–69; McClellan, *I Rode*, p. 321; Freeman, *Lee's Lieutenants*, vol. 3, pp. xi, xxxii.

73. OR, vol. 27, pt. 2, p. 321; Gallagher, ed., *Lee: The Soldier*, p. 14.

74. OR, vol. 27, pt. 2, pp. 443, 613; Wert, *Sword*, p. 264; Latrobe, Diary, VHS; Diary, Alexander Papers, UNC; *Annals*, p. 419.

75. William D. Lyon to Brother George, July 18, 1863, Lyon Papers, NC; Bud to My Dear Sister, July 18, 1863, Bud Letter, NYHS; Iowa M. Royster to Ma, June 29, 1863, Royster Papers, UNC; William A. Miller to Sister, July 1, 1863, 18th Virginia Infantry File, GNMP; Diary of James B. Clifton, Brake Collection, USAMHI; John Garibaldi to Wife, July 19, 1863, Garibaldi Letters, VMI.

76. OR, vol. 27, pt. 3, pp. 942–43; Wiley, *Life*, pp. 47–48; Wyckoff, *History*, p. 163; James P. Williams to Pa, June 28, 1863, Williams Papers, UNC; Jeremiah Tate to sister Mary, July 19, 1863, Tate Letters, NYHS; I. V. Reynolds to Wife, July 20, 1863, Reynolds Papers, DU; Benjamin L. Farinholt to Lelia, July 1, 3, 1863, Farinholt Papers, VHS; Stevens, *War Reminiscences*, p. 107; Charles J. Batchelor to My dear Father, October 18, 1863, Batchelor Papers, LSU.

77. Eugene Blackford to My dear Father, June 22, 1863, Blackford Letters, USAMHI; Stephens, ed., *Intrepid Warrior*, p. 184; William A. Miller to Sister, July 1, 1863, 18th Virginia Infantry File, GNMP.

78. Latrobe, Diary, VHS; Diary, Alexander Papers, UNC; *Annals*, p. 419; Ross, *Cities and Camps*, p. 42; L. M. Blackford to William M. Blackford, June 28, 1863, Blackford Family Papers, UVA.

79. Lord, ed., *Fremantle Diary*, pp. 197, 198; Moses, "Autobiography," p. 54, UNC; James Longstreet to Osmun Latrobe, May 28, 1886, Latrobe Diary, VHS.

80. Hunton, *Autobiography*, p. 86.

81. Hood, *Advance and Retreat*, p. 55; Maurice, ed., *Aide-De-Camp*, p. 218.

82. Longstreet, *From Manassas to Appomattox*, pp. 324, 333; B&L, vol. 3, p. 249; Sorrel, *Recollections*, p. 152.

83. *Annals*, p. 419; Sorrel, *Recollections*, p. 155; Longstreet, *From Manassas to Appomattox*, pp. 346, 347; John W. Fairfax to James Longstreet, November 12, 1877, Fairfax Papers, VHS.

84. John W. Fairfax to James Longstreet, November 12, 1877, Fairfax Papers, VHS; Longstreet, *From Manassas to Appomattox*, p. 383n.

85. OR, vol. 27, pt. 2, pp. 316, 443; pt. 3, pp. 943–44.

86. Gallagher, ed., *First Day at Gettysburg*, p. 14.

87. SHSP, vol. 4, pp. 82, 99; Cozzens, ed., B&L, vol. 5, p. 369.

88. OR, vol. 27, pt. 2, pp. 307, 317; Latrobe, Diary, VHS; Wert, *Cavalryman*, pp. 277–79.

89. OR, vol. 27, pt. 2, pp. 607, 637; Sears, *Gettysburg*, p. 137.

90. OR, vol. 27, pt. 2, p. 607; SHSP, vol. 4, p. 157.

91. Gallagher, ed., *Fighting*, p. 230; Lord, ed., *Fremantle Diary*, p. 199; Stiles, *Four Years*, p. 228.

92. Wert, *Sword*, pp. 265, 266, 267.

93. Ibid., pp. 267–69.

94. Ibid., pp. 271, 272.

95. W. Taylor, *Four Years*, p. 101; Gallagher, ed., *Fighting*, p. 222; *SHSP*, vol. 4, pp. 82, 98, 99; Styple, ed., *Writing and Fighting Confederate War*, pp. 236, 237, 238; Iowa M. Royster to Ma, June 29, 1863, Royster Papers, UNC; Dickert, *History*, p. 223; Lord, *Fremantle Diary*, p. 205.

96. Longstreet, *From Manassas to Appomattox*, p. 383n.

Chapter Nine

1. Longstreet, *From Manassas to Appomattox*, pp. 351, 352; Latrobe, Diary, VHS; Lord, ed., *Fremantle Diary*, p. 203; Gallagher, ed., *First Day at Gettysburg*, p. 45; Myers, Diary, MC; OR, vol. 27, pt. 2, p. 607.

2. Long, *Memoirs*, p. 277; Gallagher, ed., *Lee: The Soldier*, p. 14; *Annals*, p. 420.

3. Sears, *Gettysburg*, p. 165; *SHSP*, vol. 4, p. 126.

4. Wert, *Sword*, pp. 274–75; OR, vol. 27, pt. 2, p. 637.

5. Wert, *Sword*, pp. 275–76.

6. Ibid., p. 276; Gallagher, ed., *First Day at Gettysburg*, p. 101; Sears, *Gettysburg*, pp. 172–79.

7. Wert, *Sword*, pp. 276–77.

8. OR, vol. 27, pt. 2, pp. 287, 444, 552.

9. Ibid., pp. 444, 445, 468; Busey and Martin, *Regimental Strengths*, pp. 16, 284, 289, 297, 302; Sears, *Gettysburg*, p. 194.

10. OR, vol. 27, pt. 2, p. 444; Trudeau, *Gettysburg*, p. 210.

11. *SHSP*, vol. 4, p. 126; *Annals*, p. 420; T. L. Jones, ed., *Campbell Brown's Civil War*, pp. 204, 205.

12. Sears, *Gettysburg*, pp. 196, 197; T. L. Jones, ed., *Campbell Brown's Civil War*, p. 206; OR, vol. 27, pt. 2, p. 697; Wert, *Cavalryman*, p. 282.

13. Morrison, ed., *Memoirs*, p. 175.

14. Sears, *Gettysburg*, pp. 197–99.

15. Ibid., pp. 199–201; J. F. Coghill to Pappy, Ma, and Mit, July 17, 1863, Coghill Papers, UNC; Busey and Martin, *Regimental Strengths*, p. 587; W. C. Davis, ed., *Confederate General*, v. 3, p. 143.

16. Runge, ed., *Four Years*, p. 50.

17. Sears, *Gettysburg*, pp. 203–4, 206–9; Busey and Martin, *Regimental Strengths*, pp. 23, 27, 28; Wert, *Brotherhood*, p. 259.

18. Wert, *Brotherhood*, pp. 259–60.

19. Ibid., pp. 261, 262; Busey and Martin, *Regimental Strengths*, pp. 125, 298.

20. Sears, *Gettysburg*, pp. 217–18; Busey and Martin, *Regimental Strengths*, p. 305.

21. Sears, *Gettysburg*, p. 218; Busey and Martin, *Regimental Strengths*, p. 303; Wert, *Brotherhood*, p. 263.

22. OR, vol. 27, pt. 2, pp. 554, 567, 587; Norman, *Portion*, p. 183; A. M. Parker to My Dear Sir, May 29, 1891, Ramseur Papers, NCDAH; Wert, *Brotherhood*, p. 264.

23. OR, vol. 27, pt. 2, pp. 468, 469, 479, 492; CV, vol. 12, p. 193; Wert, *Sword*, p. 281.

24. Wert, *Brotherhood*, pp. 264–65; "Account of Gettysburg, Sept. 23, 1863," Daniel Papers, VHS.

25. *SHSP*, vol. 4, p. 127; *Annals*, p. 308.

26. D. C. Pfanz, *Richard S. Ewell*, pp. 308–9.

27. Ibid., p. 310; Walter Taylor to John W. Daniel, July 14, 1903, Daniel Papers, UVA; J. P. Smith, *With Stonewall Jackson*, p. 57; Sears, *Gettysburg*, p. 227.

28. D. C. Pfanz, *Richard S. Ewell*, p. 311; T. L. Jones, ed., *Campbell Brown's Civil War*, p. 211.

29. D. C. Pfanz, *Richard S. Ewell*, pp. 311, 312; T. L. Jones, ed., *Campbell Brown's Civil War*, pp. 212, 213; Account of Major J. W. Bruce in Charlottesville *Progress*, March 22, 1904; J. W. Bruce to John W. Daniel, April 8, 1904, Daniel Papers, UVA.

30. E. P. Alexander to Frederick Colston, October 31, 1906, Campbell-Colston Family Papers, UNC; Gallagher, ed., *Lee: The Soldier*, p. 14; *SHSP*, vol. 33, p. 144; Freeman, *Lee's Lieutenants*, vol. 3, pp. 171, 172; Douglas, *I Rode*, p. 247.

31. Busey and Martin, *Regimental Strengths*, p. 16; D. C. Pfanz, *Richard S. Ewell*, p. 322; *SHSP*, vol. 5, p. 168.

32. Wert, *Sword*, p. 281; *SHSP*, vol. 4, pp. 66–67; vol. 5, p. 168; Samuel Johnston to George Peterkin, December 26, [?], Johnston Papers, VHS; Jubal Early to Armistead L. Long, April 3, 1876, Long Papers, UNC.

33. Gallagher, ed., *First Day at Gettysburg*, p. 55; D. C. Pfanz, *Richard S. Ewell*, pp. 312, 324.

34. Gallagher, ed., *First Day at Gettysburg*, pp. 46, 47, 55; OR, vol. 27, pt. 2, pp. 317–18, 607.

35. Gallagher, ed., *First Day at Gettysburg*, p. 47; Trudeau, *Gettysburg*, p. 247; OR, vol. 27, pt. 2, pp. 317–18.

36. Samuel Johnston to George Peterkin, December 26 [?], Johnston Papers, VHS.

37. Longstreet, *From Manassas to Appomattox*, p. 358; *Annals*, pp. 420, 421; Lord, *Fremantle Diary*, pp. 190, 202.

38. In his various postwar writings, Longstreet gave different versions of his and Lee's words; see Longstreet, *From Manassas to Appomattox*, pp. 358–59; *B&L*, vol. 3, pp. 339–40; *Annals*, p. 421.

39. Wert, *General James Longstreet*, pp. 258, 259.

40. Gallagher, ed., *Fighting*, p. 237; *B&L*, vol. 3, p. 246; James Longstreet to Lafayette McLaws, July 25, 1873, McLaws Papers, UNC.

41. James Longstreet to Lafayette McLaws, July 25, 1873, McLaws Papers, UNC.

42. *SHSP*, vol. 4, p. 98; Gallagher, ed., *Lee: The Soldier*, p. 15; Longstreet, *From Manassas to Appomattox*, p. 334; W. Taylor, *Four Years*, p. 91.

43. OR, vol. 27, pt. 2, p. 308.

44. Ibid., p. 308.
45. Gallagher, ed., *Fighting*, p. 265; *Annals*, p. 421; E. M. Thomas, *Robert E. Lee*, p. 302.
46. Longstreet, *From Manassas to Appomattox*, p. 361; *Annals*, p. 421; Wert, *General James Longstreet*, p. 259; Lord, ed., *Fremantle Diary*, p. 205; Moses, "Autobiography," pp. 60, 61, UNC; London *Times*, August 18, 1863.
47. Samuel Johnston to George Peterkin, December 26, [?], Johnston Papers, VHS; "A Notable Conference," Participants' Accounts, Ewell File, GNMP; D. C. Pfanz, *Richard S. Ewell*, pp. 312, 313.
48. D. C. Pfanz, *Richard S. Ewell*, pp. 313, 314; "The Gettysburg Campaign," Alexander Papers, UNC.
49. OR, vol. 27, pt. 3, pp. 461, 465–68; Wert, *Sword*, pp. 283, 284.
50. Wert, *Sword*, p. 284.
51. Ibid., pp. 284, 285.
52. Ibid., pp. 271, 272, 285.
53. Wert, *General James Longstreet*, p. 260.
54. Freeman, *R. E. Lee*, vol. 3, p. 86; Longstreet, *From Manassas to Appomattox*, p. 362; James Longstreet to John P. Nicholson, July 15, 1877, Nicholson Papers, HL; *Annals*, pp. 414, 439.
55. Gallagher, ed., *Second Day at Gettysburg*, pp. 29, 30, 32; W. Taylor, *Four Years*, p. 96; Ross, *Cities and Camps*, p. 76.
56. Gallagher, ed., *Lee: The Soldier*, p. 17; Gallagher, ed., *Second Day at Gettysburg*, pp. 30–31; Gallagher, ed., *Fighting*, pp. 120, 234; Scheibert, *Seven Months*, p. 118.
57. *Annals*, p. 422; Samuel R. Johnston to My dear General, June 27, 1892, Johnston Papers, VHS; *SHSP*, vol. 4, p. 147; London *Times*, August 18, 1863.
58. London *Times*, August 18, 1863; Scheibert, *Seven Months*, p. 113; Philadelphia *Weekly Press*, February 15, 1888; *SHSP*, vol. 4, p. 147; Hood, *Advance and Retreat*, p. 57.
59. Samuel R. Johnston to Fitz Lee, February 11, 16, 1878; to My Dear General, June 27, 1892; to George Peterkin, December 26, [?], Johnston Papers, VHS.
60. Samuel R. Johnston to Fitz Lee, February 11, 1878, Johnston Papers, VHS; Freeman, *Lee's Lieutenants*, vol. 3, p. 174; H. W. Pfanz, *Gettysburg*, p. 107.
61. Coddington, *Gettysburg Campaign*, p. 374; Freeman, *Lee's Lieutenants*, vol. 3, pp. 113, 114; H. W. Pfanz, *Gettysburg*, pp. 110, 111; "Longstreet at Gettysburg," February 20, 1888; Lafayette McLaws to James Longstreet, June 12, 1873, McLaws Papers, UNC; Samuel R. Johnston to My dear General, June 27, 1892, Johnston Papers, VHS.
62. *SHSP*, vol. 4, p. 101; vol. 5, p. 202; Gallagher, ed., *Fighting*, p. 235, 236; Sorrel, *Recollections*, p. 157; Hood, *Advance and Retreat*, p. 57.
63. Sorrel, *Recollections*, p. 157.
64. Gallagher, ed., *Fighting*, pp. 233, 234; E. P. Alexander to Frederick Colston, July 22, 1903, Campbell-Colston Family Papers, UNC.

65. *Annals*, p. 422; H. W. Pfanz, *Gettysburg*, pp. 113, 114; *SOR*, vol. 5, p. 381.
66. *OR*, vol. 27, pt. 2, pp. 308, 318.
67. Quoted words are in *SHSP*, vol. 5, p. 91; see also Scheibert, *Seven Months*, p. 220; Gallagher, ed., *Third Day at Gettysburg*, p. 43.
68. Busey and Martin, *Regimental Strengths*, pp. 170, 178; Samuel R. Johnston to Fitz Lee, February 11, 1878, Johnston Papers, VHS; Meyers, "Kershaw's Brigade," GNMP; H. W. Pfanz, *Gettysburg*, pp. 120, 490n.
69. Busey and Martin, *Regimental Strengths*, p. 16; Wert, *Sword*, pp. 286, 287; Gettysburg Clipping Books, vol. 4, p. 78, GNMP.
70. Savannah *Morning News*, January 8, 1878.
71. Gallagher, ed., *Fighting*, p. 237; E. P. Alexander to Frederick Colston, April 7, 1898, Campbell-Colston Family Papers, UNC; Sanger, "Was Longstreet a Scapegoat?," p. 42; Freeman, *Lee's Lieutenants*, vol. 3, pp. 118, 175.
72. Lafayette McLaws to Wife, July 7, 1863; "Longstreet at Gettysburg," McLaws Papers, UNC; Savannah *Morning News*, January 8, 1878; Philadelphia *Weekly Press*, February 15, 1888; *B&L*, vol. 3, pp. 340–41; Cutrer, ed., *Longstreet's Aide*, p. 158; John Fairfax to James Longstreet, November 12, 1877, Fairfax Papers, VHS; H. W. Pfanz, *Gettysburg*, pp. 153–54, 497n; Dickert, *History*, p. 235.
73. Hood, *Advance and Retreat*, pp. 57, 58; Longstreet, *From Manassas to Appomattox*, pp. 380n, 381n; Sorrel, *Recollections*, pp. 159, 160; John Fairfax to James Longstreet, November 12, 1877, Fairfax Papers, VHS.
74. Gottfried, *Brigades of Gettysburg*, p. 412; Dickert, *History*, p. 234; Hattaway and Jones, *How the North Won*, p. 407.
75. *Annals*, p. 424; John Haskell to E. P. Alexander, September 7, 1901, Alexander Papers, UNC; H. W. Pfanz, *Gettysburg*, p. 431; Styple, ed., *Writing*, p. 227.
76. Gottfried, *Brigades of Gettysburg*, pp. 435, 438, 442, 451; Polley, *Hood's Texas Brigade*, p. 142; "The Gettysburg Campaign," Alexander Papers, UNC: Theodore Fogel to Father and Mother, July 7, 1863, Fogel Papers, EU.
77. Bass, Letter, July 8, 1863, FSNMP: D. M. DuBose to Porter, August 23, 1866, Alexander Papers, UNC; Wert, *Sword*, pp. 287, 288.
78. H. W. Pfanz, *Gettysburg*, pp. 231–36, quote on p. 231.
79. Ibid., pp. 228–30, 236; Simpson, *Hood's Texas Brigade*, p. 277; Powell, *Recollections*, p. 16; Polley, *Hood's Texas Brigade*, p. 173.
80. Busey and Martin, *Regimental Strengths*, pp. 260, 262, 263; Polley, *Hood's Texas Brigade*, p. 173; Stevens, *War Reminiscences*, p. 20; "Notes for E. P. Alexander," Benning Papers, UNC.
81. Lafayette McLaws to Emily, July 7, 1863; James Longstreet to Lafayette McLaws, July 28, 1873, McLaws Papers, UNC.
82. H. W. Pfanz, *Gettysburg*, pp. 246, 272; Gottfried, *Brigades of Gettysburg*, p. 417; Philadelphia *Weekly Times*, June 2, 1883; Parrish, *Wiregrass*, pp. 121, 123; Humphreys, *Semmes America*, pp. 388, 392, 393.
83. H. W. Pfanz, *Gettysburg*, pp. 246, 272; Busey and Martin, *Regimental Strengths*, pp. 32, 47, 48, 171, 178; Gallagher, ed., *Fighting*, p. 242.

84. Wert, *Sword*, pp. 289, 290; Trudeau, *Gettysburg*, p. 363.

85. Gottfried, *Brigades of Gettysburg*, pp. 415, 416; Gerald, "Battle of Gettysburg," GNMP; Benjamin G. Humphreys to Lafayette McLaws, January 6, 1878, McLaws Papers, UNC; CV, vol. 1, p. 206; Wert, *General James Longstreet*, p. 275.

86. Wert, *Sword*, p. 291; W. C. Davis, ed., *Confederate General*, vol. 1, p. 59; Moore, *Life*, p. 153.

87. H. W. Pfanz, *Gettysburg*, pp. 292–302, 390–402.

88. *Annals*, p. 425; Goode Bryan to Sir, December 10, 1877, McLaws Papers, UNC; Lafayette McLaws to Isaac R. Pennypacker, n.d., Participant Accounts, McLaws File, GNMP; Busey and Martin, *Regimental Strengths*, pp. 260, 266.

89. "Longstreet at Gettysburg," McLaws Papers, UNC.

90. H. W. Pfanz, *Gettysburg*, pp. 414, 415; Polley, *Hood's Texas Brigade*, p. 194.

91. Freeman, *Lee's Lieutenants*, vol. 3, pp. 124, 125, 126, 129; OR, vol. 27, pt. 2, p. 490.

92. H. W. Pfanz, *Gettysburg*, pp. 404–24; Busey and Martin, *Regimental Strengths*, p. 311.

93. Freeman, *Lee's Lieutenants*, vol. 3, pp. 129–32; Wert, *Gettysburg*, pp. 53, 54.

94. Wert, *Gettysburg*, pp. 53, 54.

95. Freeman, *Lee's Lieutenants*, vol. 3, pp. 132–35; Busey and Martin, *Regimental Strengths*, pp. 284, 286; Krick, *Lee's Colonels* (5th edition), p. 37.

96. Gallagher, ed., *Fighting*, p. 242; W. Taylor, *Four Years*, p. 99.

97. Wert, *Sword*, p. 286.

98. Ibid., pp. 294, 296.

99. *Annals*, p. 429; OR, vol. 27, pt. 2, p. 320; Douglas, *I Rode*, p. 249.

100. OR, vol. 27, pt. 2, p. 697; Freeman, *Lee's Lieutenants*, vol. 3, p. 139; Wert, *Cavalryman*, pp. 282, 284, 285.

101. Wert, *Gettysburg*, pp. 59, 90.

102. "The Gettysburg Campaign," Alexander Papers, UNC.

103. Gallagher, ed., *Third Day at Gettysburg*, pp. 45, 46. Longstreet claimed in a postwar letter that Pickett's division while at Chambersburg was under Lee's direct authority, and Lee should have ordered the command to the field on July 3. See James Longstreet to H. T. Owen, April 21, 1878, Owen Papers, VHS.

104. *Annals*, pp. 429, 433; B&L, vol. 3, pp. 342, 343; James Longstreet to Lafayette McLaws, July 25, 1873, McLaws Papers, UNC; OR, vol. 27, pt. 2, p. 359.

105. *Annals*, p. 429; James Longstreet to Henry Heth, February 14, 1897, Longstreet Papers, MC.

106. Wert, *Gettysburg*, chapters 3 and 4, quote on p. 61.

107. Ibid., quotes on pp. 61, 64, 89.

108. Ibid., pp. 101, 102; Busey and Martin, *Regimental Strengths*, pp. 271, 297, 298, 299, 304, 305, 307, 308; Ernsberger, *Also for Glory*, pp. 33–82; James Longstreet to Henry Heth, February 14, 1897, Longstreet Papers, MC.

109. Wert, *Gettysburg*, pp. 101, 146; Griffith, *Battle Tactics*, p. 143.

110. Coddington, *Gettysburg Campaign*, p. 463; Wert, *Gettysburg*, pp. 104, 105; Glatthaar, *General Lee's Army*, pp. 286–87.

111. Coddington, *Gettysburg Campaign*, p. 457; *SHSP*, vol. 4, p. 79; Sorrel, *Recollections*, p. 162.

112. Wert, *Gettysburg*, pp. 113, 114; Sorrel, *Recollections*, p. 48; Moses, "Autobiography," UNC.

113. Wert, *Gettysburg*, pp. 114–18; Morrison, ed., *Memoirs*, pp. 174, 175.

114. *Annals*, pp. 431–32; Ernsberger, *Also for Glory*, pp. 33–82; Wert, *Gettysburg*, pp. 128–30; Coddington, *Gettysburg Campaign*, pp. 461, 462, 463.

115. Wert, *Gettysburg*, pp. 167–81, quotes on pp. 167, 168, 175, 181.

116. Ibid., pp. 183–86.

117. *B&L*, vol. 3, p. 345; *Annals*, p. 431, George E. Pickett to [Sallie Corbell], July 9, 1863, Brake Collection, USAMHI; Gallagher, ed., *Fighting*, pp. 260, 261.

118. Wert, *Gettysburg*, pp. 187–98, quotes on pp. 194, 195.

119. Ibid., chapter 10, quotes p. 198; W. B. Robertson to Mattie, July 28, 1863, Daniel Papers, UVA.

120. Wert, *Gettysburg*, chapter 11.

121. Ibid., chapter 11, quotes on pp. 210, 216.

122. Ibid., chapter 12, pp. 240, 241.

123. Ibid., pp. 137, 244; Coddington, *Gettysburg Campaign*, pp. 463, 529; OR, vol. 27, pt. 2, pp. 320–21, 360, 368, 614–15, 620.

124. Charles Marshall to H. T. Owen, January 28, 1878, Owen Papers, VHS; Thomas J. Goree to James Longstreet, May 17, 1875, Longstreet Papers, UNC; Gallagher, ed., *Fighting*, p. 266; Cadmus Wilcox to Thomas S. Mills, July 17, 1863, Wilcox Papers, LC; Busey and Martin, *Regimental Strengths*, pp. 271, 297; S. L. Blackford, ed., *Letters*, p. 190.

125. Wert, *Cavalryman*, pp. 283–90.

126. OR, vol. 27, pt. 2, p. 309; William A. Allison to Stock, July 18, 1863, Allison Letters, NYHS.

Chapter Ten

1. Runge, *Four Years*, p. 52; Wert, *Sword*, p. 303.

2. Diary of George K. Griggs, Griggs Book, MC; W. J. Kinchelve to Sister, July 10, 1863, Daniel Papers; James L. Kemper to A. P. Pollock, January 12, 1865, Janney-Pollock Family Papers, UVA; Weigley, *Great Civil War*, p. 253.

3. Busey and Martin, *Regimental Strengths*, p. 16, 169; Wise, *Long Arm*, p. 694.

4. Freeman, *Lee's Lieutenants*, vol. 3, p. 190; W. C. Davis, ed., *Confederate General*, vol. 1, p. 38; vol. 3, p. 121; vol. 4, p. 7; vol. 5, pp. 11, 25; vol. 6, p. 61.

5. Krick, *Lee's Colonels* (5th edition), *passim*; Allardice, *Confederate Colonels*, p. 15; Freeman, *Lee's Lieutenants*, vol. 3, pp. 195, 196; Turner, ed., *Ted Barclay*, p. 93.

6. Wert, *Cavalryman*, pp. 292–93, 296.

7. Ibid., pp. 296–97.

8. Ibid., pp. 297–98.

9. Wert, *Sword*, pp. 308, 309.

10. Noble, "A 'G.I.' View," UM; Samuel B. Carter to Vincent B. Brewer, July 9, 1863, Carter Letter, USAMHI; David E. Beem to My dear Wife, July 5, 1863, Beem Collection, IHS; Toledo *Blade*, July 11, 1863; Adams, *Our Masters*, p. 147.

11. [?] to Ma, July 18, 1863, Letter to Mother, USAMHI; Thomas C. Edler to My Dear Wife, July 15, 1863, Elder Papers, VHS; Stephen D. Ramseur to My Heart's Darling, July 16, 1863, Ramseur Papers; Cadwallader Jones to Sister, August 28, 1863; J. S. Bartlett, Recollections, p. 4, UNC; John Imboden to S. O. Dounde, August 4, 1891, Participant Accounts, Imboden File, GNMP; Newspaper clipping, letter of John S. Lewis to My very dear Mother, July 21, 1863, Lewis Papers, DU; Wilkinson and Woodworth, *Scythe of Fire*, p. 261; R. E. Lee to His Excellency, July 27, 1863, Lee Papers, NYHS; Raymer, *Confederate Correspondent*, p. 89.

12. A. S. Van de Graaff to My dear Wife, July 8, 1863, 5th Alabama Infantry File, GNMP; Jedediah Hotchkiss to My Darling, July 14, 1863, Hotchkiss Papers, LC; Rozier, ed., *Granite Farm Letters*, p. 125; Tower, ed., *Lee's Adjutant*, p. 62; Stephens, ed., *Intrepid Warrior*, p. 248; Oeffinger, ed., *Soldier's General*, p. 200.

13. Gallagher, ed., *Third Day at Gettysburg*, p. 1; Raymer, *Confederate Correspondent*, p. 88; William D. Lyon to Brother George, July 18, 1863, Lyon Papers, NC; Richard W. Waldrop to Father, July 18, 1863, Waldrop Papers, UNC.

14. Jacob B. Click to Old Friend Lucius, July 17, 1863, Click Papers; T. W. Holley to Eliza, July 22, 1863, Holley Papers, DU; Marcus Hefner to Wife, July 10, 1863, Hefner Papers, NCDAH; Theodore Fogel to Father and Mother, July 7, 1863, Fogel Papers, EU; William J. Hatchett to My Dear Parents, July 7, 1863, Hatchett Family Papers, USAMHI; Leonidas Polk to My own dear Wife, July 12, 1863, Polk Papers, UNC; Charles E. Denoon to Sister, July 17, 1863, Denoon Papers, LVA.

15. Stephen D. Ramseur to My Heart's Darling, July 8, 1863, Ramseur Papers, UNC; Rozier, ed., *Granite Farm Letters*, p. 115; William H. Sanders to Matthew, July 16, 1863, Sanders Papers, ADAH; David E. Maxwell to Father, July 8, 1863, Maxwell Papers, VHS; J. J. Young to Mr. Governor, July 4, 1863, Vance Papers, NCDAH; Krick, *Parker's Virginia Battery*, p. 191.

16. Alex McNeil to Wife, July 7, 1863, McNeil Letters, GNMP; Rozier, ed., *Granite Farm Letters*, p. 115; Eugene Blackford to My dear Mother, July 8, 1863, Blackford Letters, USAMHI; Theodore Fogel to Sister, July 16, 1863, Fogel Papers, EU; Polley, *Soldier's Letters*, p. 132.

17. Freeman, ed., *Lee's Dispatches*, pp. 108, 110.

18. OR, vol. 27, pt. 2, p. 321; CV, vol. 21, p. 62; Gallagher, ed., *Lee: The Soldier*, pp. 14, 15.

19. Wert, *Cavalryman*, pp. 300, 301, 302; Sears, *Gettysburg*, p. 504; E. P. Alexander to Colston, February 9, 1904, Campbell-Colston Family Papers, UNC; Gallagher, ed., *Fighting*, p. 110.

20. E. M. Thomas, *Robert E. Lee*, p. 303; Gallagher, ed., *First Day at Gettysburg*, p. 11; *Confederate History Symposium*, p. 24; Sword, *Courage under Fire*, p. 229.

21. Weigley, *Great Civil War*, p. 255; Griffith, *Battle Tactics*, p. 38; Scheibert, *Seven Months*, p. 118; Cozzens, ed., *B&L*, vol. 5, p. 372; S. W. Smith, ed., *Freeman on Leadership*, p. 72.

22. Dowdey and Manarin, eds., *Wartime Papers*, pp. 289–90.

23. OR, vol. 29, pt. 2, pp. 639, 640.

24. Cozzens, ed., *B&L*, vol. 5, pp. 366, 367.

25. Wert, *Sword*, pp. 310–22.

26. SHSP, vol. 4, p. 153; Gallagher, ed., *Wilderness Campaign*, pp. 42, 43.

27. Carmichael, ed., *Audacity*, pp. 11, 12; Nolan, *Lee Considered*, p. 101.

28. Stephens, ed., *Intrepid Warrior*, pp. 342–43; Gallagher, ed., *Wilderness Campaign*, p. 36, 44, 49, 50.

29. Gallagher, ed., *Fighting*, pp. 345, 346; Dickert, *History*, p. 340.

30. Gallagher, ed., *Fighting*, p. 346; Dickert, *History*, p. 341; A. B. Simms to Sister, May 4, 1864, Simms Family Papers, AHC.

31. Wert, *Sword*, pp. 326, 327, 329.

32. Ibid., pp. 333, 334–65, 366.

33. Freeman, *Lee's Lieutenants*, vol. 3, pp. 358, 359, 365, 510; Wert, *Cavalryman*, pp. 356–62.

34. Freeman, *Lee's Lieutenants*, vol. 3, pp. 557–68.

35. Weigley, *Great Civil War*, pp. 347, 348, 356–57, 363–67.

36. Wert, *Sword*, pp. 375–80; E. M. Thomas, *Robert E. Lee*, 339.

37. Wert, *Sword*, pp. 389–90.

38. Weigley, *Great Civil War*, pp. 386–96, 416–22.

39. Wert, *Sword*, pp. 400–405.

40. Wert, *General James Longstreet*, pp. 401, 402, 403.

41. Ibid., p. 404; Freeman, *Lee's Lieutenants*, vol. 3, p. 746–52.

42. Freeman, *Lee's Lieutenants*, vol. 3, p. 752; E. M. Thomas, *Robert E. Lee*, p. 367.

43. Maurice, *Robert E. Lee*, pp. 83–84; Harsh, *Confederate Tide Rising*, pp. 67–68.

44. Gallagher, *Confederate War*, pp. 85, 139, 140; Boritt, ed., *Why the Confederacy Lost*, p. 107.

45. Wert, *Gettysburg*, p. 43; Boritt, ed., *Why the Confederacy Lost*, p. 106.

46. S. W. Smith, ed., *Freeman on Leadership*, pp. 153, 155; A. Jones, *Civil War Command*, p. 228; Harsh, *Confederate Tide Rising*, pp. 68, 69.

47. Newspaper interview, Gettysburg Clipping Books, vol. 6, p. 82, GNMP; Wert, *Gettysburg*, p. 44; Hess, *Rifle Musket*, pp. 6, 208.

48. Harsh, *Confederate Tide Rising*, p. 68.

49. Weigley, *Great Civil War*, pp. 255, 256; Hess, *Rifle Musket*, p. 199; McWhiney and Jamieson, *Attack and Die*, p. 8; Gallagher, ed., *First Day at Gettysburg*, p. 7; Nolan, *Lee Considered*, p. 84; Gallagher, *Confederate War*, p. 137; Wert, *Sword*, pp. 123, 136, 153, 169, 204, 252.
50. Allardice, *Confederate Colonels*, p. 13, 15; Krick, *Lee's Colonels*, p. xiii.
51. Freeman, *Lee's Lieutenants*, vol. 3, p. 204.
52. *Confederate History Symposium*, p. 68; Weigley, *Great Civil War*, p. 256; Harsh, *Confederate Tide Rising*, p. 62.
53. A. Jones, *Civil War Command*, p. 228.
54. Nolan, *Lee Considered*, p. 71; Weigley, *Great Civil War*, p. 256.
55. Gallagher, *Confederate War*, p. 138; Weigley, *Great Civil War*, p. 256.
56. Cozzens, ed., *B&L*, vol. 5, p. 688; W. B. Robertson to Mattie, July 28, 1863, Daniel Papers, UVA; Pryor, *Reading the Man*, p. 359.
57. Sword, *Southern Invincibility*, p. 169.
58. Glatthaar, *General Lee's Army*, p. 257.

Bibliography

Unpublished Sources

ALABAMA DEPARTMENT OF ARCHIVES AND HISTORY, MONTGOMERY.

Sanders, William Henry. Papers.

ANTIETAM NATIONAL BATTLEFIELD, LIBRARY, SHARPSBURG, MD.

Andrews, William H. " 'Johnny Reb' at Antietam." Typescript. First Georgia Infantry File.

Carman, Ezra. Papers.

Douglas, Henry K. Personal library (marginal notes).

5th Virginia Infantry File.

Peebles, Dudley Thomas. Memoir.

Robbie. Member of the Stonewall Brigade. Letter. 33rd Virginia Infantry File.

Wardlaw, Andrew B. Letters and Diary. Typescript. 1st South Carolina Infantry File.

ATLANTA HISTORY CENTER, KENAN RESEARCH CENTER, ATLANTA, GA.

Simms Family Papers.

BROWN UNIVERSITY, JOHN HAY LIBRARY, PROVIDENCE, RI.

Hawkins, Rush. Statement of James Longstreet, March 16, 1870.

Inman, Arthur Crew. Papers.

CHICAGO HISTORY MUSEUM.

Longstreet, James. Papers.

COLLEGE OF WILLIAM AND MARY, EARL GREGG SWEM LIBRARY, WILLIAMSBURG, VA.

Johnston, Joseph E. Papers.

Southall, George Washington. Papers.

DUKE UNIVERSITY, RARE BOOK, MANUSCRIPT, AND SPECIAL
COLLECTIONS LIBRARY, DURHAM, NC.

Bedinger-Dandridge Family Papers.
Belcher, Granville W. Papers.
Click, Jacob B. Papers.
Cooke, John Esten. Papers.
Dickenson, George W. Papers.
Elliott, Thomas J. Papers.
Fletcher, Lucy Muse (Walton). Diary.
Holley, Turner W. Papers.
Holliday, Frederick W. M. Papers.
Jones, Charles E. Papers.
Magruder, John B. Papers.
Martin, Rawley White. Papers.
McLaws, Lafayette. Papers.
Munford-Ellis Family Papers.
Pickett, George Edward. Papers.
Porter, John Richardson. Papers.
Reynolds, Isaac V. Papers.
Robertson, John F. "Memoirs." *Confederate Veteran* Papers.
Wise, George N. Papers.

EMORY UNIVERSITY, SPECIAL COLLECTIONS AND ARCHIVES,
ROBERT W. WOODRUFF LIBRARY, ATLANTA, GA.

Bowden, John Malachi. "Some of My Experiences as a Confederate Soldier, in
the Camp and on the Battle Field, in the Army of Northern Virginia."
Typescript. Confederate Miscellany IIa.
Brooke, Noble John. Papers.
Dobbins, John S. Papers.
Fogle, Theodore T. Papers.
Longstreet, James. Papers.
Shuler, Spartan McCain. Letters.

FREDERICKSBURG-SPOTSYLVANIA NATIONAL MILITARY PARK,
LIBRARY, FREDERICKSBURG, VA.

Bass, Maston G. Letter, July 8, 1863.
Beard, James E. Diary.
Cooper, Calhoun L. Letters.
Grinnan, A. G. "General Lee's Movement against Pope, August 1862." Type-
script.
Hamilton, Matilda. Diary. Typescript.
McLaws, Lafayette. Letter. Typescript.
Montgomery, J. G. Letter.
"Reminiscences of Gettysburg by Unidentified Member of the 16th Georgia Vol-
unteers,"

2nd Virginia Infantry File.
Slifer, George W. Letters.
23rd Virginia Infantry File.
Weirman, B. B. Letters. Typescript.
Woods, Joseph White. "Reminiscences."

GEORGIA DEPARTMENT OF ARCHIVES AND HISTORY, ATLANTA.
Longstreet, James. Papers.

GEORGIA HISTORICAL SOCIETY, SAVANNAH.
Longstreet, James. Papers.

GETTYSBURG NATIONAL MILITARY PARK, LIBRARY, GETTYSBURG, PA.
18th Virginia Infantry File.
5th Alabama Battalion File.
Gerald, G. B. "The Battle of Gettysburg." Barksdale Brigade File.
Gettysburg Clipping Books.
McNeill, Alexander. Letters. Kershaw Brigade File.
Meyers, Alonzo. "Kershaw's Brigade at Peach Orchard." *National Tribune*, January 21, 1926. Kershaw's Brigade File.
9th Virginia Infantry File.
Participant accounts.
2nd South Carolina Infantry File.
Stillwell, William Ross. Diary. 53rd Georgia Infantry File.
37th Infantry File.
Wilcox, Cadmus M. File.

HANDLEY REGIONAL LIBRARY, ARCHIVES, WINCHESTER, VA.
Crawford, Louisa. Collection.

HARVARD UNIVERSITY, HOUGHTON LIBRARY, CAMBRIDGE, MA.
Dearborn, Frederick M. Collection.
Dearborn Collection of Confederate Civil War Papers.
Hamlin, Augustus C. Papers. Mollus Collection.

HENRY E. HUNTINGTON LIBRARY, SAN MARINO, CA.
Nicholson, John P. Papers.
Stuart, James Ewell Brown. Papers.

HISTORICAL SOCIETY OF PENNSYLVANIA, PHILADELPHIA.
Humphreys, Andrew A. Papers.
Longstreet, James. Papers.

INDIANA HISTORICAL SOCIETY, INDIANAPOLIS.
Beem, David E. Collection.

KRICK, ROBERT K., FREDERICKSBURG, VA, COPIES IN POSSESSION OF:

Carlisle, John W. Letter. Typescript.

Stuart, J. E. B. Letters.

LIBRARY OF CONGRESS, WASHINGTON, D.C.

Ewell, R. S. Papers.

Floyd-McAdoo Family Papers.

Hotchkiss, Jedediah. Papers.

Shuler, Michael. Diary.

Wigfall, Louis T. Papers.

Wilcox, Cadmus M. Papers.

LIBRARY OF VIRGINIA, RICHMOND.

Boulware, James Richmond. Fragment of diary of Doctor James Richmond Boulware, 6th South Carolina Volunteers, C. S. Army, 1862–1863. Typescript.

Denoon, Charles E. Papers.

Hill, Daniel H. Papers.

Sale, John F. Papers.

Taylor, Walter H. Papers.

Welsh, John P. Letters.

Winsmith, John Christopher. Letters.

LOUISIANA STATE UNIVERSITY, SPECIAL COLLECTIONS, HILL MEMORIAL LIBRARY, BATON ROUGE.

Batchelor, Albert A. Papers.

MANASSAS NATIONAL BATTLEFIELD PARK, LIBRARY, MANASSAS, VA.

Berkeley, Edmund. "War Reminiscences and Others of a Son of the Old Dominion." Typescript. 8th Virginia Infantry File.

Choice, William. "Memoirs." Typescript. 5th South Carolina Infantry File.

Clack, Spencer. Letters. 9th Alabama File.

Hendricks, J. F. Civil War account. Hampton, South Carolina, Legion File.

Jackson, J. W. 47th Alabama File.

Letter, September 14, 1862. Athens (GA) *Weekly Banner*, October 1, 1862. Phillips (GA) Legion File.

Lewis, Charles J. "Account of Second Manassas."

Longstreet, James. Letter regarding Second Manassas to Francis J. Lippitt. Typescript.

Position, Organization, Longstreet's Corps: Corse's Report of August 30.

Young, M. O. "History of the First Brigade—Antietam."

MISSISSIPPI DEPARTMENT OF ARCHIVES AND HISTORY, JACKSON.

Peel, William. Diary.

MUSEUM OF THE CONFEDERACY, ELEANOR S. BROCKENBROUGH LIBRARY, RICHMOND, VA.

Anderson, Richard H. Papers.

Armistead, Lewis A. Ledger.

Griggs, George K. Book.

Herndon, Thomas. "Reminiscences of the Civil War—1861–1865." Typescript.

Hill, Daniel H. Papers.

Longstreet, James. Papers.

Myers, Robert P. Diary.

Schenck Collection.

Smith, James Power. Correspondence.

NAVARRO COLLEGE, PEARCE CIVIL WAR COLLECTION, CORSICANA, TX.

Alexander, E. Porter. Papers.

Barkley, John B. Papers.

Buchanan, Samuel T. Papers.

Butner, Augustus. Papers.

Erskine, A. M. Papers.

Goulding, G. W. Papers.

Harris, Hilary Valentine. Papers.

Hill, Daniel Harvey. Papers.

Lee, T. E. Papers.

Longstreet, James. Papers.

Lyon, William D. Papers.

Mosby, John S. Papers.

Polley, Joseph Benjamin. Papers.

Wardlaw, James L. Papers.

Warrenton, M. Papers.

NATIONAL ARCHIVES, WASHINGTON, D.C.

Compiled Service Records. Records Group 109.

NEW-YORK HISTORICAL SOCIETY, GILDER LEHRMAN COLLECTION, NEW YORK.

Allison, William A. Letters.

Bud. Letter.

Hill, A. P. Letter.

Lee, Robert E. Papers.

Marshall, Charles. "Substance of a letter written to the President by Gen Lee on the 18th September, and not recorded."

Semmes, Paul Jones. Letter.

Stafford, Robert. Correspondence.

Tate, Jeremiah M. Letters.

NEW YORK PUBLIC LIBRARY, MANUSCRIPT AND ARCHIVES DIVISION, NEW YORK.

Law, E. M. Papers. *Century* Company Records.

NORTH CAROLINA DIVISION OF ARCHIVES AND HISTORY, RALEIGH.

Brown, Henry C. Papers.
Clifton, James Beverly. Collection.
Hefner, Marcus. Papers.
Ramseur, Stephen D. Papers.
Vance, Zebulon B. Correspondence.
Winston, Francis D. Papers.

PENNSYLVANIA STATE UNIVERSITY, HISTORICAL COLLECTIONS AND LABOR ARCHIVES, PATTEE-PATERNO LIBRARY, UNIVERSITY PARK, MARY DYLA MCDOWELL COLLECTION.

Leasure, Daniel. Letters.
Wiley, William Campbell. Papers.

PICERNO, NICHOLAS P., SR., COLLECTION, BRIDGEWATER, VA.

Nye, George H. Papers.

STATE HISTORICAL SOCIETY OF WISCONSIN, MADISON.

Dawes, Rufus R. Papers.
Haskell, Frank A. Letters. Typescript.
Young, Henry F. Papers.

TULANE UNIVERSITY, HOWARD-TILTON MEMORIAL LIBRARY, NEW ORLEANS.

Walton, J. B. Papers.

UNION PRESBYTERIAN SEMINARY, WILLIAM SMITH MORTON LIBRARY, RICHMOND, VA.

Dabney, R. L. Papers.

UNITED STATES ARMY MILITARY HISTORY INSTITUTE, CARLISLE BARRACKS, PA.

Brake, Robert L. Collection.
Civil War Miscellaneous Collection.
    Compton, Edward Howard. "Reminiscences of Edward Howard Compton: A Survivor of Second Battle of Manassas and the Battle of Gettysburg."
    Goggin, James M. Letter.
    McIntosh, David G. Papers.
    Miller Family Letters.
Civil War Times Illustrated Collection:
    Devin, Thomas C. Letter. Typescript.
    Hatchett Family Papers.

Heffelfinger, Jacob. Diary. Typescript.
Neff, John F. Papers.
Perkins, Charles E. Civil War letters. Typescript.
Dunlap, Ferdinand J. Letters.
Hill, Daniel Harvey. Collection.
Jay Luvaas Collection:
    Taggart, Robert. Diary. Typescript.
Lewis Leigh Collection:
    Blackford, Eugene. Letters.
    Carter, Samuel B. Letter.
    Crenshaw, R. F. Letter.
    Eager, Charles H. Letters.
    Hawks, Wells J. Letter.
    Hege, Constantine A. Letters.
    Letter to Mother from Camp, Bunker Hill, VA.
    Pearson, Henry H. Letter and Map.
    Powers, Philip. Letters.
    Robinson, Frank O. Letter.
    Semmes, Paul. Letters.
Mosby, John S. Papers.
Wiley Sword Collection:
    Thickstun Family Papers.
    Van Aernum, Henry. Papers.

UNIVERSITY OF ALABAMA, HOOLE LIBRARY, TUSCALOOSA.
Sanders, John C. Correspondence.

UNIVERSITY OF GEORGIA, SPECIAL COLLECTIONS, HARGRETT RARE BOOK AND MANUSCRIPT LIBRARY, ATHENS.
Deloney, William Gaston Family. Papers.
Duggan, Ivy. Papers.
Gordon Family Papers.

UNIVERSITY OF MICHIGAN, BENTLEY HISTORICAL LIBRARY, ANN ARBOR.
Noble, Alfred. "A 'G.I.' View of the Civil War: The Diary of Alfred Noble."
    Alfred Noble Papers.

UNIVERSITY OF NORTH CAROLINA, WILSON LIBRARY, SOUTHERN HISTORICAL COLLECTION, CHAPEL HILL.
Alexander, Edward Porter. Papers.
Allen-Simpson Papers.
Baker, William B. Papers.
Bartlett, J. C. Papers.
Benning, Henry L. Papers.

Campbell-Colston Family Papers.
Cheatham, Benjamin Franklin. Papers.
Cobb-Hunter Papers.
Coghill, J. F. Papers.
Colston, Raleigh E. Papers.
Grimes, Bryan. Papers.
Hoyle, Lemuel J. Papers.
James, Cadwallader J. Papers.
Kendrick, H. D. Papers.
Kennedy, Francis Milton. Diary. Typescript.
Lewis, Harry. Papers.
Long, Armistead L. Papers.
McIntosh, David Gregg. "A Ride on Horseback in the Summer of 1910 over
    Some of the Battlefields of the Great Civil War with Some Notes of the
    Battles."
McLaws, Lafayette. Papers.
Moore, Samuel J. C. Papers.
Moses, Raphael J. "Autobiography."
Pendleton, William N. Papers.
Pettit, William B. Papers.
Pfohl, Christian Thomas. Papers.
Polk, Leonidas Lafayette. Papers.
Price, R. Channing. Papers.
Ramseur, Stephen D. Papers.
Reeve, Edward Payson. Papers.
Royster Family Papers.
Saunders, Joseph. Papers.
Todd, Westwood A. Reminiscences.
Tucker, Glenn. Papers.
Venable, Charles Scott. Papers.
Waldrop, Richard Woolfolk. Papers.
Whittle, Lewis N. Papers.
Williams, James Peter. Papers.

UNIVERSITY OF SOUTH CAROLINA, SOUTH CAROLINIANA LIBRARY,
COLUMBIA.
Ballenger, David. Papers.
Conner, Henry Calvin. Papers.

UNIVERSITY OF VIRGINIA, SPECIAL COLLECTIONS, UNIVERSITY OF
VIRGINIA LIBRARY, CHARLOTTESVILLE.
Blackford Family Papers. No. 5088.
Blackford, W. W. Annotations. No. 5859.
Daniel, John Warwick. Papers. No. 158.

Gordon and Rosser Family Papers. No. 1171.

Hands, Washington. Memoir.

Heth-Selden Papers. No. 5071.

Janney-Pollock Family Papers. No. 5209.

Norris, Jefferson Davis. Papers. No. 2454.

Phelps, Charles R. Papers. No. 2920.

Pollock, Thomas Gordon. Papers. No. 8458.

Robinson, Leigh. Papers. No. 438.

Smiley, Thomas. Correspondence. No. 1807-A.

Venable, Charles Scott. "Personal Reminiscences of the Confederate War." McDowell Family Papers. No. 2969-A.

VIRGINIA HISTORICAL SOCIETY, RICHMOND.

Armistead and Blanton Family Papers.

Armstrong, Sally. Diary.

Bayol, J. H. and F. E. Bayol. Letters.

Bemiss Family Papers.

Carson, Robert P. Memoirs. Typescript.

Cocke Family Papers.

Coleman, Beverly Mosby. Papers.

Collins, John Overton. Papers.

Cooke Family Papers.

Daniel, John Warwick. Papers.

Dearing, James. Papers.

Dunn Family Papers.

Elder, Thomas C. Papers.

Fairfax, John Walter. Papers.

Farinholt, Benjamin Lyons. Papers.

Johnston, Samuel R. Papers.

Jones Family Papers.

Latrobe, Osmun. Diary, 1862–1865.

Lee Family Papers.

Lee, Robert E. Letterbook. June 7, 1863–October 12, 1864. Army of Northern Virginia, CSA.

Maury, Matthew F. Papers.

Maxwell, David Elwell. Papers.

McClellan, Henry B. Papers.

McGuire, Hunter Holmes. Papers.

McIntosh, David C. Papers.

Mooney, George McCulloch. Memoir.

Mosby, John Singleton. Papers.

Owen, Henry Thweatt. Papers.

Ridley Family Papers.

Shipp Family Papers.

Stuart, James Ewell Brown. Papers.
Talley, Henry M. Papers.
Watkins, Richard Henry. Papers.
Wight Family Papers.

VIRGINIA MILITARY INSTITUTE, ARCHIVES, PRESTON LIBRARY, LEXINGTON.

Bentley, William W. Letter.
Coleman, Clayton C. Papers.
Dedrick, Henry H. Civil War papers.
Fulkerson Family Papers.
Garibaldi, John. Letters. Typescript.

VIRGINIA TECH UNIVERSITY, SPECIAL COLLECTIONS, BLACKSBURG.

Baylor, William Smith Hanger. Correspondence.
Charlton Family Papers.

WASHINGTON AND LEE UNIVERSITY, SPECIAL COLLECTIONS, LEYBURN LIBRARY, LEXINGTON, VA.

Dix, Edward. Letters.
Lee, Robert E. Letter. January 25, 1866.
Lee, Robert E. Papers.
Lyle, John Newton. "Stonewall Jackson's Guard: The Washington College Company."
Welsh Family Papers.

WERT, JEFFRY D. COLLECTION, CENTRE HALL, PA.

WESTERN RESERVE HISTORICAL SOCIETY, CLEVELAND, OH.

Lee, Robert E. Papers.

Newspapers

Atlanta *Journal.*
Buffalo *Evening News.*
Charlotte (NC) *Western Democrat.*
Columbus (GA) *Daily Sun.*
Lexington (KY) *Gazette.*
London *Times.*
Loudoun *Times Mirror*
Macon (GA) *Telegraph.*
Mobile *Advertiser and Register.*
New York *Times.*
Philadelphia *Inquirer.*
Philadelphia *Press.*
Philadelphia *Weekly Press.*

Richmond *Dispatch*.

Richmond *Enquirer*.

Richmond *Southern Opinion*.

Richmond *Sentinel*.

Richmond *Times Dispatch*.

Savannah *Morning News*.

Savannah *Republican*.

Staunton *Vindicator*.

Toledo *Blade*.

Washington *Post*.

Published Books and Articles

Adams, Michael C. C. *Our Masters the Rebels: A Speculation on Union Military Failure in the East 1861–1865*. Cambridge, MA: Harvard University Press, 1978.

Alexander, E. P. *Military Memoirs of a Confederate*. Edited and with an introduction and notes by T. Harry Williams. Bloomington: Indiana University Press, 1962.

Allan, William. *The Army of Northern Virginia in 1862*. Reprint, Dayton, OH: Press of Morningside Bookshop, 1984.

Allardice, Bruce S. *Confederate Colonels: A Biographical Register*. Columbia: University of Missouri Press, 2008.

Allen, Randall, and Keith S. Bohannon, editors. *Campaigning with "Old Stonewall": Confederate Captain Ujanirtus Allen's Letters to His Wife*. Baton Rouge: Louisiana State University Press, 1998.

Andrews, Marietta Minnigerode, editor. *Scraps of Paper*. New York: E. P. Dutton, 1929.

Andrews, W. H. *Footprints of a Regiment: A Recollection of the 1st Georgia Regulars—1881–1865*. Atlanta, GA: Longstreet Press, 1992.

The Annals of the War Written by Leading Participants North and South. Reprint, Dayton, OH: Morningside House, 1988.

Bandy, Ken, and Florence Freeland, editors. *The Gettysburg Papers*. 2 volumes. Dayton, OH: Press of Morningside Bookshop, 1978.

Bean, W. G. *Stonewall's Man: Sandie Pendleton*. Reprint, Wilmington, NC: Broadfoot Publishing, 1987.

Bee, Robert L., editor. *The Boys from Rockville: Civil War Narratives of Sgt. Benjamin Hirst, Company D, 14th Connecticut Volunteers*. Knoxville: University of Tennessee Press, 1998.

Bigelow, John, Jr. *The Campaign of Chancellorsville: A Strategic and Tactical Study*. Reprint, Dayton, OH: Morningside House, 1985.

Blackford, Susan Leigh, editor. *Letters from Lee's Army, or Memoirs of Life in and out of the Army in Virginia During the War between the States*. New York: Charles Scribner's Sons, 1947.

Blackford, W. W. *War Years with Jeb Stuart*. New York: Charles Scribner's Sons, 1945.

Bond, Natalie Jenkins, and Osmun Latrobe Coward, editors. *The South Carolinians: Colonel Asbury Coward's Memoirs*. New York: Vantage Press, 1968.

Boritt, Gabor S., editor. *Why the Confederacy Lost*. New York: Oxford University Press, 1992.

Boyd, David French. *Reminiscences of the War in Virginia*. Edited by T. Michael Parrish. Austin, TX: Jenkins Publishing, 1989.

Bridges, Hal. *Lee's Maverick General: Daniel Harvey Hill*. New York: McGraw-Hill, 1961.

Brown, Phillip F. *Reminiscences of the War of 1861–1865*. Richmond, VA: Whittet & Shepperson, 1917.

Buck, Samuel D. *With the Old Confeds: Actual Experiences of a Captain in the Line*. Reprint, Staunton, VA: Lot's Wife Publishing, 2007.

Burton, Brian K. *Extraordinary Circumstances: The Seven Days Battles*. Bloomington: Indiana University Press, 2001.

Busey, John W., and David G. Martin. *Regimental Strengths and Losses at Gettysburg*. 4th edition. Hightstown, NJ: Longstreet House, 2005.

Caldwell, J. F. J. *The History of a Brigade of South Carolinians, Known First as "Gregg's," and Subsequently as "McGowan's Brigade."* Reprint, Marietta, GA: Continental, 1951.

Carmichael, Peter S., editor. *Audacity Personified: The Generalship of Robert E. Lee*. Baton Rouge: Louisiana State University Press, 2004.

———. *Lee's Young Artillerist: William R. J. Pegram*. Charlottesville: University Press of Virginia, 1995.

Casler, John O. *Four Years in the Stonewall Brigade*. Reprint, Dayton, OH: Press of Morningside Bookshop, 1971.

Chamberlayne, C. G., editor. *Ham Chamberlayne—Virginian: Letters and Papers of an Artillery Officer in the War for Southern Independence 1861–1865*. Richmond, VA: Dietz, 1932.

Chesnut, Mary Boykin. *A Diary from Dixie*. Edited by Ben Ames Williams. Boston: Houghton Mifflin, 1949.

Clark, Walter, editor. *Histories of the Several Regiments and Battalions from North Carolina in the Great War, 1861–'65*. 5 volumes. Reprint, Wendell, NC: Broadfoot's Bookmark, 1982.

Clary, James B. *A History of the 15th South Carolina Volunteer Infantry Regiment: 1861–1865*. Wilmington, NC: Broadfoot Publishing, 2009.

Coddington, Edwin B. *The Gettysburg Campaign: A Study in Command*. New York: Charles Scribner's Sons, 1968.

Coffman, Richard M., and Kurt D. Graham. *To Honor These Men: A History of the Phillips Georgia Legion Infantry Battalion*. Macon, GA: Mercer University Press, 2007.

Collins, George K. *Memoirs of the 149th Regt. N.Y. Vol. Inf. 3rd Brigade, 2d Div., 12th and 20th A.C.* Reprint, Hamilton, NY: Edmonston Publishing, 1995.

Colt, Margaretta Barton. *Defend the Valley: A Shenandoah Family in the Civil War.* New York: Orion Books, 1994.

Confederate History Symposium, 1984. Hillsboro, TX: Hill Junior College, 1984.

Confederate Veteran Magazine. 40 volumes. Reprint, Wilmington, NC: Broadfoot Publishing, 1987–1988.

Connelly, Thomas Lawrence. *The Marble Man: Robert E. Lee and His Image in American Society.* New York: Knopf, 1977.

Cooling, Benjamin Franklin. *Counter-Thrust: From the Peninsula to the Antietam.* Lincoln: University of Nebraska Press, 2007.

Cormier, Steven A. *The Siege of Suffolk: The Forgotten Campaign, April 11–May 4, 1863.* Lynchburg, VA: H. E. Howard, 1989.

Cowper, Pulaski. *Extracts of Letters of Major-General Bryan Grimes to His Wife.* Edited by Gary W. Gallagher. Wilmington, NC: Broadfoot Publishing, 1986.

Cozzens, Peter, editor. *Battles and Leaders of the Civil War.* Volumes 5 and 6. Urbana: University of Illinois Press, 2002–2004.

———. *Shenandoah 1862: Stonewall Jackson's Valley Campaign.* Chapel Hill: University of North Carolina Press, 2008.

Cozzens, Peter, and Robert I. Girardi, editors. *The New Annals of the Civil War.* Mechanicsburg, PA: Stackpole Books, 2004.

Cutrer, Thomas W., editor. *Longstreet's Aide: The Civil War Letters of Major Thomas J. Goree.* Charlottesville: University Press of Virginia, 1995.

Dabney, R. L. *Life and Campaigns of Lieut.-Gen. Thomas J. Jackson (Stonewall Jackson).* Reprint, Harrisonburg, VA: Sprinkle Publications, 1977.

Dameron, J. David. *General Henry Lewis Benning, "This Was a Man": A Biography of Georgia's Supreme Court Justice and Confederate General.* Westminster, MD: Heritage Books, 2008.

Davis, Sam B. *A History of the 3rd South Carolina Infantry Battalion (James Battalion): 1861–1865.* Wilmington, NC: Broadfoot Publishing, 2009.

Davis, William C., editor. *The Confederate General.* 6 volumes. Gettysburg, PA: National Historical Society, 1991.

de Trobriand, Regis. *Four Years with the Army of the Potomac.* Reprint, Gaithersburg, MD: Ron R. Van Sickle Military Books, 1988.

Dickert, D. Augustus. *History of Kershaw's Brigade.* Reprint, Dayton, OH: Morningside Bookshop, 1973.

Dinkins, James. *1861–1865 by an Old Johnnie: Personal Recollections and Experiences in the Confederate Army.* Reprint, Dayton, OH: Press of Morningside Bookshop, 1975.

Douglas, Henry Kyd. *I Rode with Stonewall.* Chapel Hill: University of North Carolina Press, 1940.

Dowdey, Clifford, and Louis H. Manarin, editors. *The Wartime Papers of R. E. Lee.* Boston: Little, Brown, 1961.

Driver, Robert J., Jr. *52nd Virginia Infantry.* Lynchburg, VA: H. E. Howard, 1986.

Driver, Robert J., Jr., and H. E. Howard. *2nd Virginia Cavalry.* Lynchburg, VA: H. E. Howard, 1995.

Durkin, Joseph T., editor. *Confederate Chaplain: A War Journal of Rev. James B. Sheeran, c.ss.r 14th Louisiana, C.S.A.* Milwaukee: Bruce Publishing, 1960.

———, editor. *John Dooley Confederate Soldier: His War Journal.* Washington, D.C.: Georgetown University Press, 1945.

Dyer, John P. *The Gallant Hood.* Indianapolis: Bobbs-Merrill, 1950.

Early, Jubal A. *Lieutenant General Jubal Anderson Early C.S.A.: Autobiographical Sketch and Narrative of the War between the States.* With Notes by R. H. Early. Reprint, Wilmington, NC: Broadfoot Publishing, 1989.

Eckert, Edward K., and Nicholas J. Amato, editors. *Ten Years in the Saddle: The Memoir of William Woods Averell.* San Rafael, CA: Presidio, 1978.

Eggleston, George Gary. *A Rebel's Recollections.* Reprint, Bloomington: Indiana University Press, 1959.

An English Combatant. *Battle-Fields of the South, from Bull Run to Fredericksburg.* Reprint, Alexandria, VA: Time-Life Books, 1984.

Ernsberger, Don. *Also for Glory Muster: The Story of the Pettigrew Trimble Charge at Gettysburg.* N.p.: Xlibris, 2008.

Everett, Donald E., editor. *Chaplain Davis and Hood's Texas Brigade.* San Antonio, TX: Principia Press of Trinity University, 1962.

Fields, Frank E., Jr. *28th Virginia Infantry.* Lynchburg, VA: H. E. Howard, 1985.

Fitzgerald, O. P. *Judge Longstreet: A Life Sketch.* Nashville, TN: Methodist Episcopal Church, South, 1891.

Fleming, Francis P., editor. *Memoir of Capt. C. Seton Fleming, of the Second Florida Infantry, C.S.A.* Reprint, Alexandria, VA: Stonewall House, 1985.

Fletcher, William Andrew. *Rebel Private Front and Rear.* Reprint, Washington, D.C.: Zenger Publishing, 1985.

Fox, John J., III. *Red Clay to Richmond: Trail of the 35th Georgia Infantry Regiment, C.S.A.* Winchester, VA: Angle Valley Press, 2004.

Freeman, Douglas Southall, editor. *Lee's Dispatches: Unpublished Letters of General Robert E. Lee, C.S.A., to Jefferson Davis and the War Department of the Confederate States of America, 1862–1865.* With additional dispatches and foreword by Grady McWhiney. New York: G. P. Putnam's Sons, 1957.

———. *Lee's Lieutenants: A Study in Command.* 3 volumes. New York: Charles Scribner's Sons, 1942–1944.

———. *R. E. Lee: A Biography.* 4 volumes. New York: Charles Scribner's Sons, 1934–1935.

Furgurson, Ernest B. *Ashes of Glory: Richmond at War.* New York: Knopf, 1996.

Gallagher, Gary W., editor. *Antietam: Essays on the 1862 Maryland Campaign.* Kent, OH: Kent State University Press, 1989.

———, editor. *Chancellorsville: The Battle and Its Aftermath.* Chapel Hill: University of North Carolina Press, 1996.

———. *The Confederate War.* Cambridge, MA: Harvard University Press, 1997.

———, editor. *Extracts of Letters of Major-General Bryan Grimes, to His Wife.* Reprint, Wilmington, NC: Broadfoot Publishing, 1986.

————, editor. *Fighting for the Confederacy: The Personal Recollections of General Edward Porter Alexander.* Chapel Hill: University of North Carolina Press, 1989.

————, editor. *The First Day at Gettysburg: Essays on Confederate and Union Leadership.* Kent, OH: Kent State University Press, 1992.

————, editor. *The Fredericksburg Campaign: Decision on the Rappahannock.* Chapel Hill: University of North Carolina Press, 1995.

————. *Lee and His Army in Confederate History.* Chapel Hill: University of North Carolina Press, 2001.

————, editor. *Lee: The Soldier.* Lincoln: University of Nebraska Press, 1996.

————, editor. *The Richmond Campaign: The Peninsula and the Seven Days.* Chapel Hill: University of North Carolina Press, 2000.

————, editor. *The Second Day at Gettysburg: Essays on Confederate and Union Leadership.* Kent, OH: Kent State University Press, 1993.

————, editor. *The Third Day at Gettysburg and Beyond.* Chapel Hill: University of North Carolina Press, 1994.

————, editor. *The Wilderness Campaign.* Chapel Hill: University of North Carolina Press, 1997.

Gallagher, Gary W., and Joseph T. Glatthaar, editors. *Leaders of the Lost Cause: New Perspectives on the Confederate High Command.* Mechanicsburg, PA: Stackpole Books, 2004.

Glatthaar, Joseph T. *General Lee's Army: From Victory to Collapse.* New York: Free Press, 2008.

Gordon, John B. *Reminiscences of the Civil War.* Reprint, Gettysburg, PA: Civil War Times Illustrated, 1974.

Goree, Langston James, V., editor. *The Thomas Jewitt Goree Letters,* Volume 1: *The Civil War Correspondence.* Bryan, TX: Family History Foundation, 1981.

Gott, John K. *High in Old Virginia Piedmont: A History of Marshall (Formerly Salem), Fauquier County, Virginia.* Marshall, VA: Marshall National Bank & Trust Company, 1987.

Gottfried, Bradley M. *Brigades of Gettysburg: The Union and Confederate Brigades at the Battle of Gettysburg.* Cambridge, MA: Da Capo Press, 2002.

Gramm, Kent, editor. *Battle: The Nature and Consequences of Civil War Combat.* Tuscaloosa: University of Alabama Press, 2008.

Greene, A. Wilson. *Whatever You Resolve to Be: Essays on Stonewall Jackson.* Baltimore: Butternut & Blue, 1992.

Griffith, Paddy. *Battle Tactics of the Civil War.* New Haven: Yale University Press, 1989.

Haines, William P. *History of the Men of Co. F, with Description of the Marches and Battles of the 12th New Jersey Vols.* Camden, NJ: C. S. Magrath, 1897.

Hamlin, Augustus Choate. *The Battle of Chancellorsville.* Bangor, ME: Published by the author, 1896.

Harsh, Joseph L. *Confederate Tide Rising: Robert E. Lee and the Making of Southern Strategy, 1861–1862.* Kent, OH: Kent State University Press, 1998.

———. *Sounding the Shadows: A Confederate Companion for the Maryland Campaign of 1862.* Kent, OH: Kent State University Press, 2000.

———. *Taken at the Flood: Robert E. Lee and Confederate Strategy in the Maryland Campaign of 1862.* Kent, OH: Kent State University Press, 1999.

Haskell, John Cheves. *The Haskell Memoirs.* Edited by Gilbert E. Govan and James W. Livingood. New York: G. P. Putnam's Sons, 1960.

Hassler, William W., editor. *The General to His Lady: The Civil War Letters of William Dorsey Pender to Fanny Pender.* Chapel Hill: University of North Carolina Press, 1965.

Hattaway, Herman, and Archer Jones. *How the North Won: A Military History of the Civil War.* Urbana: University of Illinois Press, 1983.

Hennessy, John. *Historical Report on the Troop Movements for the Second Battle of Manassas, August 28 through August 30, 1862.* Denver, CO: National Park Service, 1985.

———. *Return to Bull Run: The Campaign and Battle of Second Manassas.* New York: Simon & Schuster, 1993.

Hess, Earl J. *Field Armies and Fortifications in the Civil War: The Eastern Campaigns, 1861–1864.* Chapel Hill: University of North Carolina Press, 2005.

———. *Lee's Tar Heels: The Pettigrew-Kirkland-MacRae Brigade.* Chapel Hill: University of North Carolina Press, 2002.

———. *The Rifle Musket in Civil War Combat: Reality and Myth.* Lawrence: University Press of Kansas, 2008.

Hood, John B. *Advance and Retreat: Personal Experiences in the United States and Confederate States' Armies.* Edited by Richard N. Current. Bloomington: Indiana University Press, 1959.

Hopkins, C. A. Porter, editor. "The James J. Archer Letters: A Marylander in the Civil War, Part I." *Maryland Historical Magazine,* June 1961.

Hotchkiss, Jedediah, editor. *Confederate Military History.* Volume 3. Reprint, Dayton, OH: Press of Morningside Bookshop, 1975.

Houghton, W. R., and M. B. Houghton. *Two Boys in the Civil War and After.* Montgomery, AL: Paragon Press, 1912.

Hubbell, Jay B., editor. "The War Diary of John Esten Cooke." *Journal of Southern History* 7, no. 4 (1941).

Hubbs, G. Ward, editor. *Voices from Company D: Diaries by the Greensboro Guards, Fifth Alabama Infantry Regiment, Army of Northern Virginia.* Athens: University of Georgia Press, 2003.

Humphreys, Anderson. *Semmes America.* Memphis, TN: Humphreys Ink, 1989.

Hunton, Eppa. *Autobiography of Eppa Hunton, 1822–1908.* Richmond, VA: William Byrd Press, 1933.

Jackson, Mary Anna. *Memoirs of Stonewall Jackson.* Reprint, Dayton, OH: Press of Morningside Bookshop, 1976.

Jensen, Les. *32nd Virginia Infantry.* Lynchburg, VA: H. E. Howard, 1990.

Johnson, Curt, and Richard C. Anderson Jr. *Artillery Hell: The Employment of Artillery at Antietam.* College Station: Texas A.&M. University Press, 1995.

Johnson, Robert Underwood, and Clarence Clough Buel, editors. *Battles and Leaders of the Civil War*. 4 volumes. Reprint, New York: Thomas Yoseloff, 1956.

Joinville, Prince de. *The Army of the Potomac: Its Organization, Its Commander, and Its Campaign*. New York: Anson D. F. Randolph, 1862.

Jones, Archer. *Civil War Command and Strategy: The Process of Victory and Defeat*. New York: Free Press, 1992.

Jones, J. B. *A Rebel War Clerk's Diary at the Confederate States Capital*. 2 volumes. Reprint, New York: Time-Life Books, 1982.

Jones, Terry L., editor. *Campbell Brown's Civil War: With Ewell and the Army of Northern Virginia*. Baton Rouge: Louisiana State University Press, 2001.

———. *Lee's Tigers: The Louisiana Infantry in the Army of Northern Virginia*. Baton Rouge: Louisiana State University Press, 1987.

Keller, S. Roger. *Crossroads of War: Washington County, Maryland in the Civil War*. Shippensburg, PA: Burd Street Press, 1997.

Krick, Robert E. L. *40th Virginia Infantry*. Lynchburg, VA: H. E. Howard, 1985.

Krick, Robert K. *The 14th South Carolina Infantry Regiment, of the Gregg-McGowan Brigade, Army of Northern Virginia*. Wilmington, NC: Broadfoot Publishing, 2008.

———. *Lee's Colonels: A Biographical Register of the Field Officers of the Army of Northern Virginia*. Dayton, OH: Press of Morningside Bookshop, 1979.

———. *Lee's Colonels: A Biographical Register of the Field Officers of the Army of Northern Virginia*. 5th edition. Wilmington, NC: Broadfoot Publishing, 2009.

———. *Parker's Virginia Battery, C.S.A.* Wilmington, NC: Broadfoot Publishing, 1989.

———. *The Smoothbore Volley That Doomed the Confederacy: The Death of Stonewall Jackson and Other Chapters on the Army of Northern Virginia*. Baton Rouge: Louisiana State University Press, 2002.

———. *Stonewall Jackson at Cedar Mountain*. Chapel Hill: University of North Carolina Press, 1990.

Lasswell, Mary, editor. *Rags and Hope: The Recollections of Val. C. Giles, Four Years with Hood's Brigade, Fourth Texas Infantry 1861–1865*. New York: Coward-McCann, 1961.

Lee, Robert E. *Recollections and Letters of General Robert E. Lee*. Garden City, NY: Garden City Publishing, 1924.

Levin, Alexandra Lee. *"This Awful Drama": General Edwin Gray Lee, C.S.A., and His Family*. New York: Vantage Press, 1987.

Lewis, John H. *Recollections from 1860 to 1865*. Washington, D.C.: Peake and Company, 1895.

Livermore, Thomas L. *Numbers and Losses in the Civil War In America, 1861–1865*. Reprint, Dayton, OH: Morningside House, 1986.

Loehr, Charles T. *War History of the Old First Virginia Infantry Regiment, Army of Northern Virginia*. Reprint, Dayton, OH: Morningside Bookshop, 1970.

Long, A. L. *Memoirs of Robert E. Lee*. New York: J. M. Stoddart, 1887.

Longacre, Edward G. *Lee's Cavalrymen: A History of the Mounted Forces of the Army of Northern Virginia*. Mechanicsburg, PA: Stackpole Books, 2002.

Longstreet, Helen D. *Lee and Longstreet at High Tide: Gettysburg in the Light of the Official Records*. Reprint, Wilmington, NC: Broadfoot Publishing, 1989.

Longstreet, James. *From Manassas to Appomattox: Memoirs of the Civil War in America*. Edited by James I. Robertson Jr. Bloomington: Indiana University Press, 1960.

Lord, Walter, editor. *The Fremantle Diary*. Boston: Little, Brown, 1954.

Lowe, Jeffrey C., and Sam Hodges, editors. *Letters to Amanda: The Civil War Letters of Marion Hill Fitzpatrick, Army of Northern Virginia*. Macon, GA: Mercer University Press, 1998.

Mast, Greg. *State Troops and Volunteers: A Photographic Record of North Carolina's Civil War Soldiers*. Volume 1. Raleigh: North Carolina Department of Cultural Resources, Division of Archives and History, 1995.

Maurice, Frederick, editor. *An Aide-de-Camp of Lee: Being the Papers of Colonel Charles Marshall Sometime Aide-de-Camp, Military Secretary and Assistant Adjutant General on the Staff of Robert E. Lee, 1862–1865*. Boston: Little, Brown, 1927.

———. *Robert E. Lee the Soldier*. Boston: Houghton Mifflin, 1926.

McCarthy, Carlton. *Detailed Minutiae of Soldier Life in the Army of Northern Virginia 1861–1865*. Reprint, Alexandria, VA: Time-Life Books, 1982.

McClellan, H. B. *I Rode with Jeb Stuart: The Life and Campaigns of Major General J. E. B. Stuart*. Introduction and notes by Burke Davis. Bloomington: Indiana University Press, 1958.

McDonald, Archie P., editor. *Make Me a Map of the Valley: The Civil War Journal of Stonewall Jackson's Topographer*. Dallas: Southern Methodist University Press, 1973.

McGrath, Thomas A. *Shepherdstown: Last Clash of the Antietam Campaign, September 19–20, 1862*. Lynchburg, VA: Schroeder Publications, 2007.

McKim, Randolph H. *A Soldier's Recollections: Leaves from the Diary of a Young Confederate*. Reprint, Alexandria, VA: Time-Life Books, 1984.

McMullen, Glenn, editor. *A Surgeon with Stonewall Jackson: The Civil War Letters of Dr. Harvey Black*. Baltimore: Butternut and Blue, 1995.

McMurry, Richard M. *Two Great Rebel Armies: An Essay in Confederate Military History*. Chapel Hill: University of North Carolina Press, 1989.

———. *Virginia Military Institute Alumni in the Civil War*. Lynchburg, VA: H. E. Howard, 1999.

McPherson, James M. *Crossroads of Freedom: Antietam*. Oxford: Oxford University Press, 2002.

———. *For Cause and Comrades: Why Men Fought in the Civil War*. New York: Oxford University Press, 1997.

McWhiney, Grady, and Perry D. Jamieson. *Attack and Die: Civil War Military Tactics and the Southern Heritage*. Tuscaloosa: University of Alabama Press, 1982.

Mewborn, Horace, editor. *"From Mosby's Command": Newspaper Letters and Articles by and about John S. Mosby and His Rangers.* Baltimore: Butternut & Blue, 2005.

Montgomery, Horace. *Howell Cobb's Confederate Career.* Tuscaloosa, AL: Confederate Publishing, 1959.

Montgomery, Walter A. *Life and Character of Major-General W. D. Pender.* Raleigh, NC: Edwards & Broughton, 1894.

Moore, Robert A. *A Life for the Confederacy.* Edited by James W. Silver. Reprint, Wilmington, NC: Broadfoot Publishing, 1987.

Morrison, James L., Jr., editor. *The Memoirs of Henry Heth.* Westport, CT: Greenwood Press, 1974.

Moseley, Ronald H., editor. *The Stilwell Letters: A Georgian in Longstreet's Corps, Army of Northern Virginia.* Macon, GA: Mercer University Press, 2002.

Murfin, James V. *The Gleam of Bayonets: The Battle of Antietam and the Maryland Campaign of 1862.* New York: Thomas Yoseloff, 1968.

Murray, Elizabeth Dunbar. *My Mother Used to Say: A Natchez Belle of the Sixties.* Boston: Christopher Publishing, 1959.

Musselman, Homer D. *47th Virginia Infantry.* Lynchburg, VA: H. E. Howard, 1991.

Nanzig, Thomas P., editor. *The Civil War Memoirs of a Virginia Cavalryman: Lt. Robert E. Hubard, Jr.* Tuscaloosa: University of Alabama Press, 2007.

Neese, George M. *Three Years in the Confederate Horse Artillery.* Reprint, Dayton, OH: Press of Morningside Bookshop, 1983.

Nichols, G. W. *A Soldier's Story of His Regiment (61st Georgia).* Reprint, Kennesaw, GA: Continental, 1961.

Nisbet, James Cooper. *Four Years on the Firing Line.* Edited by Bell Irvin Wiley. Reprint, Jackson, TN: McCowat-Mercer Press, 1963.

Nolan, Alan T. *Lee Considered: General Robert E. Lee and Civil War History.* Chapel Hill: University of North Carolina Press, 1991.

Norman, William M. *A Portion of My Life.* Winston-Salem, NC: John F. Blair, 1959.

Oates, William C. *The War between the Union and the Confederacy and Its Lost Opportunities.* Reprint, Dayton, OH: Press of Morningside Bookshop, 1985.

Oeffinger, John C., editor. *A Soldier's General: The Civil War Letters of Major General Lafayette McLaws.* Chapel Hill: University of North Carolina Press, 2002.

O'Reilly, Francis Augustin. *The Fredericksburg Campaign: Winter War on the Rappahannock.* Baton Rouge: Louisiana State University Press, 2003.

O'Sullivan, Richard. *55th Virginia Infantry.* Lynchburg, VA: H. E. Howard, 1989.

Owen, William Miller. *In Camp and Battle with the Washington Artillery of New Orleans.* Reprint, Gaithersburg, MD: Butternut Press, n.d.

Parrish, James W. *Wiregrass to Appomattox: The Untold Story of the 50th Georgia Infantry Regiment, C.S.A.* Winchester, VA: Angle Valley Press, 2009.

Patterson, Gerard. *Rebels from West Point.* New York: Doubleday, 1987.

Paxton, John Gallatin, editor. *The Civil War Letters of General Frank "Bull" Pax-*

ton, CSA. *A Lieutenant of Lee and Jackson*. Hillsboro, TX: Hill Junior College Press, 1978.

Pearce, T. H., editor. *Diary of Captain Henry A. Chambers*. Wendell, NC: Broadfoot's Bookmark, 1983.

Pfanz, Donald C. *Richard S. Ewell: A Soldier's Life*. Chapel Hill: University of North Carolina Press, 1998.

Pfanz, Harry W. *Gettysburg: The Second Day*. Chapel Hill: University of North Carolina Press, 1987.

Phillips, Jason. *Diehard Rebels: The Confederate Culture of Invincibility*. Athens: University of Georgia Press, 2007.

Pierro, Joseph, editor. *The Maryland Campaign of September 1862: Ezra A. Carman's Definitive Study of the Union and Confederate Armies at Antietam*. New York: Routledge, 2008.

Piston, William Garrett. "Lee's Tarnished Lieutenant: James Longstreet and His Image in American History." PhD dissertation, University of South Carolina, 1982.

Polley, J. B. *Hood's Texas Brigade: Its Marches, Its Battles, Its Achievements*. Reprint, Dayton, OH: Press of Morningside Bookshop, 1988.

———. *A Soldier's Letters to Charming Nellie*. Reprint, Gaithersburg, MD: Butternut Press, 1984.

Powell, Robert M. *Recollections of a Texas Colonel at Gettysburg*. Edited by Gregory A. Coco. Gettysburg, PA: Thomas Publications, 1990.

Priest, John M. *Antietam: The Soldiers' Battle*. Shippensburg, PA: White Mane Publishing, 1989.

Pryor, Elizabeth Brown. *Reading the Man: A Portrait of Robert E. Lee through His Private Letters*. New York: Viking, 2007.

Quaife, Milo M., editor. *From the Cannon's Mouth: The Civil War Letters of General Alpheus S. Williams*. Detroit: Wayne State University Press and Detroit Historical Society, 1959.

Raab, Steven S., editor. *With the 3rd Wisconsin Badgers: The Living Experience of the Civil War through the Journals of Van R. Willard*. Mechanicsburg, PA: Stackpole Books, 1999.

Rable, George C. *Fredericksburg! Fredericksburg!* Chapel Hill: University of North Carolina Press, 2002.

Rafuse, Ethan S. *Robert E. Lee and the Fall of the Confederacy, 1863–1864*. Lanham, MD: Rowman & Littlefield, 2008.

Ratchford, J. W. *Some Reminiscences of Persons and Incidents of the Civil War*. Reprint, Austin, TX: Shoal Creek Publishers, 1971.

Raymer, Jacob Nathaniel. *Confederate Correspondent: The Civil War Reports of Jacob Nathaniel Raymer, Fourth North Carolina*. Edited by E. B. Munson. Jefferson, NC: McFarland, 2009.

Reid, J. W. *History of the Fourth Regiment of S.C. Volunteers, from the Commencement of the War until Lee's Surrender*. Reprint, Dayton, OH: Press of Morningside Bookshop, 1975.

Reidenbaugh, Lowell. *33rd Virginia Infantry*. Lynchburg, VA: H. E. Howard, 1987.

———. *27th Virginia Infantry*. Lynchburg, VA: H. E. Howard, 1993.

Robertson, James I., Jr. *General A. P. Hill: The Story of a Confederate Warrior*. New York: Random House, 1987.

———. *Stonewall Jackson: The Man, The Soldier, The Legend*. New York: Macmillan, 1997.

Robson, John S. *How a One-legged Rebel Lives: Reminiscences of the Civil War*. Reprint, Gaithersburg, MD: Butternut Press, 1984.

Roland, Charles P. "Lee's Invasion Strategy." *North & South* 1, no. 6 (1998).

———. *Reflections on Lee: A Historian's Assessment*. Mechanicsburg, PA: Stackpole Books, 1995.

Roper, John Herbert. *Repairing the "March of Mars": The Civil War Diaries of John Samuel Apperson, Hospital Steward in the Stonewall Brigade, 1861–1862*. Macon, GA: Mercer University Press, 2001.

Ross, Fitzgerald. *Cities and Camps of the Confederate States*. Edited by Richard Barksdale Harwell. Urbana: University of Illinois Press, 1958.

Rozier, John, editor. *The Granite Farm Letters: The Civil War Correspondence of Edgeworth and Sallie Bird*. Athens: University of Georgia Press, 1988.

Runge, William H., editor. *Four Years in the Confederate Artillery: The Diary of Private Henry Robinson Berkeley*. Chapel Hill: University of North Carolina Press, 1961.

Sanger, Donald Bridgmen. "Was Longstreet a Scapegoat?" *Infantry Journal* 43 (January–February 1936).

Sawyer, Merrill C., Betty Sawyer, and Timothy C. Sawyer, editors. *Letters from a Civil War Surgeon: The Letters of Dr. William Child of the Fifth New Hampshire Volunteers*. Solon, ME: Polar Bear, 2001.

Scheibert, Justus. *Seven Months in the Rebel Army During the North American War, 1863*. Edited by William Stanley Hoole. Tuscaloosa, AL: Confederate Publishing, 1958.

Schenck, Martin. *Up Came Hill: The Story of the Light Division and Its Leaders*. Harrisburg, PA: Stackpole, 1958.

Schipke, Norman Carrington. *We Can Hear the Yankee Drums Beating: Sim Carrington and the Bloody 6th North Carolina*. N.p., 2001.

Scott, W. W. *A History of Orange County, Virginia*. Reprint, Berryville, VA: Chesapeake, 1962.

Sears, Stephen W. "America's Bloodiest Day: The Battle of Antietam." *Civil War Times Illustrated* 26, no. 2 (1987).

———. *Chancellorsville*. Boston: Houghton Mifflin, 1996.

———. *Gettysburg*. Boston: Houghton Mifflin, 2002.

———. *Landscape Turned Red: The Battle of Antietam*. New York: Ticknor & Fields, 1983.

———. "Lee's Lost Opportunity: The Battle of Glendale." *North & South* 5, no. 1 (2001).

————, editor. On Campaign with the Army of the Potomac. New York: Cooper Square Press, 2001.

————. To the Gates of Richmond: The Peninsula Campaign. New York: Ticknor & Fields, 1992.

Sheehan-Dean, Aaron. Why Confederates Fought: Family and Nation in Civil War Virginia. Chapel Hill: University of North Carolina Press, 2007.

Simpson, Harold B. Hood's Texas Brigade: Lee's Grenadier Guard. Reprint, Gaithersburg, MD: Olde Soldier Books, 1994.

Sloan, John A. Reminiscences of the Guilford Grays, Co. B, 27th N.C. Regiment. Reprint, Wilmington, NC: Broadfoot Publishing, 1999.

Small, Harold A., editor. The Road to Richmond: The Civil War Memoirs of Major Abner R. Small of the Sixteenth Maine Volunteers. Together with the Diary Which He Kept When He Was a Prisoner of War. New York: Fordham University Press, 2000.

Smith, James Power. With Stonewall Jackson in the Army of Northern Virginia. Reprint, Gaithersburg, MD: Zullo & Van Sickle, 1982.

Smith, Stuart W., editor. Douglas Southall Freeman on Leadership. Shippensburg, PA: White Mane Publishing, 1993.

Smith, W. A. The Anson Guards: Company C, Fourteenth Regiment North Carolina Volunteers 1861–1865. Reprint, Wendell, NC: Broadfoot's Bookmark, 1978.

Snell, Mark A., editor. The Maryland Campaign of 1862 and Its Aftermath. Campbell, CA: Regimental Studies, 1998.

Sorrel, G. Moxley. Recollections of a Confederate Staff Officer. Edited by Bell Irvin Wiley. Jackson, TN: McCowat-Mercer Press, 1958.

Southern Bivouac. 6 volumes. Reprint, Millwod, NY: Kraus, 1993.

Southern Historical Society Papers. 52 volumes. Reprint, Wilmington, NC: Broadfoot Publishing, 1990–1992.

Sparks, David S., editor. Inside Lincoln's Army: The Diary of Marsena Rudolph Patrick, Provost Marshal General, Army of the Potomac. New York: Thomas Yoseloff, 1964.

Squires, Charles W. "The 'Boy Officer' of the Washington Artillery, Part I." Civil War Times Illustrated 14, no. 2 (1975).

Stephens, Robert Grier, Jr., editor. Intrepid Warrior: Clement Anselm Evans Confederate General from Georgia, Life, Letters, and Diaries of the War Years. Dayton, OH: Morningside House, Inc., 1992.

Stevens, John W. War Reminiscences of the Civil War. Reprint, Powhatan, VA: Derwent Books, 1982.

Stiles, Robert. Four Years Under Marse Robert. Reprint, Dayton, OH: Press of Morningside Bookshop, 1977.

Stone, DeWitt Boyd, Jr., editor. Wandering to Glory: Confederate Veterans Remember Evans' Brigade. Columbia: University of South Carolina Press, 2002.

Sturkey, O. Lee. Hampton Legion Infantry C.S.A. Wilmington, NC: Broadfoot Publishing, 2008.

Styple, William B., editor. *Writing and Fighting from the Army of Northern Virginia.* Kearny, NJ: Belle Grove, 2003.

——, editor. *Writing and Fighting the Confederate War: The Letters of Peter Wellington Alexander Confederate War Correspondent.* Kearny, NJ: Belle Grove, 2002.

Supplement to the Official Records of the Union and Confederate Armies. 95 volumes. Wilmington, NC: Broadfoot Publishing, 1994–1999.

Sutherland, Daniel E. *Seasons of War: The Ordeal of a Confederate Community, 1861–1865.* New York: Free Press, 1995.

Sword, Wiley. *Courage under Fire: Profiles in Bravery from the Battlefields of the Civil War.* New York: St. Martin's Press, 2007.

——. *Southern Invincibility: A History of the Confederate Heart.* New York: St. Martin's Press, 1999.

Taylor, Richard. *Destruction and Reconstruction: Personal Experiences of the Late War.* Edited by Richard B. Harwell. New York: Longmans, Green, 1955.

Taylor, Walter. *Four Years with General Lee.* Edited by James I. Robertson Jr. Bloomington: Indiana University Press, 1962.

——. *General Lee: His Campaigns in Virginia, 1861–1865, with Personal Reminiscences.* Reprint, Dayton, OH: Press of Morningside Bookshop, 1975.

Thomas, Emory M. *Robert E. Lee: A Biography.* New York: Norton, 1995.

Thomas, Henry W. *History of the Doles-Cook Brigade Army of Northern Virginia, C.S.A.* Reprint, Dayton, OH: Press of Morningside Bookshop, 1981.

Thomason, John W., Jr. *Jeb Stuart.* New York: Charles Scribner's Sons, 1930.

Thompson, William Y. *Robert Toombs of Georgia.* Baton Rouge: Louisiana State University Press, 1966.

Tower, R. Lockwood, editor. *Lee's Adjutant: The Wartime Letters of Colonel Walter Herron Taylor, 1862–1865.* Columbia: University of South Carolina Press, 1995.

Trudeau, Noah Andre. *Gettysburg: A Testing of Courage.* New York: Harper Collins, 2002.

Tucker, Glenn. *High Tide at Gettysburg: The Campaign in Pennsylvania.* Indianapolis: Bobbs-Merrill, 1958.

Tumilty, Victor. "Filling Jackson's Shoes." *Civil War Times Illustrated* 42, no. 2 (2003).

Turner, Charles W., editor. *Captain Greenlee Davidson, C.S.A. Diary and Letters 1851–1863.* Verona, VA: McClure Press, 1975.

——, editor. *Ted Barclay, Liberty Hall Volunteers: Letters from the Stonewall Brigade (1861–1864).* National Bridge Station, VA: Rockbridge, 1992.

U.S. War Department. *The War of the Rebellion: A Compilation of the Official Records of the Union and Confederate Armies.* 128 volumes. Washington, D.C.: U. S. Government Printing Office, 1880–1902.

Vandiver, Frank E. *Mighty Stonewall.* New York: McGraw-Hill, 1957.

——. *Rebel Brass: The Confederate Command System.* Baton Rouge: Louisiana State University Press, 1956.

Wallace, Lee A., Jr. *5th Virginia Infantry*. Lynchburg, VA: H. E. Howard, 1988.

Warner, Ezra J. *Generals in Gray: Lives of the Confederate Commanders*. Baton Rouge: Louisiana State University Press, 1959.

Weigley, Russell F. *A Great Civil War: A Military and Political History, 1861–1865*. Bloomington: Indiana University Press, 2000.

Wert, Jeffry D. *A Brotherhood of Valor: The Common Soldiers of the Stonewall Brigade, C.S.A., and the Iron Brigade, U.S.A.* New York: Simon & Schuster, 1999.

———. *Cavalryman of the Lost Cause: A Biography of J. E. B. Stuart*. New York: Simon & Schuster, 2008.

———. *General James Longstreet: The Confederacy's Most Controversial Soldier—A Biography*. New York: Simon & Schuster, 1993.

———. *Gettysburg: Day Three*. New York: Simon & Schuster, 2001.

———. *The Sword of Lincoln: The Army of the Potomac*. New York: Simon & Schuster, 2005.

West, John C. *A Texan in Search of a Fight: Being the Diary and Letters of a Private Soldier in Hood's Texas Brigade*. Reprint, Waco, TX: Texian Press, 1969.

Wiley, Bell Irvin. *The Life of Johnny Reb: The Common Soldier of the Confederacy*. Indianapolis: Bobbs-Merrill, 1943.

Wilkinson, Warren, and Steven E. Woodworth. *A Scythe of Fire: A Civil War Story of the Eighth Georgia Infantry Regiment*. New York: William Morrow, 2002.

Williams, Edward B., editor. *Rebel Brothers: The Civil War Letters of the Truehearts*. College Station: Texas A.&M. University Press, 1995.

Wilson, LeGrand James. *The Confederate Soldier*. Edited by James W. Silver. Memphis, TN: Memphis State University Press, 1973.

Winschel, Terrence J. "Heavy Was Their Loss: Joe Davis' Brigade at Gettysburg, Part II." *Gettysburg Magazine*, no. 3 (July 1990).

Winslow, Richard Elliott, III. *General John Sedgwick: The Story of a Union Corps Commander*. Novato, CA: Presidio, 1982.

Wise, Jennings Cropper. *The Long Arm of Lee: The History of the Artillery of the Army of Northern Virginia*. Reprint, New York: Oxford University Press, 1959.

Wood, William Nathaniel. *Reminiscences of Big I*. Edited by Bell Irvin Wiley. Jackson, TN: McCowat-Mercer Press, 1956.

Woodworth, Steven E. *Davis and Lee at War*. Lawrence: University Press of Kansas, 1995.

Worsham, John H. *One of Jackson's Foot Cavalry*. Edited by James I. Robertson Jr. Reprint, Jackson, TN: McCowat-Mercer Press, 1964.

Wyckoff, Mac. *A History of the 3rd South Carolina Regiment: Lee's Reliables*. Wilmington, NC: Broadfoot Publishing, 2008.

Younger, Edward, editor. *Inside the Confederate Government: The Diary of Robert Garlick Hill Kean*. New York: Oxford University Press, 1957.

Index

Page numbers in *italics* refer to maps.

APR - - 2013